HISPANIC
AMERICAN
LITERATURE

M.

HISPANIC AMERICAN LITERATURE

An Anthology

Rodolfo Cortina

University of Houston

NTC Publishing Group

a division of NTC/CONTEMPORARY PUBLISHING COMPANY
Lincolnwood, Illinois USA

Executive Editor: Marisa L. L´Heureux
Editor: Sue Schumer
Cover and interior design: Kristy Sheldon
Cover illustration: Diego Rivera, *The Flower Carrier* (formerly, *The Flower Vendor*), 1935,
  oil and tempura on masonite, 48 x 47 3/4 in. (121.9 x 121.3 cm)
Design Manager: Ophelia Chambliss
Production Manager: Margo Goia

Acknowledgments begin on page 409, which is to be considered an extension of this copyright
page.

ISBN 0-8442-5730-3 (student edition)
ISBN 0-8442-5731-1 (instructor's edition)

Library of Congress Cataloging-in-Publication Data

Hispanic American Literature : an anthology / [compiled by] Rodolfo
  Cortina.
    p. cm.
  Includes index.
    ISBN 0-8442-5730-3 (alk. paper)
    1. American literature—Hispanic American authors. 2. American
literature—Hispanic American authors—Problems, exercises, etc.
3. Hispanic Americans—Literary collections. I. Cortina, Rodolfo
J.
PS508.H57H554 1997
810.8'0868—dc21   97-315505
                                                 CIP

7 8 9 0 VL 0 9 8 7 6 5 4 3 2 1

CONTENTS

Foreword   xi

Introduction   xiii

CHAPTER ONE
A SENSE OF PLACE   1

from *The Account*
Álvar Núñez Cabeza de Vaca 2

Canto III
Gaspar Pérez de Villagrá 13

from *Memorial*
Gonzalo Solís de Merás 27

from *The Memoirs of Bernardo Vega*
Bernardo Vega 38

Our America
José Martí 45

CHAPTER TWO
THE ORAL TRADITION   55

The Ballad of Gregorio Cortez
Américo Paredes 57

Indigenous Profile
María Cadilla de Martínez 62

The Prize of Freedom
Lydia Cabrera 70

Corridos
María Herrera-Sobek 74

La Llorona
Anonymous 79

CHAPTER THREE
THE VALUE OF FAMILY

81

familia
Tato Laviera 82

Progress Report for a Dead Father
To My Father
Judith Ortiz Cofer 85

Black & White Photo
Pedro Pietri 89

Dear Tía
Carolina Hospital 91

The Moths
Helena María Viramontes 93

CHAPTER FOUR
INNOCENCE IS A CHILD

99

from *Bless Me, Ultima*
Rudolfo A. Anaya 100

The Indian Ruins
José Martí 112

Tales Told Under the Mango Tree
Judith Ortiz Cofer 120

My Name
Sandra Cisneros 131

The Night Before Christmas
Tomás Rivera 134

CHAPTER FIVE
COMING OF AGE

142

Doubt
José Gautier Benítez 142

A Perfect Hotspot
Virgil Suárez 144

An Awakening . . . Summer 1956
Nicholasa Mohr 151

from *The Greatest Performance*
Elías Miguel Muñoz 158

night vigil
Evangelina Vigil-Piñón 165

CHAPTER SIX
LOVE AND ROMANCE 171

from *Dear Rafe*
Rolando Hinojosa 172

A Romeo and Juliet Story in Early New Mexico
Fray Angélico Chávez 178

Transference
Sandra María Esteves 186

Eva and Daniel
Tomás Rivera 189

First Love
Gary Soto 194

CHAPTER SEVEN
STRANGERS AT HOME 199

from *Nilda*
Nicholasa Mohr 200

Sun Images
Estela Portillo-Trambley 207

from *A Stranger in One's Land*
Rubén Salazar 229

Bitter Sugar: Why Puerto Ricans Leave Home
Jesús Colón 237

CHAPTER EIGHT

MIGRANTS AND EXILES   243

For the Color of My Mother
Cherríe Moraga 245

from *Our House in the Last World*
Oscar Hijuelos 248

Thoughts on a Sunday Afternoon
Joan Báez 265

Borinkins in Hawaii
Victor Hernández Cruz 269

CHAPTER NINE

EMPOWERING THE PEOPLE   275

Nuyorican Lament
Gloria Vando 277

Los Vendidos
Luis Valdez 281

Murrieta on the Hill
Sergio Elizondo 292

Arise, Chicano
Angela de Hoyos 296

I Am Joaquín
Rodolfo "Corky" Gonzales 229

CHAPTER TEN

DEFINING WOMANHOOD,
ASSUMING MANHOOD   303

Filomena
Roberta Fernández 304

Shooting Stars
Denise Chávez 321

A Thanksgiving Celebration (Amy)
Nicholasa Mohr 331

To Be a Man
Gary Soto 340

Women Are Not Roses
Ana Castillo 343

The Goat Incident
Virgil Suárez 345

CHAPTER ELEVEN
CONSTRUCTING THE SELF   **351**

Seeing Snow
Dedication
Gustavo Peréz Firmat 352

To Free Cuba
Evangelina Cossío y Cisneros 355

The Angel Juan Moncho
Ed Vega 359

from *Becky and Her Friends*
Rolando Hinojosa 374

Amigo Brothers
Piri Thomas 379

CHAPTER TWELVE
THE COSMIC RACE   **389**

La Doctora Barr
Mary Helen Ponce 390

San Antonio phantasmagoria
Barrios of the world
Latinos
Ricardo Sánchez 395

A Child to Be Born
Alberto Urista (Alurista) 401

puerto rican
Tato Laviera 404

My Race
José Martí 406

Acknowledgments 409

Author-Title Index 413

FOREWORD

A Scotsman, the Reverend Sydney Smyth, once said there was no furniture so charming as books. In this anthology, the compiler, Professor Rodolfo Cortina, has furnished us with a complete suite of such furniture.

Wide-ranging in time, from the 16th-century explorer Álvar Núñez Cabeza de Vaca to the contemporary Judith Ortiz Cofer, this book reveals both an extensive as well as an intensive view of the contributions to overall American literature by writers with a Spanish-language background.

One of the most interesting aspects of this book is its inclusivity: there is some history and some anthropology, two necessary elements that serve to provide glimpses of any people's culture, which is then reflected through its literature.

From ballads to poetry, from short stories to excerpts from novels by premier men and women writers, the book not only attempts to present varied cultures through time, it also succeeds in doing so. And this last is important, for a people reveals itself through its actions and through that most permanent of its structures, the written word.

This anthology, then, fulfills what its title says it is, *Hispanic American Literature*, and does so admirably.

Rolando Hinojosa-Smith

INTRODUCTION

The selections in *Hispanic American Literature* have been carefully chosen to reflect the richness and variety of Hispanic literature in the United States.

This anthology begins with the dawn of Hispanic literature in the United States, including historical chronicles and memoirs of the Spanish explorers who were "conquering the New World" and recording their experiences with indigenous/Native American groups in the 1500s. What is now "America" was just beginning to evolve into a cultural and racial mix of Amerindians, Africans, and Europeans. The literature of the Hispanic American oral tradition—for instance, the *corrido* or traditional ballad—is also included in an early chapter of the book.

What makes this collection distinctive is its thematic organization and the inclusion of those early texts mentioned above with the literature of contemporary Mexican Americans, Cuban Americans, and Puerto Ricans. For many, the study of Hispanic American or Latino literature is marked as beginning in the 1960s with the struggle for civil rights and, in particular, with the rise of the Chicano (Mexican American) political and cultural movement, but Hispanic American literature began long before that point. It is hoped that this collection will open a door to a new, broader vision of Hispanic literature of the United States.

A QUESTION OF LABELS AND CULTURAL IDENTITIES

For the purposes of this anthology, Hispanic American literature is defined as the oral and written literature of Hispanics (descendants of Spanish-speaking peoples) of what is now the United States. Works by Mexican American, Puerto Rican, and Cuban American authors are included in this collection, also referred to as Latino/Latina literature.

For the most part, the literature included in this collection was written in English, with some literature being of a bilingual nature. The historical chronicles as well as literature of the oral tradition are generally translations from the original Spanish.

The use of the term *Hispanic American* to identify persons in the United States of America whose ancestry lies in the Hispanic world (Spain and/or Spanish America), is of relatively recent coinage. It is important to note two specific areas of controversy with the term.

First, *America* theoretically denotes the New World from pole to pole, but when the thirteen British colonies declared independence from Great Britain, they adopted the name United States of America. Some to the south felt that this was a bit of a usurpation of the name America as the colonies represented only a part of its totality. Logically, the New World should have been named Columbia for Columbus, and not America for cartographer Amerigo Vespucci. The issue of the two Americas has surfaced several times since the early nineteenth century and continues to be a model for analysis of the New World: Anglo America and Spanish America.

A second area of controversy is that the term *Hispanic* is currently a politically contested term in the United States. Many groups claim the term was invented by the federal government and that it reduces all groups of people to the lowest common denominator (descended from Spanish-speaking peoples) and denies various ethnic groups (Mexican Americans, Puerto Ricans, Cuban Americans, as well as Caribbean and South American groups) their specific cultural identities. Some prefer the alternate term, *Latino/a*, which is a reference to Latin American origins.

MEXICAN AMERICAN NOMENCLATURE

Focusing on Mexican American literature and culture, the reader will encounter the specific label *Chicano*, which was originally selected as a self-label by Mexican Americans involved in the Civil Rights Movement during the late 1960s and 1970s. Chicano/Chicana came to be used as a label for the literature and authors emerging from that movement. Today, many use the terms *Mexican American* and *Chicano* interchangeably, with Mexican American currently being used more often in general reference to the national group.

In Texas, on the other hand, many Mexican Americans call themselves *tejano* while in northern New Mexico, the term *hispano* is often used, reflecting a connection to "New Spain" and a distancing from Mexico, particularly after the Mexican Revolution in 1810.

PUERTO RICAN NOMENCLATURE

Likewise, the term *Puerto Rican*, which may encompass both inhabitants of the island of Puerto Rico, a commonwealth of the United States, and those Puerto Ricans living in the mainland United States, can be replaced with the Arawak (native/Indian) word *Boricua* or *Borinqueño*. This is the name for the island of Puerto Rico in Taíno, the native language of Puerto Rico, which was colonized by the Spanish in the late 1400s before becoming part of the United States in 1898.

Another variant label for Puerto Rican is *Nuyorican,* a word combining New York and Puerto Rican (New York Rican), reflecting the identity of a person of Puerto Rican ancestry born and/or raised in New York City. However, not all persons of Puerto Rican heritage are connected to New York City. Many Puerto Ricans emigrated directly from Puerto Rico to Chicago, or to Milwaukee. Were they to become Chicago Ricans? Or Milwaukee Ricans?

During the 1970s, the debate raged on about this partition of the name Puerto Rican. After the onslaught from the island's intelligentsia, the term *Neorican* has become more generally accepted, which is not such a strong reference to New York. Nevertheless, some would insist on Nuyorican for all, regardless of where the Puerto Rican lives in the United States.

CUBAN AMERICAN NOMENCLATURE

Cubans who have emigrated to the United States or their descendants generally refer to themselves as *Cuban Americans.* During the 1960s and early 1970s, when increasing numbers of Cubans fled Fidel Castro's communist regime, the label *Cuban Americans* gave way slightly, as a number of the those who were forced to flee Cuba abhorred the label *Cuban American* and preferred to call themselves Cuban exiles. Their children, however, who were born in the United States and had no memory of Cuba, refer to themselves as Cuban Americans.

A HISTORICAL OVERVIEW OF HISPANIC AMERICAN LITERARY TRADITIONS

Some knowledge of history, how the Spanish came to the New World— what is now considered Mexico, Latin America, and the United States—and how Hispanic American literature formed, is essential to understanding the works of Hispanic writers of the United States.

The Era of Discovery and the Colonial Period

From 1492 through the end of the seventeenth century in the New World, Hispanic literature consisted mainly of records of the Spanish explorers and settlers, such as chronicles, letters, or memoirs, although it is possible to find songs, ballads, plays, and epic poems written at this time. For instance, among the chronicles and accounts is Pedro de Castañeda de Nágera's *Account of the Journey of Cíbola* which provides a very detailed descriptive narration of Francisco Vásquez de Coronado's expedition to the Southwest (now the United States), which took place in the early 1540s. *The Shepherd's Conversation* was a Nativity play that became the most well-known and most popular among the settlers in Mexico and in what is now the United States. The play tells of the group of shepherds whose journey to Bethlehem to visit Jesus is prevented by Lucifer, until the Archangel Michael appears, defeats Lucifer, and encourages them to complete it.

Two important epic poems are written in this period, Friar Alonso de Escobedo's *La Florida,* which deals with the proselytizing of twelve Franciscan missionaries in Florida in 1587, and Gaspar Pérez de Villagrá's *Historia de la Nueva Mexico,* a remarkable poem that begins with Juan de Oñate's march to New Mexico in 1596 and ends with the Indian massacre of the Spanish settlers at the Acoma Pueblo (New Mexico) in 1599.

In the period from the eighteenth to beginning of the nineteenth century, the diary as a genre of Hispanic American literature emerges, such as the one written by Fathers Francisco Atanasio Domínguez and Silvestre Vélez de Escalante (*Diary and Direction of Fathers Domínguez & Escalante to Discover the Road from the Santa Fe Presidio to Monterrey*). During that era there were also plays written, such as *Los Comanches,* a drama depicting the victory of the Spaniards over the Comanches in the area north of New Mexico, including the southern portion of Colorado.

The Nineteenth Century

By the 1800s the Hispanic literary record in the United States grew remarkably due to the establishment of newspapers published for the Spanish-speaking communities throughout the United States. Starting in 1808 in New Orleans with *El Misisipí,* probably the first Hispanic newspaper in the U.S., these newspapers become a venue for the publication of stories, poems, chronicles, even plays and serialized novels. Examples of these newspapers are the San Antonio newspaper *La Gaceta de Texas* (The Texas Gazette), *La Estrella de Los Angeles* (The Los Angeles Star), or New York's *El Mensajero Semanal* (The Weekly Messenger). An example of how the newspapers functioned in terms of literature can be seen in 1881 when *La Gaceta* (The Gazette) of Santa Barbara published the famous serialized novel *Las aventuras de Joaquín Murieta* (The Adventures of Joaquín Murrieta) based on the life of the well-known bandit and folk hero of California.

In addition there were several works published independently, although of these companies had connections with newspaper offices or printing shops. The works of Amparo Ruiz de Burton in California, that of Lola Rodríguez de Tio, and that of José Martí in New York take up, respectively, the cause of the loss of homeland among Mexican Americans and the Puerto Rican as well as Cuban struggles for independence from Spain.

The Early Twentieth Century

In the early twentieth century, due to the Mexican Revolution of 1910, many Mexicans emigrated to the Southwest and the Midwest portions of the United States. These Mexican immigrants were dubbed as the "Mexico of the Outside." Some maintained their interest in the politics of their former country. Among them was, for example, Sara Estela Ramírez who in 1901 established the Laredo (Texas) newspaper *La Corregidora* (The Co-regent or The Corrector), and in 1907 *Aurora,* a literary magazine.

Other writers, however, exhibited interest on issues in their new country. One good example is Daniel Venegas, who in 1928 wrote *Las aventuras de Don Chipote o Cuando los pericos mamen* (The Adventures of Don Chipote or When the Parakeets May Suckle Their Young), a picaresque, humorous, satirical novel of a Mexican's life in the United States.

In the Northeast the parallels are evident although the historical record is different. The *cronistas* (Hispanic newspaper columnists) in the Northeast wrote to protect Hispanic culture from assimilation into Anglo-American culture, trying to bring all of the diverse Spanish-speaking ethnic groups into one large community. These journalists created a "Tropical Manhattan" in New York, in which Caribbean culture flourished. Venezuelan author Alirio Díaz Guerra's novel *Lucas Guevara* (1917), dealing with the disillusionment of a young immigrant into New York, is similar in tone to Venegas's satirical *Don Chipote*.

A major literary contributor in the early decades of the twentieth century was a leading Afro-Cuban actor in blackface farces, Alberto O'Farrill, who wrote plays and in 1927 founded *El Gráfico,* an important theater and literary review based in New York City.

Luisa Capetillo was a prominent figure in the Hispanic literary scene in the U.S. during the early decades of the twentieth century. She worked as a lector in cigar factories in New York and Florida, reading aloud to workers as was the custom. Capetillo, who became famous for dressing in men's clothing, wrote anarchist essays in many newspapers of the time.

The Contemporary Period

The major turning point for Hispanic or Latino literature occurred when The Civil Rights Act was approved in 1964, which marked a new beginning for all minorities in the United States. The Chicano Movement, among others, started at this time.

By 1967 Mexican American Rodolfo "Corky" Gonzales published "I Am Joaquín," a poem that elaborated a version of cultural nationalism that would typify what is called "Movement" poetry. The Chicano literary movement in the U.S. began with such writers as Abelardo Delgado, Raymundo "Tigre" Pérez, Ricardo Sánchez, and Alurista (Alberto Urista).

The most important theatrical enterprise of this time was El Teatro Campesino (The Farmworkers' Theater), founded by Luis Valdez in 1965 as a propaganda arm of the United Farm Workers led by César Chávez, the union organizer. Valdez's purpose was of raising the consciousness of the audience to promote the Chicano cause.

Novelists such as José Antonio Villarreal, Raymond Barrio, and Richard Vásquez wrote about the ordeal of Mexican American life in the United States and the emergence of the Chicano Movement. Also very significant are Estela Portillo-Trambley's plays of the 1970s.

In the 1970s and 1980s great writers of prose and fiction emerged. Mexican American authors Rolando Hinojosa, Tomás Rivera, Rudolfo Anaya continue to be prolific writers today. Sandra Cisneros, whose first collection of stories was published in 1979, has become one of the most acclaimed Chicana authors of the 1990s.

Among the outstanding Chicano poets are Bernice Zamora, Angela de Hoyos, Gary Soto, Ana Castillo, Lorna Dee Cervantes, Alma Villanueva, Ray Gonzalez, and Jimmy Santiago Baca—to name just a few.

Also part of the major movement in Hispanic or Latino literature that continues today are the Puerto Rican authors who belong to the Nuyorican Movement, writers such as Miguel Piñero, Miguel Algarín, Pedro Pietri, Sandra María Esteves, and Lucky Cienfuegos. Their venue was and is the Nuyorican Poet's Cafe in New York City, where poetry, often of a political nature, is performed. Other Puerto Rican poets who publish without direct relation to the Nuyorican Movement include Víctor Hernández Cruz, Tato Laviera, and Martín Espada.

Other outstanding Puerto Rican writers today are Piri Thomas, Nicholasa Mohr, Judith Ortiz Cofer, and Ed Vega, all of whom have confronted the Puerto Rican community's heritage, dreams, joys, and problems in the U.S. through the characters in their prose fiction.

In regard to Puerto Rican theater, the presence of René Marqués has been felt both in the island of Puerto Rico and in the U.S. mainland. Dramatists Miguel Piñero, Ivette Ramírez, and Miriam Colón also figure prominently.

Moving to Cuban American literature, it is important to note that since the Cuban Revolution, three cultural groups have emerged: the exiles from the 1960s and 1970s; the Mariel group, Mariel being the name given to the exodus from Cuba in 1980; and the third group, the children of the exiles, born in the United States, who are called "the daring" or *los atrevidos*.

The Cuban exiles who started to publish when they arrived in the 1960s wrote in Spanish and condemned the Castro communist regime in Cuba. Writers Carlos Alberto Montaner and Hilda Perera are the foremost examples because they publish entirely in Spanish and attack the Castro regime without quarter. In poetry, this group's conservative attitude toward language and existential themes are embodied in the poetry of both Isel Rivero and José Kozer.

The Mariel writers had a champion in Reinaldo Arenas, whose novels both treat the agony of Cuba and also life for Cuban exiles in the United States. His work is pivotal between the exile and the Cuban American writer. The poets Jesús Barquet, Roberto Valero, Carlota Caulfield, and Belkis Cuza Malé also create that bridge between the exiles and their children with books ranging from the political to speculation about Elvis Presley's immortality.

The *Atrevidos*, who write mostly in English and construct new literary identities, include poets Lourdes Gil, Gustavo Pérez-Firmat and Carolina Hospital as well as writers of prose, such as Roberto Fernández, Elías Miguel Muñoz, Cristina García, and Virgil Suárez.

In Cuban American theater, after María Irene Fornés, Ivan Acosta and Dolores Prida figure prominently, breaking into writing and producing in English while retaining Cuban cultural identity.

Among the Cuban American writers who have recently achieved success in the American literary mainstream are José Yglesias, with novels such as *Fearless* (1993), and Oscar Hijuelos who, with his best-selling novel *The Mambo Kings Play Songs of Love* (1990), became the first Latino to win a Pulitzer Prize.

ABOUT THE FEATURES OF *HISPANIC AMERICAN LITERATURE*

This collection of literature is organized according to major themes in the Hispanic American experience. Each chapter has an introduction explaining the significance of the chapter theme to the Hispanic tradition in the U.S. Each selection is introduced by a biographical sketch of the author's life and literary accomplishments, as well as a brief introductory note describing the selection at hand. Following each selection are "Discussion Questions" and "Writing Topics."

ACKNOWLEDGMENTS

The publisher and I wish to thank the following reviewers for their helpful suggestions as this anthology was planned: Carlota Cárdenas de Dwyer, Tom C. Clark High School, San Antonio, Texas; Diego Alfranio Davalos, Chula Vista High School, Chula Vista, California; Rolando Hinojosa-Smith, University of Texas-Austin; and Ray Gonzalez, University of Illinois-Chicago.

I would also like to thank all those who helped me with this project. My thanks to my friend and colleague, Nicolás Kanellos, who has made his resources available to me, and to Marina Tristán, who assisted me with research. I am also grateful to Ivette Cortés-Bailey, whose assistance was very important as this project got under way, and to Sue Schumer, my editor. To Lynn E. Cortina, my gratitude for help with many facets of this book, including proofreading, and for allowing me the space to work on it.

Rodolfo Cortina

HISPANIC AMERICAN LITERATURE

CHAPTER ONE

A SENSE OF PLACE

For human beings, home is central to the construction of place. Home is the environment that is wonderfully familiar, and the uncertain world exists immediately beyond its walls. Then, as a child grows and his or her experiences increase, home expands to include first a neighborhood and then a community. One's sense of place comes to be defined by the local population and the economic structure and the values and the rituals that are part of living.

Words such as *homeless, refugee,* and *exile* are emotionally loaded because they invoke feelings of uncertainty and vulnerability and fear. Humans have a need to identify themselves with their home—the place they feel secure and accepted. Indeed, it is the search for and establishment of a home that sets humans apart, even when home is more an ideal than a reality. The Mexican Americans, for example, renamed the U.S. Southwest Aztlán as a means of holding claim to the territory that was now part of the United States and typically belonged to Anglo-Americans.

Imagine how the Spaniards felt as they reached the coasts of the New World and set out to explore the land. Imagine, too, the feelings of the Indians who saw the Spanish explorers approach and change their home forever. Empathize with the Mexicans or the Puerto Ricans as their homes abruptly changed status and affiliation. Feel the fear and uncertainty of the Cuban exile, forced to flee from the familiar to the United States and all its strangeness. Yet, the changes had to be accepted, and even embraced, because without a sense of place—even if it must be invented—it is difficult indeed to feel self-worth or hope or pride or even human.

FROM *THE ACCOUNT*

Álvar Núñez Cabeza de Vaca

Álvar Núñez Cabeza de Vaca was born in Jerez de la Frontera in Spain, and he died in Seville. Although the exact date of his birth is not known, it is speculated that he was born around 1490 or 1507 and that he died in 1559 or 1564. He is a sixteenth-century Spanish explorer who had come from similar stock. His grandfather was Pedro de Vera, conqueror of the Canary Islands.

Cabeza de Vaca, however, was not as lucky as his grandfather, for he was involved in the ill-fated Florida expedition led by Pánfilo de Narváez (1528). In 1536 Cabeza de Vaca returned to New Spain (today's Mexico) after crossing half of the continent along what is today the border between the United States and Mexico. He vividly described these adventures in a book that has been called *La relación* (*The Account*) or *Los naufragios* (*The Shipwrecks*) and was published in 1542. He also served as *Adelantado* of Paraguay, and his experiences there were recounted by Pedro Hernández, his secretary and scribe in the expedition.

Álvar Núñez Cabeza de Vaca's *The Account* relates his adventures in the expedition led by Pánfilo de Narváez. The following excerpts from *The Account*, translated by Martin A. Favata and José B. Fernández, may prove interesting in their portrayal of the land and of the people that Cabeza de Vaca encounters.

OF OUR SKIRMISH WITH THE INDIANS

1   When morning came, many Indians in canoes[1] came to us asking us to give them the two men they had left as hostages. The Governor said he would hand them over when they brought back the two Christians they had

---

[1] Although the first edition of *The Account* was published in Zamora in 1542, there was an earlier report that Cabeza de Vaca wrote with Andres Dorantes and Alonso del Castillo and presented to the Audiencia

taken. Five or six chiefs came with these people and they seemed to us to be the handsomest people, and with the most authority and composure we had yet seen, although they were not as tall as the others we had described. They wore their hair loose and long and wore sable mantles like those we had already obtained. Some of them were made in a very strange fashion with laces made from tawny skins and they appeared very attractive. They entreated us to go with them, saying that they would hand over the Christians and give us water and many other things. All the while many canoes were approaching us, trying to secure the mouth of the inlet. Because of this and because the country was too dangerous for us to remain, we put out to sea, where we remained with them until midday. As they would not return the Christians, and for this reason neither would we hand over the Indians, they began to throw sticks and sling rocks at us. They gave signs of wanting to shoot arrows at us, but we saw only three or four bows among all of them. While we were engaged in this skirmish, a chilly wind came up and they turned away and left us.

We sailed that day[2] until the hour of vespers, when my boat, which was in the lead, saw a point of land on the other side of which could be seen a very large river.[3] I put up at an islet at the tip of the land to wait for the other boats. The Governor did not want to approach it, and instead entered a bay very close-by in which there were many islets.[4] We gathered there and in the sea took on fresh water, because the river emptied out into the sea in a torrent. We landed on that island because we wanted to toast some of the corn we were carrying, since we had been eating it raw for two days. Since we found no firewood, we decided to enter the river which was behind the point one league away. We could not go in because the very strong current totally prevented us and carried us away from the shore despite our effort and determination. The north wind blowing from the land increased so much that it carried us out to sea and we could do nothing. Half a league out we took a sounding and found that we could not reach bottom with more than thirty fathoms. We did not know if the current was the reason we could not take a sounding. We sailed under those conditions for two days, struggling all the time to reach land. At the end of the two days, a little before sunrise, we saw many clouds of smoke along the coast. Struggling to reach them, we found ourselves in three fathoms of water. Since it was night, we did not dare to land. Having seen so many clouds of smoke, we believed

---

of Santo Domingo in 1537. This report has been lost, but its text was purported to appear in Gonzalo Fernández de Oviedo's *Historia general y natural de las Indias* (General and Natural History of the Indies) with Oviedo's own comments interpolated in the alleged report. This portion of Oviedo's text is known as the *Joint Report* and has been translated into English by Basil C. Hendrick and Carroll L. Riley *The Journey of the Vaca Party: The Account of the Narváez Expedition, 1528–1536, as Related by Gonzalo Fernández de Oviedo y Valdés* (Carbondale: Southern Illinois University Press, 1974). The usefulness of the *Joint Report* is that it complements *The Account*. According to the *Joint Report* there were twenty canoes (p. 20).

[2] Two days, according to the *Joint Report* (p. 21).

[3] The Mississippi River, according to most scholars.

[4] The islands around the Mississippi River Delta.

that we could be placing ourselves in some sort of danger again, and that we would not be able to determine what to do because of the great darkness. Therefore we decided to wait until morning. At dawn each boat had lost sight of the others.

3   I was in water thirty fathoms deep and, continuing on my way, I saw two boats at the hour of vespers. When I approached them, I saw that the first was the Governor's. He asked me what I thought we ought to do. I told him that he should join the boat ahead of us and that in no way should he lose sight of it and that together all three of our boats should proceed to wherever God should wish to take us. He responded that he could not do that because the boat was too far out to sea and he wanted to reach land. He said that if I wanted to follow suit, I should have the men in my boat row hard, since it was by the strength of arms that we could reach land. He was advised to do this by a captain named Pentoja, who was in his boat and who told him that, if he did not reach land that day, he would not reach it in six days. By that time we would die of starvation. When I saw his intentions, I took my oar and rowed with all the able-bodied men in our boat until the sun had nearly set. Since the Governor had the healthiest and strongest men, we could in no way keep up with him.

4   When I saw this, I asked the Governor to throw me a line so I could follow him, but he answered that it would be enough of a struggle for them to reach shore that night themselves. I asked him what I should do since it was almost impossible to follow him and carry out his orders. He told me that it was no longer necessary for any of us to give orders, that each of us should do what seemed best to save his life, since that is what he intended to do. Saying this, he went farther away on his boat.[5] Since I could not catch up with him, the other boat waited for me at sea until I reached it. When I approached it, I found that it was the one led by Captains Peñalosa and Téllez. We sailed in this manner together for four days, eating a daily ration of half a handful of raw corn.

5   After four days[6] a storm came up and caused the other boat to be lost.[7] We did not sink because of God's great mercy. The weather was rough, very cold and wintery. We had been suffering from hunger for many days and had been pounded so much by the sea that the following day many men began to faint. By nightfall, all the men in my boat had passed out, one on top of another, so near death that few of them were conscious and fewer than five were still upright. During the night only the sailing master and I

---

[5] The refusal on the part of Narváez, the expedition's Governor, for the boats to travel together clearly illustrates that he was a selfish leader who seemed to be more interested in his own safety than in that of his men.

[6] According to the *Joint Report* (pp. 21–22), the other boat disappeared a day after the two boats met. There are considerable differences between *The Account* and the *Joint Report* regarding the drifting of the two boats.

[7] Cabeza de Vaca did not learn the fate of the boat commanded by Téllez and Peñalosa until five years later, as is indicated later in *The Account*.

were left to sail the boat. Two hours after nightfall he told me I should take over because he was in such a condition that he thought he would die that very night; so I took the tiller. In the middle of the night, I went to see if the sailing master had died, but he told me that he was better and that he would steer until daybreak. At that time I certainly would have rather died than see so many people before me in that condition. After the sailing master took over the boat, I tried to rest some but could not, and sleep was the furthest thing from my mind.

6   Near dawn I thought I heard the roar of breakers near shore, which was very loud because the coast was low. Surprised by this, I roused the sailing master, who said he thought we were near land. We took a sounding and found that the water was seven fathoms deep. He thought that we should stay out until dawn. So I took an oar and rowed along the coast, which was a league distant. Then we set our stern to sea.

7   Near land a great wave took us and cast the boat out of the water as far as a horseshoe can be tossed.[8] The boat ran aground with such force that it revived the men on it who were almost dead. When they saw they were near land they pushed themselves overboard and crawled on their hands and knees. When they got to the beach, we lit a fire by some rocks and toasted some of the corn we had and found rain water. With the warmth of the fire, the men revived and began to regain some of their strength. We arrived at this place on the sixth of November.[9] . . .

WHAT HAPPENED TO LOPE DE OVIEDO WITH SOME INDIANS

8   Once our people had eaten, I sent Lope de Oviedo, who was stronger and fitter than the rest of us, to climb one of the trees nearby to sight the land and find out something about it. He did this and saw that we were on an island,[10] and that the land appeared to have been trampled by livestock. He thought for this reason that it must be a country of Christians, and told us so. I told him to look again very carefully to see if there were any paths that could be followed, but not to go too far because of possible danger.

---

[8] The *juego de herradura* was a horseshoe throw and was used to measure distance. A horseshoe throw was the equivalent of 14 meters or 41.7 feet, according to Cleve Hallenbeck's *Alvar Núñez Cabeza de Vaca: The Journey and Route of the First European to Cross the Continent of North America 1534–1536* (Glendale, CA: Arthur H. Clark, 1980), p. 49.

[9] According to Hallenbeck (pp. 116–17), this date may not have been correctly stated, since forty-eight or forty-nine days were spent in going from the Bay of Horses to the mouth of the Mississippi, some in sailing and some during stops. ". . . only eight days elapsed between the passing of the mouth of the Mississippi and the beaching of Núñez's craft, making a total of fifty-six or fifty-seven days since the barges left the Bay of Horses. But the inclusive dates as given by Núñez (September 22 and November 6) admit of only forty-five or forty-six days. Hence Núñez's memory was at fault somewhere."

[10] The majority of studies identify this as Galveston Island, Texas. However, Robert S. Weddle in his *Spanish Sea: The Gulf of Mexico in North American Discovery, 1500–1685* (College Station, TX: Texas A & M UP, 1985), p. 206, however, believes that the dimensions of the island given by Cabeza de Vaca suggest Follet's Island, immediately west of Galveston Island.

He found a path and followed it for half a league and found some unoccupied Indian huts, for the Indians had gone into the fields.[11] He took a pot from one of them, a small dog[12] and some mullet and started back.

9   We thought he was taking a long time to return, so I sent other Christians to look for him and find out what had happened to him. They found him near there, pursued by three Indians with bows and arrows. They were calling out to him and he was trying to speak to them through sign language. He got to where we were and the Indians stayed back a bit seated on the same shore. Half an hour later another one hundred[13] Indian bowmen appeared. We were so scared that they seemed to us to be giants, whether they were or not. They stopped near us, where the first three were. We could not even think of defending ourselves, since there were scarcely six men who could even get up from the ground. The Inspector and I went towards them and called them, and they approached us. As best we could we tried to reassure them and ourselves, and gave them beads and little bells. Each of them gave me an arrow, which is a sign of friendship. In sign language they told us that they would return in the morning and bring us food, since they did not have any at the time. . . .

HOW THE INDIANS BROUGHT US FOOD

10   The following day at sunrise, at the time the Indians had indicated, they came to us as promised, bringing us much fish, some roots[14] which they eat, the size of walnuts, some larger or smaller. Most of these are pulled with great difficulty from under the water. In the evening they returned to bring us more fish and the same kind of roots. They had their women and children come to see us and they considered themselves rich with little bells and beads that we gave them. The following days they returned to visit with the same things as before.

11   Seeing that we were provisioned with fish, roots, water and other things we requested, we agreed to embark on our voyage once again. We dug up the boat from the sand. We had to strip naked and struggle mightily to launch it, because we were so weak that lesser tasks would have been enough to exhaust us. Once we were out from the shore the distance of two crossbow shots,[15] a wave struck us quite a blow and got us all wet. Since we

---

[11] The word *campo* of Cabeza de Vaca's text would not be referring in this case to cultivated fields, but to clearings or the surrounding countryside, according to Adolf F. Bandelier in his *Contributions to the History of the Southwest Portion of the United States* (Cambridge: J. Wilson, 1890), p. 55.

[12] Thomas Buckingham Smith in his translation of *The Account in Relation of Álvar Núñez Cabeza de Vaca* (Washington, 1851) p. 66, speculates that this could have been a raccoon, rather than the mute dog of the Greater Antilles.

[13] Two hundred archers with joints of cane attached to their earlobes, according to the *Joint Report* (p. 23).

[14] According to the anthropologist W. W. Newcomb, Jr. in his *The Indians of Texas from Prehistoric to Modern Times* (Austin: U of Texas P, 1961), p. 66, these were possibly the roots of a species of American lotus or water lily.

[15] According to Edwin Tunis in his *Weapons: A Pictorial History* (Cleveland & New York: World, 1954), p. 74, the distance encompassed by a crossbow shot ranged from 55 to 110 meters, depending on the angle of the crossbow.

were naked and it was very cold, we let go of the oars. Another strong wave caused the boat to capsize. The Inspector and two other men held on to it to survive, but quite the opposite occurred because the boat pulled them under and they drowned. Since the surf was very rough, the sea wrapped all the men in its waves, except the three that had been pulled under by the boat, and cast them on the shore of the same island. Those of us who survived were as naked as the day we were born and had lost everything we had. Although the few things we had were of little value, they meant a lot to us.

12   It was November then and the weather was very cold. We were in such a state that our bones could easily be counted and we looked like the picture of death. I can say for myself that I had not eaten anything but parched corn since the previous May, and sometimes I had to eat it raw. Although the horses were slaughtered while we were building the boats, I was never able to eat them, and I had eaten fish fewer than ten times. This is but a brief comment, since anyone can imagine what shape we were in. On top of all this, the north wind began to blow, and so we were closer to death than to life. It pleased our Lord to let us find some embers among the coals of the fire we had made, and we made large fires. In this way we asked our Lord's mercy and the forgiveness of our sins, shedding many tears, with each man pitying not only himself but all the others who were in the same condition.

13   At sunset the Indians, thinking that we had not gone, looked for us again and brought us food. When they saw us in such a different state of attire and looking so strange, they were so frightened that they drew back. I went out to them and called them and they returned very frightened. I let them know through sign language that one of our boats had sunk and that three of our men had drowned. And there before their very eyes they saw two of the dead men, and those of us who were alive seemed as if we would soon join them.

14   The Indians, seeing the disaster that had come upon us and brought so much misfortune and misery, sat down with us. They felt such great pain and pity at seeing us in such a state that they all began to cry[16] so loudly and sincerely that they could be heard from afar. This went on for more than half an hour. In fact, seeing that these crude and untutored people, who were like brutes, grieved so much for us, caused me and the others in my company to suffer more and think more about our misfortune. When their crying ceased, I told the Christians that, if they agreed, I would ask those Indians to take us to their lodges. And some who had been in New Spain responded that we should not even think about it, because if they took us to their lodges they would sacrifice us to their idols. But seeing that we had no other recourse and that any other action would certainly bring us closer

---

16 According to American ethnologist Albert Gatschet in *The Karankawa Indians* (Cambridge, MA: Peabody Museum of American Archaeology and Ethnology, 1904), I, p. 66, in his research on the Karankawa, who inhabited the coastal area of Texas and who are now extinct, weeping in this manner was customary among the Indians. The reason for it is not known.

to death, I did not pay attention to what they were saying and I asked the Indians to take us to their lodges. They indicated that they would be very pleased to do this. They asked us to wait a bit and then they would do what we wanted. Then thirty of them loaded themselves with firewood and went to their lodges, which were far from there. We stayed with the others until nearly nightfall, when they held on to us and took us hastily to their lodges. Since it was so cold and they feared that someone might faint or die on the way, they had provided for four or five large fires to be placed at intervals, and they warmed us at each one. Once they saw that we had gained some strength and gotten warmer, they took us to the next one so rapidly that our feet scarcely touched the ground. In this way we went to their lodges and found that they had one ready for us with many fires lighted in it. Within an hour of our arrival they began to dance and have a great celebration that lasted all night. For us there was no pleasure nor celebration nor sleep because we were waiting to see when they would sacrifice us. In the morning they again gave us fish and roots and treated us so well that we were a little reassured and lost some of our fear of being sacrificed.

HOW WE FOUND OUT ABOUT OTHER CHRISTIANS

15   That same day I saw an Indian with a trinket which I knew was not among those we had given the Indians. Asking him where he had obtained it, I was answered by signs that other men like ourselves, who were farther back, had given it to them. Seeing this, I sent two Christians with two Indians to guide them to where those people were. Very near there they came upon them. The men were on their way to find us, since the Indians they were with had told them about us. They were Captains Andrés Dorantes and Alonso del Castillo, with all the men from their boat.[17] When they got to us they were shocked to see the condition we were in. They were very sorry that they had nothing to give us, since they were wearing the only clothes they had. They stayed there with us and told us how, about the fifth of that month,[18] their boat had run aground a league and a half from there and how they had escaped without losing anything. All of us agreed to repair their boat and leave in it with those strong enough and willing. The others would stay there until they convalesced and were able to go along the coast to wait until God would take them with us to a land of Christians. We set out to do what we planned. Before we launched the boat, Tavera, a gentleman of our company, died. And the boat that we intended to take met its end when it could not stay afloat and sank.

16   We considered the conditions we were left in, most of us naked and with the weather too severe to travel and swim across rivers and inlets. We had no

---

[17] There were forty-eight men in that group, according to an earlier portion of the text.
[18] According to Hallenbeck (*op. cit.*, p. 53), the Castillo-Dorantes boat was cast ashore a day before Cabeza de Vaca's.

provisions nor means of carrying them. Therefore we decided to do what we were forced to do and spend the winter there. We decided that the four strongest men should go to Panuco, since we thought we were near it, and that if God our Lord should be pleased to take them there, they should tell them how we were stuck on that island with great need and affliction. These were very good swimmers; one, a Portuguese carpenter and sailor, was named Álvaro Fernández; the second was named Méndez; the third, Figueroa, was a native of Toledo; the fourth, Astudillo, was a native of Zafra. They took with them an Indian from the island.

HOW FOUR CHRISTIANS DEPARTED

17   A few days after these four Christians left, the weather turned so cold and stormy that the Indians could no longer pull up roots and could catch nothing in the cane weirs[19] they used for fishing. And since their lodges offered so little shelter, people began to die. Five Christians who had taken shelter on the coast became so desperate that they ate one another one by one until there was only one left, who survived because the others were not there to eat him.[20] Their names were Sierra, Diego López, Corral, Palacios, Gonzalo Ruiz. The Indians were quite upset by this happening and were so shocked that they would have killed the men had they seen them begin to do this, and we would all have been in great difficulties. At last, in a very short time, only fifteen[21] survivors remained of the eighty[22] who had arrived there from both directions. After these sixty-five had died, the Indians of that country came down with a stomach ailment[23] that killed half of their people. They thought that we were the cause of their deaths, and were so sure of it that they plotted among themselves to kill those of us who had survived. When they were about to carry out their plan, an Indian who held me told them that they should not believe that we were causing them to die, because, if we had power over life and death, we would spare our own and not so many of us would have died helplessly. He told them that, since only a few of us remained and none of us was harming or hurting them, it would be best to leave us alone. It was our Lord's will for the others to heed this advice and opinion, and so their original plan was thwarted.

---

[19] A fencelike enclosure in a waterway for catching fish.

[20] Simars de Bellisle, a Frenchman who was cast ashore on Galveston Island in 1719, reported that the Indians practiced cannibalism. This custom may have been a legacy of the Spaniards, for anthropologists maintain that the Indians did not practice cannibalism prior to the arrival of the Spaniards in 1528. For an account of de Bellisle's experiences, see Henri Flomer "De Bellisle on the Coast of Texas," *Southwestern Historical Quarterly* 44 (October 1940): 204–31.

[21] Cabeza de Vaca later indicates that there were fourteen.

[22] According to Hallenbeck (*op. cit.*, p. 53), there were ninety-seven men who reached the island in two boats. The inspector and two other men had drowned. Cabeza de Vaca somehow did not account for another fourteen men.

[23] Cyclone Covey in his translation of *The Account, Cabeza de Vaca's Adventures in the Unknown Interior of America* (New York: Collier, 1961), p. 60, is of the opinion that the Indians contracted dysentery from the Spaniards.

18   We named this island the Isle of Misfortune. The people we found there are tall and well built.[23] They have no weapons other than bows and arrows, which they use with great skill. The men have one nipple pierced from one side to the other, and some have both pierced. Through the opening they place a reed two and a half palms in length and two fingers thick. They also pierce their lower lip through which they insert a reed about half as thick as a finger. The women do the hard work. They live on this island from October through February. They live on the roots that I mentioned, pulled from under water in November and December. They have cane weirs but there are no fish left by this season; from then on they eat the roots. At the end of February, they move on to other places to find sustenance, because at that time the roots are beginning to sprout and are not good. These people love their children more and treat them better than any other people on earth.[25] When someone's child happens to die, the parents and relatives and the whole village weep for him for a full year. The parents begin crying each morning before dawn, and then the whole village joins in. They do the same thing at midday and at sunrise. At the end of a year, they honor the dead child and wash themselves clean of the soot on their bodies. They mourn all their dead in this manner except old people, whom they ignore, saying that their time has passed and they are of little use, and that in fact they occupy space and consume food which could be given to the children. Their custom is to bury the dead, unless the dead man is a medicine man, in which case they burn the body, all dancing around the fire with much merriment. They grind the bones to a powder. A year later they honor the dead medicine man, scar themselves, and his relatives drink the powdered bones mixed with water.

19   Each one has a recognized wife. The medicine men have the greatest freedom, since they can have two or three wives, among whom there is great friendship and harmony. When someone gives his daughter in marriage, from the first day of the marriage onward, she takes all that her husband kills by hunting or fishing to her father's lodge, without daring to take or eat any of it. The husband's in-laws then take food to him. All this time the father-in-law and the mother-in-law do not enter his lodge and he does not enter their lodge nor the lodges of his brothers-in-law. If they encounter him somewhere, they move away the distance of a crossbow shot, and while they are moving away, they lower their heads and keep their eyes on the ground, because they think it is a bad thing for them to see each other. The women are free to communicate and converse with their in-laws and relatives. This

---

[24] The Capoques and the Hans, who, according to Newcomb (*op. cit.*, p. 63), were two groups of Karankawa Indians.

[25] According to Frederick W. Hodge in his *Handbook of American Indians* (Washington: Government Printing Office, 1910), p. 206, Indian children were very rarely punished.

custom is observed on the island and for a distance of more than fifty leagues inland.

20   Another custom of theirs is that, when an offspring or sibling dies, no one in the household looks for food for three months; they would sooner let themselves starve to death. Relatives and neighbors provide them with food. Since many of their people died while we were there and this custom and ritual was observed, there was great hunger in many households. Those who sought food found very little despite their great efforts because the weather was so bad. For this reason the Indians who were holding me left the island and crossed to the mainland in canoes. They went to some bays where there are many oysters. They eat nothing else and drink very bad water for three months of the year.

21   Firewood is scarce for them, but mosquitos are plentiful. Their houses are made of mats and built on oyster shells, on which they sleep naked, putting animal hides on them if they happen to have any. We stayed there until the end of April, when we went to the seacoast and ate blackberries for the entire month, during which they hold their festivals with areítos[26] and singing.[27]

DISCUSSION QUESTIONS

1. Describe the pressures the Spaniards faced. How were they related to the Indians? To the land? To the ocean? To the weather?
2. In small groups, discuss whether the sharing of food, trinkets, and emotions between the Indians and the Spaniards constituted a celebration that could be called "Thanksgiving."
3. Analyze the point of view of the narrator in *The Account*. Whose voice do we hear throughout the narrative?
4. Discuss the likelihood that some of these Spaniards have had contact with other Indians in the past. Based upon their previous experiences, how do they judge the Indians they encounter on the island?
5. Describe the Indians and their way of life from the perspective of the Spaniards.

---

26 Areítos is the Indian (*Taíno*) word that Cabeza de Vaca used to describe the dance ceremonies he witnessed.

27 All of these customs noted by Cabeza de Vaca have been studied and described by Newcomb (*op. cit.*, pp. 59–81).

WRITING TOPICS

1. Imagine that you are visiting a new country. In a short composition, recount your experiences with regard to survival (shelter, food, and transportation) and to learning about the country (communication, customs and traditions, rituals, and taboos).
2. To what extent do fear and courage play a part in the behavior of both Spaniards and Indians in this selection? In your journal, write a brief paragraph expressing your opinion.

CANTO III

Gaspar Pérez de Villagrá

Gaspar Pérez de Villagrá was born in Puebla de los Angeles, New Spain (known today as Pueblo, Mexico) in 1555. As a young man, he was sent by his parents to study at the University of Salamanca, where he received a bachelors degree. After spending several years at the court of Felipe II, he crossed the Atlantic and returned to New Spain. There he met Juan de Oñate, who was making preparations for an expedition to New Mexico. Villagrá was appointed the expedition's Procurator General, receiving the rank of captain.

In his *Historia de la Nueva México,* Villagrá conveys in epic verse the story of that expedition. He begins by describing the preparations for the journey. He recounts the origin of the Aztecs and the founding of Tenochtitlán, going on to review and summarize all previous expeditions to New Mexico. He shares biographical information about Juan de Oñate and his other captains, and gives his readers vivid descriptions of the countryside and the inhabitants of New Mexico. Finally, he concludes the poem by relating the events leading to the destruction of Acoma.

Interestingly, Pérez de Villagrá was the first writer to describe the *vaquero* (cowboy) and the *aventada*, which would later become the rodeo. Also, this expedition led to the naming of the river that today separates the United States from Mexico, the Río Bravo (known to Anglo-Americans as the Río Grande). He also give an account of the performance of a play written by Capitán Farfán in what today is El Paso. His most memorable description, however, is that of the destruction of Acoma, reminding his readers of the tempestuous conflict from which the New World emerged.

Historia de la Nueva México comprises thirty-four cantos or poems that ultimately tell the tale of a battle, though some would describe this epic as a recounting of a massacre. *Canto III,* translated and edited by Miguel Encinies, Alfred Rodríguez, and Joseph P. Sánchez, invites readers to consider the effort and perseverance of numerous conquerors and explorers in claiming New Mexico. From bloody and terrible encounters, the New Mexican population was born.

A glory high and gallant is the work,
Of memorable, illustrious fame,
Which in the sovereign, triumphant Court
And in the most militant[1] shelter where we live
5   We know is cherished and is treasured
By virtue of those heroes valorous
Who followed His immortal flag.[2]
Whose lofty peak and summit powerful
You well may note, incomparable lord,
10   In that, as scutcheon heroic and sublime,
That powerful, eternal God did wish
That man, as lofty height and triumph great,
Who repents in Trinity and in essence
His own beauty and high resemblance,
15   Taken from His own living being,
Should venerate it and esteem it much
If he should wish to see most things
Of this our life safe in fair harbor.
And thus no work shall there be seen,
20   If truly by heroic breasts t'would be received,
That God Himself in it does not shine,
Showing us clearly the beauty
Of their notable deeds and prowess.
And this, like to resplendent suns,
25   Raised there unto fourth heaven,[3]
They show us, with no small astonishment,
After in Florida they were lost
For that prolonged time,
The great and valorous negro Esteban
30   And memorable Cabeza de Vaca,
Castillo, Maldonado, without peer,
And Andrés Dorantes, most remarkable,
All being men most singular.[4]
In the most fierce and raging storm
35   Of all their miseries and trials sharp,

---

[1] Villagrá's reference is to the church triumphant, in heaven, and the church militant, still here on earth.
[2] The reference is to God's standard.
[3] In recalling Dante (*Paradiso* XIV) Villagrá appears to confuse heavenly circles: the fourth is identified with theologians and the fifth with captains and martyrs. He is, however, correct in identifying the fourth with the sun.
[4] In his chronological presentation of previous explorers of those lands, Villagrá begins, properly, with Cabeza de Vaca and his small group of survivors from a Spanish expedition which shipwrecked in Florida. Cabeza de Vaca gave an account of his travels through the southern United States in *Relación de naufragios y comentarios,* published long before the Oñate expedition to New Mexico.

Through them the Highest Power chose to work
Great store of miracles.
And as his Deity with just his breath
Infused the living spirit into men
40   And others He made well, blessed by his hand,
So these brave men thus passing on
Among those nations barbarous
Not only healed for them their sick,
their lame, the paralytic, and the blind,
45   But also gave life to their dead
Merely through blessing and their holy breath
That through their sainted mouths they did breathe forth,
Poultices, treacle, medicine
Which only in the miraculous pharmacy
50   Of God all-powerful could well be found.
Through whose high and sovereign virtue,
The unlearned Arabs[5] in suspense,
As though they all were gods,
One time, as tribute and sign of vassalage
55   Did consecrate and give and offer them
More than six hundred hearts
Of many animals they'd killed.[6]
Which is no small astonishment, and wonder,
That people stupid, barbarous, and gross
60   Should see and comprehend in every way
That, in all reason, nothing else but hearts
Ought to be sacrificed and offered
To those who did such works,
For, notwithstanding that it is scarcely enough
65   To satisfy the feeble hunger
Of a weak and fearful bird of prey,
No one denies the great fact of its nobleness,
For being in itself so small and timid
We now that the whole world will not contain it.
70   And in the little world that's man
It is the base and primary fundament
That gives the heat of life unto the whole device
Of all the edifice miraculous;
And so heroic is its greatness in itself

---

5 Villagrá will frequently use *Alarabe*, arab, as generic for enemy, probably a linguistic identification derived
  from Spain's long history of reconquering the Iberian Peninsula from the Moors.
6 The event is narrated by Cabeza de Vaca, *Naufragios,* Chapter 32.

⁷⁵ That, since all must pass and be registered
In one of the halls of judgment,
In which place the senses all preside,
All that which to the greatest height and excellence
Of the great understanding is proposed,[7]
⁸⁰ Thus comes it nothing can approach
To wound it and to hurt it unto death
Unless it first do end and quite destroy
The little world[8] and all its greatness,
For it is the last thing to die
⁸⁵ And is the last to lose its movement.
And so, in it, as in a lovely temple,
The soul's own majesty doth have its seat,
From whence to God all-powerful it sends
Its prayers so holy and devout,
⁹⁰ Its works, its thoughts, its joy,
Its true love, and its sadness,
Its tears and sighs and groans.
And thus, as the abundant fount of life
From which such mighty things do spring,
⁹⁵ To God alone the heart should be
On all occasions sacrificed
And to all other men of strength
Who follow in His blessed steps,
Noting the sacrifice inestimable
¹⁰⁰ Of these barbarian rustic savages,
Who offered there so many hearts
To these four famous men who in their lands
Throughout the time of nine laborious years
Suffered a million miseries.
¹⁰⁵ At the end of which they came at last
Unto the hot and famous province
Of Culiacán, which in other times
Most noble gentlemen had populated.
And in whose famous century of gold
¹¹⁰ That humble, zealous, Provincial,[9]
He of Seraphic Francis's order

---

[7] The philosophy somewhat confusedly expressed here (that there is nothing in the intellect that has not first been in the senses) is Aristotelian-Scholasticism, taught at the University of Salamanca which Villagrá attended.

[8] The reference is to an earlier identification of man as a microcosm or "little world." The idea was commonplace and is expressed, for example, by Cervantes: *La Galatea* IV.

[9] The provincial was the religious head of the monasteries in a given province.

Who was called Fray Martos de Niza,[10]
He having well-informed himself
From those who had discovered certain parts
115 Of these new, hidden, regions,
And as he knew already from the Indians
The story that I told you above,
That hence the Mexicans had come,
Like famed Columbus, he who gave a world
120 All new unto your royal Kingdom of Castile,
E'en so he then determined he would enter
A matter of two hundred leagues or more
With one companion only, trusting well
Unto that Highest Good which governs us.
125 And by the sickness which then came upon
His comrade, 'twas necessary to remain,
And he went on with effort high, divine,
With numerous barbarian friends,
Into the land; and, like to one who finds
130 A rich, most precious treasure,
Whose great abundance forces and invites him
To quickly come again for aid,
E'en so the mighty captain of poor folk
With swiftness great returned
135 And saying most notable good things about the land
Which he had seen and noted and discovered.
And as there is not in the universe
A thing which is more like and represents
The majesty of God than man himself,
140 As if he were God's Self he undertakes
Things which it seems must be reserved to God.
And thus, O powerful King, you here can note
That, having now of this new land
A copious tale got from this man,
145 This holy and heroic monk of Francis,
That great Cortez, the Marquis of the Valley,
Having endured the fury great
Of furious sea, having sunk
The powerful vessels of his fleet,

---

[10] Fray Marcos de Niza was the first to follow up on the news of the new lands to the north given by the members of the Cabeza de Vaca party. His glowing and mostly imaginary description of great cities to the north was paramount in encouraging further explorations. For a summary of his explorations, see H. E. Bolton, *Coronado, Knight of Pueblos and Plains* (Albuquerque: The Univ. Of New Mexico Press, 1964), 23–39.

150   Deed of such effort and such daring
As never famous man had done,[11]
Borne on by the illustrious and lofty valor
Of his person, never o'ercome,
Which ne'er could be contained by all the world,
155   Not because he did not know well
But seven feet of earth more than sufficed,[12]
But trying to discover at each step
A newer world, a hundred if he could,
In order to better raise up the edifice
160   Of our Holy Church and lift it high
In these lost lands barbaric;
Well, setting the prow of his intent
To set all sails before the wind
Following the demand of this emprise,
165   Since loving and ruling never bear
Competition to be offered them,
The same occurred to him as to the famous Caesar
With the brave Pompey over the command
Which each one necessarily desired,[13]
170   For Don Antonio refused him,
The first Vice-regent of New Spain,[14]
Telling him that to him alone the emprise,
As Viceroy, belonged,
Cutting the firm and cunning knot
175   Of true and ancient friendship
Which they had unto each other.
Now God deliver us from interest
When it breaks and shatters, and can cut deep,
For at the time that it becomes furious
180   There is no King nor reason, law, nor force so great
As to resist its diabolical impulse.
And thus the Mantuan[15] well says:
"O sacred hunger of vain wealth,
What misfortunes are there to which you do not force

---

[11] Cortez's deeds were already legendary and had been written about in at least two epics with which Villagrá was familiar, *Mexicana* and *El peregrino indiano*.

[12] The reminder, especially to New World conquerors of great empires, that seven feet of earth suffice one in the end, may be found as well, in Ercilla: *La Araucana* I, 1.

[13] The Caesar-Pompey conflict is the subject matter of Lucan's epic, one of the primary models of the Renaissance epic.

[14] Antonio de Mendoza, the first viceroy of New Spain, was appointed by Charles V in 1535. See C. Pérez Bustamante, *Don Antonio de Mendoza* (Santiago de Chile, 1928).

[15] Virgil is often referred to as the Mantuan. The quote that follows is from the *Aeneid* III, 73–74.

185 The sad hearts of mortals!"
And he gives to it this title sacrosanct,
Sovereign, lofty, grandiose,
So that no mortal ever dare
To undertake it ever against justice.
190 But as the Scripture warns us:
Who can this be that we may praise him
For having performed marvels while alive.
Well, these two quarreling upon this cause
As if they were two powerful gods,
195 Each one intended and did try
To subject all the world, if well he might.
And, deciding the matter would end ill,
Immediately the heroic Marquis claimed,
As Adelantado[16] of the South Sea,
200 This right he claimed and alleged
To make the voyage was his in fact.
And so he might not lose or let it lapse
He took at once the way to Spain
To treat with the imperial person
205 Of your most fortunate grandfather,
Carlos the Fifth, on all that case,
Whose lofty and most prudent government
Did have of empires the most notable,
Of kingdoms and of lordships in this life
210 The highest and most lofty primacy,
Being beloved, respected, and esteemed
By all the universe girds round.
As soon as he had ended his long voyage
And furled the tattered sails
215 Of that long toilsome trip,
Like powerful ship that does safely anchor
Right in the longed-for port and in an instant
We see it sink and without hope,
So came death, rude, ferocious,
220 Saying in loud and upraised voice,
"I pardon no one!",[17] and made peace,
Taking the emprise from before his gaze.
And with horrible and powerful command

---

16 Coming from the military-political tradition of the Spanish reconquest, the 'Adelantado' was charged with protecting and expanding a specific frontier area.
17 Villagrá attributes to Death the words *concedo nulli*, usually attributed in the emblematic literature of his day to Cronus, the pagan god of time.

Ordered him instantly to change his route,
225 Taking without excuse or remedy
That mournful, mortal road
So frequented and followed by the dead
(As it is never trod by those alive)
And more by those sad, miserable, ones
230 Who promise to themselves a life prolonged.
And as it many times doth hap,
A precious glass from out our hands
Doth slip, from carelessness,
Leaving us sad and in suspense
235 And almost breathless, open-mouthed,
To see it broken on the floor,
So it caused very great distress,
Astonishment and wonder, fear and dread,
To see that man fallen upon the earth,
240 All turned to dust and ashes vile,
This being he who won such vantage with his sword,
Who with it conquered a new world.
But who shall be so strong, O lord,
That his great strength may still resist
245 The furious force of death
If Kings and Popes and lofty potentates
Lie prostrate beneath its feet
As funeral spoils and trophies;
No feat, since we know it took the life
250 Of the live Son of living God,
For which cause let each one prepare,
For, without remedy, needs be we must surrender
And lie prone, without the vital spirit,
Beneath his hoe and mighty spade.
255 With this, Don Antonio de Mendoza
Took and kept all the field for his,
Like one who leaves his adversary great
Lying all pale in the arena and his soul
Gone from the miserable corpse.
260 And better to find out his goal
He made use of the third of divine gifts,[18]
The one which best doth guide and carry us,
Like a refulgent light that shows the way,
By whose clear ray he counsel took,
265 With that great, noble, famous man

---

[18] The reference is to intelligence, one of the three powers (intelligence, will, and memory) associated with the soul.

Who was called Cristóbal de Oñate,[19]
Person of great good sense and self-control,
One of the most virtuous and valorous
'Mong those of cape and sword[20] that we have seen
In all of New Spain and Kingdoms of Peru.
Him he did ask opinions and advice
270 As to the soldier most resourceful,
Experienced, astute, and strong, and most discreet
That it was possible for him to choose
That he might use him and employ him
Simply as scout for this ingress,
275 To go ahead with thirty chosen men
Before the camp entire should sally forth.
And as a good end is hastened on
In measure as beginning is well made,
As a shrewd lynx doth sharply see
280 Or royal eagle that without timidity
Doth look into the brightness of the sun,
Thus, with great quickness he spoke then,
Placing before him the person
Of that Juan de Zaldívar, his nephew,[21]
285 A valiant soldier and as much long-suffering
As he was well-prepared for all affronts.
They gave to him without discussion
A gallant squadron of Spaniards
Who numbered thirty lances stout.
290 With these he pierced deep into the land,
Where troubles very great came to them
And also a very tempest fierce of labors
So vigorous and vivid, spirited,
Naught but his valor could have borne them.
295 Meanwhile the insightful Mendoza
Quickly prepared great aid, being a man astute,
Forming a camp supplied right well
With sturdy soldiers, as excellent
As could possibly be achieved
300 By those who arrived and imparted
The art of war in all its finest points.

---

19 The father of Juan de Oñate.

20 The phrase *de capa y espada* suggested the ideal of a man socially and militarily adept.

21 He appears to have been the father of Juan and Vicente Zaldívar, who accompanied Oñate as his top military officers. But Villagrá, *Historia*, Junquera edition, 97, denies this family tie.

Now, seeing this brave levy raised,
305 There would return with them the holy Niza,
Provincial of the poor Franciscans,
Only that the voice of doctrine Evangelical
Might have free entry
Among those poor and lost barbarians.
310 And since it is quite impossible
That headless human body be, without a head,
Able to govern and command itself,
They named as Governor of this camp
A mighty knight whom they did call
315 Francisco Vázquez de Coronado,
A man of valor and of great emprise
In things of substance and of serious weight.
And that they have reverence for him
They wished to single out his person
320 By honorable title, that of general.
The Viceroy, honoring him in every way he could,
The better to inspire that party of explorers,
Came on in person to give escort
Until they pitched their camp at Compostela,
325 A distance from the City of Mexico
Of good two hundred miles,[22] long ones,
Where there came on to meet them on the way
Our Captain Zaldívar, all broken down
By the harsh and laborious trail
330 He, for him, had just then explored and discovered
By force of arms, of hunger and great thirst
And many other labors that I do not tell
That through great deserts they suffered.
And saying to the Viceroy that the land
335 He had seen, noted, and discovered
To him appeared as of no advantage
Because it was so poor and miserable
And peopled by barbarians rude;
But all this still was not a reason
340 For any to turn back a single pace,
Since just when hope is lost
Right there 'tis that most skillful hunters
Make it their custom, with great pleasure, entertainment,
To raise great game quite without thinking to.
345 And, as there never lacks to good

---

[22] The mile, as its name suggests, was measured at a thousand paces.

Someone to contradict, resist, deny it,
Here, too, there was not lacking one to say and to affirm
It was a miserable land, and for this cause
It were a terrible thing for that great camp
350 To occupy itself in things so ruinous.
The bad news touched the Viceroy to the quick,
But, like a prudent and cautious man,
Considering that great good luck
Doth often come from grave error,
355 He did dissimulate as best he might
And, just as in a sudden danger
'Tis best to quickly counsel with
A man who lives quite far from it,
Without delay he ordered that
360 They should keep silence and be quiet
In all such matter, so no thing
Should be by anyone found out.
Because 'twas necessary that this way
The peril of a dissolution of the camp be met,
365 Decision made because the expense
Was by then lost and all consumed,
With fifty thousand dollars[23] of good gold
That Cristóbal de Oñate gave him gladly,
Lending them from his generous heart
370 With the sole purpose that this journey might be made,
For it was possible that a second
Exploration be of advantage.
And as the tired hunter is often
Restored by stoic persistence,
375 Persisting, then, he ordered on the spot
That the new General should make a start
To breaking camp, and march.
And, having taken leave of all,
The Viceroy then returned to Mexico;
380 The encampment took to its route
With fury great and force of effort,
Which did carry them and bring them to
The Cities of Cibola and
To other places neighboring,
385 Where great Father Niza and the Floridians[24]

---

[23] Curtis translates Villagrá's *pesos* with the modern equivalent of "dollars"; but the latter did not exist then as a monetary unit.
[24] *Floridians* is a reference to the Cabeza de Vaca party.

And Captain Zaldívar with his squadron
Had come and returned with the news.
In this place, the General, well pleased
To see that land, did order then
390 That all should make great holiday;
And doing this, he came in person
On a great, powerful horse,
And, in a skirmish[25] which they had,
He fell from out his saddle,
395 Striking the hard ground forcibly,
So that, tormented by the fearful blow,
He was and did remain all senseless.
And as the separate members suffer pain
When they do feel the head is failing them,
400 And each does writhe and is not governed,
Just so the soldiery, seeing
The strength of government stricken,
Maimed, and sick, they then did wish,
Having so much land over which to extend,
405 To stop and curtail further work.
So, joined together in a body,
Like one who quite despairs of all,
So they despised all hope,
The one true remedy for the ends
410 Which we attempt, with such great care, to reach.
And, without seeing that 'twould have been best
For all that downcast camp
Not to have made beginning of the enterprise
Rather than turn their backs in shame
415 Once having put themselves into
The demanding test and challenge,
With all their furious grief
They turned, in greatest haste, to rear
Their hasty and impudent steps.
420 Although a many tried, like worthy men,
To stop them all with reasoning
And force of efficacious words,
Favored by the holy Provincial,
Protected, too, by Don Francisco
425 De Peralta, warrior extremely great,
And by the gallant heart of Zaldívar,
And by that gentleman most rarely famed,

---

[25] These "skirmishes" were not with any enemy, but jousting games simulating war.

Don Pedro de Tovar, father of that
Illustrious, beautiful, and generous dame,
430 As courteous as she was great in court,
That Doña Isabel who did incorporate
A virtue deep, lifted
To Sovereign love, with which she glows,
Having recourse to the roasted[26] martyr
435 In whose temple we do see she burns
And is consumed like glowing coals
In amorous passion for her Spouse,
Who is the life of both her life and soul,
All illustrious gifts inherited
440 From her father valiant and vigorous,
Who, with many other gentlemen,
Insisted that the camp should not return.
As always, the base rabble and the crowd
Would not permit what was outside their wish,
445 Nor gave to anyone the slightest heed;
Such was their harshness and obduracy
That, with a loss both great and notable,
They turned their backs upon the work.
Because they had not traveled stumbling
450 O'er many bars of gold and silver fine,
And since they saw the fountains clear,
Brooklets, and lakes did not pour out
Gilded soups, cakes, and sausages,
They set themselves to curse the land
455 And everyone who wished them to be put
And snared into such a place.
And so, all miserable and weeping,
They wailed their fate as though they had been women,
A meanness, worthy of dishonor,
460 With which they made themselves right infamous,
Withdrawing their hands from the labors
That must be suffered in war.
It would be well to wait for a new canto
If we must write about their dolorous weeping.[27]

---

26 The reference appears to be to Saint Lawrence, usually associated with a roasted martyrdom.

27 Although there is historical documentation for Coronado's fall from horseback, (Bolton, *Coronado, Knight of Pueblos and Plains,* 330), it occurred very near the end of the expedition, and the supposed desertion of his men, a diatribe that Villagrá carries over into Canto IV, is not historically accurate. The poet may have gotten such an impression, possibly, from reading Pedro de Castañeda's account of the disbanding of the army (Bolton, *Coronado,* 347) after it had reached Culiacán on the return trip.

DISCUSSION QUESTIONS

1. As he begins "Canto III," Villagrá evokes the many who came before Oñate, his expedition's leader, and himself. Who were they, and why recall them?
2. Discuss what motivates these men, according to Villagrá, to form part of the expedition to New Mexico.
3. To whom is Villagrá speaking throughout the epic poem? Is he flattering his reader? Why or why not?
4. Verses 141 through 254 recount the story of Spanish explorer Hernando Cortés—having conquered Mexico from Montezuma, the Aztec emperor, and having garnered the titles of Marqués (Marquis) and Adelantado (Forward Governor)—and his desire to rule New Mexico against Viceroy Mendoza's will. Most of the account details his greatness and his death. In small groups, discuss the ways in which the epic poem here yields to the elegy as a form.
5. What did Coronado do after being named general by Viceroy Mendoza on Oñate's advice?
6. Was the expedition successful?

WRITING TOPICS

1. Imagine you are a soldier in an army. Describe a tour of duty that neither you nor your fellow soldiers wanted to take. Write a letter to a family member detailing the struggles and discomfort you suffered.
2. As a viceroy, it is your job to seek out opportunities to expand your land holdings. The reports of the lands in which you are interested describe it as great and rich, full of vast cities of gold. Write a brief essay detailing how you would go about verifying the truth about the land and about how you would conquer it.
3. Write a brief analytical essay about the references to Indians and women in this canto.

FROM *MEMORIAL*

Gonzalo Solís de Merás

Dr. Gonzalo Solís de Merás, brother-in-law to the Spanish explorer Menéndez de Avilés, published a biography of Menéndez de Avilés entitled *Memorial* in 1567. Though little is known about Solís de Merás, much is known and debated about his subject. Solís de Merás opens the biography of Menéndez de Avilés by describing the event that occurred on June 29, 1565, when the two set sail from Cádiz to drive the French out of Florida. Philip II of Spain had appointed Pedro Menéndez de Avilés, a very able seaman, as commander.

Solís de Merás relates Menéndez's defeat of the French Huguenots and his founding of the settlement of St. Augustine in Florida. The colonial warfare between Georgians and Floridians made the former call Menéndez a Catholic bigot, and this characterization continued throughout several accounts supplied by English historians. Modern scholars, however, have re-evaluated Menéndez's life and side more with Solís de Merás, who maintained that, though Menéndez was intolerant and exacting, so were the French and English commanders in the area at that time. The *Memorial* stands as an important documentation of the life of Pedro Menéndez de Avilés and the history of Florida.

In this selection, Solís de Merás details the expedition into Florida waters, the presence of French Huguenots, and the plan to drive them out of Florida. It also tells of Menéndez de Avilés's founding of St. Augustine, one of the oldest cities in the United States.

¹   That day in the afternoon, the Adelantado commanded that all the ships' arms should be delivered to the captains, so that they should distribute them among their soldiers, who were to keep them clean and ready, and that each soldier should shoot three rounds every day until they reached Florida, in order to lose fear of the arquebuses and be trained, as they were raw recruits

for the most part. They were to shoot one round with bullets in a space arranged within the said galleon, prizes being awarded to the soldiers in the companies who shot best, and to their captains so that they should take great care to make them skillful; and with that exercise, which was done each day, they daily repeated the Christian doctrine and the litanies, saying prayers and making supplications to God Our Lord, and beseeching Him to grant them victory in everything. They sailed until August 28th, St. Augustine's Day, on which they sighted the land of Florida;[1] all of them kneeling, saying the *Te Deum Laudamus*, they praised Our Lord, all the people repeating their prayers, entreating Our Lord to give them victory in all things.

And because they knew not in what part the Lutherans had fortified themselves, and in great suspense, not knowing whether the French were north or south of where the said Adelantado was going with his armada, sailing by day and anchoring at night; and one morning he saw Indians on the coast:[2] he sent his camp master to land with 20 arquebusiers: he did not wish to land more men so that the Indians might not be frightened and flee. When the camp master disembarked among the Indians with the 20 soldiers, they came with their bows and arrows, and as our men went toward them, they retreated toward the woods: the Christians fearing that if they followed them there might be an ambuscade of many men, and they would run a risk; and that if they did not seek information from them to learn in what part the Lutherans were, it would be a bad state of things; for as the coast and sand-banks were not known either to the said Adelantado or to his pilots, if some storm should come up they were in danger of losing themselves with the fleet; to remedy this, the camp master ordered a soldier who had committed a crime, to lay down his arms and go to the Indians with certain little things as presents, and the soldier did so: the Indians awaited him, received him well and were reassured: then the camp master arrived and spoke with them, and through signs they told him that the French were about 20 leagues from there, to the north.[3] The Indians asked

---

[1] Francisco de Mendoza Grajales, the chaplain of Pedro Menéndez, also gives August 28th as the day that the Spanish fleet sighted Florida (*cf.* his "Memoria" or "Relación," Ruidíaz, *La Florida*, II, pp. 445–446). Barrientos says August 28th (*cf.* "Vida y Hechos de Pero Menéndez de Auiles," p. 39, in Genaro García, *Dos Antiguas Relaciones de la Florida*). Menéndez himself, however, says that the event occurred on August 25th (perhaps a scribe's mistake). Menéndez to the King, September 11th, 1565, A. G. de I., 54–5–16. Copies in D. H., Colección Navarrete, tomo 14, No. 40.—L. C., Papeles relativos á la Florida, pp. 31–79.—Lowery, II.—Smith, vol. for 1561–1593, pp. 292–309, from D. H.—Massachusetts Historical Society.—Published in Ruidíaz, *La Florida*, II, pp. 84–105; and in translation, in Mass. Hist. Soc. *Proceedings*, VIII, pp. 425–439.

[2] These Indians belonged to a large and important tribe of the Timucua, who controlled most of the northern part of the region today known as Florida. Many affiliated smaller tribes were included under that designation. The word has different forms: Timuqua, Timoqua, Thimogona, etc. The name of the River Tomoka, which empties into the Halifax above Ormond, on the Florida East Coast, is an English form of Timucua. For information on the Timucua, *cf.* Frederick W. Hodge, *Handbook of American Indians*, Bureau of American Ethnology, Smithsonian Institution, Washington, D.C., Part II, pp. 752–754.— Lowery, *Spanish Settlements*, 1562–1574, Appendix H, p. 407.

[3] Jean Ribaut, commanding an expedition of Huguenots or French Protestants (whom the Spaniards called the Lutherans), had attempted in 1562 to make a settlement to which he gave the name of Charlesfort, near Port Royal, in South Carolina.

whether the General of the armada was on board the ships, or among them: they were told that he was on the ships: they answered that they desired greatly to see him and know him: [the Spaniards] wanted to take them to the ships, but they would not go: they said that they were afraid and would await him there on land. And so the camp master returned to the flagship with his 20 soldiers, where was the said Adelantado, and he related to him everything that had taken place with the Indians and that they were awaiting him on shore; and because of the desire he had to see them, and to satisfy himself [of the truth] of what the Indians said by signs, that the French were 20 leagues from there toward the north; he went to land with 2 boats and 50 arquebusiers, and as soon as the Indians saw him land, leaving their bows and arrows, they came to the said Adelantado, [and] began to sing and to make gestures with their hands raised toward heaven, in manner of adoration, so that it was a wonderful thing to see. The Adelantado gave them many things and sweets to eat, which he had in one of the boats: they reiterated what they had said, that the French were 20 leagues from there; the Adelantado left them very happy and embarked on his ships and went sailing along the coast with his armada, and discovered 8 leagues from there a good harbor, with a good beach, to which he gave the name of St. Augustine, because that was the first land he discovered in Florida, and he did so on the very day of St. Augustine.[4] On the following day, three hours after noontime, as he was proceeding along the coast, he discovered four large galleons at anchor.[5] As it appeared to him that that was the harbor where the French were, that succor had come to them and that those

---

[4] "Un puerto bueno, con una buena ribera, á que puso nombre Sant Agustin, por ser allí la primera tierra que descubrió de la Florida y ser el mismo día de Sant Agustin cuando la descubrío." Merás, "Memorial," in Ruidíaz, *La Florida*, I, p. 72.

This is a misleading sentence. Merás, through the vague words, "por ser allí la primera tierra," intends to say that that whole region from Cape Canaveral up, was the first land which Menéndez discovered in Florida, after he had sighted it at the Cape on St. Augustine's Day, several days previous (cf. p. 80, note 2); instead of which the impression is conveyed that the site or neighborhood of the present city of St. Augustine is the land that Menéndez first discovered.

The sentence which comes next is equally ambiguous. When Merás writes: "On the following day," he probably means September 4th, the day after the Adelantado found "a good harbor, with a good beach"— he is not thinking of the day following August 28, St. Augustine's Day. Barrientos, at this point, is just as misleading; but the letter of Menéndez of September 11th, and the "Memoria" of Mendoza Grajales, make the dates fairly clear.

From the careless wording of these passages Lowery was led to believe that Menéndez gave the good harbor the name of St. Augustine because he had discovered it on the festival of the saint (*Spanish Settlements, 1562–1574*, p. 154), whereas the name of St. Augustine was given to it because it was on St. Augustine's day, August 28th, that Menéndez had sighted Florida off Cape Canaveral.

[5] A week elapsed before the fleet of Menéndez reached the mouth of the River of May (the St. Johns) and saw the four French galleons. In his letter of September 11th, the Adelantado mentions September 4th as the date of his arrival there (cf. *La Florida*, II, p. 76). Laudonnière mentions the same date, which is very likely the correct one. Mendoza Grajales in his "Memoria" say Wednesday, September 5th, and Le Challeux in his "Discours de l'Histoire de la Floride," says Monday, September 3d. Le Moyne, Merás and Barrientos do not give any date. Ribaut had anchored at the entrance of the River of May on August 28th, the day that Menéndez reached Florida in the vicinity of Cape Canaveral.

galleons belonged to their armada, he entered into council with his captains and told them that as he held it for certain that the French armada had come and that their fort could not be taken, nor their armed harbor, [the captains] should say to him what it seemed to them ought to be done. Different opinions were given, but most of the captains decided that the said Adelantado should return to Santo Domingo with the five ships he had, and that there he should gather most of the ships of his fleet which had become separated in the storm, and 6 others he expected from Biscay and Asturias, for he had left orders at the Canaries that they should go to Puerto Rico. He would likewise collect two armed ships and the horses, infantry and supplies that his Majesty had ordered to be given him in that island of Santo Domingo and that of Cuba; and so with everything being gathered together, he could go to Havana, and in the coming month of March he would return to Florida with large forces to accomplish whatever good result he could; [but] the said Adelantado was afraid that if he acted on that opinion he would run the risk of defeat, because his presence with his 5 ships was already revealed to the French fleet. There was no wind and the sun gave promise of fair weather, but on account of the storm they had had 4 of the ships had remained without foremasts and lacked others which had been broken, so that the French armada could pursue his, especially as he had notice that they had vessels with oars; and he answered the captains that the Frenchmen could not reasonably expect him so soon on the coast; they would have their infantry on land and be unloading the supplies, as those vessels, being large, could not enter the harbor laden; and it seemed to him that they [the Spaniards] should go to fight with them, for if they captured them, the French would not have an armada sufficient to go out in search of him on the seas; and that they could return to the port of St. Augustine, which was twelve leagues from there, and disembark in that harbor and fortify themselves, and send the ships to Hispaniola to give tidings to the armada he was in need of; and that the infantry, horses and supplies his Majesty had ordered to be given him, should all come together in March to that port of St. Augustine, and once they had arrived there, they could go against the enemy by land and sea, capturing their harbor, because they had their fort . . . leagues inland, on the river bank. In this way succor could not come to them from France; [the Spaniards] with the horses would be masters of the country, so that they [the French] could not have dealings or intercourse with the Indians, and they [the Spaniards] could wage war on the French within a brief time, without danger to the said Adelantado's fleet, nor to himself, nor to his men: this was to be done when they had reconnoitered the fort of the French, and [felt] that they were so strong that they could run the danger of giving them the assault and conquering the fort with their arms. Owing to these reasons which the said Adelantado gave, all the captains approved this opinion and advice, and before coming to a decision they prayed to Our Lord, beseeching Him to favor them in everything and grant them victory over their enemies; and when the prayer was ended, the said Adelantado told them that he had determined to attack the French armada, which they all approved. Then he ordered the captains to go to their ships and gave them instructions as to what they had to do, and he gave orders to the Admiral of the fleet[6] as to what point he was to support and what position he was to take, with two vessels he indicated to him and the one whereon he was, which made three in all; the other ship, a patache, the Adelantado commanded not to leave the side of his flagship. And so, sailing along with fair weather, they were about 3 leagues from the French armada, which was anchored off its harbor and consisted of 4 large galleons, when the wind died down, and there was much thunder and lightning and a heavy shower, which lasted until 9 o'clock at night, and then the sky became very serene and clear, and the wind shifted toward land. As it appeared to the Adelantado that it would be almost midnight when he arrived near the enemy, and that it would not be safe to grapple with the ships because of the danger from the incendiary missiles which the enemy is wont to carry; that they could better avail themselves thereof by night than by day; and if the vessels of both fleets should burn, the enemy could escape in the boats and skiffs they had at the poop; a thing they could easily do, as the land was theirs; and they would come off victorious and the said Adelantado would be defeated; he decided to anchor in front of their bows, in such manner that when the cables were let loose after the anchors had caught, the sterns of the ships of the said Adelantado would overlap the prows of the enemy's ships, and at dawn the next morning, by loosening the cables they could board the enemy, who could not be aided by their vessels which were within the harbor; as the bar was a long one, those ships could not come out by night, and at dawn it would be low tide, so that they would have to wait until it was high, and that would be at midday. And so [the Adelantado] commanded his captains to come on board his flagship, and told them his decision, which they all approved as being very good; and when they arrived near the French armada at about half past 11 at night, [the French] began to fire artillery pieces therefrom, and the balls passed through the masts and rigging of the said Adelantado's vessels without harming anything whatever; he did not permit that any artillery should be fired from his ships; on the contrary, he ordered that on all the ships and on his own all the soldiers should clear the decks so that they should not be injured, for since they were to anchor and not to board the enemy, it was not safe that they should remain on deck with the artillery; and with great courage and coolness, unmindful of the guns [the enemy] were firing, he passed by the French flagship, for the four ships were all together; and he paid no attention to them. They had flags and pennants, and on the mainmast of the flagship were hoisted a flag and a royal standard: and on the Admiral's galleon, at the

---

6 The Admiral of a fleet was under the orders of the Captain-General.

top of the foremast, was the Admiral's flag. When the said Adelantado had anchored with his 5 vessels turned with their prows toward the shore, he had the cables loosened, and the poop of his flagship was between the prows of the enemy's flagship and Admiral's galley, and their prows reached his vessels like long pikes; and then he had the trumpets sounded hailing the enemy, and they answered him, hailing him with theirs; and presently when these salutes were ended, the said Adelantado spoke to them with much courtesy, saying: "Señores, whence comes that armada?" One only replied that it came from France. He asked them again: "What is it doing here?" they said to him: "We are bringing infantry, artillery and supplies for a fort which the King of France has in this country, and for others which he is to build." Said the Adelantado to them: "Are you Catholics or Lutherans, and who is your General?" They answered that they were all Lutherans of the new religion, and that their General was Juan Ribao; and [they wanted to know] who they were, who was he who asked this, and whose armada that was; why it had come to that country and who was the General thereof.

3   The Adelantado replied to them: "He who asks this of you is called Pedro Menéndez, this armada belongs to the King of Spain and I am the General thereof; and I come to hand and behead all the Lutherans I may find on this sea and in this land; and thus do I bring instructions from my King, which I shall fulfill at dawn when I shall board your ships; and if I should find any Catholic, I will give him good treatment."

4   Many together answered many shameless and insulting words against the King our Master, calling him by his name, and against the said Adelantado, saying "Let that be for the King, Don Felipe, and this for Pedro Menéndez, and if thou beest a brave man, as they say, come and wait not until tomorrow." The Adelantado, on hearing such unseemly words to the detriment of his King, ordered the cables to be loosened to board the enemy, and as the sailors did this unwillingly, he leaped down from the bridge to hasten them. The cable was wound round the capstan; it could not be loosened so quickly: when the enemy saw this, and heard sounded the Adelantado's command, they feared him, cut the cables, unfurled the sails and fled.

5   The said Adelantado did the same with his ships, and pursued them in such manner that when he was in the midst of them, he followed [in the flagship] with a patache, the two [galleons] which took the direction of the north, and his Admiral pursued, with the three ships, the other two which turned to the south. By the patache the said Adelantado sent a message to his Admiral that by dawn he was to return off the harbor, and that he would do likewise, to see if they could capture it; and that if not, they would go to land at the port of St. Augustine, as had been agreed; for in case no ship of the said Frenchmen should be taken (because theirs outsailed those of the said Adelantado, which lacked some of the masts owing to the storm they had had) 3 or 4 days would pass before the enemy could come together again, wherein the said Adelantado would either capture their harbor, or disembark in the port of St. Augustine; as the other French vessels in the har-

bor would not dare to come out with the four [galleons] not appearing; and if they should come out, there was no reason to fear them. And thus it happened that the said Adelantado chased the two French galleons northward for about 5 or 6 leagues, until dawn, and his Admiral went as many after the other two which sailed to the south; and the said Adelantado, with his 5 ships, lay off the harbor of the French at 10 o'clock the next morning, and trying to enter it, he saw two infantry flags at the end of the bar, artillery began to fire and there were 5 vessels anchored within. As it seemed to the said Adelantado that he ran the risk of failure if he tried to capture the harbor from them, and that meantime the 4 ships which had fled might unite with the 5 which were within, and that [then] he could escape neither by land nor by sea; he decided, without losing time, to put his flagship under full sail and order the others to do likewise, and he went to the harbor of St. Augustine, where he arrived on the eve of Our Lady of September; and as soon as he reached there he landed about three hundred soldiers, and sent 2 captains with them, who were to reconnoitre at daybreak the next morning the lay of the land and the places which seemed to them strongest [for defence], in order that they might dig a trench quickly while it was being seen where they could build a fort, so that the next day when the said Adelantado should land, they could show him what they had observed, and decide what would be most proper to do about it.

6   And on the following day, the day of Our Lady of September, the said Adelantado landed near noon, when he found many Indians awaiting him there, as they had had tidings of him from the other Indians with whom he had spoken four days before: he had a solemn mass said in honor of Our Lady, and when that was ended, he took possession of the country in the name of his Majesty; he received the solemn oath of the officials of his Majesty's Royal Exchequer, the camp master and the captains, that they would all serve his Majesty with entire loyalty and fidelity, and this being done, the said Adelantado had the Indians fed and dined himself. On finishing, he went immediately to see the locations which appeared to the captains he had sent, suitable for the trench; and leaving the site marked out,[7] he returned to the ships, having first held a council and decided that within three days everything possible should be unloaded from the vessels, and that then, two of them should be sent to Hispaniola, for as they were large they could not enter the harbor, and if the French armada came, it would capture them. The diligence the Adelantado showed in unloading those ships to send them away, so that the enemy should not take them from him, as it seemed to him that on the fourth day the French armada would come upon him—was such that all who were there were astounded; for although the ships were anchored more than a league and a half away from the landing

---

[7]The site of St. Augustine was changed several times. The first was on Anastasia Island.

place, in two days and a half he took ashore the people, the artillery, the munitions and a large part of the supplies; and without waiting for the third day, one night at midnight, fearing that the French fleet would be upon him at dawn, he made them set sail for Hispaniola without trying to unload more of the provisions. He placed about 150 soldiers he had with him on board a shallop of about 100 *toneles,* and he himself got into a large boat which he carried with him astern of his flagship when he chased the French fleet; and in order the better to flee, he cut it loose, and went to anchor off the bar with that boat and the shallop, in two fathoms of water. At dawn the French armada was near there, a quarter of a league away, where the said Adelantado had been at midnight [and] whence he had sent the vessels to Hispaniola, and a ship and three shallops of the enemy came on, and because of the extreme low tide and the sea's not being very calm, it was dangerous to cross the bar. When the said Adelantado saw the enemy upon them so that they could not escape, they all prayed to God Our Lord and his precious Mother to save them from that danger; and as the Lutherans were already beside him, he cut the cable with which his boat and the shallop were anchored, and entered over the sand-bars at great risk, and Our Lord was pleased to bring him safely within the bar. The enemy feared the entrance and waited until the tide should be high. At that time the ships which the said Adelantado had sent to Hispaniola must have been about five or six leagues from them, and so they saved themselves from that peril without being discovered; and about two hours from the time the enemy were waiting for the tide to be high, God Our Lord performed a miracle; for the weather being fair and clear, suddenly the sea rose very high, and a strong and contrary north wind came up, which made the return to their fort and harbor difficult for the French. This became known to the Adelantado, who was already on land with his people, having a mass said to the Holy Ghost which he wished everyone to hear, supplicating him to enlighten him and set him on the right path in a decision he wanted to make; and when the mass was over, he entered into council with his captains, the first council he had held in the land of Florida, and none of them knew why they were summoned; and being assembled, he said to them:

7   "Gentlemen and Brothers: We are shouldering a very hard task, very full of trials and dangers, and if this were only for the King our Master, I should not be surprised if some of us should become tired and make some show of the weakness of cowards, in not being able to undergo so many hardships as confront us; but since this burden we are carrying is the enterprise of God Our Lord and of our King, that agent among us who should show weakness and not encourage the officers and soldiers in their duty should hold himself as accursed, for this is of much importance to us; and so, Gentlemen, I beg of you as a mercy, as earnestly as I can, [to consider] that since in this matter we serve God and our King, the guerdon of heaven cannot fail us; and let us not be dismayed by the scarcity of the supplies we have, or by our being left isolated in this land: I beg of you as

a favor that we may all take courage and make efforts to bear our sufferings with patience."

8   They all answered very well, each and all together offering to do their uttermost.

9   Then the Adelantado said to them, having thanked them for their favorable reply:

10   "Gentlemen, I feel impelled to tell you of a very good opportunity which presents itself to my soul and reason, for we must not lose it, and it behooves us to take advantage of it and not allow it to pass by, and it is that I consider (and this is common sense), that as the French armada fled from me four days ago and now comes in search of me, they must have strengthened themselves with part of the men they had as a garrison in their fort, and these must be from among the best [men] and captains: the wind is too contrary for them to return to their harbor and fort, and to all appearance it will last so for many days; and since these are Lutherans, and this we knew before departing from Spain through the proclamations which Juan Ribao, their General, issued in France when on the point of sailing; [to the effect] that under penalty of death no one should embark who was not of the new religion, and under the same penalty, no one should take books along which were not of that faith; and since likewise they themselves certified this to us, when our fleet lay at anchor with theirs outside their harbor, for they said there was no Catholic among them, and when I wished to punish them, they set sail and fled; for this reason the war we have with them and theirs with us, cannot be carried on save with fire and blood, as they, who are Lutherans, seek us, who are Catholics, to prevent our implanting the Holy Gospel in these provinces; and we seek them because they are Lutherans, in order that they shall not implant their evil and detestable sect in this land, nor teach their belief to the Indians; [and] it seems to me that we must take 500 men, two thirds of them arquebusiers, the other third pikemen, and rations for 8 days in our knapsacks, without any porters, carrying our arms on our backs; and that you ten captains, each with your banner and officers, with the number of 50 men to each captain, should go [with me] to reconnoitre the country and the fort where the Lutherans are, and the way to them; for although we know not the way, with our compass I shall know how to guide you, within two leagues right or left of the right directions; and wherever we find woods, we shall open a path with the hatchets so as to pass and know how to return; for I am taking a Frenchman with me who has been more than a year in that fort;[8] he says he is acquainted with the country for two leagues around and can take us to the fort; and if we see that we are not discovered, it may be that a quarter of an hour before dawn, we can

---

[8]Jean François. He was one of Laudonnière's mutineers from Fort Caroline whom Menéndez took with him to Florida, after they had been captured in the West Indies and sent to Spain by the Cuban government officials.

capture their fort by setting up twenty ladders which we shall make when we are near there, and risking the loss of 50 soldiers; and if we should find that we are discovered, since we are certain that the woods are less than a quarter of a league away, by planting our ten banners along the edge of the woods as if on [our] quarters, it will appear to them that we have a number of more than two thousand men and we can send them a trumpeter telling them that they must give up the fort to us and depart from that land, and that they will be given ships and supplies wherewith they may go to France; but that if they will not, we shall put them to the sword, every one; and if they do not [surrender], we shall have gained much in reconnoitring the country and the fort, and they will be afraid of us in such manner that it will be a reason why they will leave us here in security, this winter until next March, when we shall have forces enough to go and seek them, by sea as well as by land."

11   There was much discussion on this speech which the Adelantado made, as it appeared to some that the journey should not be made, and to others that it ought to be; it was decided that it should be made: the Adelantado ordered there and then that by the third day at dawn they should all hear mass, and when that was done they should start immediately; he commanded the camp master, who was called Don Pedro Menéndez de Valdés and was betrothed to his elder daughter, and Gonzalo de Villarroel, captain and sergeant major, to arrange at once for the selection of the men who were to go, and [said] that they should be given a sufficient amount of powder, wicks and lead so that they might make small shot and bullets; and he provided that Captain Bartolomé Menéndez, brother of the said Adelantado, should be in charge of the soldiers who were to remain there, with artillery, arms, ammunition and supplies; and that Diego Florez de Valdés, who was Admiral of the armada, should remain as captain of the artillery and General of the three ships which were left there from the fleet, having them under his charge, [and keeping] them and the sailors thereof, in readiness; and when they had come out of his junta with this agreed upon, it became public news at once throughout the camp, and [the men] began to make and provide those things which the Adelantado had ordered, whereat the whole camp showed great contentment . . .

DISCUSSION QUESTIONS

1. Describe the purpose of the expedition headed by Adelantado Pedro Menéndez de Avilés to Florida.
2. Analyze the relationship between the Spaniards and the Indians in this area.

3. The French Huguenots (Protestants), called Lutherans by the Spaniards, had attempted to settle along the southeast coast of what is now the United States. What policy did the Spanish government follow with regard to the Lutherans?
4. Who won the night battle fought between the French and the Spaniards?
5. Analyze the content and purpose of Avilés's speech to his men.

WRITING TOPICS

1. Write a newspaper report about the founding of the first city in North America, St. Augustine, on August 31, 1565. Include information on the reason for naming the city.
2. Write a report of a trip that you took with your family when you were a child, but tell it from the point of view of an older relative.

FROM *THE MEMOIRS OF BERNARDO VEGA*

Bernardo Vega

Bernardo Vega was born in 1885 in Farallón, a neighborhood outside of Cayey, Puerto Rico. From his early days he took up the trade of cigar roller or *tabaquero*. Even when Fate smiled on him and he came to have a small fortune, he remained faithful to his vocation as a *tabaquero*. Vega worked at several cigar-rolling shops at Bayamón, Caguas, Cayey, and Punta de Tierra—all in Puerto Rico. In effect, these shops were working-class universities, where a *lector* read important literary and historical books aloud while the employees worked. In 1915 Vega attended the Socialist Party's founding convention as representative for the city of Cayey. There, he fought for workers' rights and his island's independence.

In 1916 he emigrated to New York and came to be recognized as an outstanding leader in El Barrio, known today as Spanish Harlem. He and other compatriots founded the Puerto Rican and Hispanic League (Liga Puertorriqueña e Hispana) in 1926. In 1927, he launched *Gráfico*, a popular weekly magazine, serving as its editor for several years. In addition, he contributed both humorous and forthright articles to such publications as *Nuevo Mundo* and *Liberación*. As a member of Henry Wallace's Progressive Party, Vega worked as the national director of the Hispanic section, but when it no longer served his ends, he turned to the Puerto Rican Independence Party, serving as an organizational secretary at the national office. He died in 1965, and his *Memorias de Bernardo Vega* were issued posthumously in 1977 in Spanish and in 1984 in English.

Bernardo Vega's *Memoirs* are a rich source of information about Puerto Rican life in New York. This chapter offers readers a look at the working conditions for a *tabaquero* in a cigar factory. Vega conveys the workers' passionate responses as they exchanged ideas and reacted to the *lector's* readings in the working-class university environment of a cigar factory.

1   Since the day we had our street clothes stolen and had to come home from work in rags, Pepe and I started thinking of quitting work at the munitions plant. But we had no other job in mind, or time to look for one. One day I found Pepe gloomier than a rooster after a cockfight. I tried to console him, but he just broke down, crying his heart out. The job was even more unbearable for him than it was for me. He got sick and gave up.

2   I kept up that fierce daily battle for another few weeks. But one morning I caught sight of a bunch of rags on fire alongside a powder keg and, had I not grabbed an extinguisher and put out the fire just in time, right there and then I might have taken leave of the world of the living.

3   For fear of losing my skin, time had come to give notice. Payday was every two weeks, and I had worked only half that. I decided to leave that day no matter what, though I wanted to be sure of collecting what was due me. The only way I could see was to pick a fight with someone and force them to fire me. I chose as my victim the first co-worker who showed up. The foreman pulled us apart and took us to the office to fire us both. Once I got my pay, I assured the foreman that it was I who had started the trouble and that the other guy was innocent. The foreman shouted, "You son of a bitch!" That was the first time, though certainly not the last, that I was called by that name in the United States.

4   One day a few weeks later I picked up the morning newspaper and felt my heart skip a beat—that same plant had been blown to bits in an explosion!

5   With what savings I had I bought myself some clothes for winter. Having no notion yet what that season would demand, I made the sinful mistake of buying two loud-colored suits and an equally flashy overcoat. Friends who had already spent a few winters in New York made fun of my new purchases. So there I was, after all that hardship, in the same old straits—flat broke and without the clothes I needed for winter.

6   It took "El Salvaje," as Ramón Quiñones—another fellow townsman from Cayey and a first-rate *tabaquero*—was called, to get me out of my predicament. Though gentle and good-hearted, he would resort to his fists at the slightest provocation, and was always quick to seize the limelight. He never carried firearms, but tried to solve all his problems with his bare hands. That's how he got the nickname "Wild Man."

7   One day my friend "El Salvaje" took me down to Fuentes & Co., a cigar factory located on Pearl Street, near Fulton Street, in lower Manhattan. I started work immediately, but within a week they had marked down the price of my make of cigar, and I quit.[1] When "El Salvaje" found out, he

---

[1]Cigar prices varied according to the "make" or *vitola*—the quality of the tobacco and the cigarmakers' reputation. The *vitola* was indicated by the cigar ring.

Cigar factories ranged in size from the *chinchal* (workshop), which might include no more than the master cigarmaker and two or three apprentices, to *fábricas* (factories), which employed from fifty to four hundred workers. Some *fábricas* engaged in all phases of cigar production; in others, called *despalillados*, most of the workers were women, who separated the tobacco leaves from the stems.

went down to the shop in person and, as was his custom, had it out with the foreman with his bare fists. He had to pay a fine to stop them from locking him up.

8   As for me, I was actually lucky to leave that job. A few days later I found work at another cigar factory, "El Morito" ("The Little Moor"), on 86th Street off Third Avenue, a few steps from where I was living. At that wonderful place I struck up friendships with a lot of Cubans, Spaniards, and some fellow countrymen, all of whom awakened in me an eagerness to study. Among them, two Cubans who remain prominently in my mind. One of them, Juan Bonilla, had been a close friend of José Martí. He was a noted orator and one of the editors of *Patria,* the newspaper founded in New York by the Apostle of the Cuban Revolution himself. The other was T. de Castro Palomino, a man of vast erudition, who had also gained renown for his role in the liberation struggles of the Antilles.

9   Of the Spaniards I remember fondly Maximiliano Olay, still hardly more than a boy in those years, who had had to flee Spain to escape charges of complicity in an anarchist assassination of a leading political figure. He was a loyal friend of many Puerto Rican migrants; more than once I heard him claim that destiny had made him a brother of the Puerto Ricans, for one of them had once saved his life.

10   Maximiliano was born in Collota, a village in the Asturian mountains of Spain. Two of the Guardia Civil on duty in his town were from Puerto Rico. They were friends of his family, who had watched him grow up from early childhood. As a young man he got himself into serious trouble for political activities. He was arrested and the charges against him would have cost him his head. But one of the Guardia Civil hid him and arranged for his escape. He crossed the border into France and managed to get away to New York. "Now you see why all Puerto Ricans are my brothers," Maximiliano would say.

11   Another good Spaniard and dear friend of Puerto Ricans was Rufino Alonso, whom they used to call "Primo Bruto" ("Dumb Cousin"). Another of the Puerto Ricans I got to know there and still remember was Juan Hernández, the director of the workers' paper *El Internacional.* There was also the fine writer Enrique Rosario Ortiz, and J. Navas, Tomás Flores, Francisco Guevara, Ramón Rodríguez, Matías Nievese—known as "El Cojo Ravelo" ("Limping Ravelo")—all of whom were active in the cigarworkers' struggle and in the Hispanic community in general.

12   With workers of this caliber, "El Morito" seemed like a university. At the time the official "reader" was Fernando García. He would read to us for one hour in the morning and one in the afternoon. He dedicated the morning session to current news and events of the day, which he received from the latest wireless information bulletins. The afternoon sessions were devoted to more substantial readings of a political and literary nature. A Committee on Reading suggested the books to be read, and their recommendations were

voted on by all the workers in the shop. The readings alternated between works of philosophical, political, or scientific interest, and novels, chosen from the writings of Zola, Dumas, Victor Hugo, Flaubert, Jules Verne, Pierre Loti, Vargas Vila, Pérez Galdós, Palacio Valdés, Dostoyevsky, Gogol, Gorky, or Tolstoy. All these authors were well known to the cigarworkers at the time.

13   It used to be that a factory reader would choose the texts himself, and they were mostly light reading, like the novels of Pérez Escrich, Luis Val, and the like. But as they developed politically, the workers had more and more to say in the selection. Their preference for works of social theory won out. From then on the readings were most often from books by Gustave LeBon, Ludwig Buchner, Darwin, Marx, Engels, Bakunin . . . And let me tell you, I never knew a single *tabaquero* who fell asleep.

14   The institution of factory readings made the *tabaqueros* into the most enlightened sector of the working class. The practice began in the factories of Viñas & Co., in Bejucal, Cuba, around 1864. Of course there were readings before then, but they weren't daily. Emigrants to Key West and Tampa introduced the practice into the United States around 1869—at least, I was told that in that year the shop owned by Martínez Ibor in Key West had an official reader.

15   In Puerto Rico the practice spread with the development of cigar production, and it was Cubans and Puerto Ricans who brought it to New York. It is safe to say that there were no factories with Hispanic cigarworkers without a reader. Things were different in English-speaking shops where, as far as I know, no such readings took place.

16   During the readings at "El Morito" and other factories, silence reigned supreme—it was almost like being in church. Whenever we got excited about a certain passage we showed our appreciation by tapping our tobacco cutters on the work tables. Our applause resounded from one end of the shop to the other. Especially when it came to polemical matters no one wanted to miss a word. Whenever someone on the other side of the room had trouble hearing, he would let it be known and the reader would raise his voice and repeat the whole passage in question.

17   At the end of each session there would be a discussion of what had been read. Conversation went from one table to another without our interrupting our work. Though nobody was formally leading the discussion, everyone took turns speaking. When some controversy remained unresolved and each side would stick to a point of view, one of the more educated workers would act as arbiter. And should dates or questions of fact provoke discussion, there was always someone who insisted on going to the *mataburros* or "donkey-slayers"—that's what we called reference books.

18   It was not uncommon for one of the workers to have an encyclopedia right there on his worktable. That's how it was at "El Morito," where Juan Hernández, Palomino, Bonilla, Rosario, and young Olay stood out as the

arbiters of discussion. And when a point of contention escaped even their knowledge, the dogfight, as we used to call it, was laid to rest by appealing to the authority of the *mataburro*.

19   I remember times when a *tabaquero* would get so worked up defending his position that he didn't mind losing an hour's work—it was piecework— trying to prove his point. He would quote from the books at hand, and if there weren't any in the shop he'd come back the next day with books from home, or from the public library. The main issues in these discussions centered around trends in the socialist and anarchist movements.

20   In those years of World War I, a central topic was imperialism and its relation to pacifism. In "El Morito" we had just been reading Henri Barbusse's *Le feu* (*Under Fire*). The hair-raising depiction of life in the trenches gave rise to an endless discussion among the socialists, anarchists, and the handful of Germanophiles in the factory. Earlier we had read *La Hyene enragée* (*The Trial of the Barbarians*) by Pierre Loti, one of the writers often read to pass the time. But this particular book did a great deal to disarm the pacifists. The forceful description of the ruins of Rheims and Arras, the destructive avalanche of the Kaiser's soldiers, so graphically depicted, stirred us to thoughts of revenge and gained our deepest sympathy for the Allies. Just like so many of our comrades in both France and Germany, we fell prey to the call to "defend the fatherland," losing sight of the proletarian internationalism on which socialism is founded. Needless to say, Lenin and Bolshevism were still totally unknown in New York at the time.

21   When the Catholic newspapers in France took up their campaign against Marx and Marxism, we read the rigorous defense made by the socialist Jean Longuet. His articles kindled lively debates among the *tabaqueros*. For a while the sentiment in defense of France, inspired by Barbusse and Loti, began to lose support. The most militant pacifists among us struck back by arguing: "The French and the Germans both represent imperialist capitalism. We workers should not favor either one of them!" But this revolutionary position was again undermined by the reading of the Manifesto of March 1916, signed by the leaders of pacifist internationalism—Jean Grave, Carlo Malato, Paul Reclus, and Peter Kropotkin. This declaration struck a mortal blow to the worldwide anti-imperialist movement. "To talk of peace," it read, "is to play into the hands of the German government . . . Teutonic aggression is a threat not only to our hopes for social emancipation but to human progress in general. For that reason we, who are antimilitarists, archenemies of war, and ardent partisans of peace and brotherhood among all nations, stand alongside of those who resist."

22   "Those who resist," of course, were the French. As a result, a growing current of Francophilia spread among socialists. A great majority of *tabaqueros* saw France as the standardbearer of democracy and progress, if not of socialism.

23   The dominant trend among North American socialists, however, and perhaps among the people of the United States in general, was neutrality. The leading pacifist and anarchist among the Spanish-speaking workers in New York was

Pedro Esteves, who put out the paper *Cultura Proletaria*. As I mentioned before, most of the *tabaqueros* believed that the Germans had to be defeated. Many of them enlisted in the French army. Outstanding among them were Juan Sanz and Mario César Miranda, two leaders of the workers' movement who left Puerto Rico and were killed in combat in the first battle of Verdun. Florencio Lumbano, a Puerto Rican cigarworker in New York, also fell on the battlefields of France. Another *tabaquero* to take up arms was Justo Baerga. Years later I was told that he had been seen, old and sickly, in Marseilles.

24   Many, in fact, are the Puerto Ricans who have fought in defense of other countries. Perhaps for that reason, they have found themselves so alone in their own land. It was right there in "El Morito" that I first heard of the role of the *tabaqueros* in the Cuban wars of independence. There, too, I began to learn of the distinguished contribution our countrymen made to the Cuban revolution. I heard many true stories from the lips of Juan Bonilla and Castro Palomino, who had experienced them firsthand. From then on, I was determined to write an account of the participation of Puerto Ricans in the Cuban independence struggle, which after all was a struggle for the independence of Puerto Rico as well.

25   But life among the *tabaqueros* was not all serious and sober. There was a lot of fun too, especially on the part of the Cuban comrades. Many were the times that, after a stormy discussion, someone would take his turn by telling a hilarious joke. Right away tempers would cool down and the whole shop would burst out laughing.

26   None of the factories was without its happy-go-lucky fellow who would spend the whole time cracking jokes. In "El Morito" our man of good cheer was a Cuban named Angelito, who was known for how little work he did. He would get to the shop in the morning, take his place at his worktable, roll a cigar, light it, and then go change his clothes. When he returned to his table he would take the cigar from his mouth and tell his first joke. The co-workers nearest him would laugh, and after every cigar he'd tell another joke. He would announce when he had made enough cigars to cover that day's rent. Then he'd set out to roll enough to take care of his expenses. Once this goal was reached, he wouldn't make one more cigar, but would leave his work-place, wash up, get dressed, and head for the Broadway theaters.

27   A good-looking man, Angelito was tall and slender. He had a charming face and was an elegant dresser. He had arrived in the United States with a single, fixed idea in mind, which he admitted openly to anyone who would listen: he wanted to hook up with a rich woman. Pursuing his prey, he would walk up and down the streets, looking, as he himself would say, for his lottery prize. And the truth is that it didn't take him long to find it. A few months after I started at "El Morito" he landed a rich girl, who was beautiful and a violinist to boot. He married her and lived—in his own words—like a prince. But he never forgot us: time and again he would show up at the shop to tell us of his exploits and bless us with the latest addition to his vast repertoire of jokes.

28   Around that time news reached us at "El Morito" of a major strike in the sugar industry in Puerto Rico. A call went out for a rally in solidarity with the strikers. It took place on 85th Street near Lexington Avenue, and was attended by over a hundred *tabaqueros,* mostly Puerto Ricans. Santiago Rodríguez presided, and Juan Fonseca served as secretary. Many of those attending stood up to speak, including Ventura Mijón, Herminio Colón, Angel María Dieppa, Enrique Plaza, Pedro San Miguel, Miguel Rivera, Alfonso Dieppa, Rafael Correa, and Antonio Vega. The last mentioned immediately attracted my attention because of the way he spoke, and even more because of his appearance.

29   While I was listening to Antonio Vega I recalled how my father used to talk all the time about his lost brother, who had never been seen or heard from since he was very young. I'm not sure if it was the memory that did it, but I know I felt deeply moved by the man who bore my last name. He was a tall fellow, with a broad forehead, a full head of gray hair, a big handle-bar mustache, green eyes, and an oval-shaped face . . . When I went up to him he jumped to his feet with the ease of an ex-soldier and responded very courteously when I congratulated him for his speech. We then struck up a conversation, at the end of which we hugged each other emotionally. He was none other than my father's long lost brother.

DISCUSSION QUESTIONS

1. To what extent is Vega lucky in his life in New York City?
2. Describe the role the "reader" plays in the cigar factories. Would you call these factories working-class universities? Explain why or why not.
3. Discuss Vega's references to fiction and nonfiction. Does he prefer one over the other? Why?
4. What were some of the dilemmas faced by socialists during World War I?
5. Based on Vega's account, how would you describe the Hispanic community of New York at this time?

WRITING TOPICS

1. Write a brief memoir (no more than five pages) of your last two years in school. Select those events that you feel changed you in some way, and describe them as they stood out against the usual routine of school.
2. Describe a situation in which you were moved by a speech. Was your response due to the speaker, the content of the speech, or the emotional context? Explain your answer.

OUR AMERICA

José Martí

José Martí was born in Havana, Cuba, on January 28, 1853. As a young man he studied law in Spain, afterward becoming interested in the liberation of his island home. Returning to Havana, he involved himself in activities that landed him in a Spanish prison. Once released, he traveled to New York and several Central and South American countries before returning to New York, where he remained from 1880 to 1895. There, he worked as a journalist while he conspired against Spain on behalf of Cuban independence. He wrote most of his books during this fifteen-year period.

Among Martí's publications are the following books of poetry: *Ismaelillo* (1882), which he dedicated to his son, and *Versos Sencillos* (Simple Verses) (1891), in which he picks up some national symbols of another Cuban poet, José María Heredia. While in New York Martí also published a book of essays entitled *Cuba y los Estados Unidos* (Cuba and the United States) describing his life there. Perhaps more significant, however, are his collections of articles written for newspapers that offered his reading public—both in the United States and in Spanish America—his perceptions about life in the United States. In the first collection of articles, titled *North Americans,* he discusses such figures as James Fenimore Cooper, Mark Twain, David Thoreau, Washington Irving, and Generals Grant and Sheridan. In the second collection, titled *North American Scenes,* Martí depicts events such as the inauguration of the Statue of Liberty, the opening of the Brooklyn Bridge, and a summer day at Coney Island.

José Martí is remembered for more than his writings, however. In the Cuban communities of Key West, Tampa, New York, and Philadelphia he was best known for his oratorical skills. His passion made him a draw at any political rally. For his work on behalf of Cuban independence and for his martyrdom on the battlefield, he has been called the Apostle for Cuban Independence. José Martí died as a warrior in Cuba on July 21, 1895, while attacking a Spanish regiment.

For fifteen years, José Martí lived in the city where the Statue of Liberty welcomed millions of immigrants through its port. Martí was keenly aware of the enormous sacrifices and transformations required of the immigrants in order to fit into American society. In addition, he had seen how the U.S. westward colonization policy known as "Manifest Destiny" had affected Mexico. Likewise, he could not forget how the United States of *America* had appropriated that name for itself—a name that in reality belonged to the whole New World. "Our America" expresses Martí's feelings about these issues.

1   The villager fondly believes that the world is contained in his village, and he thinks the universal order good if he can be mayor, humiliate the rival who stole his sweetheart, or add to the savings in his sock—unaware of the giants with seven-league boots who can crush him under foot, or the strife in the heavens between comets, which streak through space, devouring worlds. What remains of the parochial in America must awake. These are not times for sleeping in a nightcap, but rather with weapons for a pillow, like the warriors of Juan de Castellanos: weapons of the mind, which conquer all others. Barricades of ideas are worth more than barricades of stone.

2   There is no prow that can cleave a cloud-bank of ideas. An energetic idea, unfurled in good season before the world, turns back a squadron of iron-sides with the power of the mystic banner of the judgement day. Nations that do not know one another should make haste to do so, as brothers-in-arms. Those who shake their fists at each other, like jealous brothers who covet the same land, or the cottager who envies the squire his manor, should clasp hands until they are one. Those who allege the sanction of a criminal tradition to lop off the lands of their brother, with a sword dipped in his own blood, had best return the lands to the brother punished far beyond his due, if they do not want to be called thieves. The honorable do not seek money in satisfaction of debts of honor, at so much a slap. We can no longer be a people like foliage, living in the air, heavy with blossoms, bursting and fluttering at the whim of light's caress, or buffeted and tossed by the tempest: the trees must form ranks so the giant with seven-league boots shall not pass! It is the hour of muster and the united march. We must advance shoulder-to-shoulder, one solid mass like the silver lodes in the depths of the Andes.

3   Only the seven-month birthling will lack the courage. Those who do not have faith in their country are seven-month men. They cannot reach the first limb with their puny arms, arms with painted nails and bracelets, arms of Madrid or Paris; and they say the lofty tree cannot be climbed. The ships

must be loaded with these destructive insects, who gnaw the marrow of the country that nourishes them. If they are Parisians or Madrilenians, let them stroll along the Prado under the lamplights, or take sherbet at Tortoni's. These carpenter's sons who are ashamed of their father for his trade! These American sons who are ashamed of the mother that loves them because she wears an Indian apron, and disown their sick mother, the scoundrels, abandoning her on her sick bed! Well, who is the man worthy of the name? The one who stays with his mother to nurse her in her sickness, or the one who puts her to work out of the sight of the world and lives off her labors in the decadent lands, affecting fancy cravats, cursing the womb that carried him, displaying the sign of traitor on the back of his paper cassock? These children of our America, which will be saved by its Indians, and goes from less to more, these deserters who take up arms in the armies of North America, which drowns its Indians in blood, and goes from more to less! These delicate beings, who are men but do not want to do the work of men! The Washington who forged this land, did he go to live with the English, to live with them during the years in which he saw them coming against his own country? These *incroyables* of their honor, who trail it through alien lands, like their counterparts in the French Revolution, with their dancing, their affectations, their drawling speech!

4   For in what lands can a man take greater pride than in our long-suffering republics of America, raised up from among the mute Indian masses by the bleeding arms of a hundred apostles to the sounds of battle between the book and the thurible. Never in history have such advanced and unified nations been forged in less time from such disordered elements. The fool in his pride believes that the earth was created to serve him as a pedestal because words flow easily from his pen, or his speech is colorful, and he charges his native land with being worthless and beyond salvation because its virgin jungles do not provide him with means to travel continuously abroad, driving Persian ponies and lavishing champagne, like a tycoon. The incapacity does not lie with the nascent country, which seeks suitable forms and greatness that will serve, but with those who attempt to rule nations of a unique character, and singular, violent composition, with laws that derive from four centuries of operative liberty in the United States, and nineteen centuries of French monarchy. A decree by Hamilton does not halt the charge of the *llanero*'s pony. A phrase of Sièyes does nothing to quicken the stagnant blood of the Indian race. One must see things as they are, to govern well; the good governor in America is not one who knows how government is conducted in France or Germany, but who knows the elements of which his country is composed and how they can be marshaled so that by methods and institutions native to the country the desirable state may be attained wherein every man realizes himself, and all share in the abundance that Nature bestowed for the common benefit on the nation they enrich with their labor and defend with their lives. The government must be the child of the country. The spirit of the government must be the same as that of the country. The form of government must conform to the natural constitution of

the country. Good government is nothing more than the true balance between the natural elements of the nation.

5   For that reason, the foreign book has been conquered in America by the natural man. The natural men have vanquished the artificial, lettered men. The native-born half-breed has vanquished the exotic Creole. The struggle is not between barbarity and civilization, but between false erudition and nature. The natural man is good. He respects and rewards superior intelligence, as long as his submission is not turned against him, or he is not offended by being disregarded, a thing the natural man does not forgive, prepared as he is to regain by force the respect of whoever has wounded his pride or threatened his interests. Tyrants in America have risen to power serving these scorned natural elements, and have fallen the moment they betrayed them. Republics have paid in tyrannies for their inability to recognize the true elements of their countries, to derive from them the proper form of government, and govern accordingly. To be a governor of a new country means to be a creator.

6   In nations of cultured and uncultured elements, the uncultured will govern, because it is their habit to strike and resolve all doubts by force, whenever the cultured prove incapable in office. The uncultured mass is lazy, and timid in matters of the mind. It asks only to be well-governed. But if the government hurts it, it rebels and governs itself. How can the universities be expected to produce governors, if there is not one university in America that teaches the rudimentary in the art of government, which is the analysis of the elements peculiar to America? Young men go out into the world wearing Yankee or French spectacles, and hope to govern by guesswork a nation they do not know. In the political race, all entries should be scratched who do not demonstrate a knowledge of the political rudiments. The prize in literary contests should go not to the best ode, but to the best study of the political factors in one's country. Newspapers, universities, and schools should foment the study of their country's dynamic factors. They have only to be stated, straightforward and in plain language. For whoever disregards any portion of the truth, whether by ignorance or design, is doomed to fall; the truth he lacked grows in the negligence and brings down whatever was erected without it. It is easier to determine the elements and attack the problem, than to attack the problem without knowing the elements. The natural man arrives, indignant and strong, and topples the authority based on books because he was not governed according to the obvious realities of the country. Knowledge holds the key. To know one's country, and govern it with that knowledge, is the only alternative to tyranny. The European university must give way to the American university. The history of America, from the Incas to the present, must be taught until it is known by heart, even if the Archons of the Greeks go by the board. Our Greece must take priority over the Greece that is not ours: we need it more. Nationalist statesmen must replace cosmopolitan statesmen. Let the world be grafted on our republics; but the trunk must be our own. And let the vanquished pedant

hold his tongue: for there are no lands in which a man can take greater pride than in our long-suffering American republics.

7   With the rosary as our guide, our head white and our body mottled, both Indian and Creole, we intrepidly entered the community of nations. We set out to conquer liberty under the standard of the Virgin. A priest, a handful of lieutenants, and a woman raised the Mexican Republic on the shoulders of the Indians. A few heroic students instructed in French liberty by a Spanish cleric, raised Central America against Spain under a Spanish general. In the oriflammed habits of monarchy, Venezuelans and Argentinians set out, from north to south, to deliver nations. When the two heroes collided, and the continent almost rocked, one, and not the lesser, turned back. But when the wars ended, heroism, by being less glorious, became rarer; it is easier for men to die with honor than to think with order. It was discovered that it is simpler to govern when sentiments are exalted and united, than in the wake of battle when divisive, arrogant, exotic, and ambitious ideas emerge. The forces routed in the epic conflict sought, with the feline cunning of their species, and utilizing the weight of realities, to undermine the new structure, which embraced at once the rude and singular provinces of our half-breed America, and the cities of silken hose and Parisian frock coat, beneath the unfamiliar flag of reason and liberty, borrowed from nations skilled in the arts of government. The hierarchical constitution of the colonies resisted the democratic organization of the republics. The capitals of stock and collar kept the countryside of horse-hide boots cooling its heels in the vestibule. The cultured leaders did not realize that the revolution had triumphed because their words had unshackled the soul of the nation, and that they had to govern with that soul, and not against it or without it. America began to suffer, and still suffers, from the effort of trying to find an adjustment between the discordant and hostile elements it inherited from a despotic and perverse colonizer, and the imported ideas and forms which have retarded the logical government because of their lack of local reality. The continent, disjointed by three centuries of a rule that denied men the right to use their reason, embarked on a form of government based on reason, without thought or reflection on the unlettered hordes which had helped in its redemption; it was to be the reason of all in matters of general concern, not the reason of the university over the reason of the province. The problem of the Independence was not the change in forms, but the change in spirit.

8   It was necessary to make common cause with the downtrodden, to secure the new system against the interests and habits of rule of the oppressors. The tiger, frightened off by the powder flash, returns at night to the haunts of his prey. When he dies, it is with flames shooting from his eyes and claws unsheathed. But his step cannot be heard, for he comes on velvet paws. When the prey awakes, the tiger is upon him. The colony lives on in

the republic; and our America is saving itself from its grave errors—the arrogance of the capital cities, the blind triumph of the scorned country people, the influx of foreign ideas and formulas, the wicked and unpolitic disdain in which the aboriginal race is held—through the superior virtue, backed by the necessary conviction, of the republic that struggles against the colony. The tiger lurks behind each tree, waiting at every turn. He will die with his claws unsheathed and flames shooting from his eyes.

9   But "these countries will be saved," as the Argentine Rivadavia announced, whose sin was to be gentlemanly in crude times; a silk scabbard does not become the *machete*, nor can the lance be discarded in a country won by the lance, for it becomes angry, and presents itself at the door of Iturbide's congress demanding that "the blond one be made emperor." These countries will be saved because a genius for moderation, found in Nature's imperturbable harmony, seems to prevail in the continent of light, where there emerges a new realistic man schooled for these realistic times in the critical philosophy, which in Europe has succeeded the literature of sect and opinion in which the previous generation was steeped.

10   We were a strange sight with the chest of an athlete, the hands of a coxcomb, and the brain of a child. We were a masquerade in English trousers, Parisian vest, North American jacket, and Spanish hat. The Indian circled about us in silent wonder, and went to the mountains to baptize his children. The runaway Negro poured out the music of his heart on the night air, alone and unknown among the rivers and wild beasts. The men of the land, the creators, rose up in blind indignation against the scornful city, against their own child. We were all epaulets and tunics in countries that came into the world with hemp sandals on their feet and headbands for hats. The stroke of genius would have been to couple the headband and tunic with the charity of heart and daring of the founding father; to rescue the Indian; to make a place for the able Negro; to fit liberty to the body of those who rose up and triumphed in its name. We were left with the judge, the general, the scholar and the prebendary. As if caught in the tentacles of an octopus, the angelic young men lunged toward Heaven, only to fall back, crowned with clouds, in sterile glory. The natural people, driven by instinct, swept away the golden staffs of office in blind triumph. The European or Yankee book could not provide the answer to the Hispanic-American enigma. Hate was tried, and the countries wasted away, year by year. Exhausted by the senseless struggle between the book and the lance, of reason against dogma, of the city against the country, of the impossible rule by rival city cliques over the natural nation alternately tempestuous and inert, we begin almost without realizing it to try love. The nations stand up and salute each other. "What are we like?" they ask; and they begin to tell one another what they are like. When a problem arises in Cojimar, they do not send to Danzig for the answer. The frock coat is still French, but thought begins to be American. The youth of America roll up their sleeves and plunge their hands into the dough; it rises with the leavening of their sweat.

They understand that there is too much imitation, and that creation holds the key to salvation. "Create" is the password of this generation. The wine is from plantain, and if it proves sour, it is our wine! It is understood that the forms of government must accommodate themselves to the natural elements of the country, that absolute ideas must take relative forms if they are to escape emasculation by the failure of the form, that liberty, if it is to be viable, must be sincere and complete, that the republic which does not open its arms to all, and move ahead with all, must die. The tiger within enters through the fissure, and the tiger from without. The general restrains his cavalry to a pace that suits his infantry, for if the infantry be left behind, the cavalry is surrounded by the enemy. Politics is strategy. Nations should live in continual self-criticism, because criticism is healthy; but always with one heart and one mind. Go down to the unfortunate and take them in your arms! Dissolve what is clotted in America with the fire of the heart! Make the natural blood of the nations course and throb through their veins! Erect, with the happy, sparkling eyes of workingmen, the new Americans salute one another from country to country. The natural statesman appears, schooled in the direct study of Nature. He reads to apply what he reads, not to copy. Economists study the problems at their origin. Orators begin to be lofty. Dramatists bring native characters to the stage. Academies consider practical subjects. Poetry shears off its romantic locks and hangs its red vest on the glorious tree. Prose, lively and discriminating, is charged with ideas. Governors study Indian in republics of Indians.

11   America is escaping all its dangers. The octopus still sleeps on some republics; but others, in contrast, drain the ocean from their lands with a furious, sublime haste, as if to make up for lost centuries. Some, forgetting that Juárez rode in a mule-drawn coach, hitch their coach to the wind and entrust the reins to a soap-bubble; poisonous luxury, the enemy of liberty, corrupts the frivolous and opens the door to the outlander. In others, where independence is threatened, an epic spirit produces a heightened manliness. Still others spawn a rabble-in-arms in rapacious wars against their neighbors which may yet turn and devour them. But there is yet another danger which does not come from within, but from the difference in origins, methods and interests between the two halves of the continent. The hour is fast approaching when our America will be confronted by an enterprising and energetic nation seeking close relations, but with indifference and scorn for us and our ways. And since strong countries, self-made by the rifle and the law, love, and love only, strong countries; since the hour of recklessness and ambition, of which North America may be freed if that which is purest in her blood predominates, or on which she may be launched by her vengeful and sordid masses, her tradition of expansion or the ambition of some powerful leaders, is not so near at hand, even to the most timorous eye, that there is not time to show the self-possessed and unwavering pride that would confront and dissuade

her; since her good name as a republic in the eyes of the world puts on the America of the North a brake which cannot be removed even by the puerile grievances, the pompous arrogance, or parricidal discords of our American nations, the pressing need for our America, is to show herself as she is, one in soul and purpose, swift conqueror of a suffocating tradition, stained only by the blood drawn from hands that struggle to clear away ruins, and the scars left us by our masters. The scorn of our formidable neighbor, who does not know us, is the greatest danger for our America; and it is imperative that our neighbor know us, and know us soon, so she shall not scorn us, for the day of the visit is at hand. Through ignorance, she might go so far as to lay hands on us. From respect, once she came to know us, she would remove her hands. One must have faith in the best in men and distrust the worst. If not, the worst prevails. Nations should have a pillory for whoever fans useless hates; and another for whoever does not tell them the truth in time.

12   There can be no racial hate, because there are no races. The rachitic thinkers and theorists juggle and warm over the library-shelf races, which the open-minded traveler and well-disposed observer seek in vain in Nature's justice, where the universal identity of man leaps forth from triumphant love and the turbulent lust for life. The soul emanates, equal and eternal, from bodies distinct in shape and color. Whoever foments and propagates antagonism and hate between races, sins against Humanity. But as nations take shape among other different nations, they acquire distinctive and vital characteristics of thought and habit, of expansion and conquest, of vanity and greed, which from the latent state of national preoccupation could be converted in a period of internal unrest, or precipitation of the accumulated character of the nation, into a serious threat to the neighboring countries, isolated and weak, which the strong country declares perishable and inferior. The thought is father to the deed. But it must not be supposed, from a parochial animus, that there is a fatal and ingrained evil in the blond nation of the continent, because it does not speak our tongue, nor see the world as we do, nor resemble us in its political faults, which are of a different order, nor favorably regard the excitable, dark-skinned people, nor look charitably, from its still uncertain eminence, on those less favored by History, who climb the road of republicanism by heroic stages. The self-evident facts of the problem should not be obscured for it can be resolved, to the benefit of peaceful centuries yet to come, by timely study and the tacit, immediate union of the continental soul. The hymn of oneness sounds already; the actual generation carries a purposeful America along the road enriched by their sublime fathers; from the Rio Grande to the straits of Magellan, the Great Semi, seated on the flank of the condor, sows the seed of the new America through the romantic nations of the continent and the sorrowful islands of the sea!

DISCUSSION QUESTIONS

1. How can Hispanic Americans learn to govern themselves? Do you think that imitation is the appropriate stratagem?
2. In small groups, discuss what you think Martí means by the terms *natural men* and *artificial men*. Which does he prefer? Explain your answer.
3. How should European creoles (whites born in the New World), Indians, and African Americans relate to one another?
4. In what way does the notion of national republics influence Martí's analysis. How does this apply to the notion of "Our America" versus the notion of the "Other America"?

WRITING TOPICS

1. Martí states, "There can be no racial hate, because there are no races." Write an essay explaining Martí's meaning and your reaction to it.
2. How does Martí describe Hispanic American dress? Write an essay explaining the meaning of each piece of apparel he discusses.

The Oral Tradition

Lullabies, songs, games, stories, riddles, and sayings are expressions of love and teaching and admonishment that elders share with children. These lessons and memories are inextricably woven into who we are, what we have been, and even what we will be as we grow older. For most people today, growing older means growing away from the music and the stories with which we were nurtured. As we distance ourselves, however, or as life creates in us a need to revisit what was once endearingly familiar, nostalgia leads us to that wellspring of fantasy and reality—the oral tradition.

Indeed, for some, the comfort of home is that gathering where stories are retold and customs and traditions are carried out with reverence and careful attention to detail. It is stories, songs, food and clothing, humor, language, legends, myths, heroes, and heroines that make up the texture of a culture. The oral tradition serves to enhance a sense of belonging and thus becomes critical to families who must reestablish a home in an unfamiliar place or try to recall their idealized birthplace so that it will live in their children.

Oral tradition for Spaniards, for instance, took the form of the eight-syllable verse ballad, which they called *romance*. The New Spaniards (later Mexicans) organized the same octosyllabic verses in stanzas of four, making it easier to set the thirty-two voiced syllables to music. They then sang the lyrics in a run-on fashion (in Spanish it was called *romance corrido*) until reaching the end of the stanza. As time passed the label *romance* was dropped, leaving the word *corrido* to survive in areas of Mexico and the southwestern United States. Both ballad forms had the same overall purpose: to relate the story of the deeds of a hero or heroine. The tales were of romance or of battles or of some historical occurrence, with the corrido serving the function of an oral newspaper. The themes of the ballads typically sung evolved over time, as oral tradition is an ever-changing channel through which everyday life manifests itself.

Thus, the power and influence of oral tradition must not be underestimated. Indeed, oral tradition is more than familiar tales and proverbs. Rather, it serves to strengthen and define an identity, which is then shared with the group. For individuals, oral tradition is a treasured opportunity to revisit home through an encounter with one's ancestors.

THE BALLAD OF GREGORIO CORTEZ

Américo Paredes

Américo Paredes was born on September 3, 1915, and grew up in Brownsville, Texas. He is able to trace his ancestry to the original inhabitants of Nuevo Santander (Mexico). As a young man, he attended the University of Texas to study creative writing and literary criticism and unintentionally fell into folklore when he tried to explore how to apply literary criticism to folk poetry. By age twenty Paredes had begun contributing literary pieces to *La Prensa's Lunes Literario,* a literary supplement published weekly. Thereafter, he issued his *Cantos de adolescencia* (Songs of Adolescence) (1937), and later went on to write articles on educational reform for the *Brownsville Herald.*

Most notable, however, was Américo Paredes's solid scholarship concerning Mexican and Mexican American folklore. Among his books are *With His Pistol in His Hand: A Border Ballad and Its Hero* (1958), on which the film *The Ballad of Gregorio Cortez* was based, *The Urban Experience and Folk Tradition* (1971), *Toward New Perspectives in Folklore* (1972), *A Texas-Mexican Cancionero: Folksongs of the Lower Border* (1976), and *Folktales of Mexico* (1979). In later years, Paredes returned to his own creative writing and published *Between Two Worlds* (1990), *George Washington Gómez* (1990), *Uncle Remus Con Chile* (1993), and the *Hammon and the Beans and Other Stories* (1994).

Américo Paredes began his folkloric career with a dissertation on the group of *corridos* (ballads) that told the true story of the heroic figure Gregorio Cortez. Paredes analyzed the many versions of the ballad and its portrayal of Cortez's deeds and reputed misdeeds. Naturally, Paredes chose the most complete version of the ballad for its full publication and for the preparation of the script for the film version of *The Ballad of Gregorio Cortez.* In addition, Paredes examined the cultural conflicts that have been part of life in the U.S./Mexican borderlands—the land that folklorists and historians call Old Mexico (today commonly referred to as the American Southwest).

In the county of Karnes
Look what has happened;
The Major Sheriff died,
Leaving Román badly wounded.

5 It must have been two in the afternoon
When people arrived;
They said to one another,
"It is not known who killed him."

They went around asking questions,
10 About half an hour afterward,
They found that the wrongdoer
Had been Gregorio Cortez.

Now they have outlawed Cortez
Throughout the whole state;
15 Let him be taken, dead or alive;
He has killed several men.

Then said Gregorio Cortez,
With his pistol in his hand,
"I don't regret that I killed him;
20 I regret my brother's death."

Then said Gregorio Cortez,
And his soul was all aflame,
"I don't regret that I killed him;
A man must defend himself."

25 The Americans were coming,
They were whiter than a dove,
From the fear that they had
Of Cortez and of his pistol.

Then the Americans said,
30 Then they said fearfully,
"Come, let us follow the trail;
The wrongdoer is Cortez."

They set the bloodhounds on him,
So they could follow his trail,
35 But trying to overtake Cortez
Was like following a star.

He struck out for Gonzales
Without showing any fear,
"Follow me, cowardly rangers,
40   I am Gregorio Cortez."

From Belmont he went to the ranch,
They succeeded in surrounding him,
Quite a few more than three hundred,
But there he jumped their corral.

45   When he jumped their corral,
According to what we hear,
They got into a gunfight,
And he killed them another sheriff.

Then said Gregorio Cortez,
50   With his pistol in his hand,
"Don't run, you cowardly rangers,
From just one Mexican."

Gregorio Cortez went out,
He went toward Laredo
55   They decided not to follow
Because they were afraid of him.

Then said Gregorio Cortez,
"What is the use of your scheming?
You cannot catch me,
60   Even with those bloodhounds."

Then the Americans said,
"If we catch up with him, what shall we do?
If we fight him man to man,
Very few of us will return."

65   Over by El Encinal,
According to what we hear,
They made him a corral,
And he killed them another sheriff.

Then said Gregorio Cortez,
70   Shooting out a lot of bullets,
"I have weathered thunderstorms;
This little mist doesn't bother me."

Now he has met a Mexican;
He says to him haughtily,
75   "Tell me the news;
I am Gregorio Cortez."

"It is said that because of me
Many people have been killed;
I will surrender now
80   Because such things are not right."

Cortez says to Jesús,
"At last you are going to see it;
Go tell the rangers
To come and arrest me."

85   All the rangers were coming,
Coming so fast they even flew,
For they wanted to get
The thousand dollars they were offered.

When they surrounded the house,
90   Cortez suddenly appeared before them,
"You will take me if I'm willing,
But not any other way."

Then the Major Sheriff said,
As if he was going to cry,
95   "Cortez, hand over your weapons;
We are not going to kill you."

Then said Gregorio Cortez,
Shouting to them in a loud voice,
"I won't surrender my arms
100   Until I am in a cell."

Then said Gregorio Cortez,
He said in his godly voice,
"I won't surrender my arms
Until I'm inside a jail."

105   Now they have taken Cortez,
Now matters are at an end;
His poor family
Are suffering in their hearts.

Now with this I say farewell,
110   In the shade of a cypress tree;
This is the end of the singing
Of the ballad of Cortez.

DISCUSSION QUESTIONS

1. Discuss the way the ballad presents the border conflict between Anglo-Americans and Mexican Americans.
2. Knowing that *rinches* are Texas Rangers, how does the characterization of *rinches* differ between ethnic groups?
3. The epic epithet "with his pistol in his hand" often accompanies the name of Gregorio Cortez. What do you suppose is the poetic strategy for using an epic epithet?
4. In which ways is Cortez made heroic? How is he depicted? What is his defense in justifying his killing of the Major Sheriff?

WRITING TOPICS

1. Given that Anglo-Americans won the Mexican War, how do you suppose the law acted toward Mexican Americans thereafter? Write a brief short story in which you tell of an incident similar to the action described in *The Ballad of Gregorio Cortez*.
2. Imagine that you are being hunted down, accused of a crime that you did not commit. You fear your treatment at the hands of police before you ever reach a trial. Write a poem that expresses your feelings.

INDIGENOUS PROFILE

María Cadilla de Martínez

María Cadilla de Martínez was born in Arecibo, Puerto Rico, on December 21, 1884. She attended elementary school and normal school at the Washington Institute and later taught at the public schools on the island. In 1928 she completed her Bachelors in Education and in 1930 her Master of Arts, both at the University of Puerto Rico. At the Universidad Central in Madrid, she earned a doctoral degree with a thesis on Puerto Rican popular poetry. Her dissertation was an important contribution to the study of Puerto Rican folklore.

Among her most important works are *Cuentos a Lillian* (Stories to Lillian) (1925), *Cazadora en el alba y otros poemas* (Huntress in the Dawn and Other Poems) (1933), *La poesía popular en Puerto Rico* (Puerto Rican Popular Poetry) (1933), *Costumbres y tradicionalismos de mi tierra* (Customs and Traditions from My Land) (1938), *Juegos y canciones infantiles de Puerto Rico (Puetro Rican Children's Games and Songs)* (1940), *Raíces de mi tierra* (Roots of My Land) (1941), *Hitos de la raza* (People's Markers) (1945), and *Rememorando el pasado heróico* (Remembering the Heroical Past) (1946). For her work she has received numerous honors and awards.

María Cadilla de Martínez worked as a folklorist in Puerto Rico most of her life. As a writer, she wanted to preserve some of the many tales and legends that are so prevalent in her homeland, so she collected stories and wrote them down for posterity. This story, translated from the original Spanish publication *Hitos de la raza,* recounts one of many encounters between Spaniards and Indians in Martínez's island.

¹   A mother's love has always been the spring that fertilized with blood the soils of the native land. . . . For its cause the land and the race acquired prestige and unmistakable fragrances. Casting towards the future with far-sighted wisdom, this love shortened distances. It never allowed discouragement to spread, nor any obstacle to cause its retreat. It became the magical

hand that in our world erased the word "impossible." Overcoming all dissent, it was able to constitute its own domination. In order to make a better judgement of that love, we are going to stop before the following indigenous profile:

2   There is a silence which minimizes the historical facts about the "Borinquen" woman, but within that silence an indigenous mother, despite receiving little emphasis from scholars, has not been ignored: we are referring to Iviahoca, a 1511 messenger for the Spaniards, whose life events have been noted by Gonzalo Fernández de Oviedo and Antonio de Herrera. Her name in her native tongue corresponded to her human mission of mother and to her nature: Iviahoca means "Here is to the mountain that reigns." We will consider her as a mountain of the maternal love that God has given all human creatures and that reigns in their conscience.

3   Iviahoca gave one of the bravest soldiers to our fierce indigenous armies: her son Ocoro, whom she raised alone since birth and taught to honor his father, one of the most courageous *nitaínos*[1] among the *araguacos*,[2] who was killed during an invasion. In order to preserve the new warrior, who would inherit his father's legacy—praised in all the war chants[3]—the Bodiques[4] forbade Iviahoca from sacrificing herself in the *athebeane nequen*[5] customary during *caciques* (leader) deaths. She then realized that this privilege would add a new duty to her responsibility as a mother: to destine her son to the defense of the tribe. She did not allow the magnitude of her task to prevent her from achieving her goal. Ocoro acquired, within years, such an outstanding masculinity that in the tribal Zodiac he could very well represent Pisces, while his mother, although less renowned, would be able to obtain the place of Arletis. She took her son, while he was still an infant, to the mountain in order for him to grow healthy, knowing that the mild climate and the elevation—including the celestial one—would be uplifting for the child's soul. She was hoping that Ocoro would acquire the strength of the trees; the fragrance of the wild flowers. . . . When the child's soul was ripened, according to her, she brought him down from the mountain and

---

1 Noble Indians.

2 Centuries before the Discovery, the Arawakans came from the area of the Orinoco River in South America and established themselves in the islands of the Caribbean including Puerto Rico. It was a race with beautiful physical features and very gentle. The Spaniard Oviedo suggests that they mixed with the Caribes, whom he describes as more aggressive. Actually, they are the same group that sectioned themselves because of the forced migration of the second-born teenage males. These in turn conducted raids for food and women on established communities, their speech became a variant of the standard Taíno dialect, and became known as Caribs or Caribes.

3 "Areytos bélicos" are narrative chants sung in choir that served as inspiration for the Indians. See Gonzalo Fernández de Oviedo's *Historia general y natural de las Indias,* ed. Juan Pérez de Tudela Bueso, BAE 130, (Madrid: Atlas, 1959).

4 Indian priests and healers.

5 Oviedo (*op. cit.* p. 134) talks about this ceremony as a custom among Indians and how in the Orient, especially in India, when a leader died he would be buried with his wives still alive.

turned him in over to the soldiers and priests, so that he could be taught the game of the *batey*,[6] the handling of the weapons and the legends of the men and the gods. Soon, he found himself at the service of Mabodamaca[7] who, comparing him with an *ácana*,[8] gave him an honorable position next to him during every warlike or ceremonial act. While they were together this leader expressed his desire to fight against the famous Spanish captain Don Diego de Salazar. The star of the Antillean indians suffered an extreme misfortune during that *guasábara*[9] and Ocoro, despite his honesty and his upright thought, was anxious of recognition, but was made prisoner and could not die like his leader and the way that he desired: for the motherland. If the maternal love had not saved him from an embarrassing slavery, he would have let himself die together with his fellow imprisoned countrymen and his last resort would have been the *curare*.[10]

4   After Ponce de León agreed to make a friendship pact with the principal *cacique* of the Island, Agüeybaná, as a first step for the Island's colonization, the Spaniards and the indians were in peace for two years. The indians helped the foreigners during this time, but the Spaniards—whose presence increased every day—inconsiderately deprived the indians from their freedom and their land. Prudently and patiently, Agüeybaná respected the friendly agreement, but this attitude allowed the Spaniards to become more demanding. The indians that were at their service were forced to work like slaves and were shared among the Spaniards without bearing in mind the *caciques'* rights or their category. They no longer respected the authority of the highest *cacique*. On September 24, 1510, Ponce de León awarded the land owned by the new highest *cacique*, Guaybana,[11] who had been chosen after the death of the previous friend of the Spaniards, Agüeybaná. The concession was given to Don Cristóbal de Sotomayor, Chief Justice of the Spaniards in the Island, and it included the land, the indians and the production of cassava, all of it owned by the *cacique* Guaybana. In October of the same year, Ponce de León challenged the fierce caribes in the Island and awarded two *caciques* from that race to the Spaniards:[12] the *cacique* Caguax, who, together with his land, was given to two Spaniards and the *cacique*

---

[6] Ball game described in *Costumbres y tradicionalismos de mi tierra* (San Juan: Ed. Imp. Venezuela, 1928) p. 161 *et passim*.

[7] Mabodamaca had his village in Guajataca (northwestern region of Puerto Rico). When the Indian revolt took place in 1511, he and 600 Indians challenged the Spanish captain Diego de Salazar, who only had 40 men, between Quebradillas and Isabela. Salazar defeated him, killing 150 Indians and taking numerous prisoners.

[8] The Indian tree that is best polished and treated.

[9] Warlike event, a battle.

[10] Oviedo, in Vol. I, p. 268 describes this drink that was poisonous and that was extracted from the cassava by the Indians after the arrival of the Spaniards so they wouldn't have to work or serve them. About 50 at a time would drink it and die together.

[11] The order for this distribution was brought from Spain by Sotomayor himself, and it ordered Juan Ponce de León to give him the best cacique in the Island.

[12] Francisco de Robledo and Juan de Castellanos received the "cacicazgo" of Caguax for 255 golden pesos.

Mabó, from Guaynabo, whose lands and *naborias* were also given to several Spaniards. He also distributed the land, indians and harvest owned by the *cacique* Majagua from Bayamón, and did the same with the land from Toa, owned by the *cacique* Gonzalo, despite his conversion into christianism.[13] This property distribution continued under the name of *encomiendas*, which the Spanish Crown used to favor its courtiers and servants. The natives' discontentment understandably grew. . . . Although the Spaniards inspired, in the beginning, a superstitious respect due to the belief in their immortality, the *cacique* from Añasco, Uroyoán, dispelled all uncertainty. He made them submerge the young Spaniard Diego de Salazar in the Guaorabo River and hold him under the waters until he drowned. Guaybana, who inherited the courage from the caribes and the prudence of the araucas, assembled all of his island *caciques* and warriors in the Coayuco and explained the situation urging them to resist and reasoning as it follows:

> "If he who is right feels without reason,
> if the memory of an ancient one lasts,
> every man will regret
> the critical subjection and misfortune,
> that we all suffer at present times". . . .[14]

5   Guaybana himself offered to begin the resistance by killing his master, D. Cristóbal de Sotomayor. The rest of the plan was made there and Guarionex, *cacique* from Otoao, would burn down Sotomayor's Villa in Aguada. After carrying this out they would force Diego de Salazar, who was ill in Aguada, to leave. The Spaniard, despite his courage, was only able to save a few of his fellow mates from the disaster and decided to go to Caparra with them. Ponce de León was in this area with his best forces and some captains. When he found out about the events in the East, he requested help from Santo Domingo to battle the indians. The natives were concentrated in the Yaguecas. When the Spaniards were on their way, at the Aimaco, they found out through their leaders about the challenge between Mabodamaca with his 600 men and D. Diego de Salazar. Salazar, whose belief in the Virgin made him courageous in the face of danger, was allowed by Ponce de León to step ahead and eliminate the enemy. After passing through Guajataca they confronted each other. The battle almost lasted a day and only with courage and cleverness Salazar and his small army were able to defeat such large number of enemies. After the fight Salazar was told that there were large concentrations of indians around the Guaybana land, which made the prudent captain stay until the rest of the Spanish fighters, who had been left

---

[13] The names of those favored with those distributions can be found in *Boletín histórico de Puerto Rico* I, p. 239.

[14] *Elegías de varones ilustres de Indias* [Elegies of illustrious men of Indies] by Juan de Castellanos (Madrid: Ed. Casa-Imprenta Vida de Alonso Gómez, 1856, Elegy VI).

behind with Ponce de León, Miguel Toro and Luis de Añasco as their captains, would reach them. He wrote them a letter to inform everything and just as he sealed it he heard the sentimental cry of a woman. He looked towards the area where the sound was coming from and was able to see an old indian woman who was curled up sobbing. He found out through his *lenguas*[15] that she was the mother of one of the warriors captured during the previous battle, the one named Ocoro. The grieving indian woman immediately recognized, in him, the fearsome Salazar and with pleading and anxious words did not stop speaking to him. Salazar inquired one of his interpreters as to what she was saying and was able to learn that she had come to the Christian camp after finding out about her son's imprisonment and wanted to offer her life and freedom for him. She had touched, when she arrived, the young prisoner, whom she had looked for among the others, and when she was convinced that he was not dead nor badly wounded, she requested permission to speak with him, but it was denied. The soldiers added that during the scene of the encounter between mother and her prisoner son, he, with a sweet and flashing look, allowed her to touch his body and caress him; that the soldiers had to separate her from him and that she then remained on the floor crying until Salazar noticed her. Moved by the story, the Spanish captain ordered the soldiers to bring Ocoro to his mother. As soon as she saw him next to her she smiled with tears in her eyes and caressed him. She then realized that the Spanish Chief was understanding and kind-hearted and told him:

> —Señor Salazar, I know that you must have a mother and because of her you will understand my pain. My son is young and loves his freedom. He must live to enjoy it. I am old. With him in prison, I will agonize during the rest of my days, but knowing that he is free, I would be able to live in peace, no matter how hard I would have to work. . . . Take my life and my services for his freedom. Heaven will reward you for that kind act. . . .
> —If you, woman, are able to take this letter promptly to Juan Ponce de León, who is camping out at the Aymaco, your son will be set free, as you have requested. As soon as I have proof that you have done this, I will fulfil my promise.

6   When these words were translated to the indian woman, she immediately took the letter and, just as a jaguar jumps through the density when followed, she, in spite her age, ran through the bushes jumping all the obstacles in order to deliver it. Some of the Spanish soldiers who had Becerrillo—the skilled dog which even had "soldada de ballestero"—followed her. Some

---

[15] Translator of *taíno*, the Indian language.

wanted to make sure that the letter would arrive at the right destiny and others had the selfish intention of taking it away from her in order to be the bearers of the message. Since they could not reach her running, they set Becerrillo on to her. The dog was only able to catch up with her and stop her; when she saw him she thought that he was a *hupia*[16] and fell on her knees, pleading. Face to face she told the animal:

—Señor dog, do not harm me. I am going to take this letter from the christians to your leader. Do not harm me, señor dog. . . .

7   Just as if he understood her words, or because of the miraculously and intuitive respect that old age inspires, the dog kept looking without harming the woman. Afterwards, calmly, he lifted one of his paws to relieve himself and left in the followers' direction. In vain, they tried to egg him on to go after her. When Iviahoca saw herself free, she disappeared so quickly that the Spaniards were not able to catch her and decided to return.

8   That afternoon the Indian woman returned with a letter from Juan Ponce de León to Salazar, announcing that he was on his way with his soldiers to join them. Those who had followed the indian told Salazar about the dog and he, to be sure about her veracity, interrogated her about the obstacles on her way. She, simply, answered that she had been stopped by a devilish *hupia* that wanted to obstruct her mission, but it had taken pity on her plea. As she related this, the trumpets from the other group of soldiers arriving could be heard. Salazar postponed his conversation with the indian woman and went to greet his leader, D. Juan Ponce de León and his fellow soldiers, that were going to strengthen his army with more than one hundred fighters.

9   After greeting each other, Salazar told Juan Ponce de León that he had hundreds of indians prisoners and wanted him to see them. He then, in front of Ocoro, remembered his promise to his old mother, who had received wings from her love to go back and forth in no time. He related the incident to Juan Ponce de León and his promise and both decided immediately to liberate Ocoro. Several soldiers brought Ocoro and his mother before the two captains and, through an interpreter, Salazar told them that he was to be set free, but she would remain with the hostages, to make sure that he would not fight against christians anymore. When Ocoro found out what Salazar told him he replied with dignity:

—Christian, I appreciate your generosity, but I can't accept it. It would be like enslaving an old and loving mother, who, because of love, does not deserve that destiny. I prefer to die than to have freedom at such high price or to be reduced to a slave under the rough treatment that your soldiers give to us. . . .

---

[16] The Indians believed in the existence of small devils or spirits that would take on animal shapes to do them wrong, the dog shape being the worst one.

10   Both Juan Ponce de León and Salazar were astonished at those feelings and reasons. Since they were both generous, they glanced at each other and agreed: Ponce de León spoke ordering his soldiers to untie the indian warrior, soon after, mother and son formed a moving and beautiful group. Speaking to them in a stirring voice, that electrified their hearts, the Leonese leader pronounced these words:

> —The nobility of your souls, which has been demonstrated with acts and words, assures us that you will be grateful and that we can count on your loyalty. We will set you both free and may God be with you. . . .

11   With tears in her eyes, Iviahoca kissed the hands of the captains standing before her. Ocoro, more reserved, but with happiness in his eyes bowed before them. Afterwards, they exchanged a few words in a low voice and ran in the direction of the mountain. She was running ahead, like a hare being followed by a greyhound—which in this case was Ocoro—who was behind her. The Spaniards never saw them again, but never forgot them either: the memory of their gestures and words was captured in the hearts of all of those present that day. . . . During the days and hours that they were able to live there peacefully, they were pleased to describe to their children such marvelous and dignified indigenous profile.

DISCUSSION QUESTIONS

1. The *encomienda* system was supposed to be used for the purpose of Christianizing the Indians. Did it become a form of serfdom?
2. Explain why Iviahoca takes the letter to Ponce de León. What does she hope to accomplish?
3. Did the Spaniards honor their treaties with the Indians? How does the Puerto Rican experience compare to that of the United States mainland?
4. Why is Ocoro released by Ponce de León and Salazar? Why is Iviahoca liberated? What is the meaning of the last line of the reading?

WRITING TOPICS

1. Often one hears of sacrifices that mothers make for their children. This legend tells the story of sacrifice by both mother and son. Write a story in which you tell of a sacrifice that a parent or loved one has made for you and one that you have made for that person.

2. As she ran, Iviahoca encountered the dog named Becerrillo [Little Heifer] and likened him to a *hupía* [spirit devil]. Write a diary entry of a memorable encounter you have had with an animal. Describe the appearance and nature of the animal you met. Did it seem to possess human qualities? In your writing, discuss your reactions to one another.

THE PRIZE OF FREEDOM

Lydia Cabrera

Lydia Cabrera was born on May 20, 1900, on the day Cuba celebrated its independence from Spain. Later, as a young girl sitting on the president's lap, she believed that all the parades and fanfare were in her honor, rather than in celebration of Cuba's birthday. As a child she spent a great deal of time with the black servants at home. Their influence ignited her interest in all things Afro-Cuban. She studied with a private tutor and attended classes at the San Alejandro Academy of Painting, where she drew some scenes depicting Cuban life. After her father's death she dabbled in antiques before enrolling at the École du Louvre in 1927, graduating three years later.

While in Paris the theme of negritude—knowledge of black cultural heritage—was in the air, and Cabrera's interest in it was renewed. She began to write about it and completed her first volume of short stories, *Contes negres de Cuba* (Black Stories from Cuba) (1936 in French, 1940 in Spanish). *Por qué . . .: Cuentos negros de Cuba* (1948) was her second volume of stories. To these we must add *Ayapá: Cuentos de Jicotea* (1971), a volume of Afro-Cuban trickster tales, and *Cuentos para grandes, chicos y retrasados mentales* (Stories for Adults, Children and the Mentally Retarded) (1979), a collection of stories heard during her childhood. *Francisco y Francisca: Chascarrillos de negros viejos* (Francisco and Francisca: Old Black Anecdotes) (1976) is a delightful conversation that illustrates life during the Cuban colonial period.

In addition, she has written several important books about Afro-Cuban folklore, including *El monte: Notas sobre las religiones, la magia, las supersticiones y el folklore de los negros criollos y del pueblo de Cuba* (The Country: Notes About Religions, Magic, Superstitions and the Folklore of the Black Creoles and of the Cuban People) (1954), *Refranes de Negros Viejos* (Old Black Proverbs) (1955), *La sociedad secreta Abakuá* (The Abakuá Secret Society) (1958), and a number of other books on *Santería, Palo Mayombé*, and several glossaries of African languages used in Cuba for religious purposes. Cabrera died in Miami, Florida, on September 19, 1991.

Lydia Cabrera absorbed most of the Afro-Cuban folklore that she recounted while listening as a child to the black servants in the kitchen of her parents' home. Her stories are a product of that store of memory, and they are based, of course, on the many rites, rituals, and beliefs that she studied with such great care. Many of these tales tell the origin of things, that is, why things came to be the way they are. These are called *creation* or *etiological tales,* and though simple in presentation, they are quite complex in their use of liminal characters—characters that represent a personality at the threshold of two or more dimensions or worlds. One may be an animal, a human being, or a god. "The Prize of Freedom," translated from the original Spanish by Lisa Wyant, is one such story.

1   Back when animals used to talk, were good friends with each other and got along with man, the Dog was already a slave.

In that age of never rushing, of elastic hours, the Cat, the Dog, and the Mouse were inseparable, Cuba's best pals. They usually got together in the backyard of a large house along the plaza, in whose stained-glass windows, still not so long ago, reflections from the sea went to die. There, at the foot of a laurel—murdered eventually, along with its birds, by the new age—they chatted away the early evening.

2   Once the Mouse, who was big in the book business (he was a scholar), and the Cat were singing the praises of liberty and discussing at length the rights of all the sons of the earth, including those of the air and water. The Dog realized that he was a slave and it made him sad. The next day he went to see Olofi:

3   "Bada dide odiddena!"[1] and he asked him for a license to be free.

4   The old man, the oldest of the heavens, was a bit at a loss. Narrowing his crafty eyes which saw everything in advance, and scratching behind his ear, he had serious doubts about whether he should accommodate the Dog. But at last, after shrugging his shoulders and shooting black spit out from behind his eye-tooth—which is what he always did when he made a decision—he put his signature on a sheet of parchment and, with everything in order, gave the Dog the longed-for liberty license. That same night, the Dog, feeling very pleased with himself, showed it to his friends.

5   "Listen, pal, put it away in a safe place, and guard it like gold," advised the Cat when he said good-bye. And the Dog, thinking that in no other place could it be safer—not having pockets—tucked it away in his rear-end.

---

[1] Get up, old man, get up!

But the precious document, shut up in there, stung terribly. It caused a disturbing condition that got worse with time. He was forced to walk in a grotesque way, his back paws immodestly spread apart, and didn't dare make even the slightest gesture to express any feeling with his tail. Then all of a sudden he'd feel an overwhelming need to itch, which gave rise to a violent urge to run, to rub himself desperately against the ground without measuring the consequences of such an act; when, to his shame, these outbursts took place in public, they made absolutely everyone laugh. It was torture. Constant worry over losing the document occupied his thoughts day in and day out. The fear of some careless slip that might smudge the text made the Dog abstain from eating; and at last, not knowing which to choose, freedom or martyrdom, the Dog pulled out the document and gave it to his friend the Cat for safekeeping.

6   The Cat thought that exposing a liberty license to the elements, and to risky roof-top living, was a big responsibility. So he took it to the house of his friend the Mouse, whose roof was at least over his head. The Mouse had gone to buy cheese at a bodega. The Mousewife came to the door, and having given her full instructions, the Cat entrusted her with the license. But the Mousewife was having labor pains. She grabbed the license, ripped it up, and made her nest.

7   Meanwhile the Dog had quarrelled bitterly with his owner.

8   The Dog had said, "Give me another bone!"

9   The Master had replied, "I don't feel like it."

10   The Dog stood up to the man. The man was about to lift the whip.

11   "I need to eat much more because I am free!"

12   The man said, "You were born a slave. You will eat as much as I think! You are my slave!"

13   "No Señor, my Master, I am not your slave—and his tail wildly confirmed the fact. "I have my liberty license."

14   "If that's so, show it to me immediately!"

15   The Dog went out to the backyard and called on the Cat.

16   "Hurry, my friend. My liberty license!"

17   The Cat called on the Mouse.

18   "My friend the Mouse, hurry! Your wife has our friend's liberty license."

19   The Mouse ran back with a heavy heart, and whispered into the Cat's ear. The Cat put his paws on his head, and for the first time let out a "Hissss!" and jumped, claws bared, on the Mouse; and this was the first time that the Dog jumped on the Cat and sank his fangs into the nape of his neck.

20   With eyes of green fire, the Cat defended himself, claws on all four paws bared; it made for a cycle of howling, whacking, biting and blood. The Mouse, since he was small, slipped away into his hole.

21   The Cat, bristling and battered, clambered up on the laurel; from one branch he reached the roof, and from the eaves he hissed, challenging the Dog, his back arched like a bow.

22   But the Dog went to lick the hand of his owner, throwing himself at his feet without further explanation.

DISCUSSION QUESTIONS

1. Animal tales or fables tell a story explaining why something is the way it is. Discuss what is explained in this tale.
2. What are the role of writing and the function of paper in a civilized society?

WRITING TOPICS

1. Who could you trust to keep something important for you? Write a diary entry describing an incident in which someone broke your trust.
2. Write interviews with each animal in this story to ascertain their points of view about what occurred.

CORRIDOS

María Herrera-Sobek

A professor of Spanish at the University of California at Irvine, María Herrera-Sobek has taught at California State University at Northridge and at Stanford University. In 1993, she researched Chicano literature at the Longfellow Institute at Harvard University. She has also served as a visiting professor at the Universidad de Alcalá de Henares in Spain.

Herrera-Sobek is both a scholar and a poet. She has conducted numerous studies on the oral tradition in the Hispanic literature of the United States. Her work on Chicana, Chicano, and Mexican *corridos* (traditional songs or ballads) is published in several books. Among them are *The Bracero Experience: Elitelore Versus Folklore* (1970), *The Mexican Corrido: A Feminist Analysis* (1990), and *Northward Bound: The Mexican Immigrant Experience in Ballad and Song* (1993). In addition, she has edited several books on Chicana literature, including the re-edition of Josephina Niggli's *A Mexican Village* (1994) and *Chicana Writers: On Word and Film* (1991). She also has published a book of poetry, *Islands in the Sun/Islas in el Sol.*

María Herrera-Sobek has collected modern-day *corridos* or ballads that illustrate life for migrant workers. Most of these deal with the adventures or vicissitudes of men or of families. In fact, relatively few of them address the position of women in society or the change in their traditional role within the culture. The following three *corridos* are from Herrera-Sobek's collection *Northward Bound* and are her translations of the original Spanish. Notice the different viewpoints of the women who are speaking in each *corrido.*

POOR ILLEGAL IMMIGRANT WOMEN

Sung:
Those poor illegal immigrant women
Who cross the border
Single women or married ones
Are all my countrywomen.

5 They leave their land with dreams

Leaving their loved ones behind
In search of their husbands
Crying for their children.

Suffering all kinds of humiliations
10 Some do have some luck
But others are deceived
They end up dead.

Those who manage to stay
Are always afraid
15 They fear the border patrol
They don't have any protection at all.

Those damn farm growers
Who exploit women
If they don't turn them in
20 They pay them what they please.

We see them picking cotton
Or working in the canneries
Dreaming about their coming home
All their joy is gone.

Spoken:
25 For you lonely women
To you I dedicate my song
You that suffer in silence
Your pain and disillusionment
Your hunger and your broken dreams
30 Poor women, I sing to you.

Sung:
If they happen to get married
They have to work
High-living countrymen
Tend to exploit them.

35 Then when they get divorced
They try to forget
Dancing in the dance halls
Drinking without end.

Those poor illegal immigrant women
40 When will they cease to go

They left their country
They will never return.

THE LEGAL IMMIGRANT WOMAN

Now that you've legalized your status
You think you're all American
You want to talk to no one
You feel you're superior
5 You're uppity 'cause you've got your
    documents
But they're good for nothing.

When you lived in your hometown
You had a lot of friends
Now you don't even want to talk to
    them
10 Because they're illegal aliens.
Now you don't remember how
You crossed over hiding in the bushes.

You're really flying high
Be careful you don't fall down.
15 You think just 'cause you have your
    green card
You've got the world at your feet
The world turns and turns a lot
And one of these days you'll fall
    down.

In order to get a good job
20 You became a legal immigrant
You keep earning the same amount

And you've got a lot of debts.
If you want to visit your village
You don't even have bus fare.

MODERN-DAY GIRLS

Young women today
Do not like work any more
They are always on the street
Cruising up and down.

5 Young women today
Do not want to do housework
As soon as the boyfriend comes
No one can find them.

The girls who follow fashion
10 Wear pants
And at home they don't cook
Not even a pot of beans.

Young women today
Love to go to the movies
15 They almost don't wear dresses
Only shorts and bikinis.

When they are fifteen years old
They want an expensive gift
They tell their fathers,
20 "Buy me a new car."

Young women today
When they are newly wed
They tell their husbands,
"Get me a servant."

25 Now I take my leave
'Cause I am dying from laughter
Pity the poor men
Who now iron their own shirts.

DISCUSSION QUESTIONS

1. These three *corridos* or ballads tell the story of women in different circumstances. Contrast the illegal immigrant women with the legal immigrant women as portrayed in the ballad.
2. How does the point of view of immigrant women differ from that of modern-day girls? Do the *corridos* concerning them differ in tone?
3. Consider the motivations of each of the three groups of women. Do these motivations explain their attitudes and behaviors? Defend your answer.
4. What role does *machismo*, the traditional masculine pride, play in these portrayals of Hispanic women? Are men responsible for these circumstances? Do men invoke the reader's pity?

WRITING TOPICS

1. Write an interview with a woman from one of these three *corridos*. Emphasize *her* views.
2. Write a ballad entitled "Poor Illegal Immigrant Men." Convey their ambitions and frustrations.

LA LLORONA

Anonymous

The anonymous tale of La Llorona (the Crying Woman) is believed to be from Mexico, historically known as New Spain, and sometimes is linked with the story of La Malinche or Malintzin, the Indian woman whom Hernando Cortés, Mexico's conqueror, called Marina. Because she served as Cortés's interpreter and bore him a son, Martín, she is often viewed as a traitor as well as the mother of the Mexican race.

In the legend of La Llorona, a woman—abandoned by her man— kills her children, the greatest betrayal of all. In this way the Llorona, the legend of the woman weeping near a river, calling for her "lost" children, is reminiscent of the Greek myth of Medea, a similar but unconnected story from ancient Europe. As is the case with oral literature, there are many variants of this legend. Following are just a few.

LA LLORONA IN MEXICO

1   At night, in the wind, a woman's voice was heard. "Oh my children, we are now lost!" Sometimes she said, "Oh my children, where shall I take you?"

LA LLORONA IN CALIFORNIA

2   About "la llorona," I only know that she was a woman who had three children. And that . . . she killed them in order to continue her wild life. And when she . . . had died, when she went to settle her accounts with God, well, He asked her to bring Him her children, to tell Him what she had done with them. She told Him that . . . she had thrown one down the toilet . . . another had been thrown into the sea . . . and that she had thrown the other one into . . . a river. Then God told her that in order to . . . be able to pardon her, that she should go look for her children. And since then, the woman has been searching for her children. And that's why she utters that cry . . . Ay, my children.

La Llorona in Texas

³   One of my brothers saw la llorona. He was fording a river . . . and the horse, when he saw her, stood on his hind legs and didn't want to move. Because he was afraid. And . . . and then my brother followed her. He took out his pistol and told her: "Now I'm going to kill you." And when he thought of doing it, his pistol fell out of his hand into the river. And then, he says that, when he got out of the river, that the horse whined and whined and then . . . he didn't want to turn around, but he turned around once [imitating the movement], and he could see a woman with . . . long hair, and covered with something like a sheet. But he didn't see her face. Nothing but her . . . and she wailed . . . Aaayyy . . .

Discussion Questions

1. How does the text of the legend differ for Mexico, California, and Texas, especially with regard to meaning?
2. Some versions of the legend say that La Llorona (Weeping Woman) killed her own children. How does this legend compare with the classical Greek myth of Medea?
3. The weeping in the story refers to the loss of the children, regardless of who killed them or would kill them. This lament, however, usually occurs at night. Why? Does the weeping cause readers to feel fear and repulsion or curiosity and compassion?
4. Why do modern-day versions of "La Llorona," such as the Californian and Texan versions, include sightings by the river? Do you think that the river implies that the children were drowned, or do you see the riverbank as a symbol?

Writing Topics

1. How does our society typically respond to news concerning children who were abused or murdered?
2. What is the allure of a mystery woman? Write a poem about such a creature.

CHAPTER THREE

THE VALUE OF FAMILY

As is true for many ethnic groups, throughout history Hispanics have placed great importance on the family. Manhood, or *macho*, was closely tied to the responsibility of providing for one's own. The extended family was an institution, ensuring that oral tradition would function to teach the children in the ways they were to go. In addition, customs involving rituals of healing and expressions of religious faith were practiced and perpetuated by families.

It is interesting that, in the Hispanic family, the father is regarded as more important in many respects than the mother. Not so, however, in the Indian and African families, in which the mother plays the more significant role. One must consider the effect of history on the dynamics of family relationships. For example, the institution of the Spanish family was influenced by the Roman model. In turn, the presence of Indian and African families in the New World influenced the European concept of family.

Further, one must not overlook the effect of migration on the Hispanic family. The necessity of adapting to a society whose customs and values differed so greatly served to rock the foundation of the Hispanic family. Children, exposed to alternatives, began to question and doubt the values and lifestyles that their parents and ancestors had embraced.

FAMILIA

Tato Laviera

Born in Puerto Rico on May 9, 1951, Tato Laviera has made New York his home since 1960. His talents have earned him many accolades, including the American Book Award in 1982 from the Before Columbus Foundation. Laviera has been recognized for his work on behalf of community-based organizations, his dramatic productions and his performance poetry. His poetry, in particular, is a source of joy and optimism for his community and for those who know it.

As other poets before him, Laviera uses titles of his work to comment on the general theme of migrant acculturation. In *La Carreta Made a U-Turn* (1979), Laviera chooses the symbol of the oxcart to represent Puerto Rican migration from the island to the mainland, much as the covered wagon represents the settlement of the West by Americans in the nineteenth century. Centering his song on the oral tradition of popular poetry, he decries the hardships faced by Puerto Ricans in New York City. He also refers to the Afro-Caribbean roots of his people. *Enclave* (1981) honors that African background by alluding to poets from Puerto Rico's past as well as to the musical legacy of the island. *AmeRican* (1986) suggests its theme through its title, emphasizing the Puerto *Rican* component in the word *American* in referring to the Ricans from the U.S. mainland. Finally, *Mainstream Ethics* (1988) highlights the influence of Hispanic heritage on the mainstream culture of the United States.

Tato Laviera's "familia," Spanish for *family*, concerns the value of the family both to the individual and to society. Claude Lévi-Strauss, the noted French anthropologist, has said that there are societies in which cannibalism is practiced and there are societies in which the opposite, that is, vomiting, is the norm. He explains that our modern Western society practices the latter, tending to "vomit" people away. For example, the children are institutionalized from an early age and the old are ensconced in retirement villas. In contrast, in Hispanic families the *abuelita* ("little," figuratively "dear," grandmother) remains at the center of the family.

moment's personal worth,
life ceases for a minute,
pays attention to a milestone.

moments when choke of tear,
5 adams apple above the eye.

moments when sacrifices find glory.

moments when we come together,
everlasting kinship strength.

moments when ay bendito humanity
10 flourishes and expands.

and of course,

moments when family tree
sees nuclear-expanded
attention moving upward,
15 abuelita at the center
of the trust.

DISCUSSION QUESTIONS

1. If time is considered to be the primary asset of all human beings, discuss how the poet links time to family.
2. Explain the reflection of the experiences of pride, pain, and celebration in the poem "familia."
3. The nuclear family and the expanded family are contrasted by the mention of one person in the poem. Who is that person, and what does he or she represent?
4. The anaphoric repetition of the word *moments* creates a thematic path. In what way could one change that path according to one's family experiences?

WRITING TOPICS

1. Describe your family. How many members can you name (grandparents, great-grandparents, siblings, first cousins, second cousins, aunts and uncles, in-laws)?
2. How do the family structures of some of your friends' families differ from your own? Write an essay that compares them to your family's structure.

PROGRESS REPORT FOR A DEAD FATHER

Judith Ortiz Cofer

Born in Hormigueros, Puerto Rico, on February 24, 1952, Judith Ortiz Cofer moved between the island and the mainland before settling for a time in Paterson, New Jersey, and later in Augusta, Georgia, where she attended Augusta College. After marriage and the birth of a daughter, she moved to Palm Beach County, where she taught school and obtained a graduate degree from Florida Atlantic University in 1977.

Faced with the challenges of living in the world as a woman, Judith Ortiz Cofer proposed her conditions in the 1987 poetry collection *Terms of Survival*. These conditions are to be released from the rituals of duty and of passage, and to be freed of cultural imperatives. Having received recognition for her collection *Reaching for the Mainland*, which constituted a part of the very successful title *Triple Crown*, Ortiz Cofer followed her poetic tour de force with her first novel, *The Line of the Sun* (1989). In it she portrays the migration from a Puerto Rican village to a tough immigrant community in New Jersey. This fictional reflection led her to reexamine her own personal memory in her award-winning autobiography *Silent Dancing: A Partial Remembrance of a Puerto Rican Childhood* (1990). Her autobiography received the 1991 PEN/Martha Albrand Special Citation for Nonfiction, and was selected by the New York Public Library's 1991 Best Books for the Teen Age. Her next book, *The Latin Deli,* was published in 1994.

The following two poems, "Progress Report for a Dead Father" and "To My Father," offer complimentary views of a daughter's impressions of her father. One poem centers on the rules of behavior taught and learned, and the other focuses on the terrible dilemma of fathers who are unable to express their feelings of love for their daughters.

"Keep it simple, keep it short,"
you'd say to me, "Get to the point,"
when the hoard of words I had stored for you
like bits of bright tinsel in a squirrel's nest
5 distracted you from the simple "I love you"
that stayed at tongue-tip.

Father, I am no more succinct now than when
you were alive, the years have added reams
to my forever manuscript,
10 lists rile me now in your stead,
labled "things to do today" and
"do not forget," lists of things
I will never do, lists that I write
remind me that I can never forget.

15 I can still hear you say,
"A place for everything and
everything in its place."
But chaos is my roommate now, Father,
and he entertains often.

20 Simplicity is for the strong-hearted,
you proved that through your brief
but thorough life, your days were stacked
like clean shirts in a drawer,
death was the point you drove home
25 the day your car met the wall,
your forehead split in two, not in your familiar frown,
but forever; a clean break.
"It was quick," the doctor said, "He didn't feel a thing."

It was not your fault that love could not be
30 so easily put in its right place,
where I could find it when I needed it,
as the rest of your things, Father.

TO MY FATHER

Who died thinking himself a burden
and unloved, whose fine hands grew
too rough and callused to hold
a pen or brush, or a child's hand.
5 Folded over his chest in death, the bruised
fingers would not divulge any more
than we already knew, that this man
had earned his rest. Stubborn sentinels
of his heart, they said nothing
10 of the silence that he built layer
by layer, sealing himself in the place
where he kept his private grief,
or that long ago
when hope still came in and out
15 of our house like a cat rubbing its head
on our legs, he had written love letters
to each of us, but perhaps afraid that words
would betray him, he had hidden them among
the still life of rusting tools,
20 where I find them, yellow and fragile
as unearthed bones, or relics.

DISCUSSION QUESTIONS

1. Discuss what Ortiz Cofer accomplishes by quoting her father. Does she give readers the sense that his communication with his daughter was limited to oral admonishments? Does the second poem leave readers with a different impression of the poet's father?
2. In "Progress Report for a Dead Father," how does the poet contrast her father's wishes in the past with her present life?
3. How does Ortiz Cofer portray her silent father and his avoidance of emotional communication?
4. It is said that memory demands a place for everything to be remembered. Given this, how does Ortiz Cofer remember love in the second poem, "To My Father"?

WRITING TOPICS

1. Write a letter to a friend about your father or a fatherlike figure in your life. Describe his life, his death (if he is deceased), and your feelings about him and his presence in your life.
2. Describe your father or a similar figure in a poem.

BLACK & WHITE PHOTO

Pedro Pietri

Pedro Pietri was born in Ponce, Puerto Rico, in 1944 and grew up in New York City's Upper West Side. He had lost both his parents, and later his brother Willie, and was raised by his grandmother. He adopted an unconventional lifestyle, wearing black on black and carrying a briefcase labeled "Coffin for Rent" while he rode the subways.

Pietri's writing has been characterized by his bohemian view of life and his offbeat cynicism. A bit of a stand-up comedian, he was always ready to perform his poetry, and he wrote it with performance in mind. His poems offer a surrealistic view of the world through which he explains the alienation felt by those in his community. His book *Puerto Rican Obituary* (1973) deals with the exploitation of the barrio as seen in terms of fundamentalist religion, poor living conditions, the numbers racket, and other images of urban blight amidst his people. *Traffic Violations* (1981) brings the critical vision of his first book to another period of revolt. He continues his poetic journey with *The Masses Are Asses* (1984). In addition, Pietri has published poetry in a number of journals such as *P'alante, The Rican,* and *Unidad Latina.* He has also written a book of prose entitled *Lost in the Museum of Natural History* (1981).

The respect that Hispanics have for life is likewise held for death, and birthdays are the celebration of both. In other words, each birthday celebrates a new year to live and one less year to live. Of interest here is the linking of that celebration with the ritual of celebrating Father's Day.

when Carmen Pietri
was young and younger
she celebrated her
birthday in a cemetery

5 she didn't have to
blow out the candles
because the wind kept
blowing them way out

at first I thought
10 she was a weird person
with impaired vision
destined for absurdity

until her mother said
don't make fun of her
15 your father is dead
and we are celebrating

because she was born
on father's day in june
and it is only right
20 to cut her cake here

so she can grow up
to be happy and sad
all her days of trying
not to go totally mad

DISCUSSION QUESTIONS

1. Whose voice does a reader hear in this poem?
2. Why did Carmen Pietri celebrate her birthday in a cemetery?
3. Why celebrate a birth and a death together when they did not occur on the same date?
4. Describe those elements in the poem that allude to gender differences. Discuss those differences implied by the author.

WRITING TOPICS

1. Write an essay explaining the poet's formula for "not going totally mad."
2. Describe a relative who is deceased and how you continue to honor his or her memory.

DEAR TÍA

Carolina Hospital

Carolina Hospital was born on August 27, 1957, in Havana, Cuba, and entered the United States as a child after the triumph of the Cuban Revolution in 1961. In 1984 she completed her master's thesis at the University of Florida, focusing on the writers of her generation—all Cuban Americans—whom she dubbed *los atrevidos* (the daring ones).

Hospital's poetry has appeared in magazines throughout the United States, including *The American Review* and *Bilingual Review*. She also has compiled an interesting anthology entitled *Cuban American Writers: Los Atrevidos* (1989) and has contributed to *Cuban Heritage Magazine* and *Linden Lane Magazine*.

Carolina Hospital describes her poem "Dear Tía" (*tía* being Spanish for aunt) as another black-and-white photo. In this poem her need to sing and extol exceeds her conscious memories of her homeland. Despite the vagueness of her recollections, she sees the land as intrinsic, representing the person she is.

I do not write.
The years have frightened me away.
My life in a land so familiarly foreign,
a denial of your presence.
5 Your name is mine.
One black and white photograph of your youth,
all I hold on to.
One story of your past.

The pain comes not from nostalgia.
10 I do not miss your voice urging me in play,
your smile,

or your pride when others called you my mother.
I cannot close my eyes and feel your soft skin;
listen to your laughter;
15   smell the sweetness of your bath.
I write because I cannot remember at all.

DISCUSSION QUESTIONS

1. Discuss what Hospital means by her statement "I do not write."
2. Explain what "a land so familiarly foreign" means to Hospital. Why is it both familiar and foreign?
3. Describe the feelings Hospital has concerning her aunt.
4. When Hospital says "I write because I cannot remember at all," what does she mean? Why does she feel compelled to write?

WRITING TOPICS

1. Imagine that, in another city or country, you have a relative of whom you have only vague memories and an old photograph. Write a poem about your recollections concerning him or her.
2. Interview your family members about a grandparent or other relative whom they miss. Record your questions and their responses.

THE MOTHS

Helena María Viramontes

Helena María Viramontes, a native of East Los Angeles, has chosen that area as the setting for most of her fiction. She holds a master's degree in creative writing from the University of California at Irvine and has served as editor of *Chismearte*, a cultural and literary magazine, and as the coordinator of the Los Angeles Latino Writers Association. In addition, she has edited the work of fellow writers.

Viramontes felt the need to express her own vision of women in the United States/Hispanic world, and to do so within the bounds of a particular sense of aesthetics. Her stories were published in anthologies and magazines around the country. In 1985, she wrote *The Moths and Other Stories*, a collection of work dealing with the Hispanic patriarchy's control of the female body, mind, and soul: abortion, separation, aging. She also explored the Anglo patriarchy's control: immigration, addiction, death. She studies the life of her female protagonists with great sensibility and care, going from the touchingly lyrical to the desperately violent.

Helena María Viramontes has created a gripping tale of the life of a family and the death of one of its members. For the heroine, her grandmother's house is both an exile and a haven from the home centered around her father, mother, and siblings. She feels rejected or unneeded in her father's other homes as well—the church where Catholic mass is celebrated and the chapel of undetermined denomination. Readers will find "The Moths" a sensitive study of family and one's place in it.

1   I was fourteen years old when Abuelita requested my help. And it seemed only fair. Abuelita had pulled me through the rages of scarlet fever by placing, removing and replacing potato slices on the temples of my forehead; she had seen me through several whippings, an arm broken by a dare jump off Tío Enrique's toolshed, puberty, and my first lie. Really, I told Amá, it was only fair.

2   Not that I was her favorite granddaughter or anything special. I wasn't even pretty or nice like my older sisters and I just couldn't do the girl things they could do. My hands were too big to handle the fineries of crocheting or embroidery and I always pricked my fingers or knotted my colored threads time and time again while my sisters laughed and called me bull hands with their cute waterlike voices. So I began keeping a piece of jagged brick in my sock to bash my sisters or anyone who called me bull hands. Once, while we all sat in the bedroom, I hit Teresa on the forehead, right above her eyebrow and she ran to Amá with her mouth open, her hand over her eye while blood seeped between her fingers. I was used to the whippings by then.

3   I wasn't respectful either. I even went so far as to doubt the power of Abuelita's slices, the slices she said absorbed my fever. "You're still alive, aren't you?" Abuelita snapped back, her pasty gray eye beaming at me and burning holes in my suspicions. Regretful that I had let secret questions drop out of my mouth, I couldn't look into her eyes. My hands began to fan out, grow like a liar's nose until they hung by my side like low weights. Abuelita made a balm out of dried moth wings and Vicks and rubbed my hands, shaped them back to size and it was the strangest feeling. Like bones melting. Like sun shining through the darkness of your eyelids. I didn't mind helping Abuelita after that, so Amá would always send me over to her.

4   In the early afternoon Amá would push her hair back, hand me my sweater and shoes, and tell me to go to Mama Luna's. This was to avoid another fight and another whipping, I knew. I would deliver one last direct shot on Marisela's arm and jump out of our house, the slam of the screen door burying her cries of anger, and I'd gladly go help Abuelita plant her wild lilies or jasmine or heliotrope or cilantro or hierbabuena in red Hills Brothers coffee cans. Abuelita would wait for me at the top step of her porch holding a hammer and nail and empty coffee cans. And although we hardly spoke, hardly looked at each other as we worked over root transplants, I always felt her gray eye on me. It made me feel, in a strange sort of way, safe and guarded and not alone. Like God was supposed to make you feel.

5   On Abuelita's porch, I would puncture holes in the bottom of the coffee cans with a nail and a precise hit of a hammer. This completed, my job was to fill them with red clay mud from beneath her rose bushes, packing it softly, then making a perfect hole, four fingers round, to nest a sprouting avocado pit, or the spidery sweet potatoes that Abuelita rooted in mayonnaise jars with toothpicks and daily water, or prickly chayotes that produced vines that twisted and wound all over her porch pillars, crawling to the roof, up and over the roof, and down the other side, making her small brick house look like it was cradled within the vines that grew pear-shaped squashes ready for the pick, ready to be steamed with onions and cheese and butter. The roots would burst out of the rusted coffee cans and search for a place to connect. I would then feed the seedlings with water.

6   But this was a different kind of help, Amá said, because Abuelita was dying. Looking into her gray eye, then into her brown one, the doctor said

it was just a matter of days. And so it seemed only fair that these hands she had melted and formed found use in rubbing her caving body with alcohol and marihuana, rubbing her arms and legs, turning her face to the window so that she could watch the Bird of Paradise blooming or smell the scent of clove in the air. I toweled her face frequently and held her hand for hours. Her gray wiry hair hung over the mattress. Since I could remember, she'd kept her long hair in braids. Her mouth was vacant and when she slept, her eyelids never closed all the way. Up close, you could see her gray eye beaming out the window, staring hard as if to remember everything. I never kissed her. I left the window open when I went to the market.

7   Across the street from Jay's Market there was a chapel. I never knew its denomination, but I went in just the same to search for candles. I sat down on one of the pews because there were none. After I cleaned my fingernails, I looked up at the high ceiling. I had forgotten the vastness of these places, the coolness of the marble pillars and the frozen statues with blank eyes. I was alone. I knew why I had never returned.

8   That was one of Apá's biggest complaints. He would pound his hands on the table, rocking the sugar dish or spilling a cup of coffee and scream that if I didn't go to mass every Sunday to save my damn sinning soul, then I had no reason to go out of the house, period. Punto final.[1] He would grab my arm and dig his nails into me to make sure I understood the importance of catechism. Did he make himself clear? Then he strategically directed his anger at Amá for her lousy ways of bringing up daughters, being disrespectful and unbelieving, and my older sisters would pull me aside and tell me if I didn't get to mass right this minute, they were all going to kick the holy shit out of me. Why am I so selfish? Can't you see what it's doing to Amá, you idiot? So I would wash my feet and stuff them in my black Easter shoes that shone with Vaseline, grab a missal and veil, and wave good-bye to Amá.

9   I would walk slowly down Lorena to First to Evergreen, counting the cracks on the cement. On Evergreen I would turn left and walk to Abuelita's. I liked her porch because it was shielded by the vines of the chayotes and I could get a good look at the people and car traffic on Evergreen without them knowing. I would jump up the porch steps, knock on the screen door as I wiped my feet and call Abuelita? mi Abuelita? As I opened the door and stuck my head in, I would catch the gagging scent of toasting chile on the placa. When I entered the sala, she would greet me from the kitchen, wringing her hands in her apron. I'd sit at the corner of the table to keep from being in her way. The chiles made my eyes water. Am I crying? No, Mama Luna, I'm sure not crying. I don't like going to mass, but my eyes watered anyway, the tears dropping on the tablecloth like candle wax. Abuelita lifted the burnt chiles from the fire and sprinkled water on them

[1] Final point.

until the skins began to separate. Placing them in front of me, she turned to check the menudo. I peeled the skins off and put the flimsy, limp looking green and yellow chiles in the molcajete and began to crush and crush and twist and crush the heart out of the tomato, the clove of garlic, the stupid chiles that made me cry, crushed them until they turned into liquid under my bull hand. With a wooden spoon, I scraped hard to destroy the guilt, and my tears were gone. I put the bowl of chile next to a vase filled with freshly cut roses. Abuelita touched my hand and pointed to the bowl of menudo that steamed in front of me. I spooned some chile into the menudo and rolled a corn tortilla thin with the palms of my hands. As I ate, a fine Sunday breeze entered the kitchen and a rose petal calmly feathered down to the table.

10   I left the chapel without blessing myself and walked to Jay's. Most of the time Jay didn't have much of anything. The tomatoes were always soft and the cans of Campbell soups had rusted spots on them. There was dust on the tops of cereal boxes. I picked up what I needed: rubbing alcohol, five cans of chicken broth, a big bottle of Pine Sol. At first Jay got mad because I thought I had forgotten the money. But it was there all the time, in my back pocket.

11   When I returned from the market, I heard Amá crying in Abuelita's kitchen. She looked up at me with puffy eyes. I placed the bags of groceries on the table and began putting the cans of soup away. Amá sobbed quietly. I never kissed her. After a while, I patted her on the back for comfort. Finally: "¿Y mi Amá?" she asked in a whisper, then choked again and cried into her apron.

12   Abuelita fell off the bed twice yesterday, I said, knowing that I shouldn't have said it and wondering why I wanted to say it because it only made Amá cry harder. I guess I became angry and just so tired of the quarrels and beatings and unanswered prayers and my hands just there hanging helplessly by my side. Amá looked at me again, confused, angry, and her eyes were filled with sorrow. I went outside and sat on the porch swing and watched the people pass. I sat there until she left. I dozed off repeating the words to myself like rosary prayers: when do you stop giving when do you start giving when do you . . . and when my hands fell from my lap, I awoke to catch them. The sun was setting, an orange glow, and I knew Abuelita was hungry.

13   There comes a time when the sun is defiant. Just about the time when moods change, inevitable seasons of a day, transitions from one color to another, that hour or minute or second when the sun is finally defeated, finally sinks into the realization that it cannot with all its power to heal or burn, exist forever, there comes an illumination where the sun and earth meet, a final burst of burning red orange fury reminding us that although endings are inevitable, they are necessary for rebirths, and when that time came, just when I switched on the light in the kitchen to open Abuelita's can of soup, it was probably then that she died.

14   The room smelled of Pine Sol and vomit and Abuelita had defecated the remains of her cancerous stomach. She had turned to the window and tried

to speak, but her mouth remained open and speechless. I heard you, Abuelita, I said, stroking her cheek, I heard you. I opened the windows of the house and let the soup simmer and overboil on the stove. I turned the stove off and poured the soup down the sink. From the cabinet I got a tin basin, filled it with lukewarm water and carried it carefully to the room. I went to the linen closet and took out some modest bleached white towels. With the sacredness of a priest preparing his vestments, I unfolded the towels one by one on my shoulders. I removed the sheets and blankets from her bed and peeled off her thick flannel nightgown. I toweled her puzzled face, stretching out the wrinkles, removing the coils of her neck, toweled her shoulders and breasts. Then I changed the water. . . . The scars on her back which were as thin as the life lines on the palms of her hands made me realize how little I really knew of Abuelita. I covered her with a thin blanket and went into the bathroom. I washed my hands, and turned on the tub faucets and watched the water pour into the tub with vitality and steam. When it was full, I turned off the water and undressed. Then, I went to get Abuelita.

15   She was not as heavy as I thought and when I carried her in my arms, her body fell into a V, and yet my legs were tired, shaky, and I felt as if the distance between the bedroom and bathroom was miles and years away. Amá, where are you?

16   I stepped into the bathtub one leg first, then the other. I bent my knees slowly to descend into the water slowly so I wouldn't scald her skin. There, there, Abuelita, I said, cradling her, smoothing her as we descended, I heard you. Her hair fell back and spread across the water like eagle's wings. The water in the tub overflowed and poured onto the tile of the floor. Then the moths came. Small, gray ones that came from her soul and out through her mouth fluttering to light, circling the single dull light bulb of the bathroom. Dying is lonely and I wanted to go to where the moths were, stay with her and plant chayotes whose vines would crawl up her fingers and into the clouds; I wanted to rest my head on her chest with her stroking my hair, telling me about the moths that lay within the soul and slowly eat the spirit up; I wanted to return to the waters of the womb with her so that we would never be alone again. I wanted. I wanted my Amá. I removed a few strands of hair from Abuelita's face and held her small light head within the hollow of my neck. The bathroom was filled with moths, and for the first time in a long time I cried, rocking us, crying for her, for me, for Amá, the sobs emerging from the depths of anguish, the misery of feeling half born, sobbing until finally the sobs rippled into circles and circles of sadness and relief. There, there, I said to Abuelita, rocking us gently, there, there.

DISCUSSION QUESTIONS

1. In small groups, discuss the meaning of the term *moth* in this story. Does it have the same meaning at the end of the story as at the beginning?
2. The protagonist describes her family life from her point of view. Analyze what she says and implies about her father, her mother, and her sisters. What are her attitudes about religion?
3. Cite three ways in which her *abuelita* (grandmother) helped the protagonist throughout her life.
4. Describe how the author presents death. Discuss her specific references to the body, the soul, the illness, the death itself.
5. Discuss the healing practices of the grandmother. How do they compare with the granddaughter's and the care she gives Abuelita?

WRITING TOPICS

1. Write a journal entry describing your feelings upon learning of the death of a relative or acquaintance.
2. Write a brief essay discussing the rituals surrounding death and burial in various cultures and in our society as a whole.

CHAPTER FOUR

INNOCENCE IS A CHILD

In childhood, innocence drives curiosity. Childhood is a time to discover the world and one's place in it. Stories, tales, and rituals serve as guideposts to mark the path of exploration. Within the sphere of influence of the mother and the father, whose authority, genes, and ethnicity push and pull the child this way and that, an innocent child develops his or her identity. With little understanding of what is "normal" or what is acceptable in the adult world, children have no prejudices regarding race or class or gender. Nor have they yet developed an appreciation of the collective story of their people. As a result, they accept stories of their heritage unquestioningly and at face value.

Then, as experience broadens and innocence is diminished, a child may question or reject the values or lifestyle of his or her family. Innocence and acceptance may give way to shame or rebellion. Hispanic families who migrated to the United States have been faced with their children's withdrawal from their culture and customs. The following selections consider the effects of fading innocence on migrant families.

FROM *BLESS ME, ULTIMA*

Rudolfo A. Anaya

Anaya was born on October 30, 1937, in Pastura, a village in New Mexico. Despite health problems in his youth, he was able to attend school in nearby Santa Rosa and in Albuquerque. As a young man, he enrolled at the University of New Mexico, where he earned degrees in English and guidance and counseling.

Rudolfo Anaya's most important novel was also his first. *Bless Me, Ultima* (1972) is one of Chicano literature's most important coming-of-age novels. It captures the magic of childlike innocence through the story of Antonio and his relationship with the *curandera* (healer) named Ultima. The book became one of the few Chicano bestsellers, and has brought great acclaim to Anaya. His next novel, *Heart of Aztlán* (1976), continues the development of the New Mexico trilogy with the family's move to Albuquerque. *Tortuga* (1979) tells the story of a youth who is paralyzed, encased in a cast. These three novels constitute an important view of the Chicano world.

Other work by Anaya includes *The Silence of the Llano: Short Stories* (1982), a collection of ten stories, three of which were parts of his earlier novels, and *The Legend of La Llorona* (1984), a fictional account of the weeping woman of Hispanic American legend. In *The Adventures of Juan Chicaspatas* (1985), Anaya creates a mock epic poem that depicts Aztlán and the philosophy of being Chicano. In addition, Anaya has written nonfiction books regarding New Mexico and his own travels.

Rudolfo Anaya created a marvelous character in his novel *Bless Me, Ultima.* The child-protagonist is surrounded by a mysterious world that he believes he must discover and for which he already yearns nostalgically. Knowing that one will lose the magic of innocence makes him abhor the thought of going to school, because there he will have to reckon with systematic knowledge and the outside world of society, rather than family and community. The selection that follows is the opening chapter of the novel.

1   Ultima came to stay with us the summer I was almost seven. When she came the beauty of the llano[1] unfolded before my eyes, and the gurgling waters of the river sang to the hum of the turning earth. The magical time of childhood stood still, and the pulse of the living earth pressed its mystery into my living blood. She took my hand, and the silent, magic powers she possessed made beauty from the raw, sun-baked llano, the green river valley, and the blue bowl which was the white sun's home. My bare feet felt the throbbing earth and my body trembled with excitement. Time stood still, and it shared with me all that had been, and all that was to come. . . .

2   Let me begin at the beginning. I do not mean the beginning that was in my dreams and the stories they whispered to me about my birth, and the people of my father and mother, and my three brothers—but the beginning that came with Ultima.

3   The attic of our home was partitioned into two small rooms. My sisters, Deborah and Theresa, slept in one and I slept in the small cubicle by the door. The wooden steps creaked down into a small hallway that led into the kitchen. From the top of the stairs I had a vantage point into the heart of our home, my mother's kitchen. From there I was to see the terrified face of Chávez when he brought the terrible news of the murder of the sheriff; I was to see the rebellion of my brothers against my father; and many times late at night I was to see Ultima returning from the llano where she gathered the herbs that can be harvested only in the light of the full moon by the careful hands of a curandera.[2]

4   That night I lay very quietly in my bed, and I heard my father and mother speak of Ultima.

5   "Está sola," my father said, "ya no queda gente en el pueblito de Las Pasturas—"[3]

6   He spoke in Spanish, and the village he mentioned was his home. My father had been a vaquero[4] all his life, a calling as ancient as the coming of the Spaniard to Nuevo Méjico. Even after the big rancheros and the tejanos[5] came and fenced the beautiful llano, he and those like him continued to work there, I guess because only in that wide expanse of land and sky could they feel the freedom their spirits needed.

7   "¡Qué lástima,"[6] my mother answered, and I knew her nimble fingers worked the pattern on the doily she crocheted for the big chair in the sala.[7]

8   I heard her sigh, and she must have shuddered too when she thought of Ultima living alone in the loneliness of the wide llano. My mother was not a

---

[1] Plain.

[2] A woman folk doctor; a natural healer.

[3] She's alone; there is no one left in the villge of Las Pasturas.

[4] Cowboy.

[5] Texans.

[6] What a pity.

[7] Living room.

woman of the llano, she was the daughter of a farmer. She could not see beauty in the llano and she could not understand the coarse men who lived half their lifetimes on horseback. After I was born in Las Pasturas she persuaded my father to leave the llano and bring her family to the town of Guadalupe where she said there would be opportunity and school for us. The move lowered my father in the esteem of his compadres, the other vaqueros of the llano who clung tenaciously to their way of life and freedom. There was no room to keep animals in town so my father had to sell his small herd, but he would not sell his horse so he gave it to a good friend, Benito Campos. But Campos could not keep the animal penned up because somehow the horse was very close to the spirit of the man, and so the horse was allowed to roam free and no vaquero on that llano would throw a lazo on that horse. It was as if someone had died, and they turned their gaze from the spirit that walked the earth.

9   It hurt my father's pride. He saw less and less of his old compadres. He went to the work on the highway and on Saturdays after they collected their pay he drank with his crew at the Longhorn, but he was never close to the men of the town. Some weekends the llaneros would come into town for supplies and old amigos like Bonney or Campos or the Gonzales brothers would come by to visit. Then my father's eyes lit up as they drank and talked of the old days and told the old stories. But when the western sun touched the clouds with orange and gold the vaqueros got in their trucks and headed home, and my father was left to drink alone in the long night. Sunday morning he would get up very crudo and complain about having to go to early mass.

10   "—She served the people all her life, and now the people are scattered, driven like tumbleweeds by the winds of war. The war sucks everything dry," my father said solemnly, "it takes the young boys overseas, and their families move to California where there is work—"

11   "Ave María Purísima," my mother made the sign of the cross for my three brothers who were away at war. "Gabriel," she said to my father, "it is not right that la Grande be alone in her old age—"

12   "No," my father agreed.

13   "When I married you and went to the llano to live with you and raise your family, I could not have survived without la Grande's help. Oh, those were hard years—"

14   "Those were good years," my father countered. But my mother would not argue.

15   "There isn't a family she did not help," she continued, "no road was too long for her to walk to its end to snatch somebody from the jaws of death, and not even the blizzards of the llano could keep her from the appointed place where a baby was to be delivered—"

16   "Es verdad,"[8] my father nodded.

---

[8] It's true.

17   "She tended me at the birth of my sons—" And then I knew her eyes glanced briefly at my father. "Gabriel, we cannot let her live her last days in loneliness—"

18   "No," my father agreed, "it is not the way of our people."

19   "It would be a great honor to provide a home for la Grande," my mother murmured. My mother called Ultima la Grande out of respect. It meant the woman was old and wise.

20   "I have already sent word with Campos that Ultima is to come and live with us," my father said with some satisfaction. He knew it would please my mother.

21   "I am grateful," my mother said tenderly, "perhaps we can repay a little of the kindness la Grande has given to so many."

22   "And the children?" my father asked. I knew why he expressed concern for me and my sisters. It was because Ultima was a curandera, a woman who knew the herbs and remedies of the ancients, a miracle-worker who could heal the sick. And I had heard that Ultima could lift the curses laid by brujas[9], that she could exorcise the evil the witches planted in people to make them sick. And because a curandera had this power she was misunderstood and often suspected of practicing witchcraft herself.

23   I shuddered and my heart turned cold at the thought. The cuentos[10] of the people were full of the tales of evil done by brujas.

24   "She helped bring them into the world, she cannot be but good for the children," my mother answered.

25   "Está bien,"[11] my father yawned, "I will go for her in the morning."

26   So it was decided that Ultima should come and live with us. I knew that my father and mother did good by providing a home for Ultima. It was the custom to provide for the old and the sick. There was always room in the safety and warmth of la familia for one more person, be that person stranger or friend.

27   It was warm in the attic, and as I lay quietly listening to the sounds of the house falling asleep and repeating a Hail Mary over and over in my thoughts, I drifted into the time of dreams. Once I had told my mother about my dreams and she said they were visions from God and she was happy, because her own dream was that I should grow up and become a priest. After that I did not tell her about my dreams, and they remained in me forever and ever . . .

28   *In my dream I flew over the rolling hills of the llano. My soul wandered over the dark plain until it came to a cluster of adobe huts. I recognized the village of Las Pasturas and my heart grew happy. One mud hut had a lighted window,*

---

9 Witches.
10 Stories.
11 All right.

and the vision of my dream swept me towards it to be witness at the birth of a baby.

29   *I could not make out the face of the mother who rested from the pains of birth, but I could see the old woman in black who tended the just-arrived, steaming baby. She nimbly tied a knot on the cord that had connected the baby to its mother's blood, then quickly she bent and with her teeth she bit off the loose end. She wrapped the squirming baby and laid it at the mother's side, then she returned to cleaning the bed. All linen was swept aside to be washed, but she carefully wrapped the useless cord and the afterbirth and laid the package at the feet of the Virgin on the small altar. I sensed that these things were yet to be delivered to someone.*

30   *Now the people who had waited patiently in the dark were allowed to come in and speak to the mother and deliver their gifts to the baby. I recognized my mother's brothers, my uncles from El Puerto de los Lunas. They entered ceremoniously. A patient hope stirred in their dark, brooding eyes.*

31   *This one will be a Luna, the old man said, he will be a farmer and keep our customs and traditions. Perhaps God will bless our family and make the baby a priest.*

32   *And to show their hope they rubbed the dark earth of the river valley on the baby's forehead, and they surrounded the bed with the fruits of their harvest so the small room smelled of fresh green chile and corn, ripe apples and peaches, pumpkins and green beans.*

33   *Then the silence was shattered with the thunder of hoofbeats; vaqueros surrounded the small house with shouts and gunshots, and when they entered the room they were laughing and singing and drinking.*

34   *Gabriel, they shouted, you have a fine son! He will make a fine vaquero! And they smashed the fruits and vegetables that surrounded the bed and replaced them with a saddle, horse blankets, bottles of whiskey, a new rope, bridles, chapas,[12] and an old guitar. And they rubbed the stain of earth from the baby's forehead because man was not to be tied to the earth but free upon it.*

35   *These were the people of my father, the vaqueros of the llano. They were an exuberant, restless people, wandering across the ocean of the plain.*

36   *We must return to our valley, the old man who led the farmers spoke. We must take with us the blood that comes after the birth. We will bury it in our fields to renew their fertility and to assure that the baby will follow our ways. He nodded for the old woman to deliver the package at the altar.*

37   *No! the llaneros protested, it will stay here! We will burn it and let the winds of the llano scatter the ashes.*

38   *It is blasphemy to scatter a man's blood on unholy ground, the farmers chanted. The new son must fulfill his mother's dream. He must come to El*

---

[12] Chaps; leather leggings worn over trousers, as by western ranch hands.

Puerto and rule over the Lunas of the valley. The blood of the Lunas is strong in him.

39   *He is a Márez, the vaqueros shouted. His forefathers were conquistadores, men as restless as the seas they sailed and as free as the land they conquered. He is his father's blood!*

40   *Curses and threats filled the air, pistols were drawn, and the opposing sides made ready for battle. But the clash was stopped by the old woman who delivered the baby.*

41   *Cease! she cried, and the men were quiet. I pulled this baby into the light of life, so I will bury the afterbirth and the cord that once linked him to eternity. Only I will know his destiny.*

42   The dream began to dissolve. When I opened my eyes I heard my father cranking the truck outside. I wanted to go with him, I wanted to see Las Pasturas, I wanted to see Ultima. I dressed hurriedly, but I was too late. The truck was bouncing down the goat path that led to the bridge and the highway.

43   I turned, as I always did, and looked down the slope of our hill to the green of the river, and I raised my eyes and saw the town of Guadalupe. Towering above the housetops and the trees of the town was the church tower. I made the sign of the cross on my lips. The only other building that rose above the housetops to compete with the church tower was the yellow top of the schoolhouse. This fall I would be going to school.

44   My heart sank. When I thought of leaving my mother and going to school a warm, sick feeling came to my stomach. To get rid of it I ran to the pens we kept by the molino[13] to feed the animals. I had fed the rabbits that night and they still had alfalfa and so I only changed their water. I scattered some grain for the hungry chickens and watched their mad scramble as the rooster called them to peck. I milked the cow and turned her loose. During the day she would forage along the highway where the grass was thick and green, then she would return at nightfall. She was a good cow and there were very few times when I had to run and bring her back in the evening. Then I dreaded it, because she might wander into the hills where the bats flew at dusk and there was only the sound of my heart beating as I ran and it made me sad and frightened to be alone.

45   I collected three eggs in the chicken house and returned for breakfast.

46   "Antonio," my mother smiled and took the eggs and milk, "come and eat your breakfast."

47   I sat across the table from Deborah and Theresa and ate my atole[14] and the hot tortilla with butter. I said very little. I usually spoke very little to my two sisters. They were older than I and they were very close. They usually

---

13 Mills.
14 Cornmeal gruel; cereal.

106 Rudofo A. Anaya

spent the entire day in the attic, playing dolls and giggling. I did not concern myself with those things.

48 "Your father has gone to Las Pasturas," my mother chattered, "he has gone to bring La Grande." Her hands were white with the flour of the dough. I watched carefully. "—And when he returns, I want you children to show your manners. You must not shame your father or your mother—"

49 "Isn't her real name Ultima?" Deborah asked. She was like that, always asking grown-up questions.

50 "You will address her as la Grande," my mother said flatly. I looked at her and wondered if this woman with the black hair and laughing eyes was the woman who gave birth in my dream.

51 "Grande," Theresa repeated.

52 "Is it true she is a witch?" Deborah asked. Oh, she was in for it. I saw my mother whirl then pause and control herself.

53 "No!" she scolded. "You must not speak of such things! Oh, I don't know where you learn such ways—" Her eyes flooded with tears. She always cried when she thought we were learning the ways of my father, the ways of the Márez. "She is a woman of learning," she went on and I knew she didn't have time to stop and cry, "she has worked hard for all the people of the village. Oh, I would never have survived those hard years if it had not been for her—so show her respect. We are honored that she comes to live with us, understand?"

54 "Sí, mamá," Deborah said half willingly.

55 "Sí, mamá," Theresa repeated.

56 "Now run and sweep the room at the end of the hall. Eugene's room—" I heard her voice choke. She breathed a prayer and crossed her forehead. The flour left white stains on her, the four points of the cross. I knew it was because my three brothers were at war that she was sad, and Eugene was the youngest.

57 "Mamá." I wanted to speak to her. I wanted to know who the old woman was who cut the baby's cord.

58 "Sí." She turned and looked at me.

59 "Was Ultima at my birth?" I asked.

60 "¡Ay Dios mío!"[15] my mother cried. She came to where I sat and ran her hand through my hair. She smelled warm, like bread. "Where do you get such questions, my son. Yes," she smiled, "la Grande was there to help me. She was there to help at the birth of all my children—"

61 "And my uncles from El Puerto were there?"

62 "Of course," she answered, "my brothers have always been at my side when I needed them. They have always prayed that I would bless them with a—"

---

[15] Oh, my God.

63   I did not hear what she said because I was hearing the sounds of the dream, and I was seeing the dream again. The warm cereal in my stomach made me feel sick.

64   "And my father's brother was there, the Márez' and their friends, the vaqueros—"

65   "Ay!" she cried out, "Don't speak to me of those worthless Márez and their friends!"

66   "There was a fight?" I asked.

67   "No," she said, "a silly argument. They wanted to start a fight with my brothers—that is all they are good for. Vaqueros they call themselves, they are worthless drunks! Thieves! Always on the move, like gypsies, always dragging their families around the country like vagabonds—"

68   As long as I could remember she always raged about the Márez family and their friends. She called the village of Las Pasturas beautiful; she had gotten used to the loneliness, but she had never accepted its people. She was the daughter of farmers.

69   But the dream was true. It was as I had seen it. Ultima knew.

70   "But you will not be like them." She caught her breath and stopped. She kissed my forehead. "You will be like my brothers. You will be a Luna, Antonio. You will be a man of the people, and perhaps a priest." She smiled.

71   A priest, I thought, that was her dream. I was to hold mass on Sundays, like father Byrnes did in the church in town. I was to hear the confessions of the silent people of the valley, and I was to administer the holy Sacrament to them.

72   "Perhaps," I said.

73   "Yes," my mother smiled. She held me tenderly. The fragrance of her body was sweet.

74   "But then," I whispered, "who will hear my confession?"

75   "What?"

76   "Nothing," I answered. I felt a cool sweat on my forehead and I knew I had to run, I had to clear my mind of the dream. "I am going to Jasón's house," I said hurriedly and slid past my mother. I ran out of the kitchen door, past the animal pens, towards Jasóns house. The white sun and the fresh air cleansed me.

77   On this side of the river there were only three houses. The slope of the hill rose gradually into the hills of juniper and mesquite and cedar clumps. Jasón's house was farther away from the river than our house. On the path that led to the bridge lived huge, fat Fío and his beautiful wife. Fío and my father worked together on the highway. They were good drinking friends.

78   "¡Jasón!" I called at the kitchen door. I had run hard and was panting. His mother appeared at the door.

79   "Jasón no está aquí,"[16] she said. All of the older people spoke only in

---

[16] Jasón is not here.

Spanish, and I myself understood only Spanish. It was only after one went to
school that one learned English.

80   "¿Dónde está?"[17] I asked.

81   She pointed towards the river, northwest, past the railroad tracks to the
dark hills. The river came through those hills and there were old Indian
grounds there, holy burial grounds Jasón told me. There in an old cave lived
his Indian. At least everybody called him Jasón's Indian. He was the only
Indian of the town, and he talked only to Jasón. Jasón's father had forbidden Jasón to talk to the Indian, he had beaten him, he had tried in every way
to keep Jasón from the Indian.

82   But Jasón persisted. Jasón was not a bad boy, he was just Jasón. He was
quiet and moody, and sometimes for no reason at all wild, loud sounds came
exploding from his throat and lungs. Sometimes I felt like Jasón, like I
wanted to shout and cry, but I never did.

83   I looked at his mother's eyes, and I saw they were sad. "Thank you," I
said, and returned home. While I waited for my father to return with Ultima
I worked in the garden. Every day I had to work in the garden. Every day I
reclaimed from the rocky soil of the hill a few more feet of earth to cultivate.
The land of the llano was not good for farming, the good land was along the
river. But my mother wanted a garden and I worked to make her happy.
Already we had a few chile and tomato plants growing. It was hard work. My
fingers bled from scraping out the rocks and it seemed that a square yard of
ground produced a wheelbarrow full of rocks which I had to push down to
the retaining wall.

84   The sun was white in the bright blue sky. The shade of the clouds would
not come until the afternoon. The sweat was sticky on my brown body. I
heard the truck and turned to see it chugging up the dusty goat path. My
father was returning with Ultima.

85   "¡Mamá!" I called. My mother came running out, Deborah and Theresa
trailed after her.

86   "I'm afraid," I heard Theresa whimper.

87   "There's nothing to be afraid of," Deborah said confidently. My mother
said there was too much Márez blood in Deborah. Her eyes and hair were
very dark, and she was always running. She had been to school two years and
she spoke only English. She was teaching Theresa and half the time I didn't
understand what they were saying.

88   "Madre de Dios,[18] but mind your manners!" my mother scolded. The
truck stopped and she ran to greet Ultima. "Buenos días le de Dios,
Grande,"[19] my mother cried. She smiled and hugged and kissed the old
woman.

---

[17] Where is he?
[18] Mother of God.
[19] God grant you a good morning.

89   "Ay, María Luna," Ultima smiled, "Buenos días te de Dios, a ti y a tu familia."[20] She wrapped the black shawl around her hair and shoulders. Her face was brown and very wrinkled. When she smiled her teeth were brown. I remembered the dream.

90   "Come, come!" my mother urged us forward. It was the custom to greet the old. "Deborah!" my mother urged. Deborah stepped forward and took Ultima's withered hand.

91   "Buenos días, Grande," she smiled. She even bowed slightly. Then she pulled Theresa forward and told her to greet la Grande. My mother beamed. Deborah's good manners surprised her, but they made her happy, because a family was judged by its manners.

92   "What beautiful daughters you have raised," Ultima nodded to my mother. Nothing could have pleased my mother more. She looked proudly at my father who stood leaning against the truck, watching and judging the introductions.

93   "Antonio," he said simply. I stepped forward and took Ultima's hand. I looked up into her clear brown eyes and shivered. Her face was old and wrinkled, but her eyes were clear and sparkling, like the eyes of a young child.

94   "Antonio," she smiled. She took my hand and I felt the power of a whirl-wind sweep around me. Her eyes swept the surrounding hills and through them I saw for the first time the wild beauty of our hills and the magic of the green river. My nostrils quivered as I felt the song of the mockingbirds and the drone of the grasshoppers mingle with the pulse of the earth. The four directions of the llano met in me, and the white sun shone on my soul. The granules of sand at my feet and the sun and sky above me seemed to dissolve into one strange, complete being.

95   A cry came to my throat, and I wanted to shout it and run in the beauty I had found.

96   "Antonio." I felt my mother prod me. Deborah giggled because she had the right greeting, and I who was to be my mother's hope and joy stood voiceless.

97   "Buenos días le de Dios, Ultima," I muttered. I saw in her eyes my dream. I saw the old woman who had delivered me from my mother's womb. I knew she held the secret of my destiny.

98   "¡Antonio!" My mother was shocked I had used her name instead of calling her Grande. But Ultima held up her hand.

99   "Let it be," she smiled. "This was the last child I pulled from your womb, María. I knew there would be something between us."

100   My mother who had started to mumble apologies was quiet. "As you wish, Grande," she nodded.

---

20 The same to you and your family.

101   "I have to come to spend the last days of my life here, Antonio," Ultima said to me.

102   "You will never die, Ultima," I answered. "I will take care of you—" She let go of my hand and laughed. Then my father said, "pase, Grande, pase. Nuestra casa es su casa.[21] It is too hot to stand and visit in the sun—"

103   "Sí, sí," my mother urged. I watched them go in. My father carried on his shoulders the large blue-tin trunk which later I learned contained all of Ultima's earthly possessions, the black dresses and shawls she wore, and the magic of her sweet smelling herbs.

104   As Ultima walked past me I smelled for the first time a trace of the sweet fragrance of herbs that always lingered in her wake. Many years later, long after Ultima was gone and I had grown to be a man, I would awaken sometimes at night and think I caught a scent of her fragrance in the cool-night breeze.

105   And with Ultima came the owl. I heard it that night for the first time in the juniper tree outside of Ultima's window. I knew it was her owl because the other owls of the llano did not come that near the house. At first it disturbed me, and Deborah and Theresa too. I heard them whispering through the partition. I heard Deborah reassuring Theresa that she would take care of her, and then she took Theresa in her arms and rocked her until they were both asleep.

106   I waited. I was sure my father would get up and shoot the owl with the old rifle he kept on the kitchen wall. But he didn't, and I accepted his understanding. In many cuentos I had heard the owl was one of the disguises a bruja took, and so it struck a chord of fear in the heart to hear them hooting at night. But not Ultima's owl. Its soft hooting was like a song, and as it grew rhythmic it calmed the moonlit hills and lulled us to sleep. Its song seemed to say that it had come to watch over us.

107   I dreamed about the owl that night, and my dream was good. La Virgen de Guadalupe was the patron saint of our town. The town was named after her. In my dream I saw Ultima's owl lift la Virgin on her wide wings and fly her to heaven. Then the owl returned and gathered up all the babes of Limbo and flew them up to the clouds of heaven.

108   The Virgin smiled at the goodness of the owl.

DISCUSSION QUESTIONS

1. Describe the dream that Antonio has about his birth. What does it reveal about his family? about Ultima? about his future?

---

[21] Come in, Grande, come in. Our home is your home.

2. Compare Antonio's dream with his father's dream.
3. Discuss the nature of Ultima's character. Is she a midwife, a witch, or a healer/herbalist? What does the owl in the story have to do with Ultima?
4. Analyze carefully the treatment of time and space. Consider, for example, what the subtext of the story reveals about time even as the narrator claims that time stands still. How does the story present the *llano* (the plain), including the village known as Las Pasturas, and the town of Guadalupe?

Writing Topics

1. Consider Antonio's statement "It was only after one went to school that one learned English." Write an essay in which you explore the relationship of private and public uses of language to learning.
2. Write a brief dialogue between a Márez *vaquero* (cowboy) and a Luna farmer as you imagine them at a family meeting.

THE INDIAN RUINS

José Martí

Frequent travels took José Martí from his adopted home in New York to Key West, Tampa, and Philadelphia as he sought independence for Cuba from Spain. His poetry had an intimate tone and included references to precious jewels and his love for freedom and for his Cuban homeland. He is known for his writings about the United States that made the region and the people real to Latin Americans unaware of them.

For more information on José Martí, turn to the previous biography on page 45.

For a time, José Martí published a children's magazine with the title *La Edad de Oro* (The Golden Age). In it he told the stories of real or imagined events and recounted the biographies of artists, musicians, and other people of interest. The tone of his writing reflected his respect for children as capable human beings. In the following selection, "The Indian Ruins," his rich descriptions fire the imaginations of his young readers.

1   There probably would never be a sadder or more beautiful poem than that which could be taken from the history of the Americas. You cannot read one of these old parchments, which tells about the America of the Indians, without feeling tenderness or seeing flowers and feathers in the air. They describe the Indians' cities and feasts, the excellence of their arts and the beauty of their customs. A few of the American Indian bands lived isolated and simple lives, without clothing or necessities, like primitive people. They began to paint their strange figures on the rock walls of river banks, where only the wilderness is, which makes a man think more about the wonders of nature. Other Indians had older cultures, and they lived as tribes in villages made of reeds or adobe, eating what they hunted or fished, and warring with their neighbors. Some Indian civilizations were quite advanced, with cities of one-hundred-forty-thousand buildings, palaces decorated with golden paintings, bustling trade in the streets and plazas, and marble temples with gigan-

tic statues of their gods. Their accomplishments do not resemble those of other peoples' anymore than one man resembles another. The Indians were innocent, superstitious and fierce. They created their own government, religion, art, warefare, architecture, technology and poetry. All of their creations are fascinating, daring and unique. They were an artistic, intelligent and clean race. Their histories read like novels: the Mexican Nahuatls and Mayans, the Colombian Chibchas, the Venezuelan Cumanagotans, the Peruvian Quechuas, the Bolivian Aymaras, the Uruguayan Charruas and the Chilean Araucanans.

2   The quetzal is the beautiful Guatemalan bird, a brilliant green bird with long feathers, which dies of sadness in captivity or just from the breaking of its tail feathers even when it's free. The quetzal is a bird which gleams in the light, like the heads of hummingbirds, which seem to be precious stones or iridescent jewels, that from one viewpoint might be topaz, or from another opal, or still another amethyst. So it is, when we read in the *Travels of Le Plongeon* the stories of the lovers of the Mayan Princess Ara, who refused to have the Prince Aak, who for the love of Ara killed his own brother Chaak, or in the *History of Ixtilxochitl* about the elegant and rich city life of the Mexican kings of Tenochtitlan and Tezcuco, or in the *Remembrance of Florida* by Captain Fuentes, or in the *Chronicales of Juarros*, or in the history of the conquistador Bernal Diaz del Castillo, or in the travels of the Englishman Thomas Gage, we can feel that the Indians walk before us again as if they were really here, in their white tunics, attended by messenger boys, reciting their poetry and building, and see the crowds in the cities, those wise men of Chichen, the potentates of Uxmal, the traders of Tulan, the craftsmen of Tonochtitlan, the priests of Cholula, the loving teachers and the gentle children of Utetlan. That fine race, who lived in the sun, never locked their stone houses. It does not seem like reading from an old book with yellowed pages, where the s's are like f's and words are used with great ceremony, but more like seeing the quetzal die, as he gives out his last cry when his tail is broken. With imagination things can be seen which cannot really be seen with the eyes any longer.

3   You become friends with them by reading those old books. In them are heroes, saints, lovers, poets and apostles. In those old books are descriptions of pyramids bigger than those in Egypt, as well as stories of giants who defeated beasts, battles between giants and men, gods who travel on the wind, scattering seeds of civilization over the world, kidnappings of princesses, nations in mortal combat, hand-to-hand struggles of such bravery that they seem super human, defenses of cities against powerful invaders from the north, descriptions of the varied life, pleasant and productive, in their stadiums, temples, canals, workshops, courts and markets. There were kings such as the Chichemec Netzahualpili, who killed their sons because they broke the law, the same way that the Roman Brutus allowed his son to be killed. There were orators who stood up and cried like the Tlaxcalan Xicotengal, begging his people not to let the Spaniards advance, just as

Demosthenes begged the Greeks not to allow the entry of Philip of Macedonia. There were just monarchs like Netzahualcoyotl, the great poet-king of Chichimecs, who knew how—like the Hebrew Solomon—to build justice among men with a fatherly spirit. There were sacrifices of beautiful young women to invisible gods in the sky, the same as in Greece, where the sacrifices were so numerous it wasn't necessary to erect an altar for the next ceremony, because the pile of ashes left from the last sacrifice was so tall that the priests simply placed the bodies on the ashes. There were human sacrifices like that of the Hebrew Abraham, who bound his son Isaac to a tree trunk to kill him with his own hands, because he believed he had heard voices from heaven ordering him to plunge the knife into his own son so his god would be satisfied with the blood. There were even mass sacrifices in Europe, like those that took place in the Great Plaza of Madrid in front of the bishops and the king of Spain when the Spanish Inquisition burned men alive on huge piles of firewood following pompous parades, and the ladies of Madrid watched from the balconies. Superstition and ignorance makes barbarians of men in all civilizations. The conquering Spaniards exaggerated the cases of Indian sacrifices. They invented defects in the conquered race, so that the cruelty with which they treated the Indians would seem just and proper to the rest of the world. To see the difference in opinion concerning the Indian sacrifices, you only have to read what the soldier Bernal Diaz said of them and to compare it with what the priest Bartolome de las Casas wrote. Bartolomé de las Casas is a name to be carried in your heart just like the name of your brother. He was ugly and skinny, with a big nose, and he spoke in a confused and abrupt manner, but you could see his sublime soul in the pure light of his eyes.

4   We will consider Mexico today because the engravings are from there. Mexico was first settled by the brave Toltecs, who held their wicker shields high and followed a chief who carried a gold-ringed shield. Later the Toltecs became soft with luxury, and down from the north with terrible force, dressed in skins, came the barbarous Chichemecs, who settled there and became rulers of great wisdom.

5   Later the unconquered people of the area united under the leadership of the astute Aztecs and took over the government from the Chichemecs, who lived in slovenly and degenerate ways. The Aztecs ruled like merchants, gathering riches and oppressing the people. When Cortez and his men arrived from Spain, they marched through the oppressed villages, and with the help of one hundred thousand Indian warriors who joined them, they conquered the Aztecs.

6   The Spaniards' firearms and armor did not intimidate the heroic Indians, but the fanatic people did not want to obey their war chieftans, because they believed the Spaniards were the soldiers of the god Quetzalcoatl, whom the priests had predicted would return from heaven to liberate the people from tyranny. Cortez knew the tribes' rivalries, stirred up their jealousies, separated the chiefs from their cowardly people and won the weak over with gifts

or threats. He captured or assassinated the brave and the just. The priests, who came from Spain after the soldiers, destroyed the temples of the Indian gods and built their own temples on top of the Indian ruins.

7   How beautiful was Tenochtitlan, the Aztec capital city, when Cortez came to Mexico! The whole day was like morning, and the city was always festive. Some of the streets were canals, and others were dirt. The plazas were numerous and large, and the surroundings planted with orchards. The Indian canoes travelled through the canals so quickly and skillfully that it seemed the canoes themselves knew where they were going, and there were so many that it seemed at times that you could walk on them as if on solid ground. In some they carried fruits and in still others earthen jars and cups and other things from pottery shops. The people surged in the market places, greeting each other affectionately, going from stand to stand, praising or criticizing the king, wandering and selling. The houses were made of adobe, unfired brick, or, if the owner was wealthy, cemented stone. On a five-terraced pyramid with forty small temples at its feet, the magnificent temple of Huitzilopochtli rose high above the city. It was made of ebony and jasper with cloud-like marble and fragrant cedars, and the sacred flames in the six hundred braziers were never extinguished. In the streets below, the people came and went, wearing their short sleeveless tunics, some white, some colored, others white with embroidery, and loose, soft shoes which were like boots, but open like sandals. From around a corner a group of children might emerge shooting fruit seeds with peashooters, or playing their clay flutes together on their way to school where they learned handicrafts, dance and song, along with their lessons in the use of spears and bows and arrows, and how to cultivate plants, because everyone had to learn to work in the fields and make things with their own hands, and to defend themselves. A great lord was passing by wearing a large cape adorned with feathers. At his side, his secretary followed along unfolding the notebook as he filled it with writing, making sure all the figures and signs were on the underside so that, in closing it, the fresh ink would not smear. Behind the lord walked three warriors with wooden helmets, one in the form of a snake's head, another in wolf's shape, and another in the form of a jaguar. All of these helmets were covered with skins and had openings so that the stripes for bravery, marked on the soldier's ears, could be seen. A servant was carrying a yellow and gold bird in a reed cage for the aviary of the king, who had many birds and many red and silver fish in marble fish ponds hidden in the labyrinths of his gardens. Another servant went along the street above shouting for everyone to make way for the ambassadors who were leaving the city with shields tied to their left arms and their arrows pointing down to the ground, a sign demanding captives from their tributary villages. A carpenter was singing from his doorway, carefully repairing an eagle-shaped chair, which had lost the gold and silk trimmings from its fine deer skin seat. Other men were carrying painted skins, stopping at each door to see if anyone wanted to buy a blue or red one, which were to be hung on walls like

pictures are today as decorations. The widow came back from the market with her servant following her; there were not enough hands to hold all her purchases: jars from Cholula or Guatemala, a green obsidian knife as fine as a leaf of paper, a polished stone mirror in which faces were more clearly seen than in a crystal, tightly woven fabric that would never lose its color, a fish with moving scales of silver and gold and a parrot made of enameled copper with moveable wings and beak. The people had stopped in the street to watch a pair of newlyweds with their tunics sewn together, as if to proclaim that they were joined on earth until death. Behind them ran a little boy pulling his toy wagon. Other people were gathering to listen to a traveller tell what he had seen in the wild land of the Zapotecs, where another king ruled in the temples and the royal palace itself. He never went out except when carried upon the shoulders of priests to listen to the prayers of the people, who, through him, asked favors from the one who rules the world from heaven, from the kings in the palaces and from other kings who are carried on priests' shoulders. One group of people on the side are saying how good the priest's speech was yesterday, when he told the story of the warrior who was buried, and they are describing the elaborate funeral with a flag that displayed the warrior's victories and how the servants were carrying the dead warrior's favorite foods on trays made of eight different metals.

8   In between these conversations from the street, the rustling of the trees on the patios and the noise of hammers and files could be heard. Of all that grandeur of yesteryear, hardly anything remains in the museums today, except for a small quantity of golden cups, a few yoke-like stones of polished obsidian, and a number of monotonous crafted rings! Tenochtitlan is no more, nor is Tulan, the city of great fires. The Indians of today bow their heads when they pass by the ruins, move their lips as if saying something and remove their hats until they have passed the ruins. Not one whole city or temple remains on the side of Mexico where once lived all those peoples of the same Nahuatl language and lineage who were conquering their way to the Pacific Coast.

9   Of Cholula, Cholula of the temples, which astonished Cortez, nothing more remains than the ruins of the pyramid of four terraces, which was twice as big as the famous pyramid of Cheops. In Xochicalco the only thing standing is that temple of chiselled granite, which, at the peak of its fame, was filled with tunnels and arches, made of enormous pieces so tightly joined that the junctions cannot be seen, and rock so hard that no one knows how they cut it or how they lifted the huge stones. In Centla, the ancient fortifications can be seen strewn on the ground. The Frenchman Charnay just uncovered a house in Tula of twenty-four rooms with fifteen staircases so beautiful and fancy that he says they are "a work of captivating interest." In La Quemada, the ruins of the storehouses, the fortress ramparts and columns of prophyry cover the Hill of Buildings. Mitla was the city of the Zapotecs. In Mitla in all their beauty stand the walls of the palace where the shoulder-riding prince came to tell the king what was demanded from him by the heavenly god

Pitao-Gozaana, who had created himself. The columns of carved beams without base or capital supported the roof. They have not fallen yet and, in their silence, seem more imposing than the mountains that surrounded the lush valley where Mitla was built. In the midst of weeds as tall as trees emerge beautiful walls, all covered with the finest fretwork and carvings, with no curves at all, but made of straight lines and squared angles perfectly graceful and majestic.

10   Mexico's most beautiful ruins are not these at Mitla, but rather those throughout the Mayan regions. The Mayas were a powerful warlike people who received visitors and ambassadors from coastal peoples. The celebrated city of Palenque is from the Mayans of Oaxaca with its stout-walled palace covered with carved stones, depicting men with pointed heads and very protruding mouths, dressed in ornately decorated clothes and plumed headdresses. The entrance to the palace is grandiose with fourteen doors and its stone giants standing between them. Inside and outside, the stucco that covers the wall is covered with colored paintings in red, blue, black and white. A patio surrounded by columns is in the interior. There is a Temple of the Cross, so called because on one of the carved stones there are what seems to be two priests on either side of an object like a cross, which is as tall as the priests. Only it is not a Christian cross, but rather one like the Buddhists have in their religion. Not even Palenque can be compared with the Mayan ruins of Yucatan, which are even stranger and more beautiful.

11   The empire of the Mayan princes, who had wide cheekbones and foreheads like modern white men, stretched throughout Yucatan. The ruins of Zayi are in Yucatan, with its three-story Casa Grande with a thirty-foot-wide staircase. Then there is Labna, with that strange building that has a row of stone skulls around its roof, and another ruin where two men, one standing and one kneeling, are carrying a great sphere. In Yucatan, also, is Izamal, where the famous giant face, a stone face of more than two meters, is found. Kabah is there, too, with a great stone arch, now broken on top. It is impossible to look at it without feeling its grace and nobility.

12   The Mayan cities most celebrated in the books of the American Stephens, De Brassour of Bourbourg, Charnay, Le Plongeon and his daring wife, and the Frenchman Nadaillac are Uxmal and Chichen Itza, the cities of painted palaces, houses crafted like lace, deep wells and magnificent convents. Uxmal is about three miles from Merida, which is the modern city, celebrated for its beautiful sisal fields and its good people, who receive strangers as if they were brothers. In Uxmal are many famous ruins, and all of them, as throughout all of Mexico, are on top of the pyramids, as if they were in buildings of greater value, the only ones which remained standing after more fragile houses had fallen to the earth. The most famous building is the one that the books call the *Governor's House*, which is made totally of rough stone. The building is more than two hundred eighty feet wide and thirty-six feet deep, with doors filled with richly carved wood. Another house is called the *House of Turtles*. It is very strange indeed, because one stone

turtle is enclosed in a stockade with other turtles in relief every so often. *The House of the Nuns* is truly beautiful. It is not a single house, but four, which are on top of the pyramid. They call one of them *Serpent*, because an enormous serpent has been cut in the brilliant stone outside. The serpent winds around the whole building. Another of the four houses has a crown made from the heads of idols, near the top of the wall. None of the heads is the same, and all are remarkably impressive. They are artfully arranged in groups and, just the same, seem to be there by chance. Another of these buildings still has four of the seventeen towers that it once had, and whose arch supports near the roof look like cavities in rotting teeth. Uxmal still has the *House of the Fortuneteller,* tinted with many different colors, and the *House of the Dwarf,* so tiny and well carved that it is like a wooden Chinese box, with its hundreds of carved figures. The *House of the Dwarf* is so stunningly ornate that a visitor called it "a masterpiece of art and elegance," and another said that "the House of the Dwarf is as pretty as a jewel."

13   The whole city of Chichen Itza is like the *House of the Dwarf.* Chichen Itza is like a stone book, torn, with its pages, stained and in pieces, lying on the ground, buried in the mountainous jungle. There are five hundred columns strewn on the ground of Chichen Itza. Statues without heads are leaning at the foot of the walls. The streets are choked by all the vegetation that has been growing there for centuries. Yet of that which remains there is no place without finely detailed paintings with graceful curves or nobly sculptured figures with straight noses and long beards. The wall paintings tell the story of the two mad brothers who fought each other to see who would get the Princess Ara. There are processions of priests, soldiers and animals that seem to gaze knowingly, boats with double prows, men with black beards and black men with curly hair. Everything is so clearly drawn and the colors are so fresh and bright that it seems as if the blood still coursed in the veins of the artists who left in hieroglyphics and paintings the history of this Mayan civilization, which launched its boats along the rivers and coasts of all Central America and knew of Asia by way of the Pacific and Africa by the Atlantic Ocean. There is a stone drawing in which one man is shown sending a ray of light from his half opened lips to another man seated. There are pictures and symbols, which seem to tell, in a language that cannot be read, even with the incomplete Indian alphabet of the Bishop Landa, the secrets of the civilization which built the *Amphitheater,* the *Castle,* the *Palace of Nuns,* the *Caracole* and the *Sacrificial Well.* This well of sacrifices is filled on the bottom with what seem to be white stones, that may be the remains of the bodies of the beautiful virgins who died there, smiling and singing in sacrifice to the gods, like the Christian virgins in the Coliseum of Rome died for the Hebrew god, and as the most beautiful Egyptian virgin, crowned with flowers, followed the tradition in being sacrificed to the waters of the Nile, for an Egyptian god.

14   Who carved the lacey statues of Chichen Itza? Where, oh where, has that powerful and gracious civilization gone that conceived the rounded *House of the Snail,* the little carved *House of the Dwarf* and the grand serpent of the *House of the Nuns* at Uxmal? What a beautiful novel the history of America is!

DISCUSSION QUESTIONS

1. In small groups, discuss the Indian heritage of the Americas.
2. Describe the everyday life of Aztecs as presented by Martí.
3. Analyze the architecture of the Mayas as described by Martí.
4. Describe the reasons for the fall of Mexico according to Martí.
5. In small groups, discuss the significance of the priest Bartolomé de las Casas with regard to the Native Americans.

WRITING TOPICS

1. Research and write a report on the Aztecs or the Mayas. Choose as your focus everyday life, architecture, the arts, or another specific aspect of interest to you.
2. Write an essay comparing and contrasting the Mayas and the Aztecs.

TALES TOLD UNDER THE MANGO TREE

Judith Ortiz Cofer

"Tales Told Under the Mango Tree" is a selection drawn from Judith Ortiz Cofer's book *Silent Dancing*. More than simply a collection of folklore, the book is a combination autobiography/anthology, including poetry, Puerto Rican folklore, essays, and memoirs. Her work mirrors the influences of her bilingual and bicultural childhood on her development as a writer, an artist, and a woman.

For more information, turn to the previous biography on page 85.

In *Tales Told Under the Mango Tree,* Judith Ortiz Cofer recalls the stories related by her grandmother under a mango tree when her family left their New Jersey home and returned to the island of Puerto Rico. There, surrounded by cousins, aunts, and uncles, the young Judith would join "Mamá's tribe" to listen to her grandmother's stories. This selection is, in fact, a retelling of a Puerto Rican folktale, "María Sabida," related according to Cofer's recollection of her own grandmother's version. Note Cofer's subtle use of women as models of behavior and knowledge.

MARÍA SABIDA

1   Once upon a time there lived a girl who was so smart that she was known throughout Puerto Rico as María Sabida. María Sabida came into the world with her eyes open. They say that at the moment of her birth she spoke to the attending midwife and told her what herbs to use to make a special *guarapo*[1], a tea that would put her mother back on her feet immediately. They say that the two women would have thought the infant was possessed if María Sabida had not convinced them with her descriptions of life in heaven that she was touched by God and not spawned by the Devil.

---

[1] Sugarcane juice.

2   María Sabida grew up in the days when the King of Spain owned Puerto Rico, but had forgotten to send law and justice to this little island lost on the map of the world. And so thieves and murderers roamed the land terrorizing the poor people. By the time María Sabida was of marriageable age, one such *ladrón*[2] had taken over the district where she lived.

3   For years people had been subjected to abuse from this evil man and his henchmen. He robbed them of their cattle and then made them buy their own cows back from him. He would take their best chickens and produce when he came into town on Saturday afternoons, riding with his men through the stalls set up by farmers. Overturning their tables, he would yell, "Put it on my account." But of course he never paid for anything he took. One year several little children disappeared while walking to the river, and although the townspeople searched and searched, no trace of them was ever found. That is when María Sabida entered the picture. She was fifteen then, and a beautiful girl with the courage of a man, they say.

4   She watched the chief *ladrón* the next time he rampaged through the pueblo. She saw that he was a young man: red-skinned, and tough as leather. *Cuero y sangre, nada más,*[3] she said to herself, a man of flesh and blood. And so she prepared herself either to conquer or to kill this man.

5   María Sabida followed the horses' trail deep into the woods. Though she left the town far behind she never felt afraid or lost. María Sabida could read the sun, the moon, and the stars for direction. When she got hungry, she knew which fruits were good to eat, which roots and leaves were poisonous, and how to follow the footprints of animals to a waterhole. At nightfall, María Sabida came to the edge of a clearing where a large house, almost like a fortress, stood in the forest.

6   "No woman has ever set foot in that house," she thought, "no *casa*[4] is this, but a man-place." It was a house built for violence, with no windows on the ground level, but there were turrets on the roof where men could stand guard with guns. She waited until it was nearly dark and approached the house through the kitchen side. She found it by smell.

7   In the kitchen which she knew would have to have a door or window for ventilation, she saw an old man stirring a huge pot. Out of the pot stuck little arms and legs. Angered by the sight, María Sabida entered the kitchen, pushed the old man aside, and picking up the pot threw its horrible contents out of the window.

8   "Witch, witch, what have you done with my master's stew!" yelled the old man. "He will kill us both when he gets home and finds his dinner spoiled."

---

[2] Thief.
[3] Skin and blood, nothing more.
[4] Home.

9   "Get, you filthy *viejo*."[5] María Sabida grabbed the old man's beard and pulled him to his feet. "Your master will have the best dinner of his life if you follow my instructions."

10   María Sabida then proceeded to make the most delicious *asopao*[6] the old man had ever tasted, but she would answer no questions about herself, except to say that she was his master's fiancée.

11   When the meal was done, María Sabida stretched and yawned and said that she would go upstair and rest until her *prometido*[7] came home. Then she went upstairs and waited.

12   The men came home and ate ravenously of the food María Sabida had cooked. When the chief ladrón had praised the old man for a fine meal, the cook admitted that it had been *la prometida*[8] who made the tasty chicken stew.

13   "My what?" the leader roared. "I have no *prometida*." And he and his men ran upstairs. But there were many floors, and by the time they were halfway to the room where María Sabida waited, many of the men had dropped down unconscious and the others had slowed down to a crawl until they too were overcome with irresistible sleepiness. Only the chief *ladrón* made it to where María Sabida awaited him holding a paddle that she had found among his weapons. Fighting to keep his eyes open, he asked her, "Who are you, and why have you poisoned me?"

14   "I am your future wife, María Sabida, and you are not poisoned, I added a special sleeping powder that tastes like oregano to your *asopao*. You will not die."

15   "Witch!" yelled the chief *ladrón*, "I will kill you. Don't you know who I am?" And reaching for her, he fell on his knees, whereupon María Sabida beat him with the paddle until he lay curled like a child on the floor. Each time he tried to attack her, she beat him some more. When she was satisfied that he was vanquished, María Sabida left the house and went back to town.

16   A week later, the chief *ladrón* rode into town with his men again. By then everyone knew what María Sabida had done and they were afraid of what these evil men would do in retribution. "Why did you not just kill him when you had a chance, *muchacha*?"[9] many of the townswomen had asked María Sabida. But she had just answered mysteriously, "It is better to conquer than to kill." The townspeople then barricaded themselves behind closed doors when they heard the pounding of the thieves' horses approaching. But the gang did not stop until they arrived at María Sabida's house. There the men, instead of guns, brought out musical instruments: a *cuatro*, a *güiro*, *maracas*,[10] and a harmonica. Then they played a lovely melody.

---

[5] Old man.

[6] Stew.

[7] Fiancé.

[8] Fiancée.

[9] Girl.

[10] Small four-stringed guitar; musical instrument made of dried gourds; rattlelike musical instruments also made of dried gourds.

17   "María Sabida, María Sabida, my strong and wise María," called out the leader, sitting tall on his horse under María Sabida's window, "come out and listen to a song I've written for you—I call it *The Ballad of María Sabida*."

18   María Sabida then appeared on her balcony wearing a wedding dress. The chief *ladrón* sang his song to her: a lively tune about a woman who had the courage of a man and the wisdom of a judge, and who had conquered the heart of the best bandido on the island of Puerto Rico. He had a strong voice and all the people cowering in their locked houses heard his tribute to María Sabida and crossed themselves at the miracle she had wrought.

19   One of one they all came out and soon María Sabida's front yard was full of people singing and dancing. The *ladrones* had come prepared with casks of wine, bottles of rum, and a wedding cake made by the old cook from the tender meat of coconuts. The leader of the thieves and María Sabida were married on that day. But all had not yet been settled between them. That evening, as she rode behind him on his horse, she felt the dagger concealed beneath his clothes. She knew then that she had not fully won the battle for this man's heart.

20   On her wedding night María Sabida suspected that her husband wanted to kill her. After their dinner, which the man had insisted on cooking himself, they went upstairs. María Sabida asked for a little time alone to prepare herself. He said he would take a walk but would return very soon. When she heard him leave the house, María Sabida went down to the kitchen and took several gallons of honey from the pantry. She went back to the bedroom and there she fashioned a life-sized doll out of her clothes and poured the honey into it. She then blew out the candle, covered the figure with a sheet and hid herself under the bed.

21   After a short time, she heard her husband climbing the stairs. He tiptoed into the dark room thinking her asleep in their marriage bed. Peeking out from under the bed, María Sabida saw the glint of the knife her husband pulled out from inside his shirt. Like a fierce panther he leapt onto the bed and stabbed the doll's body over and over with his dagger. Honey splattered his face and fell on his lips. Shocked, the man jumped off the bed and licked his lips.

22   "How sweet is my wife's blood. How sweet is María Sabida in death— how sour in life and how sweet in death. If I had known she was so sweet, I would not have murdered her." And so declaring, he kneeled down on the floor beside the bed and prayed to María Sabida's soul for forgiveness.

23   At that moment, María Sabida came out of her hiding place. "Husband, I have tricked you once more, I am not dead." In his joy, the man threw down his knife and embraced María Sabida, swearing that he would never kill or steal again. And he kept his word, becoming in later years an honest farmer. Many years later he was elected mayor of the same town he had once terrorized with his gang of *ladrones*.

24   María Sabida made a real *casa* out of his thieves' den, and they had many children together, all of whom could speak at birth. But, they say, María

Sabida always slept with one eye open, and that is why she lived to be one hundred years old and wiser than any other woman on the Island of Puerto Rico, and her name was known even in Spain.

25 "Colorín, colorado este cuento se ha acabado."[11] Mamá would slap her knees with open palms and say this little rhyme to indicate to the children sitting around her under the giant mango tree that the story was finished. It was time for us to go play and leave the women alone to embroider in the shade of the tree and to talk about serious things.

26 I remember that tree as a natural wonder. It was large, with a trunk that took four or five children holding hands to reach across. Its leaves were so thick that the shade it cast made a cool room where we took refuge from the hot sun. When an unexpected shower caught us there, the women had time to gather their embroidery materials before drops came through the leaves. But the most amazing thing about the tree was the throne it had made for Mamá. On the trunk there was a smooth seat-like projection. It was perfect for a storyteller. She would take her place on the throne and lean back. The other women—my mother and her sisters—would bring towels to sit on; the children sat anywhere. Sometimes we would climb to a thick branch we called "the ship," to the right of the throne, and listen there. "The ship" was a thick limb that hung all the way down to the ground. Up to three small children could straddle this branch while the others bounced on the end that sat near the ground making it sway like a ship. When Mamá told her stories, we sat quietly on our crow's nest because if anyone interrupted her narrative she should stop talking and no amount of begging would persuade her to finish the story that day.

27 The first time my mother took my brother and me back to Puerto Rico, we were stunned by the heat and confused by a houseful of relatives. Mamá's *casa* was filled to capacity with grandchildren, because two of the married daughters had come to stay there until their husbands sent for them: my mother and the two of us and her older sister with her five children. Mamá still had three of her own children at home, ranging in age from a teenage daughter to my favorite uncle who was six months older than me.

28 Our solitary life in New Jersey, where we spent our days inside a small dark apartment watching television and waiting for our father to come home on leave from the navy, had not prepared us for life in Mamá's house or for the multitude of cousins, aunts and uncles pulling us into their loud conversations and rough games. For the first few days my little brother kept his head firmly buried in my mother's neck, while I stayed relatively close to her, but being nearly six, and able to speak as loudly as anyone, I soon joined Mamá's tribe.

29 In the last few weeks before the beginning of school, when it was too hot for cooking until it was almost dark and when mothers would not even let

---

[11] "Bright color, red, this story is finished," a formula ending for a story, much like "And they lived happily ever after."

their boys go to the playgrounds and parks for fear of sunstroke, Mamá would lead us to the mango tree, there to spin the web of our *cuentos*[12] over us, making us forget the heat, the mosquitos, our past in a foreign country, and even the threat of the first day of school looming just ahead.

30   It was under that mango tree that I first began to feel the power of words. I cannot claim to have always understood the point of the stories I heard there. Some of these tales were based on ancient folklore brought to the colonies by Spaniards from their own versions of even older myths of Greek and Roman origins—which, as I later discovered through my insatiable reading, had been modified in clever ways to fit changing times. María Sabida became the model Mamá used for the "prevailing woman"—the woman who "slept with one eye open"—whose wisdom was gleaned through the senses: from the natural world and from ordinary experiences. Her main virtue was that she was always alert and never a victim. She was by implication contrasted to María La Loca, that poor girl who gave it all up for love, becoming a victim of her own foolish heart.

31   The mango tree was located at the top of a hill, on land that belonged to "The American," or at least to the sugar refinery that he managed. *La Central,* as it was called, employed the majority of the pueblo's men. Its tall chimney stacks loomed over the town like sentinels, spewing plumes of grey smoke that filled the air during cane season with the syrupy thick aroma of burnt sugar.

32   In my childhood the sugarcane fields bordered both sides of the main road, which was like a part on a head of spiky, green hair. As we approached the pueblo on our way coming home, I remember how my mother sat up in the back seat of the *carro público,* the taxi, we had taken from the airport in San Juan. Although she was pointing out the bell tower of the famous church of La Monserrate, I was distracted by the hypnotizing motion of men swinging machetes in the fields. They were shirtless, and sweat poured in streams down their backs. Bathed in light reflected by their blades, these laborers moved as on a ballet stage. I wondered whether they practiced like dancers to perfect their synchronicity. It did not occur to me that theirs was "survival choreography"—merely a safety measure—for wild swinging could lead to lost fingers and limbs. Or, as I heard one of the women say once, "there are enough body parts in the cane fields to put one whole man together."

33   And although trucks were already being used in most *centrales,*[13] in our town, much of the cane harvest was still transported from the fields to the mill in oxen-drawn carts which were piled so high with the stalks, that, when you followed one of them you could see neither the cart driver nor the beasts in front: It was a moving haystack.

---

[12] Stories.
[13] Sugar refineries.

34   To car drivers they were a headache and a menace on the road. A good wind could blow the cane off the top of the cart and smash a windshield. But what most drivers hated was getting stuck behind one that would take up the whole road traveling at five miles per hour and ignore the horn, the mad hand waving and the red-faced man shouting invectives. In later years this vehicle would be almost totally replaced by the open-bed trucks that were also loaded to the limit, traveling the roads of the Island at sixty or seventy miles per hour, granting no other vehicle (except police cars) right-of-way. The driver would keep his hand on the horn and that was all the warning a passenger car received. Pulling over as if for an emergency vehicle, was usually the best plan to follow.

35   We sucked on little pieces of sugar cane Mamá had cut for us under the mango tree. Below us a pasture rolled down to the road and the cane fields could be seen at a distance; the men in their perpetual motion were tiny black ants to our eyes. You looked up to see the red roof of the American's house. It was a big white house with a large porch completely enclosed by mosquito screens (on the Island at that time this was such a rarity that all houses designed in that way were known as "American"). At Mamá's house we slept cozily under mosquito nets, but during the day we fought the stinging, buzzing insects with bare hands and, when we lost a battle, we soothed our scratched raw skin with calamine lotion.

36   During the first few weeks of our visits both my brother and I, because we were fresh, tender meat, had skin like a pink target, dotted with red spots where the insects had scored bulls-eyes. Amazingly, either we built up a natural resistance, or the mosquitoes gave up, but it happened every time: a period of embarrassment as pink "turistas," followed by brown skin and immunity. Living behind screens, the American couple would never develop the tough skin needed for Island survival.

37   When Mamá told stories about kings and queens and castles, she would point to the big house on the hill. We were not supposed to go near the place. In fact, we were trespassing when we went to the mango tree. Mamá's backyard ended at the barbed-wire fence that led to the American's pasture. The tree stood just on the other side. She had at some point before my time, placed a strong stick under the barbed wire to make an entrance; but it could only be pulled up so much, so that even the children had to crawl through. Mamá seemed to relish the difficulty of getting to our special place. For us children it was fun to watch our mothers get their hair and clothes caught on the wire and to listen to them curse.

38   The pasture was a magical realm of treasures and secret places to discover. It even had a forbidden castle we could look at from a distance.

39   While the women embroidered, my girl-cousins and I would gather leaves and thorns off a lemon tree and do some imaginative stitch work of our own. The boys would be in the "jungle" gathering banana leaves they built tepees with. Imitating the grownups who were never without a cigarette hanging from their mouths, we would pick the tightly wrapped buds of

the hibiscus flowers, which, with their red tips, looked to us like lighted cig-arettes. We glued wild flower petals to our fingernails and, although they did not stay on for long, for a little while our hands, busy puncturing the leaves into patterns with lemon tree thorns, looked like our mother's with their red nail polish, pushing needle and thread through white linen, creating improbable landscapes of trailing vines and flowers, decorating the sheets and pillowcases we would sleep on.

40   We picked ripe guavas in their season and dumped them on Mamá's capacious lap for her to inspect for worms before we ate them. The sweet-ness of a ripe guava cannot be compared to anything else: its pink, gooey inside can be held on the tongue and savored like a caramel.

41   During mango season we threw rocks at the branches of our tree, hang-ing low with fruit. Later in the season, a boy would climb to the highest branches for the best fruit—something I always yearned to do, but was not allowed to: too dangerous.

42   On days when Mamá felt truly festive she would send us to the store with three dollars for ten bottles of Old Colony pop and the change in assorted candies: Mary Janes, Bazooka gum, lollypops, tiny two-piece boxes of Chicklets, coconut candy wrapped in wax paper, and more—all kept in big glass jars and sold two for one penny. We would have our reckless feast under the mango tree and then listen to a story. Afterwards, we would take turns on the swing that touched the sky.

43   My grandfather had made a strong swing from a plank of heavy wood and a thick length of rope. Under Mamá's supervision he had hung it from a sturdy lower branch of the mango tree that reached over the swell of the hill. In other words, you boarded the swing on level ground, but since the tree rose out of the summit, one push and you took off for the sky. It was almost like flying. From the highest point I ever reached, I could see the big house, as a bird would see it, to my left; the church tower from above the trees to my right; and far in the distance, below me, my family in a circle under the tree, receding, growing smaller, then, as I came back down to earth, looming larger, my mother's eyes glued to me, reflecting the fear for my safety that she would not voice in her mother's presence and thus risk overriding the other's authority. My mother's greatest fear was that my brother or I would hurt ourselves while at Mamá's, and that she would be held accountable by my excessively protective father when he returned from his tour of duty in Europe. And one day, because fear invites accident, I did fall from a ride up to the clouds.

44   I had been catapulting myself higher and higher, when out of the corner of my eye I saw my big cousin, Javier, running at top speed after his little brother, swinging a stick in front as if to strike the younger boy. This hap-pened fast. The little boy, Roberto, ran towards Mamá, who at that moment, was leaning towards my mother in conversation. Trying to get to his brother before he reached safe haven, Javier struck, accidently hitting my mother square on the face. I saw it happening. I saw it as if in slow motion.

I saw my mother's broken glasses fly off her face, and the blood began to flow. Dazed, I let go of the swing ropes and flew down from the clouds and the treetops and onto the soft cushion of pasture grass and just rolled and rolled. Then I lay there stunned, tasting grass and dirt until Mamá's strong arms lifted me up. She carried me through the fence and down to her house where my mother was calling hysterically for me. Her glasses had protected her from serious injury. The bump on her forehead was minor. The nosebleed had already been contained by the age-old method of placing a copper penny on the bridge, between the eyes. Her tears upset me, but not as much as the way she made me stand before her, in front of everyone, while she examined my entire body for bruises, scratches, and broken bones. "What will your father say," she kept repeating, until Mamá pulled me away. "Nothing," she said to my mother, "if you don't tell him." And, leaving her grown daughters to comfort each other, she called the children out to the yard where she had me organize a game of hide-and-seek that she supervised, catching cheaters right and left.

45   When it rained, the children were made to take naps or play quietly in the bedroom. I asked for Mamá's monumental poster bed, and, when my turn came, I got it. There I lay four or five feet above ground inhaling her particular smells of coconut oil, (which she used to condition her thick black hair) and Palmolive soap. I would luxuriate in her soft pillows and her mattress which was covered with gorgeously embroidered bed linens. I would get sleepy listening to the drone of the women's conversation out of the parlor.

46   Beyond the double doors of her peacock blue bedroom, I could hear Mamá and her older daughters talking about things that, at my age, would not have interested me: They read letters received from my father traveling with the navy in Europe, or letters from any of the many relatives making their way in the barrios of New York and New Jersey, working in factories and dreaming of returning "in style" to Puerto Rico.

47   The women would discuss the new school year, and plan a shopping trip to the nearest city, Mayagüez, for materials to make school uniforms for the children, who by September had to be outfitted in brown and white and marched off to the public school looking like Mussolini's troops in our dull uniforms. Their talk would take on more meaning for me as I got older, but that first year back on the Island I was under María Sabida's spell. To entertain myself, I would make up stories about the smartest girl in all of Puerto Rico.

48   When María Sabida was only six years old, I began, she saved her little brother's life. He was dying of a broken heart, you see, for he desperately wanted some sweet guavas that grew at the top of a steep, rocky hill near the lair of a fierce dragon. No one had ever dared to climb that hill, though everyone could see the huge guava tree and the fruit, as big as pears, hanging from its branches. María Sabida's little brother had stared at the tree until he had made himself sick from yearning for the forbidden fruit.

49   Everyone knew that the only way to save the boy was to give him one of the guavas. María Sabida's parents were frantic with worry. The little boy was

fading fast. The father tried climbing the treacherous hill to the guava tree, but the rocks were loose and for every step forward he took, he slipped back three. He returned home. The mother spent her days cooking delicious meals with which to tempt her little son to eat, but he just turned his sad eyes to the window in his room from where he could see the guava tree loaded with the only food he wanted. The doctor came to examine the boy and pronounced him as good as gone. The priest came and told the women they should start making their black dresses. All hope seemed lost when María Sabida, whose existence everyone seemed to have forgotten, came up with an idea to save her brother one day while she was washing her hair in the special way her grandmother had taught her.

50   Her mamá had shown her how to collect rainwater—water from the sky—into a barrel, and then, when it was time to wash her hair, how to take a fresh coconut and draw the oil from its white insides. You then took a bowl of clear rainwater and added the coconut oil, using the mixture to rinse your hair. Her mamá had shown her how the rainwater, coming as it did from the sky, had little bits of starshine in it. This starstuff was what made your hair glossy, the oil was to make it stick.

51   It was while María Sabida was mixing the starshine that she had the brilliant idea which saved her brother. She ran to her father who was in the stable feeding the mule and asked if she could borrow the animal that night. The man, startled by his daughter's wild look (her hair was streaming wet and she still held the coconut scraps in her hands) at first just ordered his daughter into the house, thinking that she had gone crazy with grief over her brother's imminent death. But María Sabida could be stubborn, and she refused to move until her parents heard what she had to say. The man called his wife to the stable, and when María Sabida had finished telling them her plan, he still thought she had lost her mind. He agreed with his desperate wife that at this point anything was worth trying. They let María Sabida have the mule to use that night.

52   María Sabida then waited until it was pitch black. She knew there would be no moon that night. Then she drew water from her rainbarrel and mixed it with plenty of coconut oil and plastered her mule's hoofs with it. She led the animal to the bottom of the rocky hill where the thick, sweet smell of ripe guavas was irresistible. María Sabida felt herself caught in the spell. Her mouth watered and she felt drawn to the guava tree. The mule must have felt the same thing because it started walking ahead of the girl with quick, sure steps. Though rocks came tumbling down, the animal found footing, and in so doing, left a shiny path with the bits of starshine that María Sabida had glued to its hoofs. María Sabida kept her eyes on the bright trail because it was a dark, dark night.

53   As she approached the guava tree, the sweet aroma was like a liqiud that she drank through her nose. She could see the fruit within arms-reach when the old mule stretched her neck to eat one and a horrible scaly arm reached out and yanked the animal off the path. María Sabida quickly grabbed three guavas and ran down the golden trail all the way back to her house.

54   When she came into her little brother's room, the women had already gathered around the bed with their flowers and their rosaries, and because María Sabida was a little girl herself and could not see past the crowd, she thought for one terrible minute that she was too late. Luckily, her brother smelled the guavas from just this side of death and he sat up in bed. María Sabida pushed her way through the crowd and gave him one to eat. Within minutes the color returned to his cheeks. Everyone rejoiced remembering other wonderful things that she had done, and why her middle name was "Sabida."[14]

55   And, yes, María Sabida ate one of the enchanted guavas herself and was never sick a day in her long life. The third guave was made into a jelly that could cure every childhood illness imaginable, from a toothache to the chicken pox.

56   "Colorín, colorado . . ." I must have said to myself, "Colorín colorado . . ." as I embroidered my own fable, listening all the while to that inner voice which, when I was very young, sounded just like Mamá's when she told her stories in the parlor or under the mango tree. And later, as I gained more confidence in my own ability, the voice telling the story became my own.

DISCUSSION QUESTIONS

1. Describe the children's impressions of Puerto Rico as the land of their family.
2. Discuss in small groups the tale of María Sabida. Can you compare it to any other such tale you may have heard?
3. Compare the children's life in New Jersey with their life in Puerto Rico.
4. What did the narrator learn from the story-telling sessions under the mango tree?
5. Describe the narrator's efforts at making up her own stories about María Sabida. Discuss their meaning.

WRITING TOPICS

1. Write an original story about one of your favorite characters in this story.
2. Prepare a report of your visit to a relative's or friend's home in another area. Describe the people you met and your activities there.

---

[14] In Spanish, *sabida* means "learned or wise woman."

My Name

Sandra Cisneros

Sandra Cisneros considers herself primarily a poet and a short story writer. Born in 1954 in Chicago, Cisneros experienced a great deal of uncertainty as a child, since her Mexican-American family moved around often until her parents were able to purchase a house in a mostly Puerto Rican neighborhood in Chicago. Interestingly, that neighborhood provided her with inspiration for many eccentric characters who populate her writing.

Cisneros began her writing career with *Bad Boys* (1980), a chapbook whose seven poems reflected her interests. She became famous with *The House on Mango Street* (1983), a best-selling book for a small publishing house, in which she recounts her experiences growing up in Chicago. *My Wicked, Wicked Ways* (1987), her M.F.A. thesis at the University of Iowa, is a poetry collection depicting episodes from her autobiography. Her most recent work, *Woman Hollering Creek and Other Stories* (1991), is an absorbing collection of short stories, some of which she refers to as buttons, because she claims that they represent preconstructed scenes that she will later incorporate into longer works. Presently she is at work on a novel.

Sandra Cisneros has written some very noteworthy short pieces in her career. "My Name" is one most often remembered. From *The House on Mango Street,* a novel of short, poetic prose pieces, "My Name" commands the reader's attention because it focuses on one of the two gifts that parents give to their children: life and a name. In the Hispanic tradition, names are chosen for their connection to ancestors. Often they are the names of grandparents or granduncles revered by family members. But many names are not bilingual, nor are they easily pronounced or readily shortened in the manner Americans like to abbreviate names. Thus cultural adaptation is not always easy or comfortable.

1   In English my name means hope. In Spanish it means too many letters. It means sadness, it means waiting. It is like the number nine. A muddy color. It is the Mexican records my father plays on Sunday mornings when he is shaving, songs like sobbing.

2   It was my great-grandmother's name and now it is mine. She was a horse woman too, born like me in the Chinese year of the horse—which is supposed to be bad luck if you're born female—but I think this is a Chinese lie because the Chinese, like the Mexicans, don't like their women strong.

3   My great-grandmother. I would've liked to have known her, a wild horse of a woman, so wild she wouldn't marry until my great-grandfather threw a sack over her head and carried her off. Just like that, as if she were a fancy chandelier. That's the way he did it.

4   And the story goes she never forgave him. She looked out the window all her life, the way so many women sit their sadness on an elbow. I wonder if she made the best with what she got or was she sorry because she couldn't be all the things she wanted to be. Esperanza. I have inherited her name, but I don't want to inherit her place by the window.

5   At school they say my name funny as if the syllabes were made out of tin and hurt the roof of your mouth. But in Spanish my name is made out of a softer something like silver, not quite as thick as sister's name Magdalena which is uglier than mine. Magdalena who at least can come home and become Nenny. But I am always Esperanza.

6   I would like to baptize myself under a new name, a name more like the real me, the one nobody sees. Esperanza as Lisandra or Maritza or Zeze the X. Yes. Something like Zeze the X will do.

DISCUSSION QUESTIONS

1. Describe the feelings of the narrator regarding her parents' culture.
2. Discuss at least three places in which the author makes comparisons to the Chinese or Mexican cultures.
3. Discuss the qualities of tin and silver and their significance in pronouncing *Esperanza* in English and in Spanish.
4. The narrator describes her great-grandmother in a pose by the window. In small groups, discuss what this means with regard to the meaning of the name they have in common.
5. Discuss the narrator's preference for a new name and the reasons the names she mentioned appeal to her.

WRITING TOPICS

1. Write an essay in which you discuss your name and its meaning, and whether you like your name. Would you prefer a different name? Why?
2. Write a letter to your parents explaining your choice of name for their grandchild. Explain the reason for your choice of names.

THE NIGHT BEFORE CHRISTMAS

Tomás Rivera

Tomás Rivera is the author of *The Harvest* (1989) and *The Searchers: Collected Poetry* (1990). He is best known, however, for the celebrated . . . *y no se lo tragó la tierra (. . . and the Earth Did Not Part)* (Quinto Sol, 1971, translated by Herminio Ríos; Arte Publico Press, 1990, translated by Evangelina Vigil-Piñón as . . . *and the Earth Did Not Devour Him;* Arte Publico Press, and retold in Anglo-Texas style in 1993 as *This Migrant Earth* by Rolando Hinojosa). In Rivera's words, his purpose for writing it was "to document the migrant worker for all time." Rivera writes with compassion about the laborers who seem helpless to escape their lot.

A former migrant worker himself, Rivera was born in Crystal City, Texas. From humble rural-labor origins, he rose to the highest levels of university administration. He received degrees from Southwest Texas State and the University of Oklahoma before returning to his native Texas to teach at Sam Houston State University (1969–71) and at the University of Texas-San Antonio (1971–79), where he also served as associate dean, vice-president, and executive vice-president. In 1979 he was appointed chancellor of the University of California-Riverside. He died on May 16, 1984. Later, in 1992, Arte Publico Press honored his exemplary life and work, reflective of the Mexican-American experience, by publishing *Tomás Rivera: The Complete Works*.

Rivera's "The Night Before Christmas" is taken from the novel . . . *and the Earth Did Not Devour Him,* a story of a child's coming of age. In this chapter anticipation makes the children innocently place enormous pressure on their parents. The parents, for their part, appeal to their own cultural heritage, and keep the flame of hope alive in the children. Somehow, Rivera manages to make a poignant story fearfully suspenseful.

1   Christmas Eve was approaching and the barrage of commercials, music and Christmas cheer over the radio and the blare of announcements over the loud speakers on top of the stationwagon advertising movies at the Teatro Ideal resounded and seemed to draw it closer. It was three days before Christmas when Doña María decided to buy something for her children. This was the first time she would buy them toys. Every year she intended to do it but she always ended up facing up to the fact that, no, they couldn't afford it. She knew that her husband would be bringing each of the children candies and nuts anyway and so she would rationalize that they didn't need to get them anything else. Nevertheless, every Christmas the children asked for toys. She always appeased them with the same promise. She would tell them to wait until the sixth of January, the day of the Magi, and by the time that day arrived the children had already forgotten all about it. But now she was noticing that each year the children seemed less and less taken with Don Chon's[1] visit on Christmas Eve when he came bearing a sack of oranges and nuts.

2   "But why doesn't Santa Claus bring us anything?"

3   "What do you mean? What about the oranges and nuts he brings you?"

4   "No, that's Don Chon."

5   "No, I'm talking about what you always find under the sewing machine."

6   "What, Dad's the one who brings that, don't think we don't know that. Aren't we good like the other kids?"

7   "Of course, you're good children. Why don't you wait until the day of the Reyes Magos.[2] That's when toys and gifts really arrive. In Mexico, it's not Santa Claus who brings gifts but the Three Wisemen. And they don't come until the sixth of January. That's the real date."

8   "Yeah, but they always forget. They've never brought us anything, not on Christmas Eve, not on the day of the Three Kings."

9   "Well, maybe this time they will."

10   "Yeah, well, I sure hope so."

11   That was why she made up her mind to buy them something. But they didn't have the money to spend on toys. Her husband worked almost eighteen hours a day washing dishes and cooking at a restaurant. He didn't have time to go downtown and buy toys. Besides, they had to save money every week to pay for the trip up north. Now they even charged for children too, even if they rode standing up the whole way to Iowa. So it cost them a lot to make the trip. In any case, that night when her husband arrived, tired from work, she talked to him about getting something for the children.

12   "Look, viejo,[3] the children want something for Christmas."

13   "What about the oranges and nuts I bring them."

---

[1] A localized version of a Santa Claus-like character.
[2] Three Kings or Three Wisemen.
[3] Old man.

14   "Well, they want toys. They're not content anymore with just fruits and nuts. They're a little older now and more aware of things."

15   "They don't need anything."

16   "Now, you can't tell me you didn't have toys when you were a kid."

17   "I used to *make* my own toys, out of clay . . . little horses and little soldiers . . ."

18   "Yes, but it's different here. They see so many things . . . come on, let's go get them something . . . I'll go to Kress myself."

19   "You?"

20   "Yes, me."

21   "Aren't you afraid to go downtown? You remember that time, in Wilmar, out in Minnesota, how you got lost downtown. Are you sure you're not afraid?"

22   "Yes, yes, I remember, but I'll just have to get up my courage. I've thought about it all day long and I've set my mind to it. I'm sure I won't get lost here. Look, I go out to the street. From here you can see the ice house. It's only four blocks away, so Doña Regina tells me. When I get to the ice house I turn to the right and go two blocks and there's downtown. Kress is right there. Then, I come out of Kress, walk back towards the ice house and turn back on this street, and here I am."

23   "I guess it really won't be difficult. Yeah. Fine. I'll leave you some money on top of the table when I go to work in the morning. But be careful, vieja[4], there's a lot of people downtown these days."

24   The fact was that Doña María very rarely left the house. The only time she did was when she visited her father and her sister who lived on the next block. And she only went to church whenever someone died and, occasionally, when there was a wedding. But she went with her husband, so she never took notice of where she was going. And her husband always brought her everything. He was the one who bought the groceries and clothing. In reality, she was unfamiliar with downtown even though it was only six blocks away. The cemetery was on the other side of downtown and the church was also in that direction. The only time that they passed through downtown was whenever they were on their way to San Antonio or whenever they were returning from up north. And this would usually be during the wee hours of the morning or at night. But that day she was determined and she started making preparations.

25   The next day she got up early as usual, and after seeing her husband and children off, she took the money from the table and began getting ready to go downtown. This didn't take her long.

26   "My god, I don't know why I'm so fearful. Why, downtown is only six blocks from here. I just go straight and then after I cross the tracks turn right. Then go two blocks and there's Kress. On the way back, I walk two blocks and then I turn to the left and keep walking until I'm home again.

---

4 Old woman. In Mexican Spanish, *vieja* can either be a term of endearment or a disdainful expression. Here it is the former.

God willing, there won't be any dogs on the way. And I just pray that the train doesn't come while I'm crossing the tracks and catches me right in the middle . . . I just hope there's no dogs . . . I hope there's no train coming down the tracks."

27   She walked the distance from the house to the railroad tracks rapidly. She walked down the middle of the street all the way. She was afraid to walk on the sidewalk. She feared she might get bitten by a dog or that someone might grab her. In actuality there was only one dog along the entire stretch and most of the people didn't even notice her walking toward downtown. She nevertheless kept walking down the middle of the street and, luckily, not a single car passed by, otherwise she would not have known what to do. Upon arriving at the crossing she was suddenly struck by intense fear. She could hear the sound of moving trains and their whistles blowing and this was unnerving her. She was too scared to cross. Each time she mustered enough courage to cross she heard the whistle of the train and, frightened, she retreated and ended up at the same place. Finally, overcoming her fear, she shut her eyes and crossed the tracks. Once she got past the tracks, her fear began to subside. She got to the corner and turned to the right.

28   The sidewalks were crowded with people and her ears started to fill up with a ringing sound, the kind that once it starts it doesn't cease. She didn't recognize any of the people around her. She wanted to turn back but she was caught in the flow of the crowd which shoved her onward toward downtown and the sound kept ringing louder and louder in her ears. She became frightened and more and more she was finding herself unable to remember why she was there among the crowd of people. She stopped in an alley way between two stores to regain her composure a bit. She stood there for a while watching the passing crowd.

29   "My god, what is happening to me? I'm starting to feel the same way I did in Wilmar. I hope I don't get worse. Let me see . . . the ice house is in that direction—no it's that way. No, my god, what's happening to me? Let me see . . . I came from over there to here. So it's in that direction. I should have just stayed home. Uh, can you tell me where Kress is, please? . . . Thank you."

30   She walked to where they had pointed and entered the store. The noise and pushing of the crowd was worse inside. Her anxiety soared. All she wanted was to leave the store but she couldn't find the doors anywhere, only stacks and stacks of merchandise and people crowded against one another. She even started hearing voices coming from the merchanise. For a while she stood, gazing blankly at what was in front of her. She couldn't even remember the names of the objects. Some people stared at her for a few seconds, others just pushed her aside. She remained in this state for a while, then she started walking again. She finally made out some toys and put them in her bag. Then she saw a wallet and also put that in her bag. Suddenly she no longer heard the noise of the crowd. She only saw the people moving

about—their legs, their arms, their mouths, their eyes. She finally asked where the door, the exit was. They told her and she started in that direction. She pressed through the crowd, pushing her way until she pushed open the door and exited.

31   She had been standing on the sidewalk for only a few seconds, trying to figure out where she was, when she felt someone grab her roughly by the arm. She was grabbed so tightly that she gave out a cry.

32   "Here she is . . . these damn people, always stealing something, stealing. I've been watching you all along. Let's have the bag."

33   "But . . ."

34   Then she heard nothing for a long time. All she saw was the pavement moving swiftly toward her face and a small pebble that bounced into her eye and was hurting a lot. She felt someone pulling her arms and when they turned her, face up, all she saw were faces far away. Then she spotted a security guard with a gun in his holster and she became terrified. In that instant she thought about her children and her eyes filled with tears. She started crying. Then she lost consciousness of what was happening around her, only feeling herself drifting in a sea of people, their arms brushing against her like waves.

35   "It's a good thing my compadre happened to be there. He's the one who ran to the restaurant to tell me. How do you feel?"

36   "I think I must be insane, viejo."

37   "That's why I asked you if you weren't afraid you might get sick like in Wilmar."

38   "What will become of my children with a mother who's insane? A crazy woman who can't even talk, can't even go downtown?

39   "Anyway, I went and got the notary public. He's the one who went with me to the jail. He explained everything to the official. That you got dizzy and that you get nervous attacks whenever you're in a crowd of people."

40   "And if they send me to the insane asylum? I don't want to leave my children. Please, viejo, don't let them take me, don't let them. I shouldn't have gone downtown."

41   "Just stay here inside the house and don't leave the yard. There's no need for it anyway. I'll bring you everything you need. Look, don't cry anymore, don't cry. No, go ahead and cry, it'll make you feel better. I'm gonna talk to the kids and tell them to stop bothering you about Santa Claus. I'm gonna tell them there's no Santa Claus, that way they won't trouble you with that anymore."

42   "No, viejo, don't be mean. Tell them that if he doesn't bring them anything on Christmas Eve, it's because the Reyes Magos will be bringing them something."

43   "But . . . well, all right, whatever you say. I suppose it's always best to have hope."

44   The children, who were hiding behind the door, heard everything, but they didn't quite understand it all. They awaited the day of the Reyes Magos as they did every year. When that day came and went with no arrival of gifts, they didn't ask for explanations.

DISCUSSION QUESTIONS

1. In small groups, discuss the pressure that parents feel during the Christmas holidays as celebrated in America.
2. Compare an adult's and a child's perspective regarding the importance of receiving gifts at Christmas.
3. Discuss the social significance of geographical space delineated in a small town by railroad tracks.
4. Describe the anxiety that Doña María, the children's mother, felt when she went downtown. What reasons might have been behind her fears?

WRITING TOPICS

1. Write an account of the last holiday as a child that you remember well. What customs were followed? If gift-giving was involved, what was your reaction to your presents?
2. Write a newspaper account of the incident created by Doña María at the Kress store.

CHAPTER FIVE

COMING OF AGE

Coming-of-age is not simply a marker along the path to maturity. It is, in fact, a frontier between two different and distinct worlds. It is a time of desire and insecurity, of confidence and questioning. It is a time when one discriminates between what one has been taught and what one finds to be true.

In *bildungsroman,* the German word for the literary genre about personal growth, we find the stories of young girls or boys becoming young women or men. Writers begin by presenting life as it was prior to the loss of innocence. The discoveries that youths make about themselves during this period of transition are crucial in determining who they will be as adults. Coming-of-age can be likened, perhaps, to Marine Corps boot camp, in which participants are no longer civilians, but not yet soldiers. During the transition they experience a spectrum of physical and mental effects. They also may question their ability to succeed.

The selections in this chapter focus on Latino youth and their coming-of-age experiences. Some of the readings are centered on familial expectations associated with the transition, while others address individual aspirations. Coming-of-age may also be seen in terms of one's perception of self with regard to race and ethnicity. For some, this aspect may be a particularly painful realization for a child, when he or she recognizes that the judgments of others greatly determine how one may live in society.

Doubt

José Gautier Benítez

José Gautier Benítez was born on April 12, 1848, in Humacao, Puerto Rico (though others maintain he was born on November 12, 1851, in Caguas). As a young man, Gautier Benítez served in the Spanish military as an ensign and went on to study Spanish military strategy before returning to Puerto Rico in 1871. There, using the pen name of Gustavo, he began writing for *El Progreso* and the *Revista Puertorriqueña*, as well as other island periodicals. His writing was no doubt influenced by the sadness he experienced during that period of his life. For example, despite his passionate love for Carmen O'Neill, Gautier Benítez married his cousin. Then in 1879, his mother, having survived his father some twenty-three years, passed away. In the following year Gautier Benítez died from tuberculosis.

More than anyone else, Gautier Benítez represents Puerto Rico's Romantic verse. He was influenced by Spanish and French poets of his day—already post-Romantics—as well as the Parnassians, especially Theophile Gautier's writing. His lyrical work is fairly evenly divided between political poetry and personal verse. He wrote five major poems in which he sings of his island, as well as a number of poetic compositions in which he considers love, God, and death.

In "Doubt," translated from the original Spanish, José Gautier Benítez explores the limits of knowledge, or, more precisely, how one is sure that what one thinks is so. Philosophers refer to this study of the nature of knowledge as epistemology. At the time Gautier Benítez wrote the poem, Puerto Rico was seeking to become autonomous from Spain, though some felt that what Puerto Rico needed was to be independent.

You count with so few Aprils
that I ask myself, my dear,
if there be in your girlish body
the heart of a woman.
5 I doubt it when I contemplate
your bright innocence
and your childlike happiness;
but I note an ineffable air
in the fixity of your gaze
10 of voluptuous rapture,
that I renew my doubtfulness
of which I first spoke to you:
If there be in your girlish body
the heart of a woman?

DISCUSSION QUESTIONS

1. Describe the narrator's dilemma in your own words.
2. Discuss the characteristics of the child that make the narrator wonder if the subject of his love is a grown woman.
3. Discuss the characteristics of the woman that make him doubt that she is a child.
4. Analyze the repetition and the form of the question in the poem.

WRITING TOPICS

1. Write a story about a teenager who seems at once to be both an adult and a child.
2. Write a journal entry in which you reflect on the maturity of someone you know.

A PERFECT HOTSPOT

Virgil Suárez

Born in Cuba, Virgil Suárez emigrated to the United States in 1974 after spending four years in Spain. His writing centers on the hopes and struggles of Cubans and Cuban families who have had to abandon the island to live and work in the United States. He sensitively portrays their dreams and their disappointments as they seek to make their way. Suárez has taught writing at several universities, including the University of Miami, Florida International University, and Miami Dade Community College. Currently, he teaches at Florida State University.

A prolific writer, Suárez has written three novels—*Latin Jazz* (1989), *The Cutter* (1991), and *Havana Thursdays* (1995), a novella and five stories collected as *Welcome to the Oasis* (1992), and a collection of Latino writing entitled *Iguana Dreams: New Latino Voices* (1992), which he edited with Delia Poey. He has also published numerous articles and reviews in newspapers and magazines, including *Vista: The Hispanic Magazine, The Americas Review, The Miami Herald,* the *Los Angeles Times* and the *Philadelphia Inquirer.* In addition, he has written some plays and screenplays and is currently at work on several other books.

Cuban-American writers tend to have memories of childhood or of youth either in Cuba or in the United States—frequently in Miami. In the following selection by Virgil Suárez, a son's relationship with his father is predicated on their shared role as merchants of the fulfillment of desire.

1   This idea of selling ice cream during the summer seems ridiculous, pointless. I'd much rather be close to water. The waves. Where I can hear them tumble in and then roll out, and see the tiny bubbles left behind on the sand pop one by one. Or feel the undercurrents warm this time of year. Swimming. Watching the girls in bikinis with sand stuck to the backs of their

thighs walk up and down the boardwalk. At this time of the morning, the surfers are out riding the waves.

2   Instead I'm inside an ice cream truck with my father, selling, cruising the streets. The pumps suck oil out of the ground rapidly with the creaking sounds of iron biting iron in a fenced lot at the end of the street. They look like giant rocking horses. Father turns at the corner, then, suddenly, he points to another ice cream truck.

3   "There's the competition," he says. "If the economy doesn't improve soon, these streets'll be full of them."

4   He's smoking, and the smoke floats back my way and chokes me. I can't stand it. Some of the guys on the swim team smoke. I don't understand how they can smoke and do their best when it's time for competition. I wouldn't smoke. To do so would be like cheating myself out of winning.

5   All morning he's been instructing me on how to sell ice cream.

6   "Tonio," he says now, "come empty your pockets."

7   I walk to the front of the truck, stick my hands deep into my pockets and grab a handful of coins—what we've made in change all morning. The coins fall, overlap and multiply against the sides of the grease-smudged change box. I turn my pockets inside-out until the last coin falls. He picks out the pieces of lint and paper from the coins.

8   When he begins to explain the truck's quirks, "the little problems," as he calls the water leaks, burning oil, and dirty carburetor, I return to the back of the truck and sit down on top of the wood counter next to the window.

9   "Be always on the lookout for babies," father says. "The ones in pampers. They pop out of nowhere. Check your mirrors all the time."

10   A CAUTION CHILDREN cardboard sign hangs from the rearview mirror. Running over children is a deep fear that seems to haunt him.

11   All I need, I keep reminding myself, is to pass the CPR course, get certified, and look for a job as a beach lifeguard.

12   "Stop!" a kid screams, slamming the screen door of his house open. He runs to the grassy part next to the sidewalk. Father stops the truck. The kid's hand comes up over the edge of the window with a dollar bill forked between his little fingers.

13   "What do you want?" I say.

14   "A Froze Toe," he says, jumping up and down, dirt rings visible on his neck. He wets the corners of his mouth with his cherry, Kool-aid-stained tongue. I reach inside the freezer and bring out a bar. On its wrapper is the picture of an orange foot with a blue bubble gum ball on the big toe.

15   "See what else he wants," father says. "Make sure they always leave the dollar."

16   The kid takes his ice cream, and he smiles.

17   "What else?" I ask him.

18   He shrugs his shoulders, shakes his head, and bites the wrapper off. The piece of paper falls on the grass. I give him his change; he walks back to his house.

19   "Should always make sure they leave all the money they bring," father says. "They get it to spend it. That's the only way you'll make a profit. Don't steal their money, but exchange it for merchandise." His ears stick out from underneath his L.A. Dodgers cap. The short hair on the back of his head stands out.

20   I grin up at the rearview mirror, but he isn't looking.

21   "Want to split a Pepsi, Tonio?" he says.

22   "I'm not thirsty."

23   "Get me some water then."

24   The cold mist inside the freezer crawls up my hand. After he drinks and returns the bottle, I place it back with the ice cream.

25   "Close the freezer," he says, "before all the cold gets out and they melt."

26   If the cold were out I'd be at the natatorium doing laps.

27   On another street, a group of kids jumps and skips around a short man. The smallest of the kids hangs from the man's thigh. The man signals my father to stop, then walks up to the window. The kids scream excitedly.

28   "Want this one, daddy," one of the girls says.

29   "This one!" a boy says.

30   The smallest kid jumps, pointing his finger at the display my father has made with all the toys and candies.

31   "No, Jose," the man says, taking the kid by the wrist. "No candy."

32   The kid turns to look up at his father, not fully understanding, and then looks at me. His little lips tremble.

33   "Give me six Popsicles," the man says.

34   "I don't want no Pop—"

35   "Popsicles or nothing. I don't have money to buy you what you want."

36   "A Blue Ghost. I want a Blue Ghost."

37   "No, I said."

38   The smallest kid cries.

39   "Be quiet, Jose, or I'm going to tell the man to go away."

40   I put the six Popsicles on the counter.

41   "How much?" the man asks. The skin around his eyes is a darker brown than that of his nose and cheeks.

42   "A dollar-fifty," I say.

43   He digs inside his pockets and produces two wrinkled green balls which he throws on the counter. The two dollar bills roll. I unfold the bills, smooth them, and give them to father, who returns the man his change through the front window.

44   The man gives each kid a Popsicle, then walks away with his hands in his pockets. Jose, still crying, grabs his as he follows his father back to their house.

45   "He doesn't want to spend his beer money," father says, driving away from the curb.

46   After that, we have no more customers for hours. Ever since he brought

the truck home two years ago, father has changed. Ice creams have become his world. According to father, appearance and cleanliness isn't important as long as the truck passes the Health Department inspection in order to obtain the sales license. The inside of the truck is a mess: paint flakes off, rust hides between crevices, the freezer lids hold layer upon layer of dirt and melted ice cream. Here I'll have to spend the rest of my summer, I think, among the strewn Doritos, Munchos, and the rest of the merchandise.

47   The outside of the truck had been painted by father's friend, Gaspar, before mother died. I remember how Gaspar drank beer after beer while he painted the crown over the K in KING OF ICE CREAM and assured mother, who never missed one of my swim meets and who always encouraged me to become the best swimmer I could be, that I was going to make it all right in the end.

48   Father lives this way, I know, out of loneliness. He misses mother as much as I do.

49   I count the passing of time by how many ice creams I sell. It isn't anything like swimming laps. Doing laps involves the idea of setting and breaking new limits.

50   "How much do you think we have?" my father asks. The visor of his cap tilts upward.

51   "I don't know." I hate the metallic smell money leaves on my fingers.

52   "Any idea?"

53   "No."

54   "A couple of months on your own and you'll be able to guess approximately how much you make."

55   A couple of months, I think, and I'll be back in high school. Captain of the varsity swim team. A customer waits down the street.

56   "Make the kill fast," father says.

57   A barefooted woman holding a child to her breast comes to the window. She has dirty fingernails, short and uneven, as if she bites them all the time. Make the kill fast, I think.

58   Ice creams on the counter, I tell her, "Two dollars."

59   She removes the money out of her brassiere and hands it to me, then she walks away. She has yellow blisters on the back of each heel.

60   After that, he begins to tell me the story of the wild dog. When he was a kid, a wild bitch came down from the hills and starting killing my grandfather's chickens. "Seeing the scattered feathers," father says, "made your grandfather so angry I thought his face would burst because it'd turned so red."

61   "Anyway," he continues, "the wild dog kept on killing chickens."

62   Not only my grandfather's, but other farmers' as well. The other farmers were scared because they thought the wild dog was a witch. One morning my grandfather got my father out of bed early and took him up to the hills behind the house with a jar of poison. A farmer had found the bitch's litter. My grandfather left my father in charge of anointing the poison all over the

puppies' fur so that when the mother came back, if he hadn't shot it by then, she'd die the minute she licked her young. My father didn't want to do it, but my grandfather left him in command while he went after the wild dog to shoot it. The dog disappeared and the puppies licked each other to death.

63   When he finishes telling me the story, father looks at the rearview mirror and grins, then he drives on. He turns up the volume in the music box and now *Raindrops Keep Falling On My Head* blares out of the speakers. The old people'll complain, he says, because the loud music hurts their eardrums, but the louder the music, the more people'll hear it, and more ice creams'll get sold.

64   Farther ahead, another kid stops us. The kid has his tongue out. His eyes seem to be too small for his big face. Though he seems old, he still drools. He claps his small hands quickly.

65   "Does he have money?" father asks.

66   "Can't see."

67   The kids walks over to the truck and hangs from the edge of the window.

68   "Get him away from the truck," father says, then to the kid, "Hey, move away."

69   "Come on," I tell the kid, "you might fall and hurt yourself."

70   "Wan icleam," the kid says.

71   "We'll be back in a little while," father tells him.

72   "Wan icleam!" He doesn't let go. "Wan icleam!"

73   "Move back!" father shouts. "Tonio, get him away from the truck."

74   I try to unstick the kid's pudgy fingers from the metal edge of the window, but he won't let go. His saliva falls on my hands.

75   "Wan icleam!"

76   I reach over to one of the shelves to get a penny candy for him so that I can bait him into letting go, but father catches me.

77   "Don't you dare," he says.

78   He opens the door and comes around the back to the kid, pulling him away from the truck to the sidewalk where he sets the kid down, and returns.

79   "Can't give your merchandise away," he says. "You can't make a profit that way, Tonio."

80   The kid runs after us shouting, waving his arms. I grab a handful of candies and throw them out the window to the sidewalk, where they fall on the grass and scatter.

81   The sun sets slowly, and, descending, it spreads Popsicle orange on the sky. Darkness creeps on the other side of the city.

82   If I don't get a job as a lifeguard, I think, then I'm going to travel southeast and visit the islands.

83   "How are the ice creams doing?" father asks. "Are they softening?"

84   I check by squeezing a bar and say, "I think we should call it a day."

85   "Tonio," he says. He turns off the music, makes a left turn to the main street, and heads home. "Why didn't you help me with that kid? You could have moved him. What will happen when you're here by yourself?"

86   "Couldn't do it."

87   "Here," he says, giving me the change box. "Take it inside when we get home."

88   "I'll get it when we get there."

89   He puts the blue box back down on top of the stand he built over the motor. Cars speed by. The air smells heavy with exhaust and chemical fumes. In the distance columns of smoke rise from factory smokestacks.

90   He turns into the driveway, drives the truck all the way to the front of the garage, and parks underneath the long branches of the avocado tree.

91   "Take the box inside," he says, turning off the motor. He steps down from the truck and connects the freezer to the extension cord coming out of the kitchen window.

92   I want to tell him that I won't come out tomorrow.

93   "Come on, Tonio. Bring the box in."

94   "You do it," I say.

95   "What's the matter, son?"

96   "I'd rather you do it."

97   "Like you'd rather throw all my merchandise out of the window," he says, growing red in the face. "I saw you."

98   He walks toward me, and I sense another argument coming. Father stops in front of me and gives me a wry smile. "Dreamers like you," he says, "learn the hard way."

99   He turns around, picks up the change box, and says, "I'm putting the truck up for sale. From now on you're on your own, you hear. I'm not forcing you to do something you don't want to."

100   I don't like the expressionless look on his face when usually, whenever he got angry at me, his face would get red and sweaty.

101   He unlocks the kitchen door and enters the house.

102   I jump out of the truck, lock the door, and walk around our clapboard house to the patio. Any moment now, I think, father'll start slamming doors inside and throwing things around. He'll curse. I lean against the wall and feel the glass of the window behind me when it starts to tremble.

DISCUSSION QUESTIONS

1. How does the narrator wish he could spend the summer? Does the father seem to be aware of his son's wish?
2. What experience has bonded the father and son?
3. Discuss the value for the son of learning how to sell ice cream. Is there value for the father in teaching his son?

WRITING TOPICS

1. Write an essay describing your summer job and your enjoyment or dislike of it.
2. Imagine yourself in a situation like Tonio's and write a letter to a parent explaining why you do not want to work at a particular job during the summer.

AN AWAKENING . . . SUMMER 1956

Nicholasa Mohr

Nicholasa Mohr was born on November 1, 1935, in New York City's El Barrio (Spanish Harlem) of immigrant Puerto Rican parents. As a young woman, she studied at the Art Students' League of New York (1953–56), the Brooklyn Museum Art School (1959–66), and the Pratt Center for Contemporary Printmaking (1966–69).

After working in the art world for eighteen years, Mohr began writing fiction at the urging of a business friend. Her first book, *Nilda* (1973), is a novel composed of a series of vignettes related to her growing up in El Barrio. The novel won the Jane Addams Children's Book Award and was selected by *School Library Journal* as a Best Book of the Year in 1973. The book jacket, which Mohr designed, received the Citation of Merit from the Society of Illustrators. Encouraged by her success, she made writing her career, though she did not completely abandon her art. She went on to publish *El Bronx Remembered* (1975), a novella with other stories for which she also did the jacket illustrations, and three semi-autobiographical novels for juvenile audiences: *In Nueva York* (1977), *Felita* (1979), and *Going Home* (1986). Her first adult audience book is *Rituals of Survival: A Woman's Portfolio* (1985), a series of powerfully written stories.

Mohr's work is an important source for readers interested in family and community life in post-World War II Spanish Harlem. In "An Awakening . . . Summer 1956," Mohr makes several provocative propositions: that negation invites affirmation, that classification in preexisting categories makes for poor science, and that power resides within a person. The story invites the reader to speculate about these ideas as the protagonist makes a journey that is quite different from the journey at the beginning of the story.

FOR HILDA HIDALGO

1   The young woman looked out of the window as the greyhound bus sped by the barren, hot, dry Texas landscape. She squinted, clearing her vision against the blazing white sunlight. Occasionally, she could discern small adobe houses clumped together like mushrooms, or a gas station and diner standing alone and remote in the flat terrain. People were not visible. They were hiding, she reasoned, seeking relief indoors in the shade. How different from her native Puerto Rico, where luscious plants, trees and flowers were abundant. Green was the color of that Island, soothing, cool, inviting. And people were seen everywhere, living, working, enjoying the outdoors. All of her life had been spent on her beloved land. For more than a decade she had been in service of the church. Now, this was a new beginning. After all, it had been her choice, her sole decision to leave. At the convent school where she had been safe and loved, they had reluctantly bid her farewell with an open invitation to return. Leaving there had been an essential part of working it all out, she thought, one had to start somewhere. Still, as she now looked out at all the barrenness before her, she felt a stranger in a foreign land and completely alone.

2   She was on her way to spend the summer with her good friend Ann. They were going to discuss the several directions in which she might continue to work. After all, she had skills; her degrees in elementary education and a master's in counseling. There was also the opportunity offered her of that scholarship toward a doctorate in Ohio. The need to experience the world independently, without the protection of the church, was far more compelling than her new apprehension of the "unknown."

3   The young woman checked her wristwatch.

4   "On time . . ." she whispered, and settled back in her seat.

5   Her friend Ann was now a social worker with the working poor and the Mexican American community in a small town in rural Texas. The invitation to spend most of this summer with Ann and her family had appealed to the young woman, and she had accepted with gratitude.

6   "You know you are welcome to stay with us for just as long as you want," Ann had written. "You will be like another member of the family."

7   The knowledge that she would once more be with her good friend, discussing ideas and planning for the future, just as they had done as co-workers back home, delighted and excited her.

8   "Clines-Corners . . ." the bus driver announced. The next stop would be hers.

9   "Now, please wait at the bus depot, don't wander off. Promise to stay put, in case of a change in schedule, and we will pick you up," Ann had cautioned in her last letter.

10   "Sentry!" the bus driver shouted as the bus came to a sudden halt. She jumped down and the bus sped off barely missing a sleeping dog that had placed itself comfortably under the shade of a large roadside billboard. The

billboard picture promised a cool lakeside ride on a motorboat, if one smoked mentholated cigarettes.

11   She found herself alone and watched a cloud of dust settle into the landscape as the bus disappeared into the horizon. She approached the depot building where two older Mexican men and a young black man, laborers, sat shaded on a wooden porch, eating lunch. She smiled and waved as she passed them. They nodded in response.

12   Inside at the ticket booth, a tall man with very pink skin peered out at her from under a dark green sun visor.

13   "Good day," she cleared her throat. The man nodded and waited. "I was wondering . . . eh, if there was some message for me?"

14   "What?" he asked.

15   Feeling self conscious and embarrassed, she repeated her question, adding, "I'm sorry, but it is that my English is not too perfect. I am not used to speaking English very often."

16   "What's you name? I can't know if there's a message for you if I don't know your name." She told him, speaking clearly and spelling each letter with care.

17   "Nope," he shook his head, "ain't nothing here for nobody by that name." The man turned away and continued his work.

18   The young woman stood for a moment wondering if her friends had received her wire stating she would arrive several hours earlier than expected. Checking the time she realized it was only twelve thirty. They were not expecting her until five in the late afternoon. She walked to the pay phone and dialed Ann's number. She waited as it rang for almost two full minutes before she replaced the receiver. Disappointed, she approached the clerk again.

19   "Excuse me, sir . . . can I please leave my luggage for a while? There is not an answer where my friends are living."

20   The man motioned her to a section of luggage racks.

21   "Cost you fifty cents for the first three hours, and fifteen cents for each hour after that. Pay when you come back." He handed her a soiled blue ticket.

22   "Thank you very much. Is there a place for me to get a cold drink? It is very hot . . . and I was riding on the bus for a long time."

23   "There's a Coke machine by the garage, right up the street. Can't miss it."

24   "Well, I would like a place to sit down. I think I saw a small restaurant up on the main street when I got off the bus."

25   "Miss, you'd be better off at the Coke machine. Soda's nice and cold. You can come back and drink it in here if you like." He looked at the young woman for a moment, nodded, and returned once more to his work.

26   She watched him somewhat confused and shrugged, then walked out into the hot empty street. Two mangy, flea-bitten mutts streaked with oil spots walked up to her wagging their tails.

27   "Bueno . . ." she smiled, "you must be my welcoming committee." They followed her as she continued up the main street. The barber shop and the hardware store were both closed. Out to lunch, she said to herself, and a nice siesta . . . now that's sensible.

28   Playful shouts and shrieking laughter emanated from a group of Mexican children. They ran jumping and pushing a large metal hoop. She waved at them. Abruptly, they stopped, looking with curiosity and mild interest at this stranger. They glanced at each other and, giggling, quickly began once more to run and play their game. In a moment they were gone, heading into a shaded side street.

29   The red and white sign above the small store displayed in bold printed letters: NATHAN'S FOOD AND GROCERIES—EAT IN OR TAKE OUT. On the door a smaller sign read, OPEN. Thankful, she found herself inside, enjoying the coolness and serenity of the small cafe. Two tables set against the wall were empty and except for a man seated at the counter, all the stools were unoccupied. No one else was in sight. She took a counter seat a few stools away from the man. After a minute or two, when no one appeared, the young woman cleared her throat and spoke.

30   "Pardon me . . . somebody. Please, is somebody here?" She waited and before she could speak again, she heard the man seated at the counter shout:

31   "ED! Hey Ed, somebody's out here. You got a customer!"

32   A middle-aged portly man appeared from the back. When he saw the young woman, he stopped short, hesitating. Slowly he walked up to her and silently stared.

33   "Good day," she said. "How are you?" The man now stood with his arms folded quite still without replying. "Can I please have a Pepsi-Cola." Managing a smile, she continued, "It is very hot outside, but I am sure you know that . . ."

34   He remained still, keeping his eyes on hers. The young woman glanced around her not quite sure what to do next. Then, she cleared her throat and tried again.

35   "A Pepsi-Cola, cold if you please . . ."

36   "Don't have no Pepsi-Colas," he responded loudly.

37   She looked around and saw a full fountain service, and against the rear wall, boxes filled with Pepsi-Colas.

38   "What's that?" she asked, confused.

39   The man gestured at the wall directly behind her. "Can't you read English."

40   Turning, she saw the sign he had directed her to. In large black letters and posted right next to the door she read:
NO COLOREDS
NO MEXICANS
NO DOGS
WILL BE SERVED ON THESE
PREMISES

41   All the blood in her body seemed to rush to her head. She felt her tongue thicken and her fingers turn as cold as ice cubes. Another white man's face appeared from the kitchen entrance and behind him stood a very black woman peering nervously over his shoulder.

42   The silence surrounding her stunned her as she realized at the moment all she was—a woman of dark olive complexion, with jet black hair; she spoke differently from these people. Therefore, she was all those things on that sign. She was also a woman alone before these white men. Jesus and the Virgin Mary . . . what was she supposed to do? Colors flashed and danced before her embracing the angry faces and cold hateful eyes that stared at her daring her to say another word. Anger and fear welled up inside her, and she felt threatened even by the shadows set against the bright sun; they seemed like daggers menacing her very existence. She was going to fight, she was not going to let them cast her aside like an animal. Deeply she inhaled searching for her voice, for her composure, and without warning, she heard herself shouting.

43   "I WOULD LIKE A PEPSI-COLA, I SAID! AND, I WANT IT NOW . . . RIGHT NOW!!" The words spilled out in loud rasps. She felt her heart lodged in her throat, and swallowed trying to push it back down so that she could breathe once more.

44   "Can't you read . . . girl?" the man demanded.

45   "I WANT A PEPSI. DAMN IT . . . NOW!" With more boldness, this time her voice resounded, striking the silence with an explosion. Taking out her change purse she slammed several coins on the counter. "NOW!" she demanded staring at the man. "I'm not leaving until I get my drink."

46   As the young woman and the middle-aged portly man stared, searching each others' eyes, that moment seemed an eternity to her. All she was, all she would ever be, was here right now at this point in time. And so she stood very still, barely blinking and concentrated, so that not one muscle in her body moved.

47   He was the first to move. Shaking his head, he smiled and with slow deliberate steps walked over to the cases by the wall and brought back a bottle of Pepsi-Cola, placing it before her. As she picked up the bottle, she felt the heat of the liquid, it was almost too hot to hold.

48   "Very well," she said, surprised at the calmness in her voice. "May I please have an opener?"

49   "Girl . . . we ain't got no openers here. Now you got your damned drink . . . that's it. Get the hell out of here!" He turned, ignoring her, and began to work arranging cups behind the counter.

50   Her eyes watched him and just for an instant the young woman hesitated before she stood, grabbed the bottle and lifted it high above her bringing it down with tremendous force and smashing it against the counter edge. Like hailstones in a storm, pieces of glass flew in every direction, covering the counter and the space around her. The warm bubbling liquid drenched her. Her heavy breathing sucked in the sweetness of the cola.

51   "KEEP THE CHANGE!" she shouted. Quickly she slammed the door behind her and once again faced the heat and the empty street.

52   She walked with her back straight and her head held high.

53   "BITCH!" she could hear his voice. "YOU DAMNED MEXICAN COLORED BITCH! CAN'T TREAT YOU PEOPLE LIKE HUMAN BEINGS . . . you no good . . ."

54   His voice faded as she walked past the main street, the bus depot and the small houses of the town. After what seemed a long enough time, she stopped, quite satisfied she was no longer in that town near that awful hateful man. The highway offered no real shade, and so she turned down a side road. There the countryside seemed gentler, a few trees and bushes offered some relief. A clump of bushes up on a mound of earth surrounded a maple tree that yielded an oasis of cool shade. She climbed up the mound and sat looking about her. She enjoyed the light breeze and the flight of large crows that dotted the sky in the distance. The image of the man and what had happened stirred in her a sense of humiliation and hurt. Tears clouded her view and she began to cry quietly at first, and then her sobs got louder. Intense rage overtook her and her sobbing became screams that pierced the quiet countryside. After a while, her crying subsided and she felt a sharp pain in her hand. She looked down and realized she still clenched tightly the neck of the broken Pepsi-Cola bottle. The jagged edges of glass had penetrated between her thumb and forefinger; she was still bleeding. Releasing her grip, the young woman found a handkerchief in her pocket. Carefully she pressed it to the wound and in moments the bleeding stopped. Exhausted, she closed her eyes, leaned against the tree, and fell asleep.

55   She dreamt of that cool lakeside and the motorboat on the billboard, that might take her back home to safety and comfort. Friends would be there, waiting, protection her just for the asking.

56   "Wake up . . . it's all right. It's me, Ann." She felt a hand on her shoulder and opened her eyes. Ann was there, her eyes filled with kindness and concern. Again, the young woman cried, openly and without shame, as she embraced her friend.

57   "I know, we got your wire, but only after we got home. By then it was late, around three o'clock, and we went looking for you right away. This is a very small town. You caused quite a stir. I should have warned you about things out here. But, I thought it would be best to tell you when we were together. I'm so sorry . . . but don't worry . . . you re safe and with us. We are proud of you . . . the way you stood up . . . but, never mind that now. Let's get you home where you can rest. But, you were wonderful . . . .

58   In the weeks that followed, the young woman worked with Ann. She made lifetime friends in the small Texas community. There were others like her and like Ann, who would fight against those signs. Civil rights had to be won and the battles still had to be fought. She understood quite clearly in that summer of 1956, that no matter where she might settle, or in which direction life would take her, the work she would commit herself to, and

indeed her existence itself, would be dedicated to the struggle and the fight against oppression. Consciously for the very first time in her life, the young woman was proud of all she was, her skin, her hair and the fact that she was a woman.

59   Riding back East on the bus, she looked at her hand and realized the wound she had suffered had healed. However, two tiny scars remained, quite visible.

60   "A reminder . . . should I ever forget," she whispered softly.

61   Settling back, she let the rhythmic motion of the large bus lull her into a sweet sleep. The future with all its uncertainties was before her; now she was more than ready for this challenge.

DISCUSSION QUESTIONS

1. Describe the setting—time and place of this story—and the experience of the young woman upon her arrival.
2. Discuss the incident brought on by the young woman's search for a cold drink on a hot day.
3. What is the "awakening" that is mentioned in the title? What brings it about in the story?
4. Discuss the various ways the young woman could have reacted toward her experience in 1956.

WRITING TOPICS

1. Write a journal entry describing some incident that caused you to learn something about yourself.
2. Cite examples from the story of the warnings the young woman was given regarding the town's racism.

FROM *THE GREATEST PERFORMANCE*

Elías Miguel Muñoz

Elías Miguel Muñoz was born in Ciego de Avila, Camagüey, Cuba, on September 29, 1954. He left Cuba in exile in 1968. He studied in the United States at California State University and the University of California at Irvine. He later worked at El Camino Community College, at Coastline Community College, at Saddleback Community College, and at Wichita State University.

After directing the literary magazine *Fénix*, Muñoz began writing poetry and published *En estas tierras* (*In These Lands*) (1988) and *Desde esta orilla: poesía cubana del exilio* (*From the Shore: Cuban Poetry in Exile*) (1988). His first novel, *Los viajes de Orlando Cachumbambé* (1980), was followed by *Crazy Love* (1988), and by his masterpiece *The Greatest Performance* (1991). His narrative grows progressively better as he experiments with form. At first, he writes without much discipline. Then, in his second book, he undertakes three novelistic forms: the epistolary novel, the immigration novel, and the coming-of-age novel. Finally, he explores the personality and identity of Hispanics in the United States, writing two biographies with dialogue that merges into one voice—a great performance, indeed.

Elías Miguel Muñoz tells of Rosita's difficulty in adapting to life in a suburb of Los Angeles and her reluctance to adopt the ways and language of the United States. The reader learns of her father's prejudices concerning Mexicans and about his denial of his cultural connections to Cuba. Rosita's father wants his daughter to be American, not Cuban—certainly not Mexican. Through this story, Muñoz emphasizes the irony in the desire of many immigrants to forget the past and embrace the future, even as they focus on the values to be passed on to their children.

¹ The first couple of months in California I did nothing but bitch and ask that I be sent back to Spain. There was life there, good life. There were good-looking people who spoke pure Spanish and there was gorgeous music

and crowded plazas. Here, in Garden Shore (a name that didn't fit the place at all), there were only cars, freeways and solitary houses. Nobody walked. The streets were always empty. How I detested that world. How I still detest it today, whenever I take a good look around me.

2   California was one enormous cemetery. Its inhabitants seemed ugly and haggard. Its music, *Baby baby baby I love you baby baby baby,* they called that unimaginative crap music. The weather was supposed to be the best on the entire globe. It was hot like Cuba's. Some rain, very little cold in the winter. And it would be easy for Papi to find employment there. Unfortunately not in an office, the way he would've liked to. But in a factory, where he could make lots of money right away. Yes, California was the promised land. Home away from home. Arcadia. But to me it became the vivid representation of hell.

3   Guess what I'm holding. What do you mean you can't tell? Records, you dope! Can't you see the faces on the covers? Look closely, *chico.* I know it's a super-old photo but try, look at it.

4   I found out through a Channel 35 commercial that there was a record store in Los Angeles, on Broadway, that sold Spanish music. The place, Discoteca Latina, was owned by a Cuban man, Señor Enrique, and most of his employees were Cuban. Reluctantly, Papi took me to Discoteca Latina one Saturday afternoon. He hated Los Angeles; he still does. He claimed that it was full of Mexican Indians and he hadn't come to the United States to mingle with an inferior race. That's why he tried to get our family located in Orange County, where there were more white people. We couldn't afford the ritzy places like Anaheim and Newport Beach, but Garden Shore—we were told by the Immigration authorities—was clean and moderately affluent, a predominantly middle-class city with a booming aircraft industry. It was far from the Mexican community of Santa Ana, and even further from downtown Los Angeles.

5   My record albums, yes. Papi complained the whole way to the music store. Why did I have to buy Spanish records, anyway? Weren't we in the United States? I should be studying English and listening to the American hits on the radio, not making him drive his '65 Rambler through those Indian-infested streets of the Angeleno metropolis. If anything happened to us, I'd be held responsible, he warned me. We'd risk our lives just to please me, the little lady, Baby Rosita. Why did I always have to have my way, he asked. Why did I consider myself so special?

6   I told him that I didn't consider myself special at all, that I was not a spoiled baby. My argument was simple: I hated American music and if I didn't find some way of entertaining myself, of alleviating my Cuban depressions, I'd surely commit suicide, as cut and dried as that. Suicide.

7   I bought, against his will, two Raphael's, one Massiel, one Karina, and one Marisol. "A fortune!" cried Papi. "Money I sweated for, money I bled for, wasted despicably on records!" Three of the albums turned out to be

damaged; they were scratched and you could tell they were used or poorly manufactured. All of them, actually, were of the poorest quality. I was so broken-hearted. Papi drove me back to Discoteca Latina the next weekend, so we could return the damaged merchandise and get our money back. That's what you were supposed to do in America, he said; it was your right. But we were in for a not-so-American surprise.

8   "Impossible!" screamed one of the Cuban salesladies. "We don't take records back!" Papi was hyperventilating. "Well, you're gonna have to!" he wailed. But the lady was firm, "Don't blame us, blame your daughter! She was the one who ruined the records!" By now three other Cuban cows had shown up. You know the type: huge hips and butt, talcum-white skin, beady eyes heavily made-up, fake pearls and bracelets hanging from every limb, thinly disguised fuzz on the upper lip, the cow type. They were all telling Papi that if he didn't leave, he would have to deal with Mister Enrique himself, the owner, *El Dueño*." "Bring out that gangster! Tell him I wanna see him! Tell him I think he's a thief!"

9   Señor Enrique answered the call of duty, as was to be expected. He was predictably heavy-set, like his employees, had a black-bean belly and hairy arms, was balding and wore a *guayabera*.[1] They just didn't make them more typical than that, I thought. (Oh, I guess he was missing the Havana cigar.) "How dare you speak that way to these ladies? Have you no manners?" he asked like a true Cuban gentleman. "Gangsters!" responded Papi. Mister Henry turned to one of his employees, the one who had been dealing with my father. "What seems to be the reason for the complaint?" he inquired. "This man!" she spat out her words, "this man came in here claiming that our records are bad! The nerve!" "My money back!" Papi restated his case. "Or I'll burn down your filthy pigsty!"

10   And just as Papi grabbed Señor Enrique's neck, and just as Señor Enrique's faced turned red like a tomato, and just as Papi moved his fist into Señor Enrique's nose, the choking man shouted, "Give him back every penny!" Papi let go of his neck, leaving the clearly visible marks of his fingers on it. "That's more like it," said my father. And Mister Henry, trembling, handed him the money, twenty-five bucks more or less. "Don't you ever come here again!" the owner admonished. "Don't worry," Papi told him as we headed for the door, "I don't do business with pigs!"

11   On our way home Papi and I reveled in a wonderful fantasy. We'd buy a can of gasoline, we'd go to Discoteca Latina at night, when the store was closed and there was no one inside, and we'd set the whole place on fire. But maybe that would be dangerous, we could get burned ourselves. Better yet: we'd go into the store during the day, wearing disguises so they wouldn't recognize us, and we'd hide a bomb under a stack of albums. We would time

---

[1] Loose-fitting men's pleated shirt (Cuban), often worn in lieu of a suit jacket.

the mechanism so it would explode later that night, so that it wouldn't hurt anybody. Just as long as it left the entire rats' nest in ruins.

12   "*Coño!*[2] They make me feel ashamed to be a Cuban!" Papi kept saying. "*Coño!* Ashamed!"

13   That picture was taken when I was a Freshman in high school. Can't you tell? The name of the school is right behind me, see it on the wall? GARDEN SHORE HIGH. And here's a picture of my friends; I took this one. That's Leticia and that's Marco and that's Ramón and that's Luisita. The cute guy on the left, that's Francisco. He sort of had the hots for me. No, he wasn't my boyfriend. And I didn't have a girlfriend either! Are you kidding? I was totally and pathetically repressed in those days.

14   God, I was bored to tears with life in the great North! The world seemed flat and predictable, nothing moved me. No, not even gorgeous blonde Gringas or the prospect of speaking the American language fluently. I was convinced that I had left my heart buried behind, on the island, just like the song said. *Cucudo salí de Cuba . . .*[3]

15   I hated English and refused to speak it unless it was absolutely necessary. Papi used to get so pissed at me. Because, you see, I didn't always feel like translating his gross remarks when he was arguing with some clerk (which happened a lot). He'd tell me that I was stupid and lazy and that what the hell had he brought me to the North for and how did I expect to get ahead in life and get rich or catch a Gringo millionaire if I didn't "espeekee de eengleesh"?

16   My only source of happiness was the trips Mami and I took to downtown Los Angeles on Sundays to see old movies from Mexico at the Million Dollar Theatre. In that theatre that reeked of urine, I rediscovered, in ecstasy, handfuls of Mexican melodramas that took me right back to Cuba. Incredible, huh, that those dime-store stories and slapsticks featuring María Félix, Arturo de Córdoba, Sara García, Cantinflas, would make me long for Cuba. But they did. And I cried like a baby. Until one day when I got sick and tired of crying and decided not to go to the Million Dollar anymore. I need to stop living off memories the way my parents do, I said to myself. I began to see nostalgia as my enemy. And the images of my homeland that I carried inside as an obstacle for my success.

17   I stashed my Spanish albums away, my photos, my letters, my Cuban memories in the closet. And I started to go to American movies with Pedro, because now I thought I was ready to understand them. The first American film I remember enjoying was *Valley of the Dolls*. The first American song I sang was "Aquarius." The first one I detested was "It's Your Thing." And the first American meal I remember savoring with gusto was a Sir Burger Supreme, with cheese. The rest I guess you could say is history.

---

[2] In Cuban Spanish, *coño* means "damn."
[3] *When I Left Cuba*, a song about Cuban exile in the 1960s.

18   Do you recognize me? Hard to believe that's me. Excellent polaroid shot, though, don't you think? That picture was taken right after I started high school. I was confused to the marrow. But fashionable. My hair dyed blonde, or rather what I thought was blonde (in reality a strange shade somewhere between red and brown, a barf-inducing color); wearing those dreadful bell-bottoms with the waist line below the hip, and that wide, scaly, worn-out leather belt, I was hot to trot.

19   The American students, compared to the ones in Madrid, seemed to me like people from another planet: tall, dead-white, distant, incomprehensible. Skinny girls with false eyelashes made of broom straw. Straight hair teased on top in the form of a nest, loose below, long and hanging as if all of a sudden there were a million greasy baby boas coming out of the high nest. Eyeshadow in blue, green, purple or all three colors smeared on their eye-lids. Miniskirts that displayed long, feeble legs dressed in grey stockings. Platform shoes that forced them to drag themselves like war tanks.

20   Among the boys, needless to say, the blonde-boy type with T-shirts and pestilent tennis shoes predominated. The Koreans were gaining a reputation for being smart. Through a dirty trick of fate they had ended up first in Argentina and then in "America," so they spoke fluent Spanish with a Tango accent. There was also a species called Low-riders, drivers of Impalas, Chevrolets and Cadillacs at the level of asphalt. Mean-looking dudes who smoked marijuana and lived in Santa Ana. And the Blacks! How they had warned me at home to stay away from those Negroes! (Which I did, Heaven forbid.)

21   My GSH gang: The Colombian Leticia, who would one day become a flight attendant for Avianca and vanish into sidereal space. The Korean boy, Ramón (the name the Gauchos gave him), who would become a wealthy and stressed-out restaurateur. Marco the Ecuadorian, who would marry a Cheerleader and work in a factory all his life. Luisita the Cuban, whom I lusted after, today a mother of three and the resigned wife of a Marielito. Of all of them, I miss Francisco the most. Francisco El Mexicano.

22   Since I couldn't speak English, the school authorities "assigned" me to this Mexican guy, Francisco Valdés, from day one of my freshman year. He was an exemplary student, considering his "language handicap." I was told that he would help me with my classes and serve as my guide, until I felt ready to fend for myself. Whatever grades Francisco got (all of them Bs), I'd get, they informed me.

23   "Why are they doing this?" I asked Francisco. "Because," he said, amiably, smiling, "they don't know what to do with the recent arrivals."

24   And while we're on the subject: Those ESL classes! English as a Second Language. The darned classes didn't teach us a thing. They were taught by a thin, stooped old man who didn't speak a word of Spanish, much less Korean. Mister "I-Don't-Know-What" would stand in front of us every morning and tell us jokes. I knew they were jokes because he laughed whole-heartedly at his own words. He talked and talked and cracked up and talked

and once in a while he'd write a verb on the board, asking us to repeat: *I eat, you eat, he eats, she eats* . . .

25   Francisco and I became accomplices in lunch-time escapades to the corner diner. I smoked my first and last cigarette with him. He was the only one with whom I spoke of my Cuban nostalgia. He listened. And he hardly ever talked about Guadalajara, his hometown, or about his absent family. I tried my first burrito and my first taco with Francisco. He used to tell me that Mexican cuisine was the most varied and flavorful in the whole world. Sure! How could he talk of variety and flavor when everything Mexican people ate was so spiced up that you could hardly taste anything but a raging fire? And besides, corn tortillas smelled of bats. No, I had never even seen a bat, but if I had, and if bats possessed a particular smell, it would definitely be the same smell as the tortillas. Little did I suspect at the time that I would eventually turn into a voracious and regular Taco Shell customer.

26   Francisco kissed me once, while we were walking to the diner. And I gave him the usual lines, you know: I liked him as a friend, not as a boyfriend. And I was too young to get involved with anyone, anyway. We drifted apart gradually, starting half-way through my freshman year. I was now excited by the prospect of being on my own, without an assigned classmate, and without a Latin clique to assuage my exile longings.

27   I had a know-it-all feeling about things when my sophomore year began. Sure of myself and determined to work for my own Bs, I was speaking perfectly accented broken California English, much to Papi's satisfaction. And I had decided to get the high school phase (without Prom and Grad night, please) out of the way as soon as possible so I could go to a good university, preferably one far from home. That was the American way: Move out to go to college. That's what most of my American classmates were planning to do. And I wanted to do as they did.

DISCUSSION QUESTIONS

1. Describe the way the narrator compares California with Spain and Cuba.
2. Discuss Rosita's and Papi's feelings concerning music records. Describe the scene in Discoteca Latina.
3. Why did Rosita find happiness in seeing Mexican movies in downtown Los Angeles? Discuss her decision not to return to the Million Dollar Theatre.
4. Rosita describes different ethnic groups living in and around Garden Shores. Discuss what she learned about American life through these people.

WRITING TOPICS

1. Write an essay in which you contrast your expectations about your future with your parents' expectations for you.
2. Based on the narrative, write a description of life for a student during the 1960s living in Garden Shores.

NIGHT VIGIL

Evangelina Vigil-Piñón

A native of San Antonio, Texas, Evangelina Vigil-Piñón was born in 1949 into a family of ten children. She began writing poetry in 1976. Vigil-Piñón published her first chapbook, *Nade y Nade*, in 1978 and her first book, *Thirty an' Seen a Lot*, in 1982. For her book, published by Arte Público Press, she won the American Book Award of the Before Columbus Foundation. In her second book, *The Computer Is Down* (1987), Vigil-Piñón blends her visions of the urban experience with universal themes found in traditional and popular music. Her poetic language flows in several distinct codes: she writes in English, in Spanish, in Caló (slang), and in alternating sequences of all of these. As an editor of the influential *The Americas Review,* this Mexican-American writer paved the way for poetic expression for beginning and developing poets. Particularly noteworthy is her edited collection *Woman of Her Word: Hispanic Women Write* (1983), which brings together the creative and critical expression of over forty writers. Evangelina Vigil-Piñón also translated Tomás Rivera's *. . . y no se lo tragó la tierra* as *And the Earth Did Not Devour Him.* Indeed, she is an exemplary writer and editor.

In "night vigil," Evangelina Vigil-Piñón plays on the meaning of her surname in English and creates a sense of ambiguity. Is she the vigil, the night person? Or is she a poetic persona involved in a night vigil? The poet's meanderings through the night reveal her intimate self and the solitude she experiences in the dark of night.

in the twilight hour all is still
all lights out
except for my nocturnal eyes, fluorescent
shining on oscuridades[1]

---

[1] Dark corners.

5 spotlight rolling
exposing crevices on walls
shaded pastel surfaces
elongated door structures
furnishing converted into bultos[2] by the darkness
10 como los que te espantaron cuando niña[3]
"cúrala de susto"[4]
dijo tu abuelita:[5]
in your juvenile memory
four little broomstraws forming crosses
15 an egg, water

in night surroundings while others sleep
my heart thumps, off beat
absolutely refusing to align itself with time
ticking rhythmically
20 from faithful clock
marking time
advancing time
in night surroundings while others dream
I can taste my solitude

25 my imagination spins
images take form
I recall the splendor of beaches in the Caribbean
warmed by the sun
caressed by waters blue
30 I recall the powerful thrusts of the Atlantic
the Pacific
I envision beaches being swallowed up by night tide
the color of obsidian
moon illuminating rapture

35 I picture in my mind
receding waters
por la mañana[6]
exposing sprinklings of starfish, urchins, seashell pedals pink
nocturnal creatures slithering, crawling, stretching
40 traces of last night's liquid passion

---

[2] Shapes.
[3] Like the ones that frightened you when you were a little girl.
[4] Cure her of this illness of profound fright.
[5] Your dear grandmother said.
[6] In the morning.

(what the stars will not tell)
realization anchored in this knowledge:

      the universe is immeasureable;
      the constellations shine so

45 thoughtglow spins into silvermist, then silverblack
then into live darkness
feelings, sensations have collected themselves back inward
to self-consuming origins
in depths of memories reconcealed

50   images have disappeared before my very eyes
      like would they were they tails of comets
      or paths of falling stars

                  images have vanished in colorful flashes
                  dash by dash
55   like silk scarf streamers would
                  into elegant skillful, white-gloved hands
                  of a magician

consciousness retreats into my breathing body
I am back in this room
60 I feel calm awareness of heart pumping lifeblood rhythmically
my own body warmth sends chill through my bones
warmth regenerates
I breathe in stillness
with ease

65 solitude, darkness, quiet
envelope my once more
feelings of loneliness, forlornness gather in my chest
they weigh my heart
sentimiento[7] slowly transforms into a focused thought—
70 spotlight rolling again
mind fluorescent, sensors beaming
surveillant

sideglance:
the sky glows opaque
75 window frames silhouette of tree with winter limbs
the branches are brittle, made so by the frost

---

[7] Sentiment; feeling.

they are silver-lined with moonmist
they are beautiful, elegant
they express artistry, magic

80 closing my eyes, I turned inward
I feel fluid, serene, peaceful
my mind lies potent with imagination
all is silent around me
I am by myself
85 I am singular
the night's presence cushions me
its embrace is pillow soft

como un indio[8]
who in stillness detects stampede
90 of approaching herd
I detect
far off in the distance
an approaching train
its heavy rhythmic speed transmits velocity through my bones
95 its iron clanking sounds are muffled, sifted
by the night air thick with mist and fog
I hear its familiar whistle
its distant call slowly permeates through nightspace
it rings solitude
100 immense sadness engulfs me
it is upon me
but it quickly begins to fade
like a tumbleweed of sound
rolling by:
105 I wonder who this nightrain traveler is
I wonder how he feels about this vast sea
of nocturnal singular existence

I pull multicolored quilt over my head
mind rests assured:
110 in the morning the sea will flow aquablue
sparkling and vibrant, activated by the sun
brilliance, inspiration
will explode from within the spirit, uncontained
but tonight

---

[8] Like an Indian.

115 nocturnal naked eyes keep watch
    beholding with awe
    heart's inner vision:

    moment's pause
    del corazón[9]
120 anchored in perennial motion
    like cascades of the ocean waves
    gushing
    crowned with white lace liquid patterns
    jeweled with watermist of pearls exquisite
125 crescents volatile, explosive
    energía[10] sculpted
    by force of rolling tide

DISCUSSION QUESTIONS

1. In this poem, the persona—the author—talkes about herself while playing with the meaning of her surname (vigil). In small groups, discuss
   whether she dreams or whether she stays alert and sleepless during the
   night.
2. Describe the worlds that she sees in her night solitude.
3. Analyze the poet's use of the phrases "I turn inward" and "I am back in
   this room."

WRITING TOPICS

1. Write a poem about your dreams or night visions.
2. In your journal, write an entry about a significant event in your childhood. What aspects make it memorable?

---

[9] Of the heart.
[10] Energy.

CHAPTER SIX

LOVE AND ROMANCE

The theme of love and romance is a universal theme in literature. In a process as old as time itself, an undeniable attraction leads to romance and courtship, and usually culminates in marriage. Stories of love and romance have long intrigued poets and playwrights because they center on relationships that are fueled by human passions. As such they may be complicated or constrained by jealousy, anger, doubt, deceit, and so on, adding interest and a bit of suspense to a couple's story.

The influence of a culture on love and romance also affects the course of a relationship. For example, custom may dictate the presence of a chaperone, or that a young woman's father or mother choose his or her daughter's suitor. The issue of a dowry and the need to receive the approval or blessing of future in-laws may also be complicating factors. Then, somehow, love overcomes all of these cultural obstacles, and lives are transformed.

In the selections that follow, as in life, love's course is not necessarily smooth. Readers will be drawn to these Hispanic writers' tales of love and romance. The courting rituals described give insight into the culture and underscore the dominant role of the family in Hispanic society.

FROM *DEAR RAFE*

Rolando Hinojosa

One of Chicano literature's major authors, Rolando Hinojosa, also known as Hinojosa-Smith, was born in Mercedes, Texas, in 1929. He was raised in a border culture of conflict and perseverance, change and endurance. After serving in the United States Army, he attended the University of Texas. He worked as a teacher, data processor, and civil servant before receiving his M.A. in Spanish from New Mexico Highlands University in 1962 and his Ph.D. from the University of Illinois in 1969. Hinojosa-Smith later returned to the University of Texas, where he holds a distinguished professorship in English and creative writing.

His works include *Estampas del valle y otras obras* (1973), for which he was awarded the Quinto Sol Prize, *Klail City y sus alrededores* (1976), which earned him the Casa de las Américas Prize and was published bilingually as *Generaciones y semblanzas* in 1977, *Korean Love Songs* (1978), *Mi Querido Rafa* (1981), *Rites and Witnesses* (1982), *The Valley* (1983), and *Partners in Crime: A Rafa Buenrostro Mystery* (1985), *Claros varones de Belken* (1986), *Becky and Her Friends* (1989), and *The Useless Servants* (1993). All of these narrative works, including the poetry *Korean Love Songs*, record the struggles of Texas Mexicans and their neighbors.

Rolando Hinojosa tells an interesting tale in *Dear Rafe*. The following selection comprises the first two chapters of the novel. This is an epistolary work in which the character Jehu writes to Rafe. We, as readers, understand what the reply might have been and the nature of the relationship between the cousins. In telling the tale, the narrator shifts between first and third persons, while the story is framed in the second person, since Jehu is addressing Rafe in a letter. In *Dear Rafe,* readers get an apparently gossipy set of letters about the town—letters that are meant only for Rafe's eyes. Note the informal style and occasional "shorthand" in these letters. Interestingly, Hinojosa does not make his protagonist all pure and good, but a bit of a cynic.

1 Dear Rafe:

2 Here's wishing you a hale and hearty and hoping to hear that you're doing better, much better. According to Aaron, he claims you look as thin and pale as a whooping crane, and all I can say is "Fatten up, cousin," and you'll be up and out of that hosp. before you know it.

3 Not much to tell about the Valley right now, but things'll pick up when the primaries come around. The job at the Bank is a job at the Bank, and you'd be surprised (most prob. not) about how some people run their lives in Klail and in Belken County. Not a matter of a three-alarmer, no, but their accounts reveal that all is not well with some of the citizens in our tip of the L.S. State.

4 The trial for those killers you uncovered has been set for next Jan. 8. You're sure to be up and around by then; will you then be asked to testify?

5 Since you'll be in exile in Wm. Barrett for a while, I'll keep you up-to-date, as far as I can, on the doings here. For now, then, the primaries which are just around the corner.

6 Yesterday, and what follows is rumor, gossip, and hearsay, my boss, Noddy Perkins, called Ira Escobar into his office; it's soundproof, of course, and late that afternoon, Ira called on the interoffice phone: "Got to see you, Jehu." I initialed the teller's accounts, popped my head in Noddy's office, and said good-night to him. On my way to the back lot, there's Ira again.

7 He could hardly stand it, whatever *it* was, and then, in a rush, he said that Noddy "and some very important persons, Jehu" had talked to him seriously and on a high level. It happens that our Fellow Texans want Ira to stand for County Commissioner Place Four. And, what did I think a-that?

8 My heart didn't miss a beat, needless to s., and poor Ira felt a bit deflated. Neither of us said a word for a second or more until I hit him for a light after having first accepted one of his cigarettes. (Ira's dumb, but not *that* dumb). He saw that, far from envy, it was plain disinterestedness on my part, but he still wasn't sure about my reaction or lack of it.

9 He looked at me again and asked if I didn't have any earthly I-de-ah what THAT meant: Noddy and the very imp. pers. wanted and had *asked* him to run, and that they were ready (and standing in line, I suppose) to help him all the way.

10 Wherever that may happen to lead, say I. But, who am I to go around breaking hearts and illusions? By now you're prob. way ahead of me here since the only thing Ira was interested in was to let me know the Good News, and that was it.

11 Forward! Haaarch! The last thing he'd want from me would be some advice, and I'm not good at that either. There we were, two lonely people in a treeless parking lot, at 6 p.m., with 97 degrees F staring us in the face, and Ira saying: "Jay, Jay, don't you see? County Commissioner Place Four, the *fat* one, Jay." (Yes, he calls me *Jay*). About all I could think of was to wonder what Noddy, the Ranch, the Bank, etc. were up to this time; I mean, they already own most of the land 'in these here parts' and they have ALL

THAT MONEY, SON; so it's prob. something else in that woodpile aside from the wood, right? I finally shook his hand, or the other way round, and then he went straight home to give his wife the second surprise of her life.

12   Ira and his wife are new to Klail, and I'm fairly certain you don't know her; her name's Rebecca Caldwell (we who know and love her, call her *Becky*) and she's from Jonesville-on-the-Rio. Her father's a Caldwell, but a Mexican for a'that. Her mother's a Navarrete, and enough said. I've seen her a couple of times at a Bank party and other Bank doings and what-not.

13   The phone! A call from one of the relatives in Relámpago; Auntie Enriqueta says she's coming along nicely; nothing serious. (Remember when we used to hit Relámpago fairly often? I wonder whatever-happened-to-those-baldheaded-tattooed-twins, Doro and Thea, right?). Anyway, getting back to Becky, she's a bit of a looker. We get along, and we do look each other in the eye when we've said 'hello' and such. Nice looking face to go with a well-rounded little *bod*. We'll see.

14   Now, it could be it's a false alarm, and it may be that the Central Powers are merely testing our boy here. You never know. If Noddy *were* testing the waters, and Ira's enthusiasm showed through, Noddy could read that as our boy's willingness to serve the public.

15   Old Man Vielma sends his best; ran into him at the Blue Bar. In re his daughter who now shares a house with your former sister-in-law, Delfina, our illuminated friends are up in arms about 'those two shameless women who live together.' Why go on? As you can see with that one good eye you've got left, we're still as nice and as sweet and understanding in Klail City as ever.

16   Well, cuz, take care, eat well, and I'm sure that before either one of us knows it, you'll be back hard at work at the Court House. (Thought I'd make your day: Sheriff Parkinson, he of the big feet, is taking much of the credit for solving those murders you and Culley and Sam cleared up. Big Foot's no fool; he says it was his *office* that solved them, and since he is the sheriff . . .

17   Best,

18   Jehu

19   Dear Rafe:

20   First off: kindly do excuse the delay in answering your latest; it has to do with the work here, a rush on time, and then, before I know it, two weeks have come and gone, and I haven't dropped you line one. Second excuse: attended and participated in a sad funeral: don Pedro Zamudio's, that old Oblate of Mary Immaculate, who graced the fair city of Flora long and well.

21   It happens that he had two older brothers (yes, *older*), and they came down from God only knows what aerie of His. Black hats, hooked-noses, and as bald as Father Pedro himself. Half the world and most of Belken County showed up, and I almost broke up thinking on that grand and glo-

rious burial we gave Bruno Cano that bright Spring morning years ago. It's rained here and snowed elsewhere since that time, son. And now, sic transit.

22   On the way back to Klail, I stopped off at the old mexicano cemetery near Bascom. One of those things, I guess; I walked around reading the stones and markers, looking over the old and loved names. As you know, we're all one day nearer the grave.

23   *Public Notice*: The offer to Ira appears to be on the level. Noddy Perkins' sister (more on her in a minute) came by the Bank *eins-zwei-drei* times, and where there's smoke, there's a political barbecue, right?

24   Tidy-up time: you're wrong on the Escobar familial relationships, and I'll explain why in short order. Ira's an Escobar on his father's side (old don Nemesio Escobar, who's related to the Prado families from Barrones, Tamaulipas. Got that?) But, Ira also happens to be a Leguizamón, sad to say, and it comes from the maternal end of things: A Leguizamón-Leyva for a mother who's from Uncle Julian's generation. Of course, if you were to see Ira, you'd pick him out in a crowd, straight off. It's the nose and jaw that gives the Leguizamóns away every time. And, as far as the Bank job's concerned, he got *that* because of his Leguizamón connections (this from Noddy, by the way). That aside, if I were Ira, I'd watch Noddy P. NP's not a lost babe, and our boy Ira is, in a word, blinded by the goal that glitters. To sum up, then, he looks as easy a prey as a jackass flats bunny, wide-eyed (and blind), ears pointed up (and deaf as a door), and ready for someone to pick him off with a .22 long. He seems to love it, though. It's God's truth that there's always someone who's willing to do anything in this world.

25   Ira himself told me that he'll pay the filing fee at the Court House this p.m. I've no proofs, of course, but I'm dead sure Noddy's got something up that sleeve of his'n. Yes, he do. I've been here three years now, and I've barely scratched three or four layers in that man's make-up. And he goes much deeper'n that, believe me.

26   As for you, I've got another surprise: you know Noddy's sister. Yes, you do. Ready? No less a body than Mrs. Kirkpatrick, our old Klail H.S. typing inst. Remember this?

27   A S D F G & don't look at the key

28   Q W E R T & keep your eyes on me!

29   Yep! Powerhouse Kirkpatrick is Noddy Perkins' sib. (The first time she saw me at the bank, must be going on three years now, she spotted me in my office & said, "Are you the Buenrostro boy?")

30   Well! I knew *she* knew who I was (it's their bank, dammit, and they know who they hire) but I went along, & we both wound up laughing and what-all. Getting up in the years is Old Powerhouse, and widowed all these twenty years, Jehu, but I've got all my teeth, she says. (And all that money Tinker Kirkpatrick left her, too, sez I). Her main interests these days revolve around the Klail City Woman's Club & the Music Club. If she rules there the way she did at Klail High, God help 'em.

31   By the by, Ira's not to run for Place Four, as he'd been told. (There's a note of sadness to that 'as he'd been told,' isn't there?)

32   This is what I think the play will be.

33   Ira's to run v. Morse Terry (Place Three) in the Democratic Primary. Do you recall MT? He was up at Austin with us; speaks Spanish (natch), and he's a friend of the mexicano. Sure he is. (Same old lyrics to Love's Old Sweet Song).

34   Here's your story, Your Honor: Looks like some toes were stepped on; or maybe a double cross or two, not sure, but *something* happened. Big, too. Soooo, Noddy's lining up some of our Fellow Texans against Morse Terry, and backing Ira Escobar.

35   Talk about your strange bedfellows. The rundown: Ira v. Terry with Bank backing, and our fair-haired boy's on his way to the victory circle. I can imagine Ira at night, alone, and softly, in the bathroom, facing the mirror, that Ira sees himself as a future Congressman in Washington; how's *that* for a dream? Still, stranger things have happened, mirabile visu et dictu[1].

36   There *is* one problem, however, and thus Powerhouse's comings and goings: Noddy wants Ira's wife's admission to the Woman's Club, and that's a tall order, Chief. More on this later as soon as the news develops.

37   Next week this here cousin a-yours is off to the Big House for a kickoff Bar-B-Q; Ira's announcement, most prob. One of the girls at the Bank says that a lot of people (she put the stress on *people*) have been invited out there; I'll keep you posted.

38   And, too, word of honor and, as a relative, I'll say more in re Noddy and his antecedents although this may just be repeating something you already know. Correct me if I'm wrong.

39   Gotta go. Am enclosing a pix; the girl on the left is a current one.

40   Best,

41   Jehu

DISCUSSION QUESTIONS

1. Jehu, the narrator/author of the letters in *Dear Rafe* has taken advantage of the form with regard to perspective, language, and characterization. In small groups, discuss examples of how he does so.

2. Describe the conversation between Ira Escobar and Jehu (short for Jesús) as described in Jehu's letter. Why does Ira call Jehu *Jay*?

3. What is Jehu's interest in Becky Escobar?

---

[1] Wonderful to behold and describe (Latin).

4. Discuss the meaning of the family names mentioned and how these family members are related to one another.
5. Discuss Jehu's character and whether he is a playboy. Cite examples from the selection to support your answer.

WRITING TOPICS

1. Write a casual and conversational letter to a friend about the happenings at your school.
2. Write a letter to the editor of your newspaper in support of a candidate who is running for local office.

A ROMEO AND JULIET STORY IN
EARLY NEW MEXICO

Fray Angélico Chávez

Fray Angélico Chávez, born Manuel Chávez on April 10, 1910, in Wagon Mound, has been recognized as one of New Mexico's most distinguished writers. He has been honored by the state's governor and three of its universities. He studied at several colleges in the Midwest as well as at the St. Francis Seminary in Cincinnati. In 1937 he became a Franciscan priest in the Catholic Church. Because he liked art, his teachers dubbed him Angélico in honor of Florentine artist Fra (Friar) Angelico. Their nickname was thus the inspiration for his pen name, Fray Angélico Chávez.

Chávez has authored more than twenty books on the topics of literature, history, and religion. Best known is his *My Penitente Land: Reflections on Spanish New Mexico* (1974), a historical essay and spiritual autobiography. Previously, he had written a number of books of poetry. *Clothed with the Sun* (1939), and *Eleven Lady-Lyrics, and Other Poems* (1945) are simple lyrics that convey moments of intense emotion. *The Single Rose; the Rose Unica and Commentary of Fray Manuel de Santa Clara* (1948); and *The Virgin of Port Lligat* (1959) are more poetically complex and intellectually ambitious works.

In addition, Chávez wrote four historical narratives: *New Mexico Triptych* (1940), *La Conquistadora: The Autobiography of an Ancient Statue* (1954), *From an Altar Screen/El retablo: Tales from New Mexico* (1957), and *The Lady from Toledo* (1960). His interest in history is also reflected in *Our Lady of the Conquest* (1948) and the biography of José Manuel Gallegos, New Mexico's first United States congressman, *Très Macho—He Said* (1985).

Genaro Padilla's compilation of the short stories written by Fray Angélico Chávez—mostly unpublished and some written as early as his seminary days—round off the literary portrait of this gifted author. In "A Romeo and Juliet Story in Early New Mexico," Fray Angélico Chávez tells the story of Manuel and Francisca and their love for each other. Curiously, Chávez recasts their story as a play in imitation of Shakespeare's own script, but without a dialogue text. This charming story is told fondly and with an affectionate tone.

1   Santa Fe in 1733 was a very old town already, a small cluster of low adobe houses around a plaza and the much taller church; but the great mountain behind it lent it considerable impressiveness both winter and summer. Albuquerque was but a quarter of a century old, hence much smaller as to the number of dwellings and the size of the church; in summer it was almost lost among the cottonwoods on the flat riverbank, but the sharp outline of the high range to the east was near enough as to give it character also. Traffic between the two settlements was of the barest, due chiefly to primitive modes of travel over difficult winding trails. Yet both came close together in that year to provide the scenes for a real-life drama having the more pleasant features of Shakespeare's *Romeo and Juliet*—and some of the heart tragedy, too, even if there were no deaths or carnage to mar or prevent a happy ending.

2   It was the old story of a boy and a girl in love hounded by parental disapproval, the plot found in folklore and written classics all over the world. We owe the New Mexico version, however, not to some professional or amateur purveyor of romances who wished to regale posterity with a delectable scandal, but to a court clerk in Mexico City who sandwiched the incident, as a case in point, between dry and drawn-out legal proceedings regarding ecclesiastical jurisdiction. Other ancient archives from Sevilla, Mexico City, and Santa Fe, help us in identifying the chief persons of the play.

3   Manuel Armijo and Francisca Baca were the lovers. Their romance was as tender as that of the Veronese young couple, and they were just as handsome and sweet in each other's eyes, no matter how they might have actually looked. The dun adobe walls and rough vigas of Santa Fe and Albuquerque were a far cry from southern Europe's bright-tiled roofs and graceful colonnades, but the great Sangre de Cristo and Sandia ranges made marvelous backdrops nevertheless. The elder Bacas and Armijos, with knvies stuck in their sashes under homespun capes, and leering at each other from under low-crowned wide sombreros, were the silken-hosed, sword-wielding gentry of other times and other lands.

4   Why Francisca Baca's family objected to the match is easy to see and important to know. The girl's parents are singled out first because the Armijos are not recorded as having interfered. It was a matter of family pride among the Bacas who claimed direct descent from a First Conquistador; for Don Antonio Baca, a captain in the local militia, prided himself in being a great-great-grandson of the original Baca, Don Cristóval Baca, who had

come to New Mexico in 1600. He furthermore believed himself to be, though mistakenly, a descendant of the already legendary Nuñes Cabeza de Vaca. Antonio's wife, Doña María de Aragón, was relatively a newcomer who had arrived with her parents in 1693 at the time of the Reconquest of New Mexico by Don Diego de Vargas; this lent luster to her own family of the Aragón and Ortiz clan, over and above the important fact that, like the Baca, it passed for pure Spanish, although previously established in the Valley of Mexico for some generations.

5   The Armijos, on the other hand, were not only late-comers, having arrived fully six months after the glorious retaking of Santa Fe from the Indians by Governor de Vargas, but they very casually admitted that they were mestizos[1] from Zacatecas. Of the four grown sons who had come with their parents, Antonio Durán de Armijo was the only surgeon in "*El Reyno de la Nueva México*"[2] at the time and for many years to come, and was very dexterous with the pen as well as with the scalpel, quite an envious distiction in a crude little world of cattlemen and of part-time militiamen who could not sign their names for the most part. But at the time of this story neither Antonio Armijo nor his brothers José and Marcos had any son of marriageable age by the name of Manuel. At least there is none on record. The fourth brother, however, Vicente Durán de Armijo, had not only one but three sons with the same name: Manuel *el Primero*, Manuel *el Segundo*, and Manuel *el Tercero*.[3] So the odds are three to nothing that Vicente was the father of our hero. The first Manuel had been sent as a boy to Guadalupe del Paso in order to learn a trade as a tailor's apprentice, and there, it appears, he married and established himself. The second Manuel married a Lucero de Godoy girl in Santa Fe (a year after our story), and later moved down to Albuquerque to fill that lower part of the Río Grande valley with Armijos. Then it must be Manual III who was stirring up the coals of trouble in the exclusive Baca hearth.

6   But if Don Antonio Baca objected to Armijos in general, he had greater reason for refusing to have Manual Armijo for his son-in-law. The boy's mother was a María de Apodaca who had been born in a pueblo of an unknown Tewa father and a Spanish or part-Spanish girl who had been captured by the Indians in the Great Rebellion of 1680. Moreover, María's unfortunate mother, after she had been rescued with her child by the conquering De Vargas forces twelve long years later, later married the Governor's Negro drummer. The fact that Manuel Armijo's mother was a Negro's step-child did not better his chances at all. But now to Manuel and Francisca.

7   In early Spanish civil and church law, when a youth and a maiden fell in love but the latter's family refused to give her hand in marriage, the boy could appeal to the courts and have the girl deposited in a neutral home for

---

[1] Of mixed Spanish and Indian heritage.
[2] "The Kingdom of New Mexico."
[3] The First, the Second, the Third.

some time, where she was supposed to make up her own mind without the interference of relatives on either side. Any such interference brought on the penalty of excommunication on those breaking the law. Manuel Armijo knew his law, at least in this regard, and better than his foes had bargained for. When he appeared before the Lord Vicar and Ecclesiastical Judge to plead his case, he took along two witnesses, an itinerant shoemaker and a farm laborer from the Río Abajo district who happened to be in town. These "friends of Romeo" were to prove invaluable aids in overcoming the many obstacles thrown in Manuel's path by the very court which ought to have been an unbiased arbiter.

8   Don José de Bustamante y Tagle was the Vicar at this time. As the legal person of the Bishop of Durango twelve hundred miles away, and as a member of the late Governor's family, his sway in Santa Fe was considerable. This priest was an intimate friend of Don Antonio Baca. What is more, two of Don Antonio's brothers had married into the Bustamante social group, and a first cousin of his was the wife of the prominent Captain and merchant, Don Nicolás Ortiz, whose aunt was Don Antonio's mother-in-law. All in all, it was a welter of affinities and consanguinities in higher circles that formed a formidable bastion between poor Manual Armijo and Francisca Baca. Of necessity an integral part of this barrier, the Vicar could not approve of such a marriage. But here he was confronted by the young swain himself and his two witnesses in due legal form. It may be that he tried to dissuade Armijo from his purpose, or offered him a bribe to leave the north country and join his elder brother at Guadalupe del Paso. That sort of thing has been tried before, and ever shall be. At any rate, Armijo remained resolute, and the Vicar had no other choice than to carry out the law, although with some reservations that were already ticking in his mind.

9   First, he interviewed Francisca Baca privately, but she proved just as headstrong as her lover. This vain attempt over, he had her solemnly conducted to the home of a certain Don José Reaño y Tagle. There she was to think seriously upon the matter and, after weighing the disadvantages following a marriage with Armijo, return a negative answer. But her reply was still most affirmative when she was questioned some time later. Then the anger of Santa Fe's society broke loose upon her little head. Her uncles and cousins, not to mention her local aunts, came secretly to the house, despite the threat of excommunication, and tried to dissuade her from marrying Armijo. Her own father threatened to kill her with his own sword. Young blades among her relations were ready to do away with Armijo himself. Even the Vicar, avoiding the church penalty by appearing personally, sent her a message. Even if she were pregnant, it said, everything would be taken care of nicely and quietly. Now was the time for sorely beset Francisca, had she ever read Shakespeare, to lean out the window and cry:

"O Romeo, Romeo! wherefore art thou Romeo?
Deny thy father and refuse thy name."

10   Crazed finally by these incessant visits and threats which gave her no rest, or, what is more likely, to gain some respite for her tired mind, Francisca bowed at last to her kinfolk's wishes; only then was she taken home from the Reaño residence which to her had become a madhouse. Really, it had not been a "neutral home." Don José Reaño was also a Bustamante on his mother's side. His wife was a Roybal, another family of that closely-knit society; her brother Mateo was already engaged to Francisca's sister Gregoria; she was, moreover, a sister of the Vicar who had preceded Bustamante and who was to succeed him when all this trouble was over. Both Reaño and his wife had given Francisca no rest in the intervals left her by her more immediate relatives. In the end, it all had turned out into a pitched battle between the Spanish-born Bustamantes of the mountains of Santander and a lone youth from the hills of Santa Fe with more Indian than Spanish blood in his lovelorn heart. And Spain had won, apparently, forgetting for the nonce that all her songs and tales give true love the victory in the end.

11   Back in her father's house, Francisca recanted, to her credit and our admiration. Don Antonio Baca began fuming anew, and this time resorted to a different strategy. He put his daughter on one of his best horses and sent her under armed escort to Albuquerque "twenty-four leagues away," a tremendous distance in those days of travel by horse or ox-drawn *carreta*[4]. She was to be deposited in the home of her aunt, Doña Josefa Baca, who owned a prosperous hacienda at Pajarito.

12   How often did not Francisca look back during that first day's journey, as the horses trudged down the dusty road towards La Ciénega under a bright July sun, especially when her father's house, and her lover's home, blended in the distance with the ochre earth of which they were made. The last to fade away was the great adobe Parroquia of St. Francis which she had always imagined as the biggest building on earth; she had not been baptized in it since it was not finished until five years after her birth, and she had not been born in Santa Fe anyway, but she had often dreamed of kneeling at its high altar blazing with candles, and her Manuel at her side placing the ring on her finger and pouring the *arras*[5] into her open palms. Only the great blue and green mountain, called the Sierre Madre in those days, remained in sight all day long, seeming to raise herself even higher the further away she rode, as if telling her like a fond mother that she would not forget. But as the horses began picking their painful way down the black volcanic boulders of La Bajada, the Sierra Madre regretfully turned away and out of sight, and the Jémez range appeared in front, all purple in the glory of the crimson sunset behind it; but to Francisca that hue and the rough contour of the ridges were more like the sad purple cloth thrown over the images of saints from Passion

---

[4] Wagon.

[5] Thirteen coins given by bridegroom to the bride at a wedding; similar to a dowry, but more a symbolic gift.

Week until Good Friday. It was dark when they reached the pueblo of Santo Domingo; there the party spent the night in the houses of the Alcalde Mayor, the only Spanish home in the entire district. Next morning they started out again along the lush groves of the Río del Norte, a monotonous but easier trip now that familiar landmarks were well out of sight. At noon they stopped to rest at the post of Bernalillo, her parents' hometown where she herself had been born almost twenty-one years before, but she did not remember the place nor many of the vast Baca relationship which came to greet her. The Sandía Mountain, shaped like a mammoth watermelon when viewed from the north, now kept her interest as they rode along its precipitous western flank all afternoon, her eyes scaling each succeeding sky-scratching cliff all the way down the broadening valley, until nightfall found them approaching the ranch of Doña Josefa Baca.

13   Although Don Antonio Baca knew his sister Josefa well, he had not reckoned with her strong-willed nature, much less with her own views on love problems such as the one he was thrusting upon her. Alone and unmarried, she had developed her inheritance into a prosperous hacienda and had borne and reared six healthy children besides. One can take it for granted that Aunt Josefa quickly won her niece's confidence. She most certainly got a different version of the Santa Fe maneuvers, not only from the girl's lips, but from the Albuquerque men who had gone with Manuel Armijo before the Vicar. What Aunt Josefa did to solve the problem in the true playwright fashion may be detected in an unforgettable (yet long-forgotten) incident that took place in the Albuquerque church sometime later.

14   It was the tenth day of August, in the year 1733, the Feast of the martyr St. Lawrence. This feast day was celebrated by the Spanish population all over New Mexico in memory of those many Franciscans who had been massacred by the Indians on this very day in 1680. While the Bacas and Bustamantes and the rest of the Santa Fe folk were putting on their finery and repairing to the great Parroquia for Mass, the people of the lower valley were flocking to the nearest Mission, those around Albuquerque to the smaller church of San Francisco Xavier (today San Felipe) which faced the Sandía from the plaza by the river.

15   Doña Josefa Baca came with her children from Parajito accompanied by her niece who drew all eyes to herself—and also whispered comments among the bystanders—for her frustrated romance had become well known by now despite the difficult means of communication. Francisca and her aunt looked particularly devout that morning as both took their places far up in front near the altar. Had the congregation seen their faces during the chanting of the Mass, they might have caught a nervous twitch of apprehension now and then, or a faint smile of anticipation. No sooner was the Mass over than the people began milling and pushing their way out the front door, to watch the play of Moors and Christians and the horse races that were to follow. They had not noticed that the priest had remained at the altar instead of repairing to the sacristy as usual.

16   Doña Josefa nudged her niece and they both arose and walked close together towards the open sunlit door. As they reached the front, a young man stepped out from behind the door, grasped the young lady by the arm, and swiftly marched her up to the altar where the Padre was waiting. Soon the church filled up again when word got outside that Manuel Armijo and Francisca Baca were being married. The ceremony went on without interruption, either because everybody was so completely taken by surprise, or because there were no men present of that impious stamp who would dare to profane the holy place with violence.

17   Fray Pedro Montaño, the Franciscan pastor of Albuquerque who ended this true drama happily without the aid of fatal herbs and potions, later wrote up the case for his Superior so that the latter might present it to the Viceregal Court in the City of Mexico as an illustration of the secular Vicar's abuse of authority. In doing so, the friar makes it appear as though the incident in church was entirely spontaneous and unrehearsed; that, confronted by this unexpected action of the groom, and having questioned the parties concerning the whole matter, he had married them then and there "to avoid greater inconveniences." But through it all shines forth the genius of Doña Josefa, who had previously contacted the friar, the groom, the various witnesses, and who very likely concocted the plot that ended in such a successful coup.

18   As noted in the beginning, the more pleasant features of *Romeo and Juliet* are here present. That nameless Nurse, whom Shakespeare purposely created in rough contrast to the gentle-spoken protagonists and their high-born families, who minced no words when speaking or spoken to, and who was a most efficient go-between in the lovers' trysts and in arranging for the wedding with old Friar Lawrence, was admirably played by Doña Josefa Baca. Fray Pedro Montaño resembles Shakespeare's famous Franciscan in his human understanding if not in his outlandish way of concluding the affair. *Romeo and Juliet* ends with a churchyard scene strewn with fresh corpses after a bit of sword-play. Although there were no killings after the wedding of Manuel and Francisca, a duel did flare up as the people poured out a second time onto the walled *campo santo*[6] in front of the church. Two individuals by the name of Antonio de Chávez and Antonio Montoya, who had begun disputing as to whether the friar did the right thing or not, suddenly drew out knives from their sashes and began taking each other's measure. The crowd promptly disarmed them, however. Nor do we know who it was that took whose part, for Montoya was married to Francisca's sister Ynés, and Chávez was the husband of her cousin Antonia Baca.

19   That the Bacas in Santa Fe did not immediately approve of the marriage is shown by the fact that Manuel and Francisca did not have their *velación* (or solemn nuptial blessing with rings, coins, and candle) until two years

---

[6] Cemetery; literally holy ground.

later, when Francisca's dream came true as she knelt with her one true love before the high altar of the Santa Fe Parroquia. But in the last will and testament which Don Antonio Baca made in 1755, there appears the name of Manuel Armijo among his six sons-in-law. Doña Josefa Baca, too, drew up a will in 1746, in which she asked God's mercy for having been such a great sinner by having, though unwed, the six children who inherited her property in the order named.

DISCUSSION QUESTIONS

1. The narrator compares the story of Manuel Armijo and Francisca Baca to that of Romeo and Juliet. Discuss how he accomplishes this in his story.
2. Why does the Baca family object to the marriage of their daughter to Manuel Armijo?
3. How does Manual Armijo use the law to his advantage in his dispute with the Bacas?
4. Explain how Doña Josefa Baca accomplishes what the young people could not.

WRITING TOPICS

1. Write a newspaper account of this incident for the Sunday supplement of your hometown daily.
2. Write an account of the several folklore scenes included in this story.

TRANSFERENCE

Sandra María Esteves

Sandra María Esteves was born in the Bronx, New York, on May 10, 1948. Her father, a Puerto Rican sailor, and her mother, a Dominican, had separated before Esteves was born. While her mother worked at a needlework factory, her paternal aunt cared for her. Due to the women's fears concerning drugs and violence, at age six Esteves was sent to a boarding school on the Lower East Side of Manhattan. After completing her primary and secondary education in Catholic schools, she entered Pratt Institute and obtained a B.F.A. in 1978.

Esteves began her writing career by reading her poetry among the already well-known poets in the New York area. Her first poetry collection, *Yerba buena* (Mint) (1980), contains her early explorations of self and community from the perspective of a mainland-born Puerto Rican. Her second book, *Tropical Rains: A Bilingual Downpour* (1984), continues her search for a past and seeks to project a positive ideal for the future as does *Bluestown Mockingbird Mambo* (1990). Esteves is a debunker of identity myths in the United States, even as she creates myths of her own.

The poem "Transference" sets parameters that a woman wants to establish for a relationship with a potential partner. She wants a relationship based on who she is—not on her partner's previous experience with women and life. As she seeks to clarify the nature of the relationship she wants, she offers an invitation for partnership and dialogue.

Don't come to me with expectations
Of who you think I should be
From some past when
You were going through changes

5   I'm not your mother who didn't hold you all day long
Or kiss away the rough cuts when you fell

I'm not your sister who wouldn't play with you
Mashing up your favorite toys on purpose
I'm not the lady upstairs who keeps you up all night
10   Playing Lawrence Welk Muzac
And I'm not your girlfriend who left you flat
The one who promised forever never to go
For whom you would never love another
Or the one who used you for sex
15   And forgot your first name
I'm not the one who beat you
For ten dollars and dinner
Or ate up your cookies and milk
Or gave you the wrong kind of presents
20   I'm not the schoolgirl you followed for breakfast
Or the secretary you rapped to at lunch
Or the whore who tricked you in the evening
With a case of advanced herpes
I'm not your neighbor who hates you
25   'Cause you have more roaches than them
Or the landlord who steals your rent
And leaves you out in the cold
I'm not the meter maid who gave you $300 in parking tickets
Or the kid who plugged your tires just for fun
30   Or the psycho who smashed your front windshield
Or the truck that hit your rear bumper and ran
I'm not the traffic court judge who insists you're the liar
Or the junkie who popped your trunk lock
And tried to steal your spare tire
35   I didn't take your virginity with empty promise
Or con you with a job for sex
And I'm definitely not the one who ripped off your mind
And did not allow you to speak your own tongue
Or tried to turn you slave or dog
40   No, I'm not the bitch who denies you your true history
Or tries to hide the beauty of yourself
I am not the colonizer or the oppressor
Or the sum total of your problems, I am not the enemy
I am not the one who never called you
45   To invite you to coffee and dinner
Nor the friend who never gave you friendship
Or the lover who did not know how to love

So when you come to me, don't assume
That you know me so well as that
50   Don't come with preconceptions

Or expect me to fit the mold you have created
Because we fit no molds
We have no limitations
And when you do come, bring me your hopes
55 Describe for me your visions, your dreams
Bring me your support and your inspiration
Your guidance and your faith
Your belief in our possibilities
Bring me the best that you can

60 Give me the chance to be
Myself and create symphonies like
The pastel dawn or the empty canvas
Before the first stroke of color is released

Come in a dialogue of we
65 You and me reacting, responding
Being, something new
Discovering.

DISCUSSION QUESTIONS

1. Discuss the expectations that men have about relationships with women.
2. Describe the poet's definition of herself by negation ("I'm not . . .") in this piece.
3. What does the persona want her lover to bring to her?
4. Do two people in a relationship form a third entity that is different from the two individuals themselves?

WRITING TOPICS

1. Write a poem addressing your ideal mate.
2. Write an advertisement for the newspaper personal columns in which you describe yourself and the partner you are seeking.

EVA AND DANIEL

Tomás Rivera

The writings of Tomás Rivera use dialogue to establish the identity of his characters and their relationship to one another, to family, and to their community. To Rivera, Chicano literature seeks to convey the wisdom of a disparate yet kindred group of human beings. For more information, turn to the previous biography on page 134.

Tomás Rivera's "Eva and Daniel" is a story of the love shared by two young migrant workers. In a simple and straightforward fashion Rivera describes the dreams and uncertainties Eva and Daniel experience as they contemplate and then carry out their plan to marry. The conclusion of the story is deceptively simple, yet rich with symbolism.

1   People still remember Eva and Daniel. They were both very good look-ing, and in all honesty it was a pleasure to see them together. But that's not the reason people remember them. They were very young when they got married or, rather, when they eloped. Her parents hardly got angry at all, and, if they did, it was for a very short time and that was because everyone who knew Daniel liked him very much and had many good reasons to like him. They eloped up north during the County Fair that was held every year in Bird Island.

2   Both families lived on the same ranch. They worked together in the same fields, they went to town in the same truck and they just about had their meals together; they were that close. That's why no one was surprised when they started going together. And, even though everyone knew about it, no one let on, and even Eva and Daniel, instead of talking with one another, would write letters to each other once in a while. I remember very clearly that that Saturday when they eloped they were going happily to the fair in the truck. Their hair was all messed up by the wind, but when they got to the fair they didn't even remember to comb it.

3   They got on every ride, then they separated from the group and no one saw them again until two days later.

4   "Don't be afraid. We can take a taxi to the ranch. Move over this way, come closer, let me touch you. Don't you love me?"

5   "Yes, yes."

6   "Don't be afraid. We'll get married. I don't care about anything else. Just you. If the truck leaves us behind, we'll go back in a taxi."

7   "But they're going to get after me."

8   "Don't worry. If they do, I'll protect you myself. Anyway, I want to marry you. I'll ask your father for permission to court you if you want me to. What do you say? Shall we get married?"

9   At midnight, when all the games were closed and the lights of the fair were turned off and the explosions of the fireworks were no longer heard, Eva and Daniel still hadn't shown up. Their parents started to worry then, but they didn't notify the police. By one-thirty in the morning the other people became impatient. They got on and off the truck every few minutes and, finally, Eva's father told the driver to drive off. Both families were worried. They had a feeling that Eva and Daniel had eloped and they were sure they would get married, but they were worried anyway. And they would keep on worrying until they saw them again. What they didn't know was that Eva and Daniel were already at the ranch. They were hiding in the barn, up in the loft where the boss stored hay for the winter. That's why, even though they looked for them in the nearby towns, they didn't find them until two days later when they came down from the loft very hungry.

10   There were some very heated discussions but, finally, Eva's parents consented to their marriage. The following day they took Eva and Daniel to get their blood test, then a week later they took them before the judge and the parents had to sign because they were too young.

11   "You see how everything turned out alright."

12   "Yes, but I was afraid when father got all angry. I even thought he was going to hit you when he saw us for the first time."

13   "I was afraid too. We're married now. We can have children."

14   "Yes."

15   "I hope that they grow real tall and that they look like you and me. I wonder how they will be?"

16   "Just let them be like you and me."

17   "If it's a girl I hope she looks like you; if it's a boy I hope he looks like me."

18   "What if we don't have any?"

19   "Why not? My family and your family are very large."

20   "I'll say."

21   "Well, then?"

22   "I was just talking."

23   Things really began to change after they were married. First of all because, by the end of the first month of their marriage, Eva was vomiting often, and then also Daniel received a letter from the government telling him to be in such and such town so that he could take his physical for the army. He was afraid when he saw the letter, not so much for himself, but he immediately sensed the separation that would come forever.

24   "You see, son, if you hadn't gone to school you wouldn't have passed the examination."

25   "Oh, mama. They don't take you just because you passed the examination. Anyway I'm already married, so they probably won't take me. And another thing, Eva is already expecting."

26   "I don't know what to do, son, every night I pray that they won't take you. So does Eva. You should have lied to them. You should have played dumb so you wouldn't pass."

27   "Oh, come on, mama."

28   By November, instead of returning to Texas with his family, Daniel stayed up north, and in a few days he was in the army. The days didn't seem to have any meaning for him—why should there be night, morning or day. Sometimes he didn't care anything about anything. Many times he thought about escaping and returning to his own town so that he could be with Eva. When he thought at all, that was what he thought about—Eva. I think he even became sick, once or maybe it was several times, thinking so much about her. The first letter from the government had meant their separation, and now the separation became longer and longer.

29   "I wonder why I can't think of anything else other than Eva? If I hadn't known her, I wonder what I would think about. Probably about myself, but now . . ."

30   Things being what they were, everything marched on. Daniel's training continued at the same pace as Eva's pregnancy. They transferred Daniel to California, but before going he had the chance to be with Eva in Texas. The first night they went to sleep kissing. They were happy once again for a couple of weeks but then right away they were separated again. Daniel wanted to stay but then he decided to go on to California. He was being trained to go to Korea. Later Eva started getting sick. The baby was bringing complications. The closer she came to the day of delivery, the greater the complications.

31   "You know, viejo, something is wrong with that baby."

32   "Why do you say that?"

33   "Something is wrong with her. She gets very high fevers at night. I hope everything turns out all right, but even the doctor looks quite worried. Have you noticed."

34   "No."

35   "Yesterday he told me that we had to be very careful with Eva. He gave us a whole bunch of instructions, but it's difficult when you can't understand him. Can you imagine? How I wish Daniel were here. I'll bet you Eva would even get well. I already wrote to him saying that she is very sick, hoping that he'll come to see her, but maybe his superiors won't believe him and won't let him come."

36   "Well, write to him again. Maybe he can arrange something, if he speaks out."

37   "Maybe, but I've already written him a number of letters saying the same thing. You know, I'm not too worried about him anymore. Now I worry about Eva."

38   "They're both so young."

39   "Yes they are, aren't they."

40   Eva's condition became worse and, when he received a letter from his mother in which she begged him to come see his wife, either Daniel didn't make himself understood or his superiors didn't believe him. They didn't let him go. He went AWOL[1] just before he was to be sent to Korea. It took him three days to get to Texas on the bus. But he was too late.

41   I remember very well that he came home in a taxi. When he got down and heard the cries coming from inside the house he rushed in. He went into a rage and threw everyone out of the house and locked himself in for almost the rest of the day. He only went out when he had to go to the toilet, but even in there he could be heard sobbing.

42   He didn't go back to the army and no one ever bothered to come looking for him. Many times I saw him burst into tears. I think he was remembering. Then he lost all interest in himself. He hardly spoke to anyone.

43   One time he decided to buy fireworks to sell during Christmas time. The package of fireworks which he sent for through a magazine advertisement cost him plenty. When he got them, instead of selling them, he didn't stop until he set them all off himself. Since that time that's all he does with what little money he earns to support himself. He sets off fireworks just about every night. I think that's why around this part of the country people still remember Eva and Daniel. Maybe that's it.

DISCUSSION QUESTIONS

1. Describe the elopement of Eva and Daniel.
2. Discuss the effect of the Korean War on their marriage.

---

[1] Absent without leave.

3. What was the effect of Eva's pregnancy and subsequent illness on the couple's relationship?
4. Discuss the significance of the fireworks in the story.

WRITING TOPICS

1. Taking the role of Daniel, compose a letter to your commanding officer in the U.S. Army explaining your decision to go AWOL.
2. Write an essay about your expectations for the future and the person with whom you hope to share that time.

FIRST LOVE

Gary Soto

Gary Soto was born to Mexican-American parents in Fresno, California, on April 12, 1952. He grew up in the San Joaquin Valley and studied at Fresno City College and California State University in Fresno. While at college, Soto came under the guidance of poet Phillip Levine, and his writing career began. In 1977 he obtained a teaching position at the University of California at Berkeley and earned his tenure in English and ethnic studies.

Soto is one of the most accomplished poets in the United States. He received the Academy of American Poets Prize (1975), the *Discovery*-Nation Award (1975), the United States Award of the International Poetry Forum (1976), the Bess Hopkins Prize from *Poetry* magazine (1977), a Guggenheim Fellowship (1979), the National Association Fellowship (1981), the Levinson Award from *Poetry* magazine (1984), and the American Book Award from the Before Columbus Foundation (1984). His books include *The Elements of San Joaquin Valley* (1977), *Father Is a Pillow Tied to a Broom* (1980), *Where Sparrows Work Hard* (1981), *Black Hair* (1985), and *Who Will Know Us?* (1990). He has also published three collections of essays and stories, all of them autobiographical, including *Living Up the Street: Narrative Recollections* (1985), *Small Faces* (1986), and *Lesser Evils: Ten Quartets* (1988). His most recent book is a young adult novel titled *Baseball in April* (1990).

Soto is best known for his strong characterization and autobiographical self-consciousness. "First Love," a selection from *Small Faces,* is a sentimental recollection of the feelings that a young man has when separated from his first love. He begins by describing his efforts to avoid thinking of the girlfriend he misses so intensely. When these efforts prove to be fruitless, however, he allows himself to revel in thoughts of Carolyn.

Love

To know you're in love, you have to step outside, walk up the street, and be so alone, so flogged by your separation, that your mind will race your heart and almost win. I did this one fall when I was twenty and so dazed by the separation from my girlfriend, who was on vacation, that I thumbed her photo in my room, confessing my one lust for another woman. Guilt caught like a chicken bone in my throat. I paced the room. I looked out the window. Yellow grass. Scraggly vines. Noisy sparrows in trees that were so thin that nothing could hide behind them.

I was rooming with my brother and two artist friends: one painted monkeys reading books in different places—subways and over-stuffed chairs—and the other shaped and pressed clay into elephant feet which he sold as ashtrays. My brother, an artist also, airbrushed eggs and red balls in the blue of untraveled space. In other words, the household was crazy. I couldn't turn to any one of them, open a beer and spill out my story. Instead I put on my coat, went downstairs and, looking left, looking right, went back upstairs to drag down my bicycle. I started off slowly in high gear, but to keep from thinking of Carolyn, I rode faster. I passed City College and busy intersections into the residential streets with names like Poplar and Pine. Leaves shattered beneath my wheel and I loved the sound. I rode slowly admiring the lawns, the children puffed up in down jackets, and the feathery smoke of chimneys. The October sun was behind an overcast sky, almost breaking through, almost making shadows where there was only gray.

I stopped at a pharmacy in the Tower District and read magazines until the cashier, a woman with blue hair, adjusted her glasses so often that I finally got the message. I bought a candy and, to keep from thinking of Carolyn, I immediately picked up my bike and rode so fast that things looked blurry and confused my eyes. I pedaled in the direction of the canal where I and Benny Jeung, a friend of many years, had ridden inner tubes through languid days of our best summers. I stopped my bike. I stood at the water's edge to look down at the dark water of leaves and sticks. I sat on the weedy bank tossing rocks, and thought of Carolyn and what she might be doing in Canada on her vacation. It must be like here, I thought. Lots of leaves. Cold sky. Few people going about. I blew out a puff of white breath, and thought she might be doing the same by some river, quick with salmon. I saw her in a sleeping bag, the lantern at her side throwing out an aura of heat and light. She was writing postcards, one after another. She brushed back her hair that kept falling into her eyes as she hurried little messages to her family and her new lover, me. Growing sad, I got up and started off again because I didn't want to think about her. I rode to the Fresno Mall where I bought a bag of popcorn at Woolworth's, and walked up and down the aisles that glittered with toys, pans . . . and record albums at half-price. From there I went to Gottschalks where I dreamed of new clothes, bright Kennsington shirts and stiff Levis.

I rode to South Fresno, the place of my birth, and in an abandoned house on Sarah Street searched closets where I found overcoats, vests, and shoes seeming to sleep on their sides. On the back porch sat a stack of news-papers, musty stories from the fifties. What a find, I glowed, and carried an armful back to the apartment where, with my roommates who put down their brushes, I sat on the floor reading about deaths and weddings and housing tracts going up not far from where we lived. The four of us said very little as we bit our lips and read with knitted brows while the newspapers made a dull rustle in our hands when we turned the pages, fanning a musty smell into the air.

5   But after awhile my roommates got up, one by one, and went back to their art. I sat alone with a pile of newspapers, with their stories and ads and brown photographs of women in dresses like frilly lampshades. When the cat nudged my leg, I thought of Carolyn who was probably reading a newspa-per in Canada. She was in the lobby of her hotel, leg wagging as she waited for her friend to come back from making a telephone call in the bar. Again growing sad, I folded the newspapers and put them out onto the balcony. When I came back in, when I couldn't think of anything to do, I gave up and went to my bedroom to indulge, to hover over the photograph of my girlfriend standing by a tree, smiling. Beautiful, I smiled back. I looked out the window and things were beginning to disappear in the dusk.

6   All day I had tried to keep my mind from thinking of her, this first love. Ride a bicycle. Pick up things, put things down. Talk with my brother, with my roommates. Feed the cat fourteen times. Now I was alone, willing to sur-render myself to a deep longing. To do it right, to think of the woman who mattered in my life, I put on my jacket and went downstairs again, but instead of taking my bicycle I walked up the street that got longer with each step. The farther I got from my apartment, the clearer the picture of her became, so that after a few blocks I was talking, almost singing, as if she were right next to me, her feet moving a little quicker to my longer strides, but keeping up so that we could be together for that walk and others.

DISCUSSION QUESTIONS

1. Describe the narrator's method for confirming that one is in love.
2. Discuss the narrator's actions to distract him from thinking about Carolyn. Faced with similar circumstances how would you distract yourself?
3. Did shopping help alleviate the narrator's emotional stress, or did it intensify it? Explain your answer.
4. Discuss how physical or mental displacement affected the narrator in this story.

WRITING TOPICS

1. Write an essay describing the emotions you experience (or expect to experience) when newly in love.
2. Write a journal entry expressing your agreement or disagreement with the adage that absence makes the heart grow fonder.

CHAPTER SEVEN

STRANGERS AT HOME

Much literature has been written by Hispanic authors on the effects of being without a home. For political exiles who had anticipated returning eventually to their mother country, the writings convey a sense of emptiness and loss. For families whose lives and values are turned upside down by the changes that accompany living in a new land, the tone of the writing may be bitter and accusatory. Regardless of how they came to live in America, however, many Hispanics describe themselves as displaced outsiders.

For their children, born in America, the only reminder of their heritage may be wistful recollections shared by elderly relatives. English replaces Spanish and a Christmas turkey replaces tamales or pork. Instead of bringing gifts on the sixth of January, as did the Magi or Three Kings, Santa Claus arrives on the twenty-fifth of December.

The children are caught in the middle, speaking English because society demands it, but reverting to Spanish in the safety and familiarity of their homes. In turn, parents want their children to merge smoothly into the new society, but they resent that the price of fitting in is the loss of their heritage and the denial of their ethnicity.

FROM *NILDA*

Nicholasa Mohr

One challenge Nicholasa Mohr faced in writing an autobiographical novel was that she felt that she didn't have a clear picture of who she was when she was growing up. The American literature she read did not address Puerto Rican children, nor does it address Puerto Rican women today. Yet, although her parents were first-generation Puerto Ricans, Mohr has always chosen to do her writing in English, rather than in Spanish, believing that it stimulates her as a writer and gives life to her characters.

For more information, turn to the previous biography on page 151.

In her novel *Nilda*—itself a novel of dislocation and adaptation in the life of a young girl—Mohr masterfully re-creates the sense of displacement within her own home. The advent of Sophie and her problems absorb the household, and the young protagonist, Nilda, feels that she has lost not only her place at home, but her home itself.

EARLY NOVEMBER, 1941

1   "Nilda, you have to go this morning to the welfare food station with Sophie. I have to get ready to go see your papa in the hospital."

2   Nilda's stepfather had been home, had a relapse, and had returned to the hospital about a week ago. "Can I open the food when we get back home?"

3   "Let Sophie do it and you can help her put things away, O.K.?"

4   Nilda made a face. "All right," she said.

5   Sophie had been living with them for a week, arriving the day after her stepfather had taken ill again. There had been a timid knock on the door and Frankie had opened it up.

6   "There's some lady here to see Mama," he said.

7   Nilda went to see who it was and there stood a tall young woman with a suitcase by her side. "Hello, you wanna see my mother?" asked Nilda.

8   "Does Jimmy live here? Is this his house?" she asked.

9   "Yeah, this is his house, but he don't live here. He's gone someplace else. He's—"

10   "Who is it?" Nilda heard her mother's voice and turned to see the look of surprise and then shock on her mother's face. "Yes?" her mother asked.

11   "Does Jimmy live here? Are you Jimmy's mother?"

12   "Yes, I am. You want to come inside?"

13   The young woman shyly picked up her suitcase and walked in. She looked at the older woman and burst into tears. Putting her hand over her face, she said, "I'm sorry but I have no place to go. My mother put me out. She won't let me stay there any longer. I'm pregnant. I'm gonna have Jimmy's baby!"

14   Victor walked out of the bedroom and stood there looking at Sophie and his mother. "Hi, Sophie," he said.

15   "You know this girl?" her mother asked.

16   "Yes, she's Jimmy's girl from 102nd Street."

17   Nodding her head and half closing her eyes, Nilda's mother said, "Dios mío. All right. Sophie? That's your name? Come on in, Sophie, over to the kitchen. You want some tea, sí?" She turned to look at the children who, by now, were absolutely fascinated by the turn of events. "That's enough. Now go on about what you were doing. I'm going to talk to Sophie."

18   "Somebody raped that girl?" Aunt Delia asked Victor.

19   "No!"

20   "Then what happened? What's she doing here? She looks pregnant. She's got a suitcase!"

21   Victor bent over to talk in Aunt Delia's ear, trying not to shout so that they could not hear him in the kitchen. Nilda watched as Aunt Delia sucked her gums and looked at Victor incredulously.

22   "Is she Spanish? Puerto Rican?"

23   "Russian parents but she was born here."

24   "What? She what?" the old lady asked.

25   "No, she's not. She's American."

26   "Well," the old woman said, shrugging her shoulders, "it happens all the time in the newspapers." Victor turned and went back into the bedroom. Aunt Delia looked around her and, seeing that no one was going to listen, walked away with her newspapers tucked under her arm.

27   Sophie had moved in that night, sharing a room with Frankie and Nilda, and had been living there since. No one knew where Jimmy was.

28   Nilda resented Sophie. "Try not to fight with her," she heard her mother say. "She's older and you have to show her respeto."[1]

29   "I don't like her sometimes, Mama; she can be mean."

30   "You have to try to make an effort because she's a guest and after all you live here. Esta es tu casa."[2]

---

[1] Respect.
[2] This is your house.

31   "She calls me brat and ugly. She always finds something I do wrong. She says I eat too much and I'm too spoiled and that if I had her mother I'd really learn how to behave and . . ."

32   "She's probably teasing you and you take it too seriously."

33   "Does she have to . . . is she gonna stay here all the time? With us?"

34   "Right now she does; she has no place to go. Pobre infeliz,[3] she's pregnant and maybe she's a little nervous."

35   "All right, Mama," she said, putting her arms around her mother's waist, giving her a big hug.

36   Returning the hug, her mother rocked her and stroked her hair. "I love you," her mother said.

37   "When is Papa coming home, Mama?"

38   "Quién sabe?[4] Soon, I hope. I don't know how much longer we can hold out without his working."

39   Nilda walked along with Sophie and held her hand tightly. Now and then she would give her hand a squeeze. When she thought Sophie wasn't looking, Nilda would turn her head slightly to glance at Sophie's swollen belly. Every once in a while Sophie would slow down and stop, bringing her hand around to rub the small of her back, arching and pulling her shoulders back. Her belly would thrust upward, looking even larger. Nilda wondered if Jimmy knew about Sophie and if they were going to get married and have a wedding. Her mother had warned Nilda not to ask anything, so she said nothing. Sophie's mother must be real mean to throw her out, she thought. She remembered a part of the conversation that she had overheard between her own mother and Sophie.

40   "My mother don't like Puerto Ricans. She warned me to keep away from that spick Jimmy. Now she told me she no longer has got a daughter, that her daughter is dead." Nilda had heard her mother mumble an answer, and then Sophie crying.

41   It was a long walk to the welfare food station. They went past rows of tenements and crossed many streets. She had walked this route with her mother time and time again, going to pick up surplus food early in the morning. She never knew what they would give in the big shopping bag. Usually it was mostly canned goods, cereal, and flour. Sometimes they gave clothes and shoes that were very ugly and didn't fit right. Once they gave canned dessert, big cans of plums. Nilda closed her eyes wishing that today they would give something good. Like those good red cherries, sweet and syrupy, that come in a glass bottle.

42   It was a warm day, the last spell of Indian summer, and she was thirsty and tired when they got to the food station. There was a long line of people

[3] Poor thing.
[4] Who knows?

already waiting and they took their places at the end of the line. "Do you think we'll get something good?" she asked Sophie.

43 The young woman looked down at Nilda, shrugged and turned away. Nilda felt uneasy. Sophie had been very quiet and moody this morning and she did not quite know how to approach her. They waited and waited. She knew it was going to be a long time before their turn would come.

44 As they approached the counter Sophie looked down at Nilda. "We are going to get ice cream today," she said in a quiet voice.

45 Nilda couldn't believe her ears. Almost afraid to ask, she did. "What flavor?"

46 "Vanilla."

47 Nilda jumped and turned around. "Vanilla? Vanilla!"

48 "Shhhhh . . . don't make a fuss and scream, now. Be quiet or we won't get any."

49 "Are you sure, Sophie? They never did that before."

50 Sophie looked down at her and with a look of annoyance brought her forefinger up to her lips. "Look now, see?" She pointed over to the back of the counter. Nilda stretched up on her toes trying to see in back, beyond the long high counter. "See," Sophie said, "they are putting it into those white containers."

51 Sure enough, she could see the women in white uniforms transferring the soft velvety white substance with large ladles into white cardboard containers, sealing them, and putting thin wire handles on them. "Just like the candy store," Nilda half whispered. She turned to look at the rest of the people in line who had come after them, wanting to shout, Vanilla ice cream for everybody! Instead she smiled a knowing smile at the lady in back of them who smiled back at her briefly. She's not very excited, thought Nilda. Wait till she finds out.

52 She wanted to carry the ice cream home, but it was packed away with the other things in the large shopping bag. All the way home she wondered if there would be enough for everyone. She hoped the ice cream wouldn't melt before they got home.

53 "I'm getting thirsty. How about you?" Sophie asked.

54 "Uh huh!" nodded Nilda.

55 "I can just imagine what it tastes like, sweet, creamy, and cold," Sophie said. She went on, becoming talkative all the way home.

56 As they climbed up the stairs after the long walk, Nilda's head throbbed and her throat was unbearably dry, but she was happy to be the bearer of good news. Once she entered the apartment she went to find her mother, then remembered that she was visiting her step-father in the hospital. "We got ice cream, vanilla ice cream!" she said.

57 No one answered. Except for Aunt Delia, who was studying her newspaper, the apartment was empty.

58 "We got ice cream today, Titi[5] Delia." The old woman looked up. "We got vanilla ice cream at the food station."

---

[5] Auntie.

59   "Did you read what happened to that couple? They were stupid enough to open the door to . . ."

60   Nilda looked at her and said, "Never mind." She went back to the kitchen.

61   "Sit down, Nilda. I'll serve you a little bit now," said Sophie.

62   "Maybe we better wait for Mama."

63   "She's not gonna mind. After all, we went to get it. Right? Sit down; go on. I've already got the plate. Go on, now."

64   "O.K. then."

65   "Hurry up now before it melts." Sophie put the plate in front of Nilda.

66   Nilda noticed it looked different from regular ice cream, but scooped a spoonful into her mouth anyway. Something horrible was happening to her. She could not swallow what was in her mouth. A lumpy liquid began to drip down the sides of her mouth down to her chin. Gagging and coughing, she spit out the sticky oily substance. Lard! God, that's what it was. It was lard! she thought, closing her eyes. She could hear cackles of laughter behind her. Turning around to look, she saw Sophie. Sophie's eyes were wet and her cheeks streaked with tears as she held on to the sink to balance herself. Her large belly swayed and shook with uncontrollable laughter.

67   Nilda waited in her room. "I hate her and I wish she would drop dead! When Mama comes home I'll tell her and she'll throw her out." She had been crying in her bed with her back to the door in case Sophie walked in. "When she asks for forgiveness she'll have to eat a whole big plateful of lard. All of it! She can't leave nothing over or she can't stay. I'm gonna tell Paul so he won't think she's so nice any more." In spite of her anger she felt ashamed that she could be so easily and completely fooled. "Maybe I'll only tell Mama. They might tease me, especially that Frankie; he thinks he's so smart." A sinking feeling somewhere inside was beginning to interfere with her anger.

68   Nilda heard the front door shut, and voices. Taking a deep breath, she sat up. She wasn't crying any more but she was afraid she would burst into tears again, so she waited a little while, looking out the window. The clotheslines were full of towels, sheets, underwear, and all kinds of clothes. They were moving, flapping, swaying as the wind blew. Living on the top floor of the tenement, she could see down the alleyway in back. She could see the clotheslines going crisscross and zigzag all the way down to the bottom floors. After waiting a little while, she got up and walked to the kitchen.

69   Her mother was sitting with her elbows on the table, her face buried in her hands, supporting her head as she bent slightly forward. Aunt Delia was sitting on one side of her and Sophie was sitting on the other side. Her mother lifted her head. Her eyes were red from crying. "He might be home in about ten to fourteen days. . . . God, I don't know what I'm going to do. María Purísima."

70   "Mama, what happened?"

71   "Your papa is still very sick and he has to come home, but he can't work. Complete rest for God knows how long."

72   "Mama, I gotta tell you something, Ma." Her mother did not answer. "Mama, I gotta tell you something!"

73   "What is it? Go on, tell me!"

74   "No, I gotta tell you alone."

75   "What alone! You have something to say, Nilda, say it. Por Dios, what do you want from me, eh!"

76   Nilda could see her mother was angry, but she went on anyway. "Well, it's what Sophie did."

77   "Well, what did she do?"

78   "She told me we were getting ice cream at the food station instead of lard, and then . . . well, when we came home from the food station she gave me some lard to eat."

79   "She gave you lard to eat, and you don't know the difference between ice cream and lard?"

80   "Mama, she said it was ice cream and . . ."

81   "It was just a little joke, Mom," Sophie said. "I was just kidding."

82   "Some joke, you mean witch!"

83   "Nilda, you are too sensitive. You can't live in this world being that sensitive," Sophie added.

84   "And you are too awful and you get out of my room!"

85   "Nilda! Basta!6 Stop that right now!"

86   "But, Mama, she was laughing at me." Nilda could feel the tears swelling in her eyes.

87   "With all my problems and all the things I have to do, I have to worry that you don't know the difference between ice cream and lard." Her mother shouted, "Go to your room! Go on, get out of my sight!"

88   As Nilda ran out she could still hear her mother. "Ten years old; when I was ten I had no mother and . . ."

89   "I hate them all, I just hate them all!" Nilda whispered to herself as she lay face down on her bed.

90   As she often did when she was upset, she took her "box of things" out from under the bed. Nilda loved to draw; it was the thing that gave her the most pleasure. She sat looking at her cardboard box affectionately. Carefully she began to stack her cardboard cutouts. Her stepfather would give her the light grey cardboard that was in his shirts whenever they came back from the Chinese laundry. She cut these into different shapes, making people dolls, animals, cars, buildings, or whatever she fancied. Then she would draw on them, filling in the form and color of whatever she wanted. She had no more cardboard but she had some white, lined paper that Victor had given her. Drawing a line and then another, she had a sense of happiness. Slowly

---

6 Enough!

working, she began to divide the space, adding color and making different size forms. Her picture began to take shape and she lost herself in a world of magic achieved with some forms, lines, and color.

91   She finished her picture feeling that she had completed a voyage all by herself, far away but in a place that she knew quite well. "At last," she said. "All finished." Sticking out her tongue, she thought, I'm not showing this to Mama. She put her things away under the bed. Glancing in the mirror, she looked at herself with some interest. She was going out now; she wasn't so angry any more.

DISCUSSION QUESTIONS

1. Discuss Nilda's feelings about Sophie's presence in her home.
2. Discuss Sophie's mother's feelings about Jimmy.
3. Describe the incident with the vanilla ice cream. Why was it so upsetting for Nilda?
4. What was the economic situation of Nilda's family and those in surrounding neighborhoods?

WRITING TOPICS

1. Write an essay about the two displacements: Sophie's family's view of Jimmy and his family, and Nilda's view of Sophie's presence in her home.
2. In your journal, write an entry about a creative activity you do for comfort when you are upset or angry.

SUN IMAGES

Estela Portillo-Trambley

Winner of the prestigious Quinto Sol literary award in 1973, Estela Portillo-Trambley has achieved distinction as a poet with the haiku volume *Impressions of a Chicana* (1984), as a playwright with her plays *Days of the Swallows* (1971), *Sun Images* (1979), and *Sor Juana and Other Plays* (1983), and as a narrator with her short story collection *Rain of Scorpions* (1977) and her novel *Trini* (1986).

Born in 1936 in El Paso, Texas, Estela Portillo-Trambley is one of the best known contemporary Chicana writers. Although she has written in most genres, her fame so far has come from her work as a playwright. *Blacklight,* for example, won second place in the 1985 New York Shakespeare Festival's Hispanic-American Playwright's Competition. Also noteworthy is the achievement of having her work produced throughout the Southwest, as well as in California, New York, and Mexico.

Her themes explore problems confronted by the Chicano community, by Hispanics in general, and by most Americans. She speaks of the Hispanic family, of the existential dilemmas posed by feminism, and of the economic hardship faced by many Hispanic families. In particular, through her writing she projects the image of a strong woman whose presence and wisdom serve to guide others.

Estela Portillo-Trambley's *Sun Images,* a musical drama, connects the life of Mexicans in the United States with their memories of life back home. The setting is El Paso, Texas, and on a college campus. In this manner, Portillo-Trambley addresses themes that deal not only with border life, but also those that are contained in a microcosm of the world. The play includes a subtle treatment of political ideology, as well.

CHARACTERS:

Don Estevan
Nena
Chita
Tensha
Don Adolfo
Delfi
Marcos
Carlos

La Malcocha
Beto
Ana Escobar Smith
The Exhibitionist
The Immigration Officers
Crowd on Campus
Chuy
Dr. Refugio Smith

SETTING:

The stage is divided into three sections. Stage right represents a college campus. Up stage in this section is a door leading to a ladies room in a hall in the Students Union Building. There are some chairs and some artificial plants. At the end of this section is a signpost that acts as a divider between sets. It reads "Campus 30 miles this way." A huge arrow pointing towards hall. The second section is center stage. It is the cross-section of a bedroom in house of Don Estevan (called Don Estufas by the girls). Up stage are two doors. One leading to another bedroom. The other to the outside of the house. The bedroom contains a bed, a chest of drawers, a rocking chair, a small table, and a stool. The room is in total disarray. Clothes all over the place, dirty plates on the small table. It is obvious no one cleans the room very often. The third section of the stage is set further downstage to separate it from the middle section. This section represents a guitar shop. This area contains a counter. There is a sign over the wall that reads "Guitars." There are some guitars standing up against the wall behind the counter on a shelf. In front of the counter are several chairs. There is a high stool behind the counter where Don Adolfo works on guitars.

The guitar shop is in the barrio where Don Estevan lives. The barrio is a few miles from the border leading from El Paso, U.S.A., to Juárez, Mexico.

ACT ONE, SCENE 1

Time: the present: Saturday afternoon. Scene: the bedroom.
Lying sideways on the bed is Tensha, a girl about twenty-four. She is wearing street clothes. She seems exhausted as she stares at the ceiling. She reaches out for her purse which is laying next to her on the bed. She puts it on her stomach, opens it, takes out some money, and counts it high over her head. "Five-ten-eleven-twelve-thirteen-fourteen-fifteen," placing each bill on her chest. When she finishes, she just lies there. Nena comes in, glances at Tensha, then crosses to the rocking chair. She is about twenty-eight. She also wears street clothes. She slumps down into the chair and kicks off her shoes. Puts a box down on the floor.

NENA: What a life. My feet are killing me. What are you doing with that
          money on your chest?
TENSHA: It's my hope chest. Shall I buy goats for my dowry?
NENA: You'd be better off with straight cash.

TENSHA:	By the time I go back to Zacatecas . . . (*She jumps up from the bed with the money in her hand.*) With all my dollars.
NENA:	Ah! Méjico.
TENSHA:	When I think about going back to Zacatecas . . .
NENA:	All the fun in Zacatecas is one aqueduct.
TENSHA:	But the boys from Zacatecas. They kiss so good.
NENA:	You couldn't catch one?
TENSHA:	That's why I'm here . . . you crazy.
NENA:	You come here to catch a boy from Zacatecas?
TENSHA:	(*Goes back to bed and counts the money again on her chest.*) No stupid, I come to get the bait.
NENA:	Well, I have my man.
TENSHA:	Does he know what you're up to?
NENA:	Wait until Beto finds out, ¡Ay Dios!
TENSHA:	What do you think he would do?
NENA:	Kill me. He believes a wife's place is in the home . . .
TENSHA:	There's a letter from your mother on the table. (*Nena goes to the table, looks through some mail and finds the letter. She opens it.*)
NENA:	Ay, mamacita. I just bought her a new dress. (*Reads letter. Very alarmed.*) Oh . . . oh . . . oh . . . ¡Dios mío!
TENSHA:	What's the matter?
NENA:	Beto's coming!
TENSHA:	He's found out!
NENA:	He's coming to kill me!
TENSHA:	He won't do it. (*Puts dress on end of bed.*)
NENA:	Mama told Beto about Don Estevan.
TENSHA:	I bet that made him feel good . . .
NENA:	Mama told him about what a nice humane old man he is . . . taking us girls into his house . . . looking out for us . . .
TENSHA:	Your husband knows about men . . . eh? Don Estufas, the philanthropist!
NENA:	He's bringing his horsewhip. Poor Don Estevan . . . Poor me! Poor me! Poor me!
TENSHA:	Why don't you call him Don Estufas like Chita and I do?
NENA:	I don't know him well enough.
TENSHA:	You don't know him well enough? You have been here three weeks . . . he thinks he's one big furnace.
NENA:	It's only in his mind.
TENSHA:	Sí, hombre; a macho mind.
NENA:	Macho do about nothing.
TENSHA:	There's three of us . . . there's only one of him.
NENA:	(*She looks around at the unkempt room.*) We could clean up the place.
TENSHA:	After working for the gringa and fighting off Don Estufas?
NENA:	He cleans up on Mondays, I think.

TENSHA: Well are you ready for a weekend with Don Estufas?
CHITA: (CHITA *enters. She looks at the girls and around the room.*) Hi . . .
           Who's our housekeeper?
NENA: We could clean.
CHITA: Huh!
NENA: Look what we do to him . . . and we don't even clean up.
CHITA: It's his idea.
TENSHA: He likes it.
NENA: Fooling him isn't right.
CHITA: You have a better idea? Go to bed with him!
NENA: No . . . I won't . . . but all those lies.
TENSHA: He's happy believing them.
NENA: Saturday nights are something else.
CHITA: He passes out, eventually.
TENSHA: Thank God, for that quirk of his.
NENA: One drink . . . Poof! He's out!
CHITA: Something to do with the body chemistry.
TENSHA: So we put him to sleep.
CHITA: Coffee and brandy . . . does it every time.
NENA: And the morning after . . . the lies, we tell.
CHITA: He doesn't suspect a thing.
TENSHA: The things we do for fifteen dollars . . . . . Imagine what we go
           through for fifteen dollars!

[SONG]

NENA: We need the gringo's money.
CHITA: The whole world needs gringo money.
TENSHA: Only so much . . . then back to Zacatecas.
NENA: Chita . . . Beto's coming.
CHITA: To kill you, I bet.
NENA: What else?
CHITA: Me . . . I'm marrying my soldier boy.
NENA: You're going to marry a gringo?
CHITA: Maybe next week . . . maybe I quit my job on Monday.
NENA: Then you won't be coming back. You going to tell Don Estevan?
           (*Off stage they hear Don Estevan's voice, "Chiquititas . . . mis . . .
           gallinitas . . ."*[1])
TENSHA: Estufas is home!
DON ESTEVAN *walks in. Dressed smartly with a flower in his button hole. He
           has three boxes. The girls gather around him.*

---

[1] Little ones . . . my . . . little chicks.

CHITA: You got me my blouse! You didn't forget the size, did you? In yellow?

DON ESTEVAN: (*Handing her a box.*) A yellow blouse.

CHITA: Oh, thank you! (*She kisses him on the cheek.*)

DON ESTEVAN: Nena, (*hands her a box.*) some chocolates.

NENA: Thank you, Don Estevan.

DON ESTEVAN: Sweets for the sweet! Tensha, (*He hands Tensha the last box.*) For you my dear.

TENSHA: What is it? (*She opens it.*) Perfume! (*She kisses Don Estevan.*)

DON ESTEVAN: Now . . . are all my little chickens happy?

CHITA: Where are you taking us tonight?

DON ESTEVAN: First we have dinner at Pancho's . . . nice chiles rellenos . . . or whatever you wish . . . then we go to a nice movie.

CHITA: No . . . we go dancing.

DON ESTEVAN: Again? We go dancing every Saturday night.

TENSHA: We like to dance . . . don't we girls? (*The girls all agree.*)

CHITA: (*Deliberately.*) You get tired . . . eh . . . Don Estevan?

DON ESTEVAN: Of course not . . . I am in my prime . . . and I am a superb dancer. (*Does a tango with* TENSHA.) Tum . . . tum . . . tum . . . tum . . . (*While they're dancing,* NENA *opens up the candy box and starts eating chocolates.*)

CHITA: I'll wear my new blouse.

TENSHA: Let's use the perfume.

DON ESTEVAN: Then after a night out on the town. (*He rubs his hands and twirls his moustache.*) We'll come back here and play . . . "Blind Man's Bluff." (*Pronounces it "Bluf."*)

CHITA: (*Pinching him on the cheek.*) You ol' devil you!

TENSHA: Let's go get dressed!

All the girls go into their bedrooms to get ready. DON ESTEVAN *goes to the chest, opens a drawer, takes out a mirror, looks for a comb. When he finds one, he combs his moustache and looks at himself in various postures. When satisfied, he walks downstage and talks to the audience.*

DON ESTEVAN: It's not easy, being a great lover. It takes energy, money, intelligence. Look . . . now, you tell me . . . not everybody has these things. But if we do have them, ah! Look at me. I have three ladies. Three! What do you think about that? Even my son is jealous. He can't even handle one gal! When my wife was alive . . . God keep her in heaven safe and sound . . . and far away. I was a good husband. Walking a straight line. Now I take all the detours. Every man should do it once in his life. (*Girls return ready to go.*)

TENSHA: Here we are!

The girls parade before him for inspection; then he offers each of them his arms. With TENSHA *on one arm and* CHITA *on the other, he exits.* NENA *hesitates, goes back, picks up the box of chocolates and exits as she chooses a piece and pops it into her mouth.*

SCENE 2

Place: The guitar shop. DELFI *is listening to* CARLOS *play the guitar. Another friend,* CHUY *accompanies* CARLOS *playing.* DELFI *comes in.* MARCOS *enters and approaches* DELFI. DELFI *struggles to keep her composure.*

MARCOS: Are you talking to me?

DELFI: (*Cooly.*) You do the talking.

MARCOS: See, I knew it . . . you're not talking to me.

DELFI: Don't you want to talk about Miss Ana Escobar Smith and your engagement?

MARCOS: It was a freak accident.

DELFI: Yeah . . . two freaks got together.

MARCOS: You're mad . . . you've been my girl a long time.

DELFI: Not any more. How long have you known her?

MARCOS: A month.

DELFI: A month! Did you sweep her off her feet or did she overwhelm you?

MARCOS: She tricked me. I think she tricked me.

DELFI: Don't you know?

MARCOS: I don't quite remember . . . I mean . . . how I got engaged. Let's talk.

DELFI: I'm sorry but I have a date with Carlos.

MARCOS: Carlos! You can't have a date with Carlos. You're my girl.

DELFI: Two girls . . . eh? You're beginning to sound like your father.

MARCOS: Never mind my father.

DELFI: You want to have a harem . . . like him!

MARCOS: I don't want to fight. I just want to explain.

DELFI: You don't owe me any explanations.

MARCOS: You *know* you love me.

DELFI: Do I? Maybe you have the wrong tense. Maybe long ago . . . I *loved* you.

MARCOS: You still do.

DELFI Oh! I don't *know.* All good things come to an end. (DELFI *walks to* CHUY.) Isn't that right, Chuy?

CHUY: Like love?

DELFI: Especially love.

[SONG]

(*When the song ends,* DELFI *takes* CARLOS' *arm and walks out.*)

CHUY: (*Walking up to* MARCOS.) She's trying to make you jealous. How did it happen . . . with Ana?

MARCOS: Liquor.

CHUY: She got you drunk?

MARCOS: I woke up in her car the next morning . . . she said I had to marry her.

CHUY: That's dumb. Nobody has to get married nowadays. That's a dumb line.

MARCOS: It's the way she said it . . . so innocent . . . so helpless. Before I knew it, she took me home, introduced me to her parents and told them we were engaged.

CHUY: You stupid! Didn't you say anything? Protest? Fight?

MARCOS: I had a terrible hangover. Now . . . I've got to get out of it . . . I got to make up with Delfi.

CHUY: That's some doing.

MARCOS: They say Ana's very fickle . . . that she changes boyfriends the way she changes shoes.

CHUY: It depends then, on how long it takes for you to become an old shoe. Alli te veo.[2] (*Exits.*)

MARCOS: Todo lo bueno pasa[3] . . . that's what she thinks! (DON ADOLFO *comes into the shop and notices that* MARCOS *is disturbed.*)

DON ADOLFO: Where's Delfi?

MARCOS: Your daughter went out with Carlos.

DON ADOLFO: So that's why you're looking so sad.

MARCOS: She's mad at me.

DON ADOLFO: She showed me the news in the paper about you and Ana. She couldn't stop crying.

MARCOS: She didn't seem to mind a little while ago.

DON ADOLFO: Women play the game better than we do.

MARCOS: Love can be a lot of trouble . . .

DON ADOLFO: What would we do in a problemless world?

MARCOS: I guess at your age, you see life different. It's a view from the end of things.

DON ADOLFO: End? No . . . no . . . it is not an end. In the spring I still shiver with the winter wind. Still, I feel the newness of spring. Just like you do . . . maybe I feel it in a different way. Always like the sun . . .

MARCOS: Time does change things. You're different from me.

DON ALOLFO: I see me in you. New image . . . old image . . . are we not all images of the sun?

MARCOS: If you want to put it that way, I guess we are.

[SONG]

---

[2] I'll see you.
[3] All that is good passes.

SCENE 3

Place: The bedroom. Time : Sunday morning before dawn.
DON ESTEVAN is returning with the girls. He's singing a popular song. He opens the door and takes exaggerated bows as each girl enters. Then he dances into the room, snapping his fingers. CHITA places a finger to her lips and goes into the other bedroom to get to the kitchen. The girls know that she is preparing the special coffee for DON ESTEVAN.

DON ESTEVAN: O.K., gallinitas, it's game time! Game time! Let's see who I catch tonight! It's time for "Blind Man's Bluff."

NENA: It's a dumb game. (*TENSHA nudges for her to keep quiet. Then she goes to a drawer and takes out a handkerchief.*)

TENSHA: I will cover your eyes. Sit! (*DON ESTEVAN sits on the bed and TENSHA puts the handkerchief over his eyes.*)

DON ESTEVAN: Where's Chita? Chita must play. (*CHITA comes through the door.*) Chita.

CHITA: Here I am!

DON ESTEVAN: (*Stands up.*) Minnie . . . Minnie . . . Miny . . . Moe . . . Who am I going to catch by her little toe? (*He starts feeling the air. The girls avoid him. They go over the bed, one by one making faces at him. He misses each one; then they pick up the covers and wrap him up in it.*) Get me out! Help! Help! (*None of the girls helps him. He falls off the bed and unwinds himself. The girls giggle and laugh.*)

DON ESTEVAN: (*Huffing and puffing.*) Now, was that nice?

TENSHA: You're peeking! I can see your left eye.

DON ESTEVAN: Alright . . . alright . . . put the blindfold on again. (*Has a bright idea, suddenly.*) Why can't I chase you all around without the blindfold?

CHITA: No . . . we must play the game properly.

DON ESTEVAN: I'm tired after all that dancing.

TENSHA: One more try! (*He attempts to find them. CHITA pushes him towards NENA. NENA pushes him towards TENSHA. Then they turn him and turn him until he falls to the floor.*)

DON ESTEVAN: Enough! Enough! I'm out of breath.

CHITA: Rest a while. (*They all help him to the bed where he sits.*) I'll get you some coffee. It will wake you up. (*CHITA goes back to the kitchen and comes back with a cup of coffee. TENSHA takes off the blindfold.*)

CHITA: (*Handing him the cup of coffee.*) Good . . . eh?

DON ESTEVAN: (*Winking.*) I drink . . . then I catch. Ajúa! Ajúa![4] (*Cries like a rooster, then he drinks the coffee. Suddenly, his head drops to one side. He has passed out.*)

CHITA: (*With one finger, touches him, he falls into bed.*) There . . . another orgy for old Estufas.

NENA: (*Shaking her head.*) Never fails.

---

[4] High-pitched cry that often punctuates Mexican songs; pronounced "Ahovah, Ahovah."

TENSHA:	(*Yawning.*) It's morning and I need my beauty sleep.
CHITA:	We all need our beauty sleep. Whose turn is it to tell him about the wonderful experience tonight when he wakes up?
NENA:	It's my turn . . . but I don't want to. It isn't right. I'm a married woman.
TENSHA:	You and your scruples.
NENA:	I'm worried about Beto.
TENSHA:	Don't worry 'til it happens.
CHITA:	I'll do it, Nena. It will be my last grand performance. I'll be marrying my soldier.
TENSHA:	You tell the best. Your orgies are just like the movies.
CHITA:	That's were I get them from. (*They go towards their bedroom. NENA turns and looks at DON ESTEVAN on the bed.*)
NENA:	Shouldn't we take off his shoes?
CHITA:	Forget it! (*All exit.*)

ACT II, SCENE 1

Place: Bedroom. Time: Late Sunday afternoon. TENSHA appears from the other bedroom. CHITA and NENA follow. She looks at DON ESTEVAN who is still asleep.

CHITA:	He's snoring.
TENSHA:	He better wake up if he is going to drive us to work.
NENA:	It's terrible going to work on Sunday nights.
TENSHA:	It's better than staying here another night . . .
NENA:	We're going to be late for work. (*CHITA goes into the bedroom to get suitcase.*)
TENSHA:	(*To CHITA.*) You packed?
CHITA:	Yes. This is goodbye. (*She goes back to the bed and practically shouts.*) Don Estevan! (*He wakes with a start and sits up on the bed with a dazed look on his face. There's a knock on the door.*) Who is it?
BETO:	(*Voice from outside.*) I am looking for my wife, Nena Esquivel.
NENA:	Beto! He's come to kill me and Don Estevan!
DON ESTEVAN:	(*Hides under bed covers and peeks over covers slowly.*) Kill me?
TENSHA:	What do we do?
NENA:	He has a horsewhip.
DON ESTEVAN:	(*Looking over the cover again.*) Horsewhip! Do something! Do something! (*The girls pull DON ESTEVAN out of bed.*)
CHITA:	You got to hide.
NENA:	Maybe he has a gun.
DON ESTEVAN:	A gun! I'll hide in your room. (*He goes towards door. The girls pull him back.*)
NENA:	No, he'll look in there. He'll look everywhere . . . he's very jealous.
TENSHA:	Don Estufas, you're going to get it!
DON ESTEVAN:	Who's Don Estufas?

TENSHA: You are, you dirty old man. Let's get him under the bed. (*They try to help him under, but it is not big enough for him.*) No, that won't do. I know, the dress you bought for your mother, Nena. Get it. (*The knocking starts again.*)

NENA: (*As she exits bedroom.*) Beto's going to kill me, then him.

DON ESTEVAN: Maybe, maybe I can reason with him. I merely want to help the orphans of the world.

CHITA: Yeah . . . good looking orphans under thirty. You want to try?

DON ESTEVAN: Now that I reconsider, it is hard to reason with a madman. (*The knocking starts again.* NENA *comes back with the dress. Gives it to* TENSHA.)

TENSHA: (*To* DON ESTEVAN.) Okay, put this on.

DON ESTEVAN: A dress?

TENSHA: Don't argue. Don't you want to be saved? (*She puts the dress over his head.*) You're your own grandmother. You understand?

CHITA: The moustache! I'll get a razor.

DON Estevan: No! No! You can't do that. (*The girls grab him and sit him roughly in the rocking chair.* CHITA *comes back with the razor and a shaving mug. The others hold him down. He struggles to escape.* CHITA *lathers his face. He struggles again and escapes from them. They chase him around the room and over the bed. They catch him. The knocking becomes louder.*)

CHITA: There's no time to shave him. I know! A shawl. It will cover his face. (*She exits through the bedroom door to get the shawl. The girls lead the tired* DON ESTEVAN *to the chair again.*)

TENSHA: Alright, granny, sit down and behave yourself. (CHITA *comes back with a shawl and a rosary. They cover half the face of* DON ESTEVAN *and* CHITA *hands him the rosary.*)

CHITA: You keep your mouth shut and pray silently, you understand? You could stand a few prayers. (DON ESTEVAN *mumbles something from under the shawl.*) Shut up and pray! O.K., open the door and let me handle it. (NENA *hides behind* CHITA. *The knock is heard again.* TENSHA *goes to the door and opens it.* BETO *comes in. He carries a horsewhip. He hits the floor with it.*)

BETO: Where is he? Where is that defiler of women? (*He spies* NENA *hiding behind* CHITA. *Crosses to her and pulls her towards him.*) What have you done, woman?

NENA: Nothing! Nothing! I have not betrayed you as God is my witness.

BETO: Where's the lecher?

CHITA: Don Estevan is not here. He left town a few days ago.

BETO: (*Looking around suspiciously.*) Oh, yeah?

CHITA: Yes, look for yourself. He's not in the house.

BETO: That's what I'm going to do. (*He exits through the bedroom door to search the rest of the house. The girls cover* DON ESTEVAN'S *face.*

The shawl has slipped and his mustache shows. He has a petrified look on his face.)

CHITA: Now, pray your beads off. Your life depends on it! (DON ESTEVAN, *with bent head, prays at a great speed.* CHITA *kicks him.*) Not that fast, you knucklehead! (DON ESTEVAN *slows down with the rotation of beads.* BETO *comes out, looks suspiciously at them, searches around the room; finally notices* DON ESTEVAN.)

BETO: Who's that?

CHITA: That's granny Estufas, Don Estevan's mother.

BETO: Why is she all covered up like that?

CHITA: She's very shy.

BETO: When does she breathe?

CHITA: Oh, she only covers up with strangers.

TENSHA: We girls are like her children.

BETO: She doesn't look as if she's good for much. (DON ESTEVAN *begins to pray on his beads faster.*) Where's your son? I'm going to whip him to an inch of his life! (BETO *hits the floor around* DON ESTEVAN *mercilessly with the whip.* DON ESTEVAN *is now going around the rosary hardly touching each bead.* TENSHA *kicks him again.* BETO *looking suspiciously at* DON ESTEVAN.) What is she doing with that rosary?

TENSHA: She's a very devout person. She prays to a long list of saints every day. That's why she prays so fast.

BETO: (*Peering at* DON ESTEVAN.) She has shifty eyes. Listen, granny, how can you breathe with that shawl covering your face? Or is there another reason for covering your face?

CHITA: Of course there's a reason. She has a bad case of acne . . . very bad case. She won't let anybody look at her face.

BETO: Acne? At her age?

CHITA: It's a new disease in the U.S. . . . . old-age puberty.

BETO: I think you're all crazy. Nena, you're coming with me. Now! (*He hits the floor with the whip.*)

NENA: Yes, dear . . . my things . . .

BETO: Never mind your things. Let's go. (*He grabs his wife by the hand and pulls her to the door. He turns and looks at them suspiciously.*) If I ever catch that old satyr, you tell him for me, I'm going to skin him alive.

CHITA: We'll tell him.

NENA: Nothing happened, Beto. I swear it. He's a harmless old man.

TENSHA: We'll send your things to you.

BETO: Come on. (NENA *and* BETO *exit.* DON ESTEVAN *slides down from the rocking chair onto the floor. He's all done in.*)

CHITA: Serves you right! We should have given you to him!

TENSHA: You have to pay for your sins in this life, you stink pot! (DON

ESTEVAN *gets to his feet and musters all the dignity he can, under the circumstances.*)

DON ESTEVAN: Your girls have no right to talk to me like that! I have taken you under my roof . . . fed you . . . entertained you.

CHITA: And made a fool of yourself. (DON ESTEVAN *immediately takes off the dress and shawl, throws them on the bed. He hesitates a moment and looks towards the door.*)

DON ESTEVAN: They're gone, aren't they? They're not coming back, are they?

TENSHA: (TENSHA *goes to the door and looks out, then returns.*) They're gone and it's late.

CHITA: You'll have to drive us to work tonight, exhausted or not.

DON ESTEVAN: Yes, my pidgeons . . . but last night . . . who did I catch last night?

CHITA: (*Shaking her head.*) You'll never learn will you? (*she thinks for a moment.*) No one.

DON ESTEVAN: But . . . I always catch someone.

CHITA: Not this time . . . so there's no tale to tell. No one can tell you what a great lover you were last night. You fell asleep and snored like a pig.

DON ESTEVAN: (*Confused.*) I fell asleep? (*He scratches his stomach, then his head, and then his moustache.*) My luck! I'm going to make some coffee. (*He exits through the bedroom door to the kitchen.*)

CHITA: Someone has to tell him the facts of life . . . one of these days.

TENSHA: No thank you . . . not me. (*They sit dejectedly on the bed.*)

CHITA: I'm splitting . . . for good.

TENSHA: (*Calls out.*) Don Estevan . . . hurry up . . . we're late! (DON ESTEVAN *comes out.*)

DON ESTEVAN: Here I am, little pidgeons! (*They exit.*)

SCENE 2

Place: The College Campus. Time: One week later. ANA ESCOBAR SMITH *enters stage right with an armful of books. She wears glasses. She sits on a chair in the hall of the Student Union Building and lays her books and purse down. Then she takes one and begins to read. Suddenly she becomes aware of the audience, slams the book shut, takes off her glasses, and walks down stage.*

ANA: (*To audience.*) Hello, there! You know, it's very hard being a female. Especially now in 1976. Can I tell you a secret? Well . . . I'm still a virgin . . . and that's something that's hard to be . . . in 1976. I mean, I tell my friends, "I'm a Virgin." Some of them look at me as if I were a freak. Others look like they're sorry for me. Some just advise me to keep it to myself. You know, I'm beginning to doubt if it's such a good thing to be. (*A college boy walks by. She follows him with her eyes, enjoying herself.*) My mother thinks being a virgin is a great thing. Who am I to argue? I came to college to consume the knowledge of the world . . . to liberate myself. (*Another boy passes by and she follows him with her eyes. He stops in the hall as if waiting for someone.*) But liberation and virginity don't mix well, I think. Anyway, mother says that every girl is bound to lose her virginity and the best way to do it, is under contract. (*Another boy comes and begins to talk to the second boy.*) Well, I didn't come to college to catch a husband . . . of course not! I came to consume the knowledge of the world. (*She looks towards the boys and sighs.*) Anyway I got myself engaged recently . . . just for fun. (*Another boy comes in furtively looking from side to side. He goes into the girls' bathroom when no one is looking.*) Marcos, my fiancee, is a doll . . . but he's giving me trouble already. He's angry about our engagement. He says I should have asked him first, but I thought at the time it was all settled. The morning we got engaged, I told him we had to get married. He had a headache because he had taken one drink. One drink, mind you . . . and then . . . he passed out! (*Snaps her fingers.*) Just like that . . . one drink and he was gone. Well, the next day I told him we had to get married, and he assumed the worst just like a man. What I really meant at the time was . . . We had to get married because I felt like being engaged . . . but he never let me finish the sentence. What are we poor, defenseless, weak, tender females to do? It's a cruel, hard world for the likes of us . . . dainty and gentle as we are. Oh! I got to run! But first, I'll powder my nose. (*She picks up her books and purse and goes into the girls' bathroom. Suddenly there are screams and shouts and bangings. The boy runs out with his pants half-falling.* ANA *chases him beating him with her purse, kicking him, biting him, etc. He screams for help attempting to put up his pants and run. He finally manages to escape from her and she runs after him, yelling.*) "Stop, pervert! Police! Sex-maniac! Stop him!" (*A crowd gathers exclaiming what happened. A young professor,* DR. REFUGIO SMITH, *joins the crowd.*)

DR. SMITH: What happened?
1ST STUDENT: You wouldn't believe it! Some chick was beating on a guy.
3RD STUDENT: An exhibitionist. He attacked her in the girls' bathroom.
1ST STUDENT: That's not the way it happened.
2ND STUDENT: She attacked him.
1ST STUDENT: Yeah . . . did you see him run!
3RD STUDENT   He was in the girls' bathroom!
DR. SMITH: Alright! Alright!
2ND STUDENT: The poor dude . . . he needs help.
3RD STUDENT: She needs help. (ANA *comes back on stage with vengeance on her face.*)

ANA: He went right over the fence and I couldn't find the campus patrol. They're never around, when you need them.

1ST STUDENT: Poor dude!

ANA: (*Angrily.*) Why are you sticking up for him? I'm going to carry some tear-gas in my purse. They ought to hang him.

2ND STUDENT: Help!

DR. SMITH: Are you alright?

ANA: (*Noticing him for the first time. She changes character immediately.*) Oh! I think so . . . I was so shocked.

DR. SMITH: I can imagine.

ANA: It's so hard, you know.

DR. SMITH: What is?

ANA: Staying a virg—oops!

DR. SMITH: You had quite a scare.

ANA: (*Taking his arm.*) It's so good to have someone around to protect you. Your wife must feel so safe.

DR. SMITH: I'm not married.

ANA: (*Elated.*) Not married . . . but how could that be?

DR. SMITH: (*Jokingly.*) It's been hard for me . . . too!

ANA: You're joking!

DR. SMITH: I'm joking.

ANA: What do you teach?

DR. SMITH: Philosophy.

ANA: All about truth and beauty.

DR. SMITH: About people.

ANA: I thought that was sociology.

DR. SMITH: It all concerns people.

ANA: I never thought of it that way.

DR. SMITH: Just imagine . . . a ball of fire . . . in the sky . . . the earth taking shape . . . waiting . . . for people. (Sings "*Before the People Came.*")

ANA: Oh! I can see it! I can see it! Dr. . . . Dr. . . . You are a doctor aren't you?

DR. SMITH: Yes . . . Smith is the name.

ANA: Smith! Oh, my!

DR. SMITH: What's the matter?

Ana: I'm Smith, too! It must be fate. (*She hugs him and kisses him.*)

DR. SMITH: My, you're an impetuous young lady.

ANA: I am really a very nice girl. I take Mama's advice . . . but you're so wonderful, so full of the knowledge of the world. I would like to consume . . .

DR. SMITH: (*Clears throat.*) Well, I am already late for an appointment. (ANA *takes his arm as he starts to walk away.*)

ANA: You must come home to meet Mama and Daddy. Now, you can't say "no." I shall cook your favorite meal. Shall we say next Saturday?

DR. SMITH: I will have to look at my calendar . . .

ANA: Don't do that! Just say "yes." Yes?

DR. SMITH: Well . . .

ANA: That will do, that's a good enough "yes."

DR. SMITH: Goodbye. (*Exits.* ANA *returning. Boys and girls gather around her.*)

1ST STUDENT: You have some nerve!

ANA: Is that what you call it?

2ND STUDENT: Aren't you engaged to Marcos?

ANA: I have been engaged many times . . .

2ND STUDENT: That figures. So Marcos is scratched . . . eh?

ANA: Oh, he won't mind! He wasn't too pleased about our engagement.

1ST STUDENT: Has love anything to do with all this?

ANA: But of course! I love them all madly.

1ST STUDENT: That's the word: "madly."

ANA: I know about love. Of course, I know about love! Don't you know about love?

[Song and choreographed dance number]

Scene 3

Place: Guitar Shop. Time: Two Fridays later. CARLOS *and* CHUY *are strumming guitars.* DON ADOLFO *is polishing a guitar on his stool.*

CHUY: Hey, Carlos, how's it going between you and Delfi?

CARLOS: We're good friends.

CHUY: Is that all?

CARLOS: Marcos doubled-crossed her, and my girl doubled-crossed me. We console each other.

CHUY: Marcos is an old shoe now. He's off the hook. Ana's after some poor professor at the college.

CARLOS: Poor guy!

CHUY: Delfi knows, but I don't think she's about to forgive Marcos.

CARLOS: She will. I know that if my girl came back to town . . . I would still feel something.

CHUY: In spite of . . .

CARLOS: In spite of anything. Mistakes are mistakes.

CHUY: But your girl had . . . so many guys in . . . between.

CARLOS: When we were kids, she used to follow me around . . . all through school. Hasta que cambió . . . hasta que la perdí.[5]

CHUY: ¿La quieres todavía?[6]

CARLOS: Before the world took over. (CARLOS *sings.*)

DON ADOLFO: ¡Las heridas del amor![7] (MARCOS *enters and looks for* DON ESTEVAN *around the room.*)

---

[5] Until she changed . . . until I lost her.

[6] Do you still love her?

[7] The wounds of love.

MARCOS: Don Adolfo, have you seen my father?

DON ADOLFO: No . . . not for weeks.

MARCOS: Some immigration men were looking for him. They've found out about the girls.

DON ADOLFO: Poor Estevan!

MARCOS: I bet he's over at the Green Parrot in Juárez.

CARLOS: Isn't that the place where your ol' man interviews the girls that answer his ad in the newspaper?

MARCOS: That's the place. He's probably interviewing again . . . maybe the federales saw the ad.

CHUY: No, I think it was that guy that came for his wife a couple of weeks back. The one with the horsewhip.

MARCOS: Chita ran off to marry a soldier and Nena went back with her husband. He'll advertise again. He was down, man, when I went to see him. He always gets that way when the girls run out on him.

CHUY: How many girls have run out on him?

MARCOS: Too hard to keep count . . .

DON ADOLFO: It's hard for Estevan to accept old age.

MARCOS: You have.

DON ADOLFO: When I lost my wife. I had this shop . . . my music . . . but when Estevan lost your mother, all he had was a pension, a house, and time on his hands. And, remember when he was young he was popular in the barrio with the girls.

MARCOS: That was long ago.

DON ADOLFO: He'll run out of wind . . . one of these days. Then he'll come over and we'll play checkers, remember our youth, and enjoy the peace in our lives.

MARCOS: When immigration catches up with him, he'll be off to jail or a fine. He's a poor man . . . though he tells it different.

CHUY: Want to drive over to the Green Parrot?

MARCOS: Yeah . . . let's scout around.

CARLOS: I'll go with you.

MARCOS: Kiko, the owner, might know where he is.

DON ADOLFO: Good luck. (*As they're about to leave,* DELFI *comes in and deliberately ignores* MARCOS.)

DELFI: Hello, Carlos, Chuy.

CARLOS: Hi Delfi.

MARCOS: (*Going to her.*) No "hello" for me?

DELFI: Oh . . . did I overlook you? Hello.

MARCOS: Hello again.

DELFI: Hello.

CARLOS: Hey, you two . . . break it up. Are we going or not?

MARCOS: I have to go now, but can I see you later . . . to talk?

DELFI: I'll be here. (*They look at each other for a moment, then* MARCOS *leaves with the boys.*)

DON ADOLFO: You know, he's not engaged anymore?

DELFI: I heard.

DON ADOLFO: And you've already forgiven him.

DELFI: Oh, Papa, of course.

ACT III, SCENE 1

Place: The bedroom. Time: The same afternoon. DON ESTEVAN *comes in looking dejected. He misses the girls and is waiting for* TENSHA.

DON ESTEVAN: (*Calling out.*) Tensha . . . you home? (*No answer.*) All my gallinitas gone . . . Only Tensha . . . she's going to leave too . . . I know . . . when they start to go . . . they all go. I have to go to the Green Parrot when I feel a little better. (*He falls into the unmade bed. He just lies there and is unaware of a knock at the door. After a while the door opens and* LA MELCOCHA *enters. She's a woman about forty. She's wearing an old pair of army boots and an old hat. She wears a misshapen coat, sizes too big for her. She walks into the room and looks around shaking her head. She see* DON ESTEVAN *lying on the bed. She tip-toes over and looks down at him.*)

LA MELCOCHA: Are you awake? (DON ESTEVAN *sits up startled and looks at her.*)

DON ESTEVAN: Who are you?

LA MELCOCHA: Everyone calls me La Melcocha.

DON ESTEVAN: Melcocha . . . I hate the stuff.

LA MELCOCHA: It's good candy . . . sweet and long lasting.

DON ESTEVAN: What are you doing in my house?

LA MELCOCHA: Kiko at the Green Parrot gave me your address.

DON ESTEVAN: Kiko gave you . . . (*He gets out of bed with some difficulty, groaning and moaning. Then he looks her over.*) You look like something the cat dragged in . . . you're old.

LA MELCOCHA: What is old?

DON ESTEVAN: Kiko's not to send me prospects. I go there and choose them for myself. You say . . . he gave you my address?

LA MELCOCHA: Not exactly . . . a young girl answered your ad at the same time. We waited for you, but you didn't show up . . . so Kiko gave the address to the girl.

DON ESTEVAN: How did you get it? The newspaper ad says explicitly that I help young girls . . . not old scarecrows like you.

LA MELCOCHA: I paid the girl my last ten pesos for the address.

DON ESTEVAN: I should have gone yesterday. Look what happens when you don't do what you are supposed to. The girl, where is the girl?

LA MELCOCHA: She didn't know how to get across the bridge . . . so she gave up.

DON ESTEVAN: I usually bring the girls over in my car. Never been caught.

LA MELCOCHA: I waded across the river close to here. Look at my shoes.

DON ESTEVAN: You're one big mess. You waded across the river, eh? Well, now you can wade right back. This place is a haven for young girls.

LA MELCOCHA: Haven . . . looks more like a trap an old man, like you, would set.

DON ESTEVAN: Old! I'm not old!

LA MELCOCHA: They all leave you . . . eh? The girls fool you and then leave you, eh?

DON ESTEVAN: They leave because of extenuating circumstances. Now go!

La Melcocha: You described yourself as a lover of humanity and you don't even let me catch my breath.

DON ESTEVAN: You talk too much! As soon as you catch your breath . . . vamoose! scram! vanish!

LA MELCOCHA: I'm hungry. I haven't eaten in a long time. Point me to the kitchen. (DON ESTEVAN *points and she goes through the bedroom door to the kitchen. Calls out.*) Poor man, your house is a mess! (*He sits dejectedly on the low stool, as* TENSHA *comes in. She sees him and crosses over to him.*

TENSHA: What's the matter?

DON ESTEVAN: Oh, Tensha. Thank heavens you're here! I thought this would be the loneliest weekend of my life . . .

TENSHA: I'm going back to Mexico. I'm not staying.

DON ESTEVAN: Why . . . little pidgeon? Did you lose your job?

TENSHA: No, I quit! I have enough money for a dowry. I'm going back to Zacatecas to find myself a husband.

DON ESTEVAN: Dowry? Husband?

TENSHA: What do you care? All you ever did was chase the life out of us.

DON ESTEVAN: I gave you good times! Presents! I drove you around . . . anywhere you wanted to go. I was good to all of you.

TENSHA: I guess you were . . . in a way . . . but I'm leaving. It was hard enough for three of us to keep you in line. I'm not staying by myself.

DON ESTEVAN: But we had good times. Saturday nights, you remember. I am your passionate lover.

TENSHA: Never were! We put brandy in your coffee. Every Saturday, you passed-out cold.

DON ESTEVAN: (*Scratching his head.*) But I remember . . .

TENSHA: You remember the lies we told you the next morning.

DON ESTEVAN: Lies?

TENSHA: Lies . . .

DON ESTEVAN: But my reputation . . . everybody in the barrio knows.

TENSHA: That was a long time ago. Why don't you wise up! Is life that bad when you get old . . . that you have to fool yourself?

DON ESTEVAN: Will you marry me, Tensha?

TENSHA: No, Don Estevan, I'm young and I want somebody young.

DON ESTEVAN: There are ready-made advantages.

TENSHA: I'd rather make my own advantages with someone my age. Listen, Don Estevan, you're a nice man. Find somebody your own age. I've got to go. I have to catch a bus to Zacatecas.

DON ESTEVAN: I'll drive you to the station.

TENSHA: You've been the best of drivers . . . I'll get my things. (*She goes into the other bedroom.*)

DON ESTEVAN: (*To the audience.*) She's wrong, you know. I'm as a great a macho as ever was. There are many fish in the sea. Women are a nickel a hundred. I must have been crazy, asking that silly girl to marry me. Thank goodness she refused. (TENSHA *comes back with a bag.*)

TENSHA: I'm ready. By the way, there's a woman eating in the kitchen.

DON ESTEVAN: I must remember to throw her out when I come back. (TENSHA *looks bewildered as* DON ESTEVAN *pushes her out the door.* MELCOCHA, *still eating, opens the door of the bedroom, peeps out, watches them go. When they leave, she comes into the bedroom and looks at the room in despair.*)

LA MELCOCHA: Poor man! No wonder he's crazy! Living like this. Men are helpless! They bluster through life creating every kind of trouble. We take care of them, make them comfortable. What on earth would they do without us? (*While she is talking, she begins to pick up and straighten the room.*) I'll have him tamed and manageable in no time. (*She continues her work.*)

SCENE 2

This scene is played simultaneously in the guitar shop and on the campus. Action in the guitar shop is pantomimed, accompanied by a strobe light, to give the effect of a silent movie, while the characters in the campus scene act normally.

Campus: DR. SMITH *walks on with* ANA.

ANA: Tell me more! You're so wise. I want to consume the knowledge of the world.

DR. SMITH: So you've told me many times.

ANA: You say that the miracle of things is people because when they came upon the earth, they brought love. Weren't the other life forms doing well

Shop: Background music of "Before the People Came." MARCOS *walks in, catches* DELFI *flirting with* CARLOS *and* CHUY. *He goes up and pulls her away.* CARLOS *doesn't like it. He gets up and tells* MARCOS *to let her go.* MARCOS *refuses.* DELFI *pushes* MARCOS *away and* CARLOS *and* MARCOS *face each other; start circling each other posing with karate moves. Blackout.*

without them? I mean, the frogs and the deer and the dinosaurs couldn't care less if people were around.

DR. SMITH: Oh, but the frogs and deer and dinosaurs didn't know they were frogs and deer and dinosaurs.

ANA: You mean, they didn't have names.

DR. SMITH: Exactly! Nothing had names.

ANA: Oh, I see. Without the words, love, peace . . . there wouldn't be any.

DR. SMITH: (Scratching his head.) That is a questionable syllogism . . . but yes, you could say that.

ANA: People made up the words . . . Love! Peace!

DON ESTEVAN goes into shop with TENSHA. *They sit down.* DON ADOLFO *comes to greet them. They shake hands:* DON ADOLFO *kisses* TENSHA's *hand. Two immigration officers enter, cross to* DON ESTEVAN *and flash their credentials. Blackout.*

DR. SMITH: Or was it the other way around? Words were still energy, then the people came.

ANA: Words are important.

DR. SMITH: No, not really . . . when you think about it . . . silence is a good thing.

ANA: Silence . . . is that love and peace?

DR. SMITH: Creation . . . the den of creation is love too! Struggle . . . change.

ANA: It's confusing . . . but everybody strives for love and peace!

DON ESTEVAN *is proclaiming innocence. One of the immigration officers grabs* TENSHA *by the arm. She steps on his foot, he grabs his foot in pain. She starts to run out. The other officer catches her. She hits him over the head with her bag; he falls to the floor.* TENSHA *runs out.* DON ESTEVAN *starts to follow her, trips over officers. They all get up.* DON ESTEVAN *runs out.* DON ADOLFO *follows. Officers chase them blowing whistles. Blackout.*

ANA: I feel guilty! Let's go apologize to Marcos and Delfi. (*They exit stage right, blackout campus set. They enter guitar shop.* ANA *ignores commotions, goes over to* DELFI *with outstretched arms.* DELFI *turns her around and kicks her in the behind.* DR. SMITH *goes to the rescue and gets involved in the fracas with the boys. The fight is in full swing, while very loudly, over the speaker, the voice of* DR. SMITH *sings out the last chorus of "Before the People Came."*

SCENE 3

This is also a dual scene, focusing on the guitar shop and ESTEVAN's *bedroom. The shop is empty, except for* DELFI *who is sitting dejectedly on her father's stool. At the same time,* DON ESTEVAN *enters bedroom, and is greatly surprised to find everything in order. There are even flowers on the table.* MELCOCHA *comes in. She is dressed neatly. It is evident that she is an attractive woman.* DON ESTEVAN *is very surprised by the change in her appearance.*

DON ESTEVAN: You look . . . er different.

LA MELCOCHA: You poor man! Sit down. I heard about you being thrown in jail. (*She leads him to a chair. He doesn't resist.*) A man like you deserves so much! Life should be kinder.

DON ESTEVAN: You are right. A man like me deserves so much more.

LA MELCOCHA: You deserve everything. You have so much to offer . . . (*Sings.*) (*During the song* LA MELCOCHA *massages his neck muscles, makes him comfortable, puts her arms around him from behind the chair. When the song ends:*)

DON ESTEVAN: Ah! I need peace . . .

LA MELCOCHA: The girl, Tensha . . . she was sent back to Méjico?

DON ESTEVAN: (*Rather pleased.*) Ha! That's exactly what she wanted! (*Suddenly he jumps up in anger.*) They fined me five hundred dollars! Five hundred dollars! Me. A poor man!

LA MELCOCHA: That is the price of sin.

DON ESTEVAN: What, you say?

LA MELCOCHA: Oh nothing . . . I'm just wondering how you've been.

DON ESTEVAN: Oh . . . I have suffered, suffered, and my corns hurt.

LA MELCOCHA: Oh, sit down, let me look at your feet. (*He meekly does what she asks. She takes off his shoes, and looks at his feet. He reaches out and touches her hair.*)

DON ESTEVAN: Your hair is soft.

LA MELCOCHA: I'm going to get some warm water to soak your feet.

DON ESTEVAN: I smell something nice.

LA MELCOCHA: I'm cooking your favorite dinner. Marcos told me what your wife used to cook you.

DON ESTEVAN: Wife! I don't want a wife!

LA MELCOCHA: (*Calming him.*) There! There! Who said anything about you wanting a wife! I'm just making you comfortable. Let me get the water for your feet. (*She goes to get water.* DON ESTEVAN *watches her as she leaves. At the shop,* DELFI *stands and walks around, touching guitars, etc.*)

DON ESTEVAN: Nice . . . nice . . . She still wiggles quite well . . . good figure. Oh! I like this . . . maybe tomorrow, I'll go interview some young girls. Wife! Who needs a wife!

LA MELCOCHA: (*Coming back with the water.*) Here, put your sore feet into this. (*She places the basin at his feet. He puts his feet in it and sighs with pleasure.*) Isn't that nice? Aren't you hungry? We'll start with some nice soup. I'll bring it, you just relax. (*She goes to get the soup. Again* DON ESTEVAN *watches her.*)

DON ESTEVAN: I got to watch out for that woman. She's setting a trap! I'm too smart for that. I always had a weakness for behinds. Fine . . . fine . . . figure of a woman. (*He closes his eyes and relaxes.*)

At the guitar shop, MARCOS *enters. He walks up to* DELFI *and taps her on the shoulder. She turns and goes into his arms. They kiss as background music of "Gocé" is heard. After embrace, they walk downstage and sit on edge of stage.* DELFI *leaning on* MARCOS *as he sings.*

In middle of song. MELCOCHA *comes in with a bowl of soup. She feeds* DON ESTEVAN *a couple of spoonfuls as he sits relaxed and comfortable. Then hands him the plate, sits on stool and puts her head on his lap. He puts the bowl down on the floor next to the chair. Strokes her hair and leans back and closes his eyes. When the song ends the curtain falls.*

DISCUSSION QUESTIONS

1. Compare the relationship between Don Estevan and the girls from Mexico with that between Ana Escobar Smith and the boys from the United States.
2. Describe how Tensha, Nena, and Chita deceive Don Estevan on Saturday nights.
3. Compare Don Adolfo with Don Estevan.
4. Discuss the effect of Tensha's words to Don Estevan about why she is returning to Mexico. How is Don Estevan affected by the presence of La Melcocha?

WRITING TOPICS

1. Write a drama or musical with a political or social theme with which you are familiar.
2. Write a news article for the local paper in which you report the activities of Don Estevan and his brush with the law.

FROM *A Stranger in One's Land*

Rubén Salazar

Rubén Salazar was born on March 3, 1928, in Chihuahua, Mexico, and moved to the United States the following year. He became a naturalized citizen in 1949. During the 1950s Salazar worked as a journalist for the *El Paso Herald-Post,* the *Santa Rosa Press Democrat,* and the *San Francisco News.* In 1959 he joined the *Los Angeles Times,* where he was assigned to cover Vietnam. He later became news bureau chief for Mexico City.

Rubén Salazar's writing style reflected his journalist's perspective and his observations of life in many different places. He was killed in 1972 after covering a political demonstration in Los Angeles concerning Mexican Americans and the Vietnam draft. While sitting in a bar, he was struck by a police-fired tear-gas canister. Although his death was ruled accidental, many people in the Chicano community believed Salazar was murdered in response to his reporting, criticizing police action against the Mexican community.

Salazar has been recognized for his writing dealing with the feelings of alienation he experienced living in the United States. His introduction to and the following excerpt from his 1970 report for the U.S. Commission on Civil Rights examine the problems faced by young and old Mexican Americans caught in a powerful movement of social change. His writing captures their anger.

INTRODUCTION

1   The San Antonio hearing of the U.S. Commission on Civil Rights which probed into the social anguish of Mexican Americans was born in protest and began in controversy.

2   As the country's second largest minority, Mexican Americans had been

virtually ignored by public and private reformers. There was vague realization that they had educational, employment, and cultural problems. But it
was felt that language was the basic reason for these problems. And, it was
concluded, once this accident of birth was repaired, Mexican Americans
would melt into the Caucasian pot, just as Italians, Germans, and Poles had.

3   Then came the black revolution.

4   It exploded partly from a condition which had been known all along but
was now the basis for a black-white confrontation: the color of one's skin was
all too important in America. White was good. Black was bad.

5   Faced with an identity crisis, many young Mexican Americans—excited
by black militancy—decided that they had been misled by their elders into
apathetic confusion. It came as a shock at first: Mexican Americans felt
caught between the white and the black. Though counted as "white" by
the Bureau of the Census, Mexican Americans were never really thought
of as such. Though the speaking of foreign languages was considered
highly sophisticated, Mexican Americans were condemned for speaking
Spanish.

6   The ambivalence felt vaguely and in silence for so long seemed to crys-
tallize in the light of the black revolution. A Mexican American was neither
Mexican nor American. He was neither white nor black. What was he then
and where was he going? The young, the militant, and the angry wanted to
know.

7   When the Commission met in San Francisco in May 1967, Mexican
Americans walked out protesting there was not a Mexican American
Commissioner to represent them or enough attention accorded their problems.

8   In October of that year, the U.S. Inter-Agency Committee on Mexican
American Affairs held a hearing in El Paso on the problems of the Spanish-
speaking. The hearing, conducted at the same time President Johnson offi-
cially returned to Mexico a disputed piece of border land [El Chamizal],
ended on a sour note.

9   Governor John Connally of Texas, accused of allowing the use of Texas
Rangers to break strikes by Mexican American farm workers in the Rio
Grande Valley, was roundly booed and hooted by Mexican Americans in the
presence of President Johnson. Because the President was there, the incident
was given wide publicity and it marked a rare national exposure of rising
Mexican American militancy.

10   In other areas of the Southwest, the strike-boycott of California table
grapes led by César Chávez was becoming a national and international
cause. Reies López Tijerina's land grants struggle in New Mexico and its
adversaries introduced violence to the movement. There were the high
school walkouts in East Los Angeles by Mexican American students, and
Rodolfo (Corky) Gonzales, head of the Denver-based Crusade for
Justice, was preaching ethnic nationalism. Many Mexican Americans
joined the Poor People's Campaign in Washington, D.C., in the summer
of 1968.

11   For the first time, many Americans became aware of Mexican American discontent. There was talk now of brown power.

12   In November 1968, President Johnson named the first Mexican American to the Commission, Dr. Hector P. García, a physician from Corpus Christi, Texas, and founder of the American G.I. Forum. A Commission hearing which would center on Mexican American problems was scheduled for December 9–14, in San Antonio.

13   Protests helped bring it about. Now the controversy would begin.

14   Some Mexican American leaders charged that Washington was meddling in something it knew nothing about and so would make things worse instead of better. They felt any problems Mexican Americans might have should be solved locally, by local leadership. The younger and the more militant Chicano leadership retorted that the problems had intentionally been ignored and that national exposure would bring new, more imaginative solutions. Traditional leadership, they claimed, had failed.

15   These strong points of view, aired publicly before the Commission met, hint at the diversity of thought and feeling found among the some six to seven million Mexican Americans, most of whom live in California, Texas, New Mexico, Arizona, and Colorado.

16   There are many splits in the black movement. But there's something the American Negro knows for sure—he's black. He can easily define his problems as a race which make him part of a cohesive force. This is what has forged the beginning of black power in the United States. As yet, most Mexican Americans seem not to identify with any one single overriding problem as Americans. Though they know they're somehow different, many still cling to the idea that Mexican Americans are Caucasian, thus white, thus "one of the boys."

17   Many prove it: by looking and living like white Americans, by obtaining and keeping good jobs, and by intermarrying with Anglos who rarely think of it as a "mixed marriage," to these people, Mexican Americans are assimilating well into white American society. They felt uncomfortable about the Commission's hearing because in their eyes it would merely tend to continue the polarization of Anglos and Mexican Americans at a time in which they felt it was disappearing.

18   To many other Mexican Americans, especially the young activists, Mexican Americans have for too long been cheated by tacitly agreeing to be Caucasian in name only. They say they would rather be proud of their Indian blood than uncertain about their Caucasian status. They feel they can achieve greater dignity by identifying with pre-Anglo Mexican Indian civilizations and even the Conquistadores than by pretending that they can truly relate to the *Mayflower* and early New England Puritanism.

19   This division of feeling will continue and perhaps widen. The hearing, however, clearly showed that people who are indigenous to the Southwest seem sometimes strangers in their own land and certainly in many ways curiously alienated from fellow Americans.

AQUÍ NO SE HABLA ESPAÑOL[1]

20   You know it almost from the beginning: speaking Spanish makes you different. Your mother, father, brothers, sisters, and friends all speak Spanish. But the bus driver, the teacher, the policeman, the store clerk, the man who comes to collect the rent—all the people who are doing important things—do not. Then the day comes when your teacher—who has taught you the importance of many things—tells you that speaking Spanish is wrong. You go home, kiss your mother, and say a few words to her in Spanish. You go to the window and look out and your mother asks you what's the matter?

21   *Nada mamá*, you answer, because you don't know what is wrong. . . .

22   Howard A. Glickstein, then Acting Staff Director of the Commission asked witness Edgar Lozano, a San Antonio high school student, whether he has ever been punished for speaking Spanish at school. Yes, in grammar, in junior high, and in senior high schools, he answers.

23   ". . . they took a stick to me," says Edgar. "It really stayed in your mind. Some things, they don't go away as easy as others."

24   Edgar relates with some bitterness and anger the times he was beaten by teachers for speaking Spanish at school after "getting a lecture about, if you want to be an American, you have got to speak English."

25   Glickstein tries to ask Edgar another question and the boy, this time more sad than angry, interrupts and says:

26   "I mean, how would you like for somebody to come up to you and tell you what you speak is a dirty language? You know, what your mother speaks is a dirty language. You know, that is the only thing I ever heard at home.

27   "A teacher comes up to you and tells you, 'No, no. You know that is a filthy language, nothing but bad words, and bad thoughts in that language.'

28   "I mean, they are telling you that your language is bad. . . . Your mother and father speak a bad language, you speak a bad language. I mean you communicate with dirty words and nasty ideas.

29   ". . . that really stuck to my mind."

30   Edgar, like many Mexican Americans before him, had been scarred with the insults of an Anglo world which rejects everything except carbon copies of what it has decreed to be "American." You start being different and you end up being labeled as un-American. An Anglo-oriented school in a Mexican American barrio can do things to the teachers, too. Bad communication can sorely twist the always sensitive relation between teacher and pupil.

31   Under questioning from David Rubin, the Commission's Acting General Counsel, W. Dain Higdon, principal of San Antonio's Hawthorne Junior High School, 65 percent Mexican American, asserted that he felt there was something in the background or characteristics of the Mexican Americans which inhibits high achievement.

---

[1] Spanish not spoken here.

32   Mexicans or Mexican Americans, Higdon told the Commission, have a "philosophical concept" in dealing with life which says *lo que Dios quiera,* "what God wishes."

33   An Anglo, on the other hand, Higdon continued, says "in God we trust," not "this is how it shall be and you are limited."

34   ". . . you have unlimited horizons," Higdon explained to the Commission. "And whenever some situation befalls me [as an Anglo], I say it is my fault. Whenever some situation befalls a Mexican American, he may say it is his fault, but more generally and from a heritage standpoint he would be inclined to say, *lo que Dios quiera.*"

35   Rubin: Would it be fair to say that you feel there are genetic factors involved which account for the differences in achievements, that mixture of genes causes differences in people?

36   Higdon: Well, when you were in my office, I made that statement to you and I will stick by it. . . .

37   The Mexican American child learns early that he is different. Then he learns that speaking Spanish prevents his becoming a good American. It's at this time, perhaps, when he most needs sensitive guidance. Yet, how do some teachers see the role of their profession?

38   Rubin: Did you state in an interview with me and with another staff member that the obligations of the teacher were first to complete paperwork and secondly to maintain discipline?

39   Higdon: Yes, sir, I did.

40   Rubin: And thirdly, to teach?

41   Higdon: Yes, sir.

42   What can a school, in which teacher and student speak not only different languages but are also on different emotional wave lengths, do to a Mexican American child?

43   This kind of school, Dr. Jack Forbes of Berkeley's Far West Laboratory for Educational Research and Development, told the Commission:

44   "Tends to lead to a great deal of alienation, a great deal of hostility, it tends to lead also to a great deal of confusion, where the child comes out of that school really not knowing who he is, not knowing what he should be proud of, not knowing what language he should speak other than English, being in doubt as to whether he should completely accept what Anglo people have been telling him and forget his Mexican identity, or whether he should listen to what his parents and perhaps other people have said and be proud of his Mexican identity."

45   The word "Mexican" has been and still is in many places in the Southwest a word of contempt. Mexican Americans refer to themselves as Mexicanos or Chicanos with the ease of those who know and understand each other. But when some Anglos talk about "Mexicans" the word takes on a new meaning, almost the counterpart of "nigger."

46   The Mexican Americans' insistence on keeping the Spanish language is but one aspect of cultural differences between Anglos and Mexican Americans.

47   Values differ between these two groups for a variety of historical reasons. Mexicans have deep rural roots which have produced a sense of isolation. Spanish Catholicism has given Mexicans an attitude of fatalism and resignation. Family ties are extremely important and time, or clock-watching, is not.

48   Luis F. Hernández, assistant professor of education at San Fernando Valley State College in Los Angeles, has described the differences this way:

49   "Mexican American values can be said to be directed toward tradition, fatalism, resignation, strong family ties, a high regard for authority, paternalism, personal relations, reluctance to change, a greater orientation to the present than to the future and a greater concern for being than doing.

50   "The contrasting Anglo-American values can be said to be directed toward change, achievement, impersonal relations, efficiency, progress, equality, scientific rationalization, democracy, individual action and reaction, and a greater concern for doing than being."

51   Distortion of or deletion of Mexicans' contribution to the Southwest in history books can inhibit a Mexican American child from the beginning of his schooling.

52   State Senator Joe Bernal of Texas told the Commission that the "schools have not given us any reason to be proud" of being Mexican Americans. People running the schools "have tried to take away our language," the senator continued, and so Mexican American children very early are made to feel ashamed of the Spanish language and of being Mexican.

53   The children start building up defenses such as insisting on being called "Latin" or "Hispano" or "Spanish American" because, said Bernal, "they want no reference made to being Mexican." One of the reasons for this, Bernal told the Commission, is that "it has been inculcated" in the minds of grammar school children that the Mexican "is no good" by means of, for instance, overly and distortedly emphasizing the Battle of the Alamo and ignoring all contributions made by Mexicans in the Southwest.

54   To be Spanish, of course, is something else. Spanish has a European connotation and Europe is the motherland.

55   Carey McWilliams in his *North From Mexico* explains that "the Hispanic heritage of the Southwest has two parts: the Spanish and the Mexican-Indian. Originally one heritage, unified in time, they have long since been polarized. Carefully distinguished from the Mexican, the Spanish heritage is now enshrined throughout the Southwest. It has become the sacred or templar tradition of which the Mexican-Indian inheritance is the secular or profane counterpart. . . ."

56   Dr. Forbes noticed on his arrival in San Antonio for the hearing that things have not changed.

57   ". . . the San Antonio greeter magazine which I picked up in a hotel lobby and which had the statement about the history of San Antonio said nothing about the Mexican heritage of this region, talking only about the glorious Spanish colonial era and things of this nature. . . ."

58   To be Spanish is fine because white is important and Spain is white.

59   Dr. Forbes reminded the Commission that "first of all, the Mexican American population is in great part a native population in the Southwest. It is not an immigrant population. Now this nativity in the Southwest stems not only from the pre-1848 period during the so-called Spanish colonial and Mexican periods, but it also stems from the fact that many people who today identify as Mexican Americans or in some areas as Hispanos, are actually of local Indian descent. . . ."

60   Aurelio Manuel Montemayor who taught in San Felipe High School at Del Rio, Texas, explained to the Commission how in his view all this is ignored in the school curriculum.

61   Quoting from a State-approved textbook, Montemayor said the book related how "the first comers to America were mainly Anglo-Saxons but soon came Dutchmen, Swedes, Germans, Frenchmen, Africans, then the great 19th century period of immigration added to our already melting pot. Then later on, it [the textbook] said, the Spaniards came."

62   "So my students," continued Montemayor, "had no idea where they came from" and wondered whether "they were part of American society." This frustrated Montemayor so much, he said, that he told his students "let's see if we can write our own textbook." He instructed them to write papers on the subject, "Who Am I?"

63   "They told me in their words," Montemayor said, "that they were inferior to the standards of this country. That no matter how much they tried they could never be blonds and blue-eyed."

64   San Felipe High School is located in the San Felipe Independent School District of the city of Del Rio, which also contains the Del Rio Independent School District. San Felipe High School has about 97 percent Mexican Americans and the Del Rio High School has about 50 percent Anglos and 49 percent Mexican Americans. Though the Laughlin Air Force Base is located in the San Felipe Independent School District, the base children are bused to the more affluent and less Mexican American Del Rio High School.

65   Some of Montemayor's students, prompted by the teacher's concern with self-identity, decided to work on a project called: Does San Felipe Have an Inferiority Complex?

66   "They studied the schools, they studied the discontent in the San Felipe Community," Montemayor told the Commission. A boy and a girl interviewed parents at the air base and asked them what they thought of the San Felipe schools and whether they would allow their children to attend there.

67   The boy and girl told Montemayor that base officials had them escorted to the gate when they discovered what they were doing. But not before a base mother told the young pollsters what she thought of San Felipe.

68   Montemayor: . . . [a woman told my students] that she wouldn't send her children to [San Felipe] district schools. They had them there for a semester, the neighborhoods were so dirty and all of that, and that the schools were falling down. And, of course, the students were finding this out on their own and, of course, as far as morale, it couldn't have been lower.

69   Many Mexican American youths, despite their low morale, continue on their business as best they can even though lamenting, as some of Montemayor's students, that no matter how much they try they will never be blond and blue-eyed.

70   Others become ultramilitant as did David Sánchez, prime minister of the Brown Berets in Los Angeles, who told a newsman: "There are very few gabachos [Anglos] who don't turn me off. To the Anglo, justice means 'just us.'"

71   And many others, as did some 1,500 Mexican Americans from throughout the Southwest who last March attended a "Chicano Youth Liberation Conference" in Denver will adopt, in their anger, frustration, and disillusion, a resolution which condemns the "brutal gringo invasion of our territories."

DISCUSSION QUESTIONS

1. Discuss whether Mexican-American children today have full access to the educational opportunities afforded to Anglo-American children.
2. Compare the values of Anglo-Americans with those held by Mexican-Americans. Do you believe these groups share similar values? Explain your answer.
3. Discuss the absence of Mexican-American history from the high school textbook mentioned on page 265. Describe the impact on both Anglo-American and Mexican-American students.
4. Discuss the causes of low morale and the feelings of inferiority experienced by Mexican-American students in Salazar's report. What actions could have been taken by school administrators or the government to improve the situation?

WRITING TOPICS

1. Write a report for the U.S. Civil Rights Commission in which you describe the current social climate for Hispanics in the U.S.
2. In a personal essay, discuss problems for society that are caused by racial prejudices.

BITTER SUGAR: WHY PUERTO RICANS LEAVE HOME

Jesús Colón

Jesús Colón (1901–1974) is credited as greatly influencing the development of a Nuyorican (New York Puerto Rican) voice. Unlike most of his contemporaries, Colón chose to write in English about working class and racial issues of his day. *A Puerto Rican in New York and Other Sketches* (1961, 1982) and *The Way It Was and Other Writings* (1993) are collections of his writing. The latter title is a compilation of work, written mostly for the *Daily Worker* and collected by Edna Acosta Belén and Virginia Sánchez Korrol from the essays and memoirs curated by Nélida Pérez at the Center for Puerto Rican Studies of the City University of New York.

Colón grew up in Cayey, Puerto Rico, in a house behind a cigar factory. There he heard the works of Marx, Cervantes, Zola, and Balzac read aloud by the *lectores* (readers) while the factory workers rolled cigars. At age sixteen he stowed away on the SS *Carolina*, bound for Brooklyn. His life was dedicated to the fight for workers' rights and political organization. Colón became involved with the Communist party in New York and wrote a column for the party paper until his death. In 1952 he ran for the United States Senate on the American Labor Party ticket, advocating, among other things, the independence of Puerto Rico. He was a candidate again in 1969, this time for the Communist Party, for the position of comptroller of New York City. His legacy is his unique understanding of New York's Puerto Rican community. In this essay, also published under the title of "A Puerto Rican in New York," Colón reminisces about his realization that social classifications are based on race and wealth.

I still remember the day my teacher in San Juan gave me that fat history book: *A History of the United States*. It was around 1915. I was in the eighth grade, elementary school. I looked curiously at the maps and pictures, and for the first time looked at the oval face of George Washington and the Christlike figure of Abraham Lincoln.

2   Thumbing through the book, I chanced upon a phrase in one of the documents reproduced at the end of the book. The phrase was: "*We the people of the United States . . .*" The phrase somehow evoked a picture of all those people about whom we had been studying in our flat, cream-colored geography book. The people who picked cotton in Alabama, raised wheat in the Dakotas, and grew grapes in California. The people in the big, faraway American cities who manufactured my mother's Singer machine and the shoes we saw on sale. The people in Brooklyn and other shipyards who built the great big ships that plied the waters of the Caribbean. All these people and I, and my father and the poor Puerto Rican sugar workers and tobacco workers, we were, all together, "*the people of the United States.*" We all belonged! That is what the words meant to me, a little schoolboy in Spanish-speaking Puerto Rico, colony of the United States.

3   My eighth-grade teacher was a six-foot Montanan, Mr. Whole, by name. He was very friendly. There was always a fading smile on his lips. One day he was sitting on the wide porch of the Y.M.C.A. All of us in school had been politely obliged to bring in a quarter each as a contribution for the construction of the building. Mr. Whole hailed me from the porch and invited me to play a game of checkers. I sat in front of him, with the checkerboard between us. Somebody in authority came out and told Mr. Whole that I could not play there with him because I did not belong to the white race.

4   That incident started me thinking. In this "we the people" phrase that I admired so much, were there first and second class people? Were there other distinctions and classifications based not only on "race" but on money or social position?

5   Life and reading gave me the answer. Yes, there were classifications and divisions. The rich and the poor. The sugar planter and the sugar peon. And I soon discovered that the rich Puerto Rican sugar planter and the rich American investor belonged to the same clubs and played golf and danced and dined together. Both despised and exploited the masses of the Puerto Rican people.

6   I learned that the Americans did not come to Puerto Rico because of the altruistic and democratic reasons that General Miles[1] had stated in his famous proclamation when the Yankees invaded Puerto Rico in 1898. I learned that a race to gain control of the resources and the markets of the world was then going on. The United States was first getting into this race in earnest around 1898. I learned the meaning of the word *imperialism*. I further learned that ever since the Americans had come into Puerto Rico, our country, which had produced the varied products for our daily meals, was converted into a huge

---

[1] Nelson Miles was in charge of the U.S. military forces that invaded Puerto Rico on July 25, 1898.

sugar factory with absentee owners caring absolutely nothing about the standards of living of the agricultural workers who comprise two-thirds of the Puerto Rican population. A man's sunrise to sunset labor under the burning tropical sun, cutting sugar cane, yielded one dollar and a half a day.

7   I realized more clearly than before that all our school books, except our Spanish grammar, were written in English. It would be just as if you New Yorkers or Pennsylvanians discovered one good morning that your children's school books were all written in German or Japanese.

8   In 1917, there was a big strike of the dock workers. The police were ordered to patrol with long range rifles. Right in front of the school in Puerta de Tierra some of the strikers were marching. It was during the noon recess hour. The mounted police charged them. The dock workers and the Puerta de Tierra women—famous for their militancy—stood firm.

9   The workers were mauled down by the police. One was killed, many were wounded.

10   During my first year of high school, I was told by the workers that this legalized murder was nothing new. In the sugar plantations the owners used to burn a stretch of planted sugar cane, impute the arson to the workers and kill them like malaria mosquitoes.

11   The workers and the course of my life kept teaching me. The workers told me that we were a colony. A sort of storage house for cheap labor and a market for second-class industrial goods. That we Puerto Ricans were a part of a vast colonial system, and that not until colonialism was wiped out and full independence achieved by Puerto Rico would the condition by which we were living be remedied.

12   Colonialism made me get out of Puerto Rico thirty years ago. Colonialism, with its agricultural slavery, monoculture, absenteeism and rank human exploitation are making the young Puerto Ricans of today come in floods to the United States.

13   I didn't find any bed of roses in the United States. I found poor pay, long hours, terrible working conditions. I met discrimination even in the slums and in the low-paying factories where the bosses very dexterously pitted Italians against Puerto Ricans, and Puerto Ricans against American Negroes and Jews.

14   The same American trusts that milked us in Puerto Rico were in control in New York. And the trusts—the fountainhead of imperialism and colonialism, the meaning of which I had learned the hard way—were not only oppressing the Puerto Ricans in New York, but the other various national minorities and workers as well.

15   Today there are approximately 400,000 Puerto Ricans in greater New York. The largest number live in East Harlem, from 98th to 116th Street, between 5th and Lexington Avenues. Then comes the second largest Puerto Rican community, around Longwood and Prospect Avenues in the Bronx. The third largest concentration is around the Williamsburg section in Brooklyn. There are smaller Puerto Rican communities from Bay Ridge in Brooklyn to Yonkers.

16   Why have the reactionary newspapers unleashed a concerted campaign against the Puerto Ricans coming to New York? Why do they describe the Puerto Ricans in the worst light they can imagine? Simply because they know that colonial conditions of exploitation and the cry for their economic, social and political independence have made the Puerto Ricans a freedom-loving democratic people. Their American idol is Vito Marcantonio.[2] Because they are progressives with the right to vote as American citizens, the reactionaries hate them and are trying to intimidate them and frighten them into submission.

17   The Puerto Ricans are joining the unions and the progressive fraternal, civic and political organizations. They are looking for and achieving unity with the other national groups and progressive forces in America today. Increasing numbers are joining the Cervantes Society of the I.W.O.[3]

18   The Puerto Ricans now arriving are learning the power of unity. At the call of Representative Vito Marcantonio, a broad organization of all Puerto Ricans has been established after two great conferences of representatives from fraternal, religious, civic and political organizations. This Convention for Puerto Rico, as the organization is called, has as its main purpose the ending of the colonial status of Puerto Rico and achievement of the civil rights of the Puerto Ricans in this country.

DISCUSSION QUESTIONS

1. Describe the interpretation the narrator had for the phrase "We, the people of the United States." How did he feel as he skimmed through his eighth-grade history book?
2. Discuss the narrator's realization concerning second-class citizenship.
3. Compare the exploitation of Puerto Ricans in New York with that of Puerto Ricans on the island of Puerto Rico. Discuss the reasons for the exploitation, according to Colón.
4. Discuss specific examples of how the author's understanding of the reasons Americans had come to Puerto Rico changed from what he had learned at school.

---

[2] Italian-American Congressman from New York active in the Puerto Rican community.
[3] Colón was president of this society, which was part of the International Workers' Order.

WRITING TOPICS

1. In this selection, Jesús Colón states that "life and reading" brought him to understand the difference between what he had heard in the classroom and reality. Write an essay discussing your own experience with "life and reading" changing your perspective.

2. Imagine that you are from Puerto Rico and that you belong to the black race. Write a journal entry about how others react to you in the United States.

CHAPTER EIGHT

MIGRANTS AND EXILES

Though many Hispanics in the United States were born here, many came to America when conditions in their homeland became impossible to bear due to political or economic circumstances. Still others came to be here, not because they saw political refuge or economic opportunity, but because of war that changed territorial borders. Thus the division of an ethnic group into exiles and immigrants is based upon the circumstances that brought these people to America.

Among the Mexicans, one may find those whose families have lived here for centuries, as well as exiles who came after the Mexican Revolution and immigrants who came in search of employment. Hispanic exiles also include Cubans seeking asylum during the long series of struggles for independence from Spain or because of the Cuban Revolution, Spaniards escaping the Spanish Civil War, and some Central Americans fleeing violence at home. Other Central and South Americans, as well as Caribbeans such as the Dominicans, may be counted among the Latino immigrant populations.

Whether labeled exile or immigrant, these Hispanics suffer a similar plight: How are they to adapt to a new society, preserve the cultural traditions of their homeland, and raise their children in communities that are bilingual and bicultural. Practical issues such as their legal status also come into question. Do they have visas? Can they bring their families from their homeland to the United States? In particular, immigrants focus on issues of education and employment, while exiles concern themselves with the U.S. policy toward their home country and their ability to live and work while they await imminent return to their homeland. And in the meantime, how are their children to be educated? Should these displaced Hispanics encourage their children's adaptation to the new society, or limit it, given the exile's plan to return one day to his or her homeland?

This literature voices the laments of a displaced people. Songs of nostalgia and reminiscence set up the former homeland as a lost paradise. Reality is not imitated, but manufactured from the hopes and dreams of the exile community. Through hyperbole, a golden age is contrasted with an existence that falls far short of the lost paradise.

FOR THE COLOR OF MY MOTHER

Cherríe Moraga

Cherríe Moraga was born in Whittier, California, on September 25, 1952. Though she lived for a time in Arizona and in Tijuana, Mexico, she grew up primarily in California in a bilingual home. Her interest in storytelling and drama began in her childhood. She would sit transfixed, listening to the women tell tales in the kitchen of her home. After graduating from college in 1974, Moraga taught English in a private high school for two years. It was then that she began studying creative writing. Excited with the many possibilities that writing offered her, she used creative writing as a means to come to terms with issues of difference, culture, gender demarcation, and feminism.

In 1977, she wrote one of her best-known poems— "For the Color of My Mother." Shortly after, while working on feminist writings at San Francisco State University, she met Gloria Anzaldúa and agreed to collaborate on an anthology comprising writings of women of color. It was entitled *This Bridge Called My Back* (1981). Her search for a publisher for the anthology took her to Boston and then New York, where she co-founded Kitchen Table/Women of Color Press. At about that time Moraga embarked on a project with Alma Gómez and Mariana Romo-Carmona—to edit a collection of stories by Latina feminists. The result, *Cuentos: Stories by Latinas* (1983), was issued by their new publishing company.

In 1984 Moraga was accepted as a playwright in residency at INTAR (Hispanic American Arts Center) under the direction of María Irene Fornés. She worked on three plays, eventually publishing one entitled *Giving Up the Ghost* (1986). Since then she has also edited a special issue of *Third Woman* with Ana Castillo and Norma Alarcón and overseen the newly revised and translated reissue of *This Bridge Called My Back*. In addition, *Este puente, mi espalda: voces de mujeres tercermundistas en los Estados Unidos* (1988) was published for the Latin American market.

The following selection, "For the Color of My Mother," elaborates on the theme of identity. The poem effectively weaves elements of biography throughout her testimony.

I am a white girl gone brown to the blood color of my mother
speaking for her through the unnamed part of the mouth
the wide-arched muzzle of brown women

    at two
5   my upper lip split open
    clear to the tip of my nose
    it spilled forth a cry that would not yield
    that travelled down six floors of hospital
    where doctors wound me into white bandages
10 only the screaming mouth exposed

    the gash sewn back into a snarl
    would last for years

I am a white girl gone brown to the blood color of my mother
speaking for her

15 at five, her mouth
    pressed into a seam
    a fine blue child's line drawn across her face
    her mouth, pressed into mouthing english
    mouthing yes yes yes
20 mouthing stoop lift carry
    (sweating wet sighs into the field
    her red bandana comes loose from under the huge brimmed hat
    moving across her upper lip)

    at fourteen, her mouth
25 painted, the ends drawn up
    the mole in the corner colored in darker larger mouthing yes
    she praying no no no
    lips pursed and moving

    at forty-five, her mouth
30 bleeding into her stomach
    the hole gaping growing redder
    deepening with my father's pallor
    finally stitched shut from hip to breastbone
        an inverted V
35   *Vera*
        Elvira

I am a white girl gone brown to the blood color of my mother
speaking for her

as it should be
40 dark women come to me
                        sitting in circles
I pass through their hands
the head of my mother
painted in clay colors

45 touching each carved feature
                        swollen eyes and mouth
they understand the explosion the splitting
open   contained within the fixed expression
they cradle her silence
50   nodding to me

DISCUSSION QUESTIONS

1. Describe the events that the speaker in the poem recalls when she was two years old and five years old.
2. Compare her expectations about life as a girl of fourteen with those of a woman of forty-five.
3. What is her relationship to her mother? How did she feel about the kind of life her mother led?
4. Describe the symbolism of her actions with the dark women who come to her.

WRITING TOPICS

1. Write a poem about your mother and your relationship to her.
2. Write an essay in which you consider the issues of gender or race.

FROM *OUR HOUSE IN THE LAST WORLD*

Oscar Hijuelos

Oscar Hijuelos was born on August 24, 1951, in New York City. His Cuban parents had moved to New York in the forties. As a young man, he obtained undergraduate and graduate degrees from the City University of New York. After graduating, while working in the field of advertising, he began to write. For his efforts, Hijuelos won fellowships from the Creative Artists Program Service (1982), the Ingram Merrill Foundation (1983), the National Endowment for the Arts (1985), and the American Academy in Rome (1985), as well as the Oscar Cintas Breadloaf Writer's Conference Scholarship (1980). In 1983 he published his first novel, *Our House in the Last World*. The book is something of a reverse ethnic family autobiography in which he tells of leaving Cuba and of settling in Spanish Harlem, as well as of making a return trip to Cuba and of his suffering from a serious illness afterward. His second novel, *The Mambo Kings Play Songs of Love* (1990), won him the highly regarded Pulitzer Prize for fiction—the first awarded to a Hispanic writer in the United States. *Mambo Kings* tells the story of two Cuban musicians who come to the United States, appear on the *I Love Lucy* show, and play a song with Desi Arnaz. The novel was later released as a film and shown in major urban centers of the United States. Hijuelos's third novel, *Mr. Ives's Christmas* (1995), departs from the Cuban theme and addresses religion and the despair brought on by senseless urban crime.

The following selection from his novel *Our House in the Last World* tells of Hector and his experiences during a return trip to Cuba in 1954. In richly descriptive language, Hijuelos describes the tastes and the scents and the beauty that Hector found in Cuba.

1

CUBA, CUBA, 1954

1   And Hector? For him the journey was like a splintering film. He was so young, his memory had barely started. Impressions swooped upon him like the large-winged, white butterflies in the yard. There were quiet, floating dragonflies, star blossoms, hanging lianas, and orchids of sweet smells. The sunlight, *el señor sol*, a friendly character who came out each day. Nightingales, dirty hens, sparrows, doves, chicks, crows in the dark of trees. Orange-bottomed clouds shaped like orange blossoms, sun up in the sky, big hairy trees: acacia, tamarind, breadfruit, banana, mango, cinnamon, mamey. Rainbows arching between trees, prisms inside puddles . . . In town there were old carved church doors, Christ up to heaven, stagnant wells, a lazy turtle, the sleeping dog . . . bakery smells, white laundry sheets, a laundress. Taste of eating Hershey bar, taste of eating slice of pineapple, taste of eating chicken, taste of eating trees, taste of eating steak, taste of eating flowers, taste of eating sugar, taste of eating kisses, taste of eating fried sweet plantains. "Cuba, Cuba," repeated incessantly, "Cuba, Cuba . . ."

2   "Oh Hector! Hector!"

3   It was Aunt Luisa. She was in the kitchen, reading the dress-shop ledger book. The light of the afternoon printed a rectangle on the table and over her soft face. "Oh Hector, come and give your auntie a kiss and you'll get a delicious treat."

4   He kissed her and she laughed, patting his head.

5   "How affectionate you are," she said and pinched his cheeks. Then he waited for the treat. He loved to eat, so much so that with each day he grew a little chubbier. His legs and belly were fat. His checks, so, so plump, were red. In the evenings he was always happy to sit on the floor with his female cousins, eating snacks given by Luisa. Chewing fried toast covered in sugar with his eyes closed, listening to Aunt Luisa's soft, pleasant voice as she sewed in the half-light of the room. Chewing sounds and Luisa's voice mingled with the street noises outside: clop, clop, clop of horses, insects' songs, a dog barking, the murmur of spirits in the Cuban ghost land. Taste of sugar and bread. Luisa sighed as she put aside her sewing for the moment and leaned forward to touch Hector's face. "You're such a little blondie," she said.

6   Aunt Luisa fixed his drink, which he slowly drank down, savoring its taste. It was so good, with nutty, deep-forest flavors, sweet but not too sweet, with just enough bitterness to fill the mouth with a yawning sensation. He asked for more. She kissed him, poured another glass, and he drank that down. It went deep into his belly but shot up again, from time to time, into his sleep, night after night, for years to come. For some reason he would remember that drink, wondering what it could be, so Cuban, so delicious. Then one day, years in the future, Luisa would come to America, and he would find out its name.

7   He divided his time between the two aunts' houses, eating and drinking

everything in sight: caramel sweets, hard candies, plates of fried pork in rice, bananas, sweet papaya ice cream, leaves, twigs, soda crackers, honey-dipped flour balls, sour Cuban milk, Coca-Cola, and even water from a puddle. At Rina's house he would sit in a chair placed in front of Uncle Manny's workshop and eat his lunch. Uncle Manny was an enormous man with white hair and wire-rimmed glasses. He had a horse face and liked to wear khaki clothing and read newspapers in an enclosure of prickly bushes. He was a bookkeeper but kept this little workshop in the backyard in order to do some silversmithing and watch repair on the side. Luisa and Rina sent him customers from the dress shop. The workshop: a pine shed, boxes of watch gears and tiny screws, coils of soft wire, and a burner used for heating a little pot of coffee. Smell of metal, rubber, silver, talcum, eucalyptus.

8   Now Hector was watching him melt silver in a tiny ladle over a flame. His demitasse of coffee steamed on the wooden counter. Swirling the silver around, Manny said, "You know what this is boy? Cuban blood." Hector looked at the steaming coffee, and Manny laughed. "Not the coffee, boy, the silver. You have this in your veins." The silver swirling. "You know what you are, boy? You're Cuban. *Un Cubano*. Say it."

9   "*Cubano Cubano*, Cuba, Cuba . . ."

10   Hector sat watching Manny for a long time, wondering if the demitasse was full of the exotic, delicious Cuban drink. His eyes would dart between the ladle of Cuban blood and the coffee, and noticing this, Manny let him sip the dark espresso to which he had added sugar and dark rum. Hector spit it out, and Manny laughed again.

11   "Don't worry, you'll like it when you're older."

12   But he drank many other beverages: Coca-Cola and orange juice at Aunt Rina's. In town, at the bodega, some kind of crushed ice drink mixed with pieces of fruit and syrup. All so good, but not like what Luisa gave him. And he was always drinking Cuban water, especially on those trips he and Horacio took with Manny out to the countryside. Manny sometimes did the accounting for a pal of his who worked at a pharmaceutical warehouse. His pal used to give him free bottles of medicine and aspirin, which he would give to the poor *guajiros*—"hicks."

13   "How they can live like that," Manny used to say, shaking his head, "how they can live like that?"

14   And Manny would take the family up north to Gibara to go swimming. That was where, according to Mercedes, Hector got sick.

15   The whole family was together: Mercedes, Luisa, and Rina, the cousins, Manny, Horacio, and Hector. All the women sat under a big umbrella, reading fashion and Hollywood magazines with actors like William Holden and Cary Grant on the cover, while the men ran in and out of the warm ocean. The current whooshed Cuban sand between their toes. There were starfish by Manny's massive feet. His strong hands took Hector aloft onto his shoulders, real high up, the way Alejo used to do, back in New York. He was so high up, he could see all the palms and the Persian-looking

cabanas and the weathered boardwalk, the sea all around him, a curly blue mirror.

16   Breaking the waves, Manny marched out into the ocean, his great chest of white hair foaming. The skies overhead, zooming by. Manny's voice: something about Christopher Columbus and a ship with huge white sails, Indians, skeletons under the water, and the edge of the world . . . And he was taking Hector out deep into the Cuban sea. Hector held on for his life, his arms around Manny's bull neck, until Manny pried his hands free and let him float off.

17   But down he went.

18   "Come on, niño¹, try, try, try, don't be afraid."

19   Hector swallowed more water, went up and down.

20   "Come on, niño."

21   But Hector went down and tasted salt and his throat burned, he swallowed and coughed, so that Manny finally brought him back to shore, where Luisa cured him with kisses.

22   When Hector started feeling sick, Luisa gave him more of the delicious Cuban drink, so good in his belly. But sometimes a weariness confused him and he stayed up at night, listening to the Cuban ghosts walking around in the yard. Or he could hear Mercedes speaking in whispers to Luisa. Sometimes his back ached or his penis felt shot with lead, and he could be in a room, drinking his treat, when he would hurt but remain quiet. If he did cry out, Luisa or Rina cured him with kisses. Mercedes always said, "You were so good, a quiet, quiet boy. If only we knew . . ."

23   A Cuban infection of some kind entered him. In any case, that was what Mercedes always said. What had he done? Swim in the ocean? Drink from a puddle? Kiss? Maybe he hadn't said his prayers properly, or he had pissed in his pants one too many times or cried too much. Maybe God had turned the Cuban water against him and allowed the *micróbios²*, as Mercedes would call them, to go inside his body. Who knew? But getting sick in Cuba confused him greatly, because he had loved Cuba so much.

24   In her way Mercedes made sense of these things. This was what she said about that journey.

25   "We went there to see my poor mama, bless her soul. She was viejita, viejita, so old and happy to see us. There were other reasons we went, for a vacation, you know. Alejo couldn't take that much time off, three months, so he sent us along.

26   "When we got to Havana we took the train east to Holguín. That was a long trip, twelve hours, but at least we got to see a little of everything: the big sugarcane plantations, the ranches, the mountains, the old colonial towns with their dusty train stations and the poor farmers going everywhere with their caged, dirty, white hens. Horacio was pressed against the window,

---

¹ Little boy.
² Germs; bacteria.

looking at everything with big eyes, but Hector was too hot for the whole trip, inside a stuffy train. And, Dios mío,[3] it was hot in those days. So believe me, we were happy when we finally came to Holguín.

27   "My sisters loved both of the boys very much, and they loved my sisters back. The boys were as happy as little mice and everything was pretty: the house, the town, and the flowers that were everywhere. I remember Manny . . . his children came to America last year on a boat from Mariel Harbor. He was a big man, so good, especially with the poor. He died in 1960, young, like everyone else who's any good in this world, but in those days he took us everywhere. To the movies and out to the farm and to the ocean, where maybe Hector got sick.

28   "I tried to be good, but it's impossible to watch the children all the time, with all the running around and playing. Horacio was good, quiet, and minding his own business, but Hector . . . he made me go crazy down there. We would leave him in the yard in Luisa's house, saying, Stay put, but he wouldn't do that. Running around, he got into everything. I didn't mind that, but he went around drinking water out of puddles in the yard. There was dirty water down there, filled with little micróbios, which is why he got sick. We didn't know it then. He looked healthy, mi hijito, my little son. He was nice and chubby, and, little by little, he put on more weight. Horacio put on some weight, too, all those chorizos and plátanos[4] omelets that he liked so much. So we didn't think anything about it. We went through the days in peace, Horacio having fun and Hector so curious and happy. Who knew that he would be so sick? I didn't.

29   "Alejo was writing me nice letters, saying nice things in them, saying for us to have a good time. The only thing he asked us to do was to visit his great grandmother, old Concepción. That's where Horacio and Hector got their light hair. From old Concepción. A long time ago, when Concepción was a young girl, maybe seventeen or sixteen years of age, walking in Santiago de Cuba, she met an Irish sailor by the name of O'Connor. He was very light and fair, with blond hair. He had sailed around the world about five or six times and was looking for a place to settle, was swept off his feet by Concepción, and eventually married her. So her name became Concepción O'Connor, and his blood passed down quietly through the generations until my sons were born.

30   "In any case, we went to see her one day. She was almost one hundred years old. But she was clean and still had all her senses. Her arms were thin, like young branches, and her hair was white, white. But she had young eyes, and was so happy to see us! She always sat in one place on the patio under an umbrella so that the berries dropping from the trees wouldn't hit her in the head. She was something of a celebrity, too, having been written up in the *Sol* and *Diario de la Marina*[5] because she was so old and not yet dead. She was very happy to meet us, and when she saw Hector's little blond head, she got all happy . . . to think that more of the sailor was around!

---

[3] My God.
[4] Sausage and banana.
[5] Two local Cuban newspapers.

31   "And I took the boys to see my old house. It was just like it used to be, so beautiful, except that now we couldn't go inside. A government man lived there and had servants who wouldn't even let us peek around. There it was, a beautiful white house, so nice . . . the kind of house we could have all lived in if our luck was a little different, and if my poor papa did not die. . . .

32   "Still we had our fun. We went to the marketplace and saw a bullfight. And then I showed Horacio and Hector where a witch lived when I was a little girl, and we would pass the time watching the farmers going by on the road. Down the way there was a blind negro, un negrito muy bueno, who played the guitar and used to sing for pennies. For hours we would stand beside him or go riding around; every one of us had fun.

33   "But Hector became very sick and made trouble for me. I don't know what happened. Maybe it was the drinking water there or something in the food, but he got so sick, and Alejo blamed me for it. Maybe I should have known . . . One day we were at the beach at Gibara and Manny was taking everybody into the water. Hector was having fun on top of Manny's shoulders, going deeper and deeper into the water. You know how sometimes you can think of things, they come to you in a second? I was sitting under the umbrella, because the sun was bad for my skin, when I suddenly felt like a little girl, and as I watched everyone in the water, I had the idea that something was going to get me in trouble: I didn't want it to happen but couldn't tell what it would be, just a feeling of wanting to stop something before it started. Like knowing that there are bugs eating up your garden, but you can never find them. That was what it was like. When we left Cuba, Hector was sick but so happy and fat that we didn't know anything. He came back saying *Cuba, Cuba* and spent a lot of time with Alejo. He was a little Cuban, spouting Spanish."

THE CUBAN ILLNESS, 1954–1995

34   They were in New York for a few months when the pains returned to Hector's lower back. At night he called out to Alejo and Mercedes, and they came down the hall to see what was wrong. Alejo figured that Hector was just afraid of the dark, a phase kids go through. After all, Hector was at the age when devils and shadowy animals roam wild in the mind. Horacio had screamed from nightmares at that age. Alejo used to come down the hall and, sitting on the edge of the bed, hold down Hector's hands, say, "Estoy aquí, estoy aquí," "I am here, I am here." He would sit there with a confused expression on his face until Hector went to sleep. But sometimes Hector woke from his sleep with a violent wretching inside, jumping up and screaming as if fighting someone or something in that room. This always made Alejo a little angry, that the kid could get this way, after having such a nice time in Cuba . . . a little kid, "my son." "But don't worry, su papá está aquí."[6]

---

[6] Your papa is here.

35   Other times Mercedes took care of him. She was not always as patient or as sympathetic as Alejo. Sometimes her answer to everything was an aspirin or Alka Seltzer. She'd come into the dark room, ask what was wrong, and, hearing the usual, come back with either a glass of plain or fizzling water. Horacio, who was in the very next room at the end of the hall, used to stay up listening to Hector moan. He tried to understand why no one would take Hector to a doctor, but that was the way things were done in that house.

36   On a bad night, when Hector called out three or four times, Mercedes came down the hall, sat on the bed, and started pounding on his chest, one, two, three times.

37   "Now we're going to get the little devils out," she said, pounding his chest again. "You'll cry until it all comes out." Then she twisted his ears until he cried out, but the devils did not leave. Instead he heard a buzz, as if an angel was standing in the doorway with hand on chin, checking them out and saying, "Hmmmmmmm. . . ."

38   This continued for a few weeks. Then Mercedes finally decided to call a doctor uptown who knew about illnesses and fakery. He was from the Dominican Republic and was practicing medicine in the United States without a license. He came to the house with his wife. She dressed like a widow in black and was the witch part of the team. She performed everything from exorcisms to rituals that cured impotence and changed a man's luck with women. The doctor brought her along to gain credibility with the more superstitious clients who did not trust modern medicine or doctors. He examined Hector and told Mercedes that a specialist's help was in order, but she didn't want to believe him. Too much trouble, too much money. The doctor left some pills and went away.

39   That evening, when the screams continued, Alejo came and sat with Hector, and then Mercedes came. She was convinced that he was calling out only for attention. So she pounded his chest again and told him a story: "You know, child, if you keep complaining you'll never be able to get along in this world, like the little girl we used to hear about in Cuba. She was afraid of everything: shadows, flies, dogs, the wind, and even people in her own family. She was always standing at the window of her house looking out at the people walking by, but she wouldn't go out herself. She was so afraid, the slightest noise made her cry out for help, and someone would come along and tell her, 'You have to get along by yourself,' the way I'm telling you, child. And she said yes, but as the years went by and all her friends went to school and grew up, she never left her house. Soon she was a young woman, unmarried and without a novio. Then more years passed and she became an old woman, still unmarried. But she was lonely and called for people to help her, but no one came because she had been calling out all her life. So she finally got her nerve back, and having nothing to lose, she went outside. You know what happened? When she left the house by herself, she was run over by a truck and died."

40   Laughing, she took hold of Hector's hands and squeezed his wrists. Pounding his chest, she said, "In the morning you're going to wake up and

everything bad inside of you will have gone away." Then she left him and went back to bed.

41   Afraid of getting into trouble or being pounded, Hector didn't call out to her again. He tried to fall asleep. Finally, after a long time, he began to dream about the ocean and Spanish galleons with foamy decks, and he could feel the mattress under him soaked and cakey as if crystal wafers had been broken. He dreamed about the whoosh of the Cuban current, Manny's laughter, Mercedes's voice, and he touched his hands to the bed, which was all wet, and in the middle of the dream he woke up again, calling out, "Mama, Mama," but it was Horacio who came instead. And he really yelled, because Hector had been urinating blood.

42   In the morning Mercedes was in a panic to take Hector to the hospital. "I should've known how my luck would go," she kept saying. The kid looked sort of healthy. He was fat; his limbs and belly had bloated out, and he slept like a turtle on his back. It hurt him to move. Things were dark . . . His muscles really hurt, he was boneless, and he felt like soaked rags inside. Horacio tried to carry him out, but Hector was too heavy. Mercedes went to the window. There were kids playing stickball outside on the street, and she called to them, "Please get me a taxi," and they got him out into a cab.

43   At the hospital Mercedes and Horacio waited in the hall outside the examination room where all the complicated tests were being performed. Nurses pushed many geared machines with screens and tubes in and out of rooms. Mercedes looked down into her cupped hands, trying to have faith in science, about which she knew almost nothing. When the machines passed she looked at them in awe, as if they were saintly coffins. And she nodded to the doctors, who knew all the baffling secrets of the human body. All these machines were so new, not like what she had seen in Holguín. Medicine in Holguín was nineteenth-century medicine. People died easily. But here in America? The machines would help Hector. Miraculously, they would stop the blood, heal the broken vessels, purify the internal organs. Poor Mercedes knew practically nothing about the body, only that the heart could burst and blood was very important. And that the soul resided in the backbone and that real prayer could turn God's head so that he would squeeze out cures. She knew all kinds of old wives' tales about the curative properties of rosaries, holy water, and dreams. The power of eucalyptus, garlic, and lilies—hit-and-miss stuff that sometimes worked. Mercedes saw the body as a mystery, like a huge house with winding halls and endless rooms where food was eaten and blood pumped and where little monsters like micróbios swarmed in thick streams through the halls, a house where the walls were on the verge of collapse. She had the kind of faith in science that the ignorant have: It will do everything. She had a faith like the faith hoods with knife wounds that spill their guts have, who come to the hospitals thinking they won't die. They come walking in nonchalantly and then fall to the floor, dead.

44   Horacio drew pictures, and Mercedes prayed into the streams of thought that passed through her mind. She was thinking that Alejo was going to hit

her, call her no good, send her away, or prove her crazy. She thought about what Buita would say, that she was not fit to be a mother. She remembered the time when Buita accused her of poisoning Horacio, and Buita's threats of sending her to the asylum. Would these things happen? No, he'll get better, don't you worry. She kept telling Horacio, "He'll get better." But after a while a doctor came out and told her bluntly, "Señora Santinio, your child is most gravely ill." For hours she remained motionless, thinking about the children she knew in Cuba who died. Tuberculosis and yellow fever were the big killers. Overnight a bad fever would bring on pneumonia, and by the morning the child would be dead. Names came to mind: poor Theodocia, poor Alphonso, poor Pedro, poor Mariaelena. For a moment, Cuba became a place of disease and death. She saw tiny coffins, cemetery stones, flowers, stoic-faced families walking through cemetery gates and down winding paths, heads bowed; she saw children crying and her mother crying. She saw her father's funeral winding through the cobblestone streets of Holguín.

45   Occasionally a nurse who knew Spanish came by to speak to her, but this did nothing to allay her fears. A terrible infection had spread through Hector's body. A doctor elaborated, and this was translated by the nurse: "He may have a bad inflammation of the kidneys. This condition has gone on for months. His kidneys do not work, nothing works. He cannot get the poison out of his system. He's bloated with dirty water, and it's everywhere inside him. Already the infection has spread to his liver and heart."

46   The doctor was holding a folder that would grow thick over the years with the bird script of specialists. Three hundred pages of blood pressure and pulse readings, diagnosis, appraisal of blood samples and urinalysis . . . *All from the dirty water of Cuba?*

47   "Just tell the Señora," the doctor said, "that we don't know what will happen."

48   The room was cheerless with no windows. There were two doors with wire windows. Around eight o'clock, Alejo came in. He had been at the hotel when a family friend went to get him. He looked very confused; he would not say a word to Mercedes. She called out his name, but he did not answer. He was at the desk signing papers and presenting union insurance forms and the like. There were many questions. Citizen? Yes. Occupation? Cook. Age? Forty-two. Birthplace? San Pedro, Cuba. Date? January 17, 1912. Faith? Catholic. (*Worried? Yes, yes, yes, I'll kill that witch!*)

49   He stood patiently by the desk, smoking one cigarette after another. He signed forms, shook his head, blew smoke from his mouth. When the nurse left, Mercedes went over to him and rested her head on his shoulders. She was waiting to be lifted away from the situation, but he told her, "This is your fault, no one else's."

50   Horacio was falling asleep in a chair. His eyes kept closing and opening. In his striped shirt, he looked like a tomcat having dreams. Hector was going to die. He was sure it was going to happen. Then he would sing at the funeral. In the next few days he would go to the funeral parlors with Alejo,

pricing coffins. Just a few weeks before, Horacio had punched Hector around in anger. He came home, and boom! he hit Hector in the face and turned the lights off and twisted his arm. It was really nothing, but when he thought Hector might die, then every thought swirled into the fear that the dead would come back to get revenge. He did not like to think about it. He remained curled up in his seat, trying to sleep, but kept flinching each time he saw his pop's face and felt the sadness, thick in that room. He knew, too, things would explode once they got home.

51   Alejo sat beside Horacio, his brown felt, black-banded hat in his hands. Mercedes was beside him, but did not say a word. She kept looking off into the dark hallway, thinking about the illness. It had come almost supernaturally from the Cuban water, making her look bad before Alejo. Micróbios malos, little malicious spirits had penetrated Hector's flesh. She shook her head in confusion. The doctor said he got sick from drinking something bad. Water from the puddle? Water dripping from branches in the yard? All she could do was sit there terrified, whispering, "No me diga, no me diga"— "Don't tell me, don't tell me." She was watching the hall and Alejo's exhausted face, wishing he would move his hand a few inches closer to hers.

52   They remained overnight. Around two the next afternoon, a nurse led them to the room where Hector was sleeping. He was propped up, and there were needles and tubes of blood and more tubes sticking out from his nose. There was some kind of catheter shoved up his penis, and a thick tube coming out of his ass. Alejo looked him over for a moment and then left the room. Mercedes made the sign of the cross. Horacio stood, just watching. Hector seemed to him to be asleep, but he could also be near the land of the dead. A nurse called them out and said they might as well go home, and so they left the hospital.

53   They spent the evening with company. A Cuban family from next door brought them dinner in pots and casserole dishes, and everyone sat in the living room, eating and making small talk. Alejo disappeared. He would be gone for three days. Later, Mercedes's friend, Mary, invited Horacio upstairs to watch their television set, which he did. And Mercedes passed her time in bed, nervous and shaking, trying to sleep.

54   After a month they sent Hector to a hospital in Connecticut that was a terminal home for children. It was near Hartford, and there was a convenient cemetery along the way, shaded by drooping willow trees and dotted with white- and blue-streaked tombstones. The road curved into an estate of hilly greens, duck ponds, stone walks, and benches. It was very beautiful. Hector stayed in a ward at the end of a long corridor. There were two rows of simple metal beds and windows high up on the bare walls. Not one of the kids could leave the building. To get into the ward, you had to get past a guard and three double doors. Even the sunlight seemed to sneak in clandestinely, illuminating the faces of the other children like little El Dorados. The patients were innocent children. Most were filled with water and bad air

and with micróbios. They came to this place from all over the East Coast, and there was even a little girl with pigtails who came from California. The children were very sick and had to take pills five times a day and were required to piss in bedpans, whose contents were examined under microscopes. Blood samples, ugly in thick hypos, were taken every week. Gas was always being administered through tubes into the noses of the children, and metallic rods were shoved up into the privates, rods so cold and violating that the children's bones would leave their bodies and walk around in the outer hall waiting for the flesh's temperature to rise again. Little adorable girls, who would have certainly grown up to be real beauties, went to sleep without a mark on their faces and woke in the morning black and blue, as if they had received the worst beatings. Then they became pale like fish and started to cry. Some crawled along the floor like lizards, while others ran wildly, banging into the walls and shaking. And when the nurses came by with their medicines, the children crawled into shelves and, wracked with pain, spoke to themselves, asking to be helped. If a beam of sunshine shot through the window, spotlighting the floor, they would crawl in it, letting it warm their insides. They would sail around the floors in their boats of light, until they could not move. The pretty girls sang until their bellies cramped and they keeled over and the crying began again. Sometimes at night two men in white hats, dressed like garbage collectors, came into the ward and would lift one of the sleeping children quietly out of bed, put him in a bag, and carry him off. In the morning one of the nurses would calmly make the bed of the missing child, without so much as a word to the kids. But they knew. Another one gone to the skeletons, vanished like so many other things: like the shaky sunlight, sucked into the mirrors and never returned, like toys and tiny shoes and dolls and mirrors, one second there and then poof! gone. Like the Superman funny books! Like Mama and Papa! Like their homes and the whole world and the sun, poof! gone so fast, pulled out from under them.

55   But they had their fun. They had a television set that was the greatest wonder on Earth. Howdy Doody was a mannequin and he looked just like one of them, except Howdy could still walk around. And now and then the nurse took everyone down the corridor and let them stand on a bench to look out the window, through which they sometimes could see snow falling over the meadow and the countryside.

56   The parents came into the hospital on visiting days. The kids who were well enough were brought down the long hallway, into a visiting room. The parents sat facing the children and did not always like what they could see. The parents had faces like rubber masks stretched out on nails. They spoke quietly and gave presents but could not kiss the kids because their kisses carried too many micróbios.

57   Hector was lucky. After the third or fourth month he was allowed to see Mercedes. She started to come up every couple of weeks on Sundays, with a friend from down the street who was married to a gangster, or with Mary, who had a black Oldsmobile. The nurse would come down the long hallway

with Hector and put him into the room with the screen wall. Then, after a time, he was improved enough to sit face to face with her. They would sit on a bench by the window. Hector had no idea what was going on. She would hold him while he squirmed in her arms. He knew her face, recognized the jittery voice. Sometimes she didn't look him in the eyes and just started speaking her Spanish so fast, fast, while Hector wondered where the rest of his family and their friends had gone. He kept seeing Alejo in the shadows, but Alejo was never there. And when he asked Mercedes for Pop, she always grew uncomfortable, spoke about the weather, gossip, or the neighbors. Sometimes, at these moments, he noticed she had bruises under her eyes.

58 "Your papa," she would say in Spanish, "they won't let him in here. They say he has a cold and can't come in. He's standing outside."

59 Once she went so far as to show him the window facing the field and in the distance, a stark denuded tree about which she said, "See him over there, he's smoking a cigarette. They won't let him in until he's finished."

60 But he never finished the cigarettes and never came inside to visit Hector, who wanted to see him very much.

61 Hector looked everywhere for Alejo, squirming in Mercedes's arms and trying to break free from her grasp. No matter how hard Mercedes tried to take care of Hector she would always lose. Even though she often visited him, in the future Hector would swear that it was Alejo who made the trip every weekend, showering him with toys he got from a neighbor in the building. He would recall Alejo removing his hat by one of the large, arched, yellow windows in the hallway. Alejo with packages of gifts. Alejo kissing him. Alejo with the most concerned expression on his face. He swore he heard Alejo's soft voice saying, "Estoy aquí"—"I am here" and "I nearly died when you got sick," over the hissing radiator noises. He would remember Alejo walking through the ward of the terminal home, tipping his hat to the nurses and the staff, remember looking forward to the next week, an interminable length of time, and seeing Alejo again.

62 "Sure, Pop came every week," he would say, years later, to Horacio.

63 "He never came to see you."

64 "Sure he did. I saw him myself."

65 "Listen brother, I have no reason to lie to you. He never showed up to see you even once, not even once, because he was always out on those Sundays having a good time."

66 "Yeah, well you're just jealous."

67 "Well, you take it for the truth, brother."

68 Hector wanted to see Alejo because he remembered the good days before the illness, how Alejo emptied rooms of their sadness and used to let him sleep beside him and brought him presents and took him walking in the park on spring days and did not once fall down. Alejo wasn't like Mercedes, who filled the house with nervousness and worry. She had the high cackling laugh, the crazy eyes, she started the arguing, and she made Alejo turn red in the face and pant.

69   So maybe Hector did see Alejo in the shadows or in the light that fell onto the bedsheets or onto the walls of the hospital. He believed that Alejo had shown up even though everybody in the world swore differently. (And where was Alejo? He passed his days holed up with friends, getting stewed and worrying about bills, and crying about human mortality and about his sick kid, made sick by that woman, a thorn in his side, who couldn't even take care of the boy for a few lousy months, crying about his son named after his dead brother and now ready to go into the next world, "no, that kid isn't going to . . . no, give me a drink . . . ah, qué bueno,[7] nothing to fill up the empty like a drink . . . qué bueno.")

70   Alejo's presence made Hector feel calm, but Mercedes's presence was a punishment. The ordeal made her overly strict and protective. The few hours she saw him, she spent reminding him about how he almost died. And then she would go away, and he would be left alone, murmuring, "Cuba, Cuba . . ."

71   And that was the other thing. The origin of the disease. Cuba, as Mercedes always said. "The water made you sick." Cuba gave the bad disease. Cuba gave the drunk father. Cuba gave the crazy mother. Years later all these would entwine to make Hector think that Cuba had something against him. That it made him sick and pale . . . and excluded from that life that happy Cubans were supposed to have.

72   "Cuba, Cuba . . ."

73   Even the nurses made something of this. Hector, being a little Cuban, didn't speak much English. The nurses figured they would help him by teaching him English. After all, he was blond and fair and didn't look Spanish. There was one nurse who took special care of him: meals, bedpans, injections, tubes.

74   "Do you know something," she said to him, "you're very stupid for not speaking in English. This is your country. You live here and should know the language."

75   To teach him English she would lock him up in a closet. He would be quiet for a while then get scared and start banging on the door. She'd say, "Not until you say, 'Please let me out!'" But he wouldn't even try. He'd pull on the door of the closet and cry out in Spanish. He was afraid: All the clothes on the shelves were haunted. They had belonged at one time or another to children now dead, and they seemed to be puffed up and to move around, as if hundreds of invisible kids had crawled into them. Dead children were like normal children except their eyes were closed. He would bang on the door and scream out in Spanish, "¡Abra la puerta! ¡Abra la puerta!"—"Open the door! Open the door!" wishing in his deep dreams to open the door to Aunt Luisa's kitchen in Cuba and find a glass of the magic concoction, or to see Alejo as he went down the hall to work. He kept on saying it, in a panic, crazy, as if on fire inside. Then the voice on the other side would return, "Say it in English. *Let me out!*" Then she would shout it. "Now don't be stupid," she would tell him, "say it!"

[7] That's good.

76   The hours would drag and the door would not open.

77   Day after day, she badgered him with the same punishments and repeated phrases. In time she made him suspicious of Spanish. Spanish words drifted inside him, he dreamed in Spanish, but English began whooshing inside. English forced its way through him, splitting his skin. Sometimes he called out for Horacio and Mercedes and Alejo, Luisa and Rina, and the others, but they did not come. A few times he yelled out, "Cuba, Cuba." But no one and nothing came to save him.

78   Hector began to feel as if he deserved to be locked up. Each day was like the next. Vague, recent memories invaded him. He would be lifted from paradise in Cuba and dropped into a dark room. Each time he spoke Spanish and the nurse was nearby, she slapped his hands. The same nurse mocked his mother's ignorance of English. He was slowly improving, but his sentences were sprinkled with Spanish. Holding a glass of water before him, she would ask, "And how do you ask for this?"

79   "May I have some *agua*?"

80   "No! Water!"

81   "May I have some water?"

82   "Oh yes," she answered. "That's it!" And she kissed him.

83   In time he believed Spanish was an enemy, and when Mercedes came to visit and told him stories about home, he remained silent, as if the nurse were watching him. Even his dreams were broken up by the static of English, like a number of wasps overcoming the corner of a garden. Suddenly he could understand what his friends were saying, "Hector, I hurt. I'm so thirsty . . ."

84   This stay in the Connecticut hospital lasted for nearly a year. Tubes went into his penis, and he listened to the kids' crying and saw them shaking in the dark and watched some of the kids who had been watching Ding Dong School and Howdy Doody with him get carried off in garbage bags. He would one day remember a little girl who was carried off. She told him a story about a dog she used to have, named Fluffy, the kind of dog you throw sticks to on a fine spring day, who goes running around and pants so happily. She told him how much she missed her dog, and she kept speaking of Fluffy running in a field, his tongue feeling so nice when he came up to lick her face. And this little girl told him she would be leaving the home to play with Fluffy, but then she disappeared in the middle of the night. He never saw her again.

85   One day the doctors took Hector into the examination room, and instead of pushing a tube into his body, they stuck a needle into his arm, withdrawing blood. The doctor looked at the blood through a microscope, sent it off for the tests, and that afternoon announced ecstatically, "This one will be fine."

86   In a week Mercedes went to see the doctor, who told her she could take Hector home. The doctor behaved like a schoolteacher that day, pointing to a chart of the human body and finding the diseased kidneys, which were shaped like the island of Cuba on maps.

87   "You must be careful with him, Mrs. Santinio. The kidney is a vital organ, subject to rapid and easy deterioration, and it must be treated properly. You must be attentive when administering all antibiotics and medications. He must be careful about what he eats. His diet must contain little or no salts, fats, sweets. Everything must be boiled. No fried foods, no sweets, no rich food of any kind. Recovery is rare and there is a high incidence of recurrence, but as long as you are careful and give him all the prescribed medicines, he may live for many years . . ."

88   With such happy tidings, Mercedes went into the ward to gather his things. She was nervous about taking him back into the world. As he passed down the hall with its wobbly rectangles of sunlight cast by the corridor windows, the prospect of true sunshine excited him. It was the spring, and when the door from the hospital opened, in the sky was the astonishing sun. A beautiful spring day with smell of grass and buzz of insects in the air, and with hospital attendants lounging in short-sleeved shirts on benches by a small river that passed through the grounds. But Hector was wearing a heavy coat! Mercedes did not want to risk his catching a cold. They followed a path through the high grass, past little gardens with busy dragonflies and bees, past a gazebo, a willow tree, a lily pond. Mercedes noticed that Hector was starting to perspire, melting like a snowman. So she hurried with him to the car. Behind the wheel was the gangster from down the street, chainsmoking, and beside him, his wife, and Horacio, waiting as usual, silent because strange things were going on at home. Mercedes and Hector got into the back seat. Each time Hector tried to undo the coat's buttons, Mercedes redid them. Each time he tried to roll down the window to get some fresh air, she rolled it back up. Whenever Hector tried to get close to Horacio, she pulled him back, or else Horacio moved away. Hector possessed micróbios contracted in Cuba. He would be unable to touch anyone but Alejo for years.

89   At home Alejo was sitting in the kitchen, pretty much as if nothing had happened. When he saw Hector, he looked at him with pity and then opened his arms, and Hector ran to him. Then he started to speak to Hector in Spanish, and Hector nodded and listened but he did not speak back. When Hector finally spoke, he used English, which surprised Alejo. Alejo asked him all kinds of questions, "Why don't you speak in Spanish?" and Hector, feeling ashamed and afraid, became silent. Alejo looked at Hector, wondering if this was his son. There he was, a little blondie, a sickly, fair-skinned Cuban who was not speaking Spanish. He patted the kid on the head, turned around, and took a swig of beer. . . .

DISCUSSION QUESTIONS

1. Describe Hector's experiences with nature, food, and drink during his childhood visit to Cuba.
2. Describe Hector's illness in Cuba and in New York. How was he treated for the disease?
3. Discuss Hector's experience learning English in the Connecticut hospital.
4. Consider the conclusions about Cuba that Hector drew from his illness and from his family's response to it.

WRITING TOPICS

1. Write a story in which you, as a frightened young child, visit a loved one in a health-care facility such as a hospital or a nursing home.
2. Write an essay explaining the importance of nutrition and hygiene for good health. Direct your instructions to a young uneducated mother who does not speak your language fluently.

THOUGHTS ON A SUNDAY AFTERNOON

Joan Báez

Joan Báez, whose career spans five decades and includes composing, singing, writing, acting, and working for peace in the world, was born in Staten Island, New York, on January 9, 1941. She learned to play the guitar at age 14 and sang with her high school choir in Palo Alto, California. Her first public singing performance was with other amateurs at Club 47—a coffeehouse in Cambridge, Massachusetts. She continued performing in other establishments in the Harvard Square area from 1958 to 1960. While performing at the Gate of Horn, a Chicago folk-nightclub, she was invited to play at a folk festival in Newport, Rhode Island, in the summer of 1959 and appeared again in 1960. She soon became a celebrity and began touring nationally. Her debut at Carnegie Hall was in 1962.

She is known for her participation in civil protests, becoming a national figurehead of political demonstrations denouncing racial discrimination and involvement of the United States in the war in Vietnam. She began visiting black colleges when she learned that these African-American students were not being admitted to her concerts at white colleges in the South. In addition, she withheld from the Internal Revenue Service the sixty percent of her income taxes that she determined was destined to fund the Vietnam War.

Her book *Daybreak*, a collection of autobiographical sketches, portrays her family delicately and her commitment to nonviolent protest boldly. Her second book, *And a Voice to Sing With*, provides readers with social history together with autobiographical disclosures in a strong human voice. In the following selection, "Thoughts on a Sunday Afternoon," Joan Báez discusses identity, including her Mexican heritage, and her continued commitment to help the persecuted.

1   I have been asked if I think of myself as a Mexican or a Chicano or as being dark-skinned.

2   This is a difficult question for me to answer, since for the past ten years of my life I have made a point of not categorizing myself. I have refused to accept the title of singer, for instance. I have not particularly identified myself with any special group, but more with humanity as a whole.

3   I've always thought brown is beautiful, and every chance I've had to get into the sun I've done so, because I like being brown.

4   When I entered junior high school there was prejudice against brown people. It took me a couple of years to realize that my being brown was why I did not make friends easily.

5   I have never really regarded myself as Mexican or English. My father was Mexican and was born in Pueblo, Mexico. On my mother's side there was English and a dash of Irish. I never thought of myself as an English girl, and not too much as a Mexican. I feel distant from the cause of any particular minority group in the sense that when I throw myself into "the cause," it is that of mankind. I have never felt I should work just with browns or just with blacks or just with whites.

6   In the same way, my husband David,[1] who is in prison, has not wanted to involve himself only with political prisoners. When he was in Safford, a federal prison, about half of the prisoners were Mexicans. After he had finally got them involved in "the cause," they reached a point where they too felt that they were participating in the struggle of all persecuted people.

7   I know that color made a difference in junior high school. I think I find difficulty talking about this because I never felt I personally was badly discriminated against. When I was in junior high my father was a professor at a university, and although I looked very Mexican I did not speak Spanish. I felt that Mexican kids were getting a dirty deal, but I did not feel that I was. When my father first came to Stanford University, one of the top professors there would hardly speak to him. My father really had to struggle to break through that barrier.

8   I remember a story my parents told me. In a little town in New York State somebody called me "nigger" because they had never seen anyone as dark as I was. I said, "You ought to see me in the summertime." I loved dark-colored skin.

9   Once somebody called me a dirty Mexican, and a student asked my teacher, "Is she a Mexican?"

10   My teacher, attempting to defend me, said, "Joan is the very highest breed of Spanish."

11   I said, "What do you mean, the very highest breed of Spanish? I'm a Mexican." I made a big point of saying I was a Mexican.

12   Probably the worst place in my childhood, so far as prejudice is concerned, was southern California. For about a year my younger sister did not

---

[1] David Harris was imprisoned during the 1960s for draft evasion.

want to play with me or be seen with me. She tagged after my older sister, who was fair.

13   But I've put that thought out of my mind—perhaps because it's unpleasant, but also because I have now done all right for myself. Maybe I feel guilty about my success and don't like to harp on the times I have sensed prejudice in people.

14   There's a theory that people who have known struggle—minority-group people—may have become more sensitive, especially in their music or writing, than most white middle-class Americans.

15   I have a feeling that probably this isn't true. Ira Sandperl, my friend and co-worker, is a Jew. At times some other people get very righteous about how much their group has suffered. But Ira said, for example, "Four thousand years we have suffered, and look what we are doing in Israel now—bombing Arabs."

16   I don't know what creates sensitivity in people, but it pops up in very odd places.

17   Is it possible for us to be nonviolent in a violent world?

18   Yes, I think it is possible and necessary for us to be nonviolently active everywhere. Of course, nonviolence offers no guarantees. But the curious thing is that people who do violence don't receive any guarantees either. Statistics show that you have a much better chance of coming out alive in a nonviolent battle.

19   Too many people are hanging onto the old idea of violence. All that violence has done is to destroy people, but we are too terrified to try something different.

20   César Chávez may provide the best example of strong nonviolent action, and I am sure he does not offer any guarantees.

21   In the Institute for the Study of Nonviolence, we do not have any special training for the practice of nonviolence. We do not have a tactical approach. To root yourself in nonviolence and to be a nonviolent soldier means that you make a decision to go out into the world to confront evil and organize against it, and at the same time make the decision not to do harm to people.

22   Our approach at the Institute is more on a level of what you and I are going to do to make a change in our lives. Basically, how do we break down the nation-state—which also means breaking down smaller nationalistic groups?

23   It is assumed that deprived groups should have what everybody else has. But in this society if all the browns and blacks had what the whites have, we would be in an even more hideous situation than we are in now. If they got into the stream of what is now America, then they, too, would be exploiting others, say, in Latin America, Vietnam, Africa. America as a nation is the most destructive force in the world today. In the search for equality our vision must go farther than just wanting what other people have and what we have been deprived of.

24   In short, I would never want to see a good Mexican become a good American. I would rather that he become a brother in the brotherhood of man.

25   Browns and blacks are the targets of the most vicious attacks by the state because minorities are the easiest to manipulate. They are the brunt because America needs them. America needs a brunt to go on doing what she does in the world and at home. One of the tragedies of war is that the poor people of every nationality are the ones who carry most of the guns, fight, suffer, and die.

26   These people who are kept in ignorance and poverty will grab anything that comes to them. If they are educated as to what the nation is really like, it will be easier for them to resist what is offered. But we have to offer them alternatives that do not yet exist. Until we can offer them something that looks like a real alternative as a way of life, we can do little, and they, less. In a sense, you can say that this is what our work is all about—trying to create that alternative.

27   It is very difficult to live in a society like this. I think it is up to everyone to help find this alternative. The beautiful thing about Chávez is that he is working with poor people and together they are trying to make something out of nothing. He is building something in spite of America.

28   I feel that the sooner we become color-blind the better it is going to be. And while we attempt to become color-blind, white people should stop destroying brown and black people.

29   I don't think that an alternative can be found within the governmental institutions we have now, because when a person enters the system he has to pledge himself to the nation-state. In the nation-state when we talk about defense we are talking *not about defense of people but about defense of land*. Because the nation-state emphasizes the importance of land, people have to die to protect land. The most expendable thing turns out to be human life.

30   Obviously, it is not possible to find human alternatives within the existing judicial system. The judicial system is not there to promote justice. It is there to keep order. This is exactly why my husband is in prison. Prison is somewhere to put people whom society is afraid to have walking around the streets. True, there are some good people working in the system who try to do good things. Anytime there is a good judge, I am happy because of him; and anytime there is a lawyer who fights for someone deprived, I am happy. But the system operates primarily to prevent resistance.

31   What my husband David is saying when he talks about draft resistance is, "Claim your life." Say an absolute "No" to that system and then try to build a different basis for action.

32   What I am most aware of is people's concept of power. Power is something everyone has, and yet few people in this society truly believe they have power. If the people (not the politicians) could feel in themselves a genuine sense of power, they could behave in a very different way. They would not have to throw rocks. A lot of radicals are really into violence, and, so far as I am concerned, violence is reactionary. In fact, there is a contradiction in terms when we say "violent revolutionary," because revolution means change, and violence is a reversion to a former pattern.

33   When one raises his fist and shouts "Power," it appears to me he does this because he thinks somebody else has power and he wants to take it for

himself. But if he assumes that he is born with power, he doesn't feel the need to grasp it away from someone else. There is enough to go around when we recognize our own power.

34 To me, what is worth building and organizing is the power of love.

35 I don't think our alternative can be found within the present educational system. I think the educational system we have now should be replaced. In the context of this society, education would always end up being the same—it would wind up being nationalism.

36 The basic issues in all of life are never met in the existing educational system. How do you relate to God, no God, sex, drugs, truth, openness, honesty, fear, parents, etc.? And finally, how are you going to treat other people? Are you going to kill people or are you not going to kill people? You cannot discuss that in school because it is taken for granted that you will kill people. They call it defending your country, but it means killing people. Most of us do not see ourselves involved in the process of murder, but we very much are.

37 Revolution to me would mean people recognizing the sanctity of human life, and that's the revolution that has never happened. There have been lots of revolutions—people throwing over the government and taking other people's property. But all the good that comes out of a violent revolution comes in spite of the violence.

38 If we could learn to fight in a different way—get different weapons—then we could really have a chance to win. But for the first time since time began, men would have to recognize that there is only one thing that is really sacred, and that thing is life.

Discussion Questions

1. In small groups, discuss Báez's ideas about race, color, and ethnicity.
2. Describe her interpretation of *revolution*. How does violence enter into her understanding of the term?
3. What does Báez appreciate about the way César Chávez operates?
4. Discuss what power means to Báez. Who exercises power?

Writing Topics

1. Write an essay discussing a personal experience with discrimination.
2. In an essay, discuss your assessment of our current educational system. Does it succeed at meeting the basic issues of life? If not, how would you improve it?

BORINKINS IN HAWAII

Victor Hernández Cruz

Victor Hernández Cruz was born on February 6, 1949, in Aguas Buenas, Puerto Rico. At age five he moved with his family to New York's Spanish Harlem. Hernández Cruz attended school in New York and subsequently worked with the Gut Theater, which helped to shape his poetry into mini-dramatic dialogues.

Called a major American poet by *Life* magazine, Hernández Cruz began his career when he won a prize that earned public acclaim for his poetry. He went on to publish several poetry collections, some with major New York publishers. Among them are *Papo Got His Gun* (1966), *Snaps* (1969), *Mainland* (1973), *Tropicalization* (1976), *By Lingual Wholes* (1982), *Rhythm, Content and Flavor* (1989), and *Red Beans* (1991). In addition, he has served as editor of *Umbra* and has collaborated with Herbert Kohl to produce *Stuff: A Collection of Poems, Visions and Imaginative Happenings from Young Writers in Schools— Opened and Closed* (1970). In 1973 Hernández Cruz moved to San Francisco, where the city honors him as one of its poets in residence.

Victor Hernández Cruz's "Borinkins in Hawaii" is a poem whose title plays on the word *Borinquen*, the Arawak Indian name for the island of Puerto Rico, changing the "qu" to "k," which is the equivalent sound in English, and the "e" to "i," which rhymes with the word *Hawaii*. The poem imitates the sounds of English and Spanish in the Pacific, including exotic place names and references to sugarcane, as it tells the story of a strange migration.

FOR NORMA CARR, BLAISE SOSA AND AYALA AND HIS FAMOUS CORNER

In 1900
A ship left San Juan Harbor
Full of migrant workers
Of the fields

5 Enroute to what they believed
   To be California
   Instead something like C&H
   Which managed the vessel
   With strings like a puppet
10 From afar
   Took them to Hawaii

   When Toño who was one of them
   And Jaime who was another
   And Felipe who was a third
15 Of the many 8,000 who took
   This spin
   Saw Hawaii they thought they
   Were still in Puerto Rico
   It took movement of time
20 Show up of the wind
   It took the Japanese currents
   To convince them
   That in somewhere they were

   Sugar was the daddy on the
25 Commercial horizon
   Donuts for everybody
   Ah history was getting sweet
   If you wasn't a cane worker
   With sores on your feet
30 And corns on your hands
   Under the sun for how much
   A day
   Sugar was gonna blow flesh up
   Sugar mania
35 Sugar come from cane
   Get some cane
   Get some workers
   Get some land

   The United States talked to the
40 Old Hawaiian queen
   It was a polite conversation
   The gringo merely pointed
   To where the Marines
   Were casually placed
45 Just that
   The Hawaiian Kingdom

Pieces of cake
Littered on the Pacific

"What in the mountain got
50 Into you Toño to wanna come
From where you were
To jump on this boat
To come to this other planet.
Looka a volcano to lite your
55 Cigar, a desert for your
Camel, what is this the
End of the world, HA."

"Well Jaime look a guava
And coconut is coconut
60 See that tree where a Pana
Hangs. Smell the flowers
Fragrance like Aguas Buenas."

Thru each Pana-pen a metropopis
Of juices and texture
65 Ulus are Pana-pens in Puerto Rico
Ulus: Hawaii
Pana-pen: Puerto Rico
Breadfruit for you
Ulus hang like earrings
70 From the ears of women
On the tree
A blue dress on top
The curve is the horizon
A reminder that we all live
75 On a Pana-pen

Hawaii feudal 19th century
Catholic liturgy
Thru the flower tops
The best years of
80 Tomas-Toñon
Jaime
Felipe and the full migration
Living in camps
Box homes for workers
85 And their families
Early risers
Church on Sunday

Machete on Monday
Orange curtains thru
90   The greenery
Cuatro[1] strings
With the bird speech
The pick pickers of
Pineapple stress the
95   Decima[2]
As back in Borinkin
Ya se men
In ten lines you hem
A skirt
100 In Kohala they call it
Cachy-cachy
People jumpy-jumpy
Like roosters
The cuatro guitar chirps
105 Squeeky its note in the
Upper C high nose pitch
Sound of the Arowak
Garganta of the Areyto
Song gallery of the
110 Ancient inhabitants
Of the boat Borinkin

Broken guitars navigating
Vessels
Arrive like seed onto the
115 Ground
Whatever is in the dirt
Will come out
We're gonna finger pop
The pineapple
120 The cane is gonna fly
The mayordomos[3] will whip
Ankles
Secret hidden wood
Will get them
125 There are dark passages of night
Roads under the kona trees
In the dark the sound kaploosh
On the skull

---

[1] Four-string; a reference to a four-string guitar.
[2] Tenth; here meaning a traditional ten-line verse.
[3] Stewards or foremen of the plantation.

The mayordomos are paid
130 By the plantation owners
The wood is made by nature
At Ayalas Place
3rd & 4th generation Puerto Rican
Hawaiian
135 Eat rice and beans prepared
By Japanese woman
Soya sauce on the tables
Hawaii only Puerto Rican
Oriental community in the
140 World

A ship which left San Juan
Turn of the century
Transported workers music
And song
145 They thought they were
California bound
But were hijacked by
Corporate agriculture
Once they got to land
150 They folded over
They grew and mixed
Like Hawaii can mix
Portuguese sausage slit
Inside banana leaf
155 Filipino Japanese eyes
Stare from mulatto faces

The Portuguese brought
The ukulele to anxious fingers
Who looked at the motion of
160 Palm leaves to help them search
For a sound
They studied the designs of
The hula dancers
And made
165 A guitar which sounds like
It's being played by the
Fingers of the breeze
They all dance cachy cachy
And jumpy-jumpy
170 In places like Hilo
And Kohala

You hear the shouts
You hear the groans
You feel the wind of the
175   Cane workers' machete
And in the eyes you see
The waves of the oceans
You see beads
Which form a necklace
180   Of islands
Which have emerged out of
The tears.

DISCUSSION QUESTIONS

1. Describe how the Puerto Ricans in the poem adapt to Hawaii. How do their experiences there compare with their home?
2. Discuss the migration of Puerto Ricans to Hawaii. What were they going to do there?
3. In the poem there is an implication that migrants take their culture with them, that culture is portable. Discuss in small groups, citing examples.
4. Discuss the historical account of how the United States took control of the Hawaiian islands, as presented in the poem.

WRITING TOPICS

1. Compose a chapter in a memoir in which your Puerto Rican grandparents migrated to Hawaii. Describe how life was for them.
2. Write an essay in which you consider the New World as a place where migrants gather and redistribute themselves in it in subsequent generations.

CHAPTER NINE

EMPOWERING THE PEOPLE

The outlook and experiences of Hispanics in the United States, both native-born as well as immigrants and exiles, are affected by their histories in the United States. Rhetoric and opinions vary widely among these three groups, dividing Latinos politically among themselves.

The literature of Latinos in the United States is often a protest against a society that discriminates against them because of race and language, the point of fact being that they frequently lack a political and economic position of power. The literature often tells of Hispanics whose existence in the United States, even for generations, has been marked by police oppression and the loss of civil liberties. Many Hispanics who come to the United States want bilingual education for their children, in order to perpetuate and preserve their language and culture, and they seek better employment opportunities for themselves.

However, much of the literature of the exiled Hispanic in the U.S., one who has fled his or her native country because of political reasons or for reasons of sheer survival, is a discourse on economic opportunity. That literature celebrates the ability to vote for political leaders and to run for public office. Exiled Hispanics applaud the freedom of the press and welcome the employment and financial opportunities available in a free market. For this group of Latino individuals, their golden age lies ahead of them. They believe there is no gain in defining oneself by an imperfect past, when the present offers opportunity for a promising future.

And yet, there is a voice in the literature that represents something of a middle ground. It is the collective voice of Latino writers, born and raised in the United States, whose discourse on political freedom wavers somewhat in its effort to balance nostalgia with present circumstances and an optimistic focus for the future. This group draws enlightenment from the present—from circumstances of life as they know it now.

The following selections interweave glowing recollections of a proud and valiant heritage in the U.S. with strident protests on behalf of the immigrant and the homeless poor. Though they vary significantly in rhetoric and style, these writings do share a common aim. Through their social criticism and their rallying cries, these writers seek to empower their communities.

NUYORICAN LAMENT

Gloria Vando

Born of Puerto Rican parents, Gloria Vando was reared in New York City and attended New York University, where she studied literature and philosophy. She also studied for a year at both the University of Amsterdam and the Académie Julian in Paris. After having a family, she received her B.A. from Texas A & I University in 1974. Subsequently, she worked as an educational consultant to the City of New York and later to Kansas City.

In 1977 Gloria Vando created the celebrated *Helicon Nine: The Journal of Women's Arts & Letters,* a publication including writing, art, and music. Vando's commitment to the arts led her to serve on a multitude of boards, including the Kansas Governor's Council on the Arts and the Nebraska Arts Council, and to act as a final judge for the National Poetry Prize. She has also edited eight books with the Helicon Nine imprint.

Vando has published much of her poetic work in numerous literary magazines and anthologies, among them *The Kenyon Poetry Review, El Gato Tuerto, Women of the 14th Moon,* and the *Seattle Review.* In 1989 she was awarded a poetry fellowship from the Kansas Arts Commission, and in 1991 she won the Billee Murray Denny Poetry Prize. Her first book of poetry, *Promesas: Geography of the Impossible* (1993), was a finalist for the prestigious Walt Whitman Award and the Poetry Society of America's Alice Fay diCastagnola Prize. Currently, she publishes books and is the editor of *The Helicon Nine Reader* (1990).

In the following selection, "Nuyorican Lament," Vando compares her nostalgia for San Juan with the life she knows now in New York. Manhattan and San Juan are contrasted as the poetic persona recalls what San Juan used to be for her.

San Juan you're not for me.
My cadence quails and stumbles
on your ancient stones:

there is an inner beat here
5   to be reckoned with—
a *seis chorreao, a plena,*[1]
an imbred ¡*Oyeeee!*[2]
and ¡*mira tú!*[3] against which
my Manhattan (sorry
10 wrong island) responses fall flat.

¡*Vaya!*[4] How can I deal with that?

And yet . . . once, long ago,
your beach was mine; Luquillo
was my bridle path to ride—
15 back then, before the turning of the tide
when Teddy's blue-eyed shills
secured the hill
and tried in vain to blot
the language out. But *patria*[5]

20 is a sneaky word—it lies,
seeming to turn its back
upon itself—it lies,
through paling generations—lies
    and lies in wait:
25 the sleeping dog of nations
no translation can obliterate

(And when it's roused—
beware the bully
beware the apple pie).

30 I rode with purpose then,
back then, when
you were mine, harnessing

---

[1] A Puerto Rican folkdance and its music; a type of song.
[2] Listen! (drawn out).
[3] Hey you, look here!
[4] Come on; Get out of here; Well!
[5] Fatherland.

the strength of iron
    in my thighs—
35 my eyes blazing with self, my self
        with pride—

and once, at La Parguera,
I was baptized
on a moonless night in spring,
40 emerging purged and
reinvented, the phosphorescent
spangles clinging
to my skin, signaling
the night to bless my innocence—

45 then, only yesterday—or so it seems—
I spent my youth
in La Princesa's dungeon
for unproved crimes
against an unloved nation—yes

50 only yesterday, I knew where I belonged,
I knew my part.

And now, you see me here,
a trespasser in my own past,
tracing a faint ancestral theme
55 far back, beyond the hard rock
rhythm of the strand.
I walk down El Condado, past
Pizza Huts, Big Macs and
Coca-Cola stands
60 listening for a song—

a wisp of song—

that begs deep in my heart.

DISCUSSION QUESTIONS

1. Describe the feelings of the poetic persona as she walks through San Juan.

2. Discuss the past actions on behalf of Puerto Rico that the poetic persona has taken.
3. Has she had to pay a price for those actions? What is the price?
4. How does the poet describe the Americanization of Puerto Rico?

WRITING TOPICS

1. Write an essay about the political status of Puerto Rico.
2. Write a poem about returning to a once-familiar place. Contrast its present appearance and atmosphere with what you recall.

LOS VENDIDOS

Luis Valdez

Luis Miguel Valdez was born into a large Mexican-American family on June 26, 1940, in Delano, California. As a young boy he developed an avid interest in puppet shows and performed them for his friends and neighbors. Indeed, this experience served him well because, after winning a scholarship, he went on to study theater at San Diego State College and graduated with a B.A. in 1964.

He won a regional playwriting contest in 1961 with his one-act play *The Theft*, which stimulated him to attempt a full-length play, *The Shrunken Head of Pancho Villa* (1963). After graduation from college the following year, he joined the San Francisco Mime Troupe, where he learned the theatrical techniques of the Italian *commedia dell'arte* on which the company's work was based.

When César Chávez began organizing agricultural workers in Valdez's hometown in 1965, he went to offer assistance. With Chávez's approval he began to show farmworkers the role of theater in teaching the ideology of labor organization. He placed a sign on each of two volunteers—one representing a *huelguista* (striker) and the other an *esquirol* (scab)—and had them enact the scene they had just lived in reality. Thus was the birth of the *acto,* or the improvised scenario. El Teatro Campesino (The Farmworkers' Theatre) was founded in 1965 and became the propaganda arm of the new Chávez-led union, the United Farmworkers of America.

Valdez, after separating from the union and founding his own dramatic company, continued with a series of important plays that dealt with many issues of the day, including *Los Vendidos* (*The Sell-outs*) (1967), *Bernabé* (1970)—which followed the company's first of many European tours, *Vietnam Campesino* and *Soldado Razo*— both opposing the Vietnam War, *Dark Root of a Scream* (1971), *Las cuatro apariciones de la Virgen de Guadalupe* (*The Four Appearances of the Virgin of Guadalupe*) (1971), *La pastorela* (*The Shepherd's Play*) (1971), *La gran carpa de los Rasquachis* (*The Underdog's Great Tent*) (1971), and *El fin del mundo* (*The End of the World*) (1972).

In 1978 *Zoot Suit* represented a new challenge for Valdez. Although the play was a great success in Los Angeles, it failed in New York. The resulting film was a hit, however, and became an important milestone. Later, *La pastorela* was produced for television, and Valdez began to release his plays in book and video formats.

Luis Valdez recognized a need to identify political manipulation and reveal the truth beneath the surface. The following one-act play, *Los Vendidos*, a farce, confronts the California political establishment's solution to its problems.

1967; FIRST PERFORMANCE: BROWN BERET JUNTA, ELYSIAN PARK, EAST LOS ANGELES.

CHARACTERS:

HONEST SANCHO
SECRETARY
FARMWORKER
PACHUCO
REVOLUCIONARIO
MEXICAN-AMERICAN

Scene: HONEST SANCHO'*s Used Mexican Lot and Mexican Curio Shop. Three models are on display in* HONEST SANCHO'*s shop. To the right, there is a* REVOLUCIONARIO, *complete with sombrero, carrilleras and carabina 30-30. At center, on the floor, there is the* FARMWORKER, *under a broad straw sombrero. At stage left is the* PACHUCO, *filero in hand.* HONEST SANCHO *is moving among his models, dusting them off and preparing for another day of business.*

SANCHO: Bueno, bueno, mis monos, vamos a ver a quién vendemos ahora, ¿no? (*To audience.*) ¡Quihubo! I'm Honest Sancho and this is my shop. Antes fui contratista, pero ahora logré tener mi negocito. All I need is a customer. (*A bell rings offstage.*) Ay, a customer!
SECRETARY: (*Entering.*) Good morning, I'm Miss Jimenez from . . .
SANCHO: An, una chicana! Welcome, welcome Señorita Jiménez.
SECRETARY: (*Anglo pronunciation.*) JIM-enez.
SANCHO: ¿Qué?
SECRETARY: My name is Miss JIM-enez. Don't you speak English? What's wrong with you?

SANCHO: Oh, nothing, Señorita JIM-enez. I'm here to help you.

SECRETARY: That's better. As I was starting to say, I'm a secretary from Governor Reagan's office, and we're looking for a Mexican type for the administration.

SANCHO: Well, you come to the right place, lady. This is Honest Sancho's Used Mexican Lot, and we got all types here. Any particular type you want?

SECRETARY: Yes, we are looking for somebody suave . . .

SANCHO: Suave.

SECRETARY: Debonaire.

SANCHO: De buen aire.

SECRETARY: Dark.

SANCHO: Prieto.

SECRETARY: But of course, not too dark.

SANCHO: No muy prieto.

SECRETARY: Perhaps, beige.

SANCHO: Beige, just the tone. Asi como cafecito con leche, ¿no?

SECRETARY: One more thing. He must be hard-working.

SANCHO: That could only be one model. Step right over here to the center of the shop, lady. (*They cross to the* FARMWORKER.) This is our standard farmworker model. As you can see, in the words of our beloved Senator George Murphy, he is "built close to the ground." Also, take special notice of his 4-ply Goodyear huaraches, made from the rain tire. This wide-brimmed sombrero is an extra added feature; keeps off the sun, rain and dust.

SECRETARY: Yes, it does look durable.

SANCHO: And our farmworker model is friendly. Muy amable. Watch. (*Snaps his fingers.*)

FARMWORKER: (*Lifts up head.*) Buenos días, señorita. (*His head drops.*)

SECRETARY: My, he is friendly.

SANCHO: Didn't I tell you? Loves his patrones! But his most attractive feature is that he's hard-working. Let me show you. (*Snaps fingers.* FARMWORKER *stands.*)

FARMWORKER: ¡El jale! (He begins to work.)

SANCHO: As you can see he is cutting grapes.

SECRETARY: Oh, I wouldn't know.

SANCHO: He also picks cotton. (*Snaps.* FARMWORKER *begins to pick cotton.*)

SECRETARY: Versatile, isn't he?

SANCHO: He also picks melons. (*Snaps.* FARMWORKER *picks melons.*) That's his slow speed for later in the season. Here's his fast speed. (*Snap.* FARMWORKER *picks faster.*)

SECRETARY: Chihuahua . . . I mean, goodness, he sure is a hard worker.

SANCHO: (*Pulls the* FARMWORKER *to his feet.*) And that isn't the half of it. Do you see these little holes on his arms that appear to be pores? During those hot sluggish days in the field when the vines or the branches get so entangled, it's almost impossible to move, these holes emit a certain grease that allows our model to slip and slide right through the crop with no trouble at all.

SECRETARY: Wonderful. But is he economical?

SANCHO: Economical? Señorita, you are looking at the Volkswagen of Mexicans. Pennies a day is all it takes. One place of beans and tortillas will keep him going all day. That, and chile. Plenty of chile. Chile jalapeños, chile verde, chile colorado. But, of course, if you do give him chile, (*Snap.* FARMWORKER *turns left face. Snap.* FARMWORKER *bends over.*) then you have to change his oil filter once a week.

SECRETARY: What about storage?

SANCHO: No problem. You know these new farm labor camps our Honorable Governor Reagan has built out by Parlier or Raisin City? They were designed with our model in mind. Five, six, seven, even ten in one of those shacks will give you no trouble at all. You can also put him in old barns, old cars, riverbanks. You can even leave him out in the field overnight with no worry!

SECRETARY: Remarkable.

SANCHO: And here's an added feature: every year at the end of the season, this model goes back to Mexico and doesn't return, automatically, until next Spring.

SECRETARY: How about that. But tell me, does he speak English?

SANCHO: Another outstanding feature is that last year his model was programmed to go out on STRIKE! (*Snap.*)

FARMWORKER: ¡Huelga! ¡Huelga! Hermanos, sálganse de esos files. (S*nap. He stops.*)

SECRETARY: No! Oh no, we can't strike in the State Capitol.

SANCHO: Well, he also scabs. (*Snap.*)

FARMWORKER: Me vendo barato ¿y qué? (*Snap.*)

SECRETARY: That's much better, but you didn't answer my question. Does he speak English?

SANCHO: Bueno . . . no, pero he has other . . .

SECRETARY: No.

SANCHO: Other features.

SECRETARY: No! He just won't do!

SANCHO: Okay, okay, pues. We have other models.

SECRETARY: I hope so. What we need is something a little more sophisticated.

SANCHO: Sophisti-qué?

SECRETARY: An urban model.

SANCHO: Ah, from the city! Step right back. Over here in this corner of the shop is exactly what you're looking for. Introducing our new 1969 JOHNNY PACHUCO model! This is our fast-back model. Streamlined. Built for speed, low-riding, city life. Take a look at some of these features. Mag shoes, dual exhausts, green chartruese paint-job, dark-tint windshield, a little poof on top.

Let me just turn him on. (*Snap.* JOHNNY *walks to stage center with a* PACHUCO *bounce.*)

SECRETARY: What was that?

SANCHO: That, señorita, was the Chicano shuffle.

SECRETARY: Okay, what does he do?

SANCHO: Anything and everything necessary for city life. For instance, survival: he knife fights. (*Snaps.* JOHNNY *pulls out a switchblade and swings at* SECRETARY. SECRETARY *screams.*) He dances. (*Snap.*)

JOHNNY: (*Singing.*) "Angel Baby, my Angel Baby . . ." (*Snap.*)

SANCHO: And here's a feature no city model can be without. He gets arrested, but not without resisting, of course. (*Snap.*)

JOHNNY: En la madre, la placa. I didn't do it! I didn't do it! (JOHNNY *turns and stands up against an imaginary wall, legs spread out, arms behind his back.*)

SECRETARY: Oh no, we can't have arrests! We must maintain law and order.

SANCHO: But he's bilingual.

SECRETARY: Bilingual?

SANCHO: Simón que yes. He speaks English! Johnny, give us some English. (*Snap.*)

JOHNNY: (*Comes downstage.*) Fuck-you!

SECRETARY: (*Gasps.*) Oh! I've never been so insulted in my whole life!

SANCHO: Well, he learned it in your school.

SECRETARY: I don't care where he learned it.

SANCHO: But he's economical.

SECRETARY: Economical?

SANCHO: Nickels and dimes. You can keep Johnny running on hamburgers, Taco Bell tacos, Lucky Lager beer, Thunderbird wine, yesca . . .

SECRETARY: Yesca?

SANCHO: Mota.

SECRETARY: Mota?

SANCHO: Leños . . . marijuana. (*Snap.* JOHNNY *inhales on an imaginary joint.*)

SECRETARY: That's against the law!

JOHNNY: (*Big smile, holding his breath.*) Yeah.

SANCHO: He also sniffs glue. (*Snap.* JOHNNY *inhales glue, big smile.*)

JOHNNY: Tha's too much man, ese.

SECRETARY: No, Mr. Sancho, I don't think this . . .

SANCHO: Wait a minute, he has other qualities I know you'll love. For example, an inferiority complex. (*Snap.*)

JOHNNY: (*To* SANCHO.) You think you're better than me, huh, ese? (*Swings switchblade.*)

SANCHO: He can also be beaten and he bruises. Cut him and he bleeds, kick him and he . . . (*He beats, bruises and kicks* PACHUCO.) Would you like to try it?

SECRETARY: Oh, I couldn't

SANCHO: Be my guest. He's a great scape goat.

SECRETARY: No really.

SANCHO: Please.

SECRETARY: Well, all right. Just once. (*She kicks* PACHUCO.) Oh, he's so soft.

SANCHO: Wasn't that good? Try again.

SECRETARY: (*Kicks* PACHUCO.) Oh, he's so wonderful! (*She kicks him again.*)

SANCHO: Okay, that's enough, lady. You'll ruin the merchandise. Yes, our Johnny Pachuco model can give you many hours of pleasure. Why, the LAPD just bought 20 of these to train their rookie cops on. And talk about maintenance. Señorita, you are looking at an entirely self-supporting machine. You're never going to find our Johnny Pachuco model on the relief rolls. No, sir, this model knows how to liberate.

SECRETARY: Liberate?

SANCHO: He steals. (*Snap.* JOHNNY *rushes to* SECRETARY *and steals her purse.*)

Johnny: ¡Dame esa bolsa, viejá! (*He grabs the purse and runs. Snap by* SANCHO, *he stops.* SECRETARY *runs after* JOHNNY *and grabs purse away from him, kicking him as she goes.*)

SECRETARY: No, no, no! We can't have any more thieves in the State Administration. Put him back.

SANCHO: Okay, we still got other models. Come on, Johnny, we'll sell you to some old lady. (SANCHO *takes* JOHNNY *back to his place.*)

SECRETARY: Mr. Sancho, I don't think you quite understand what we need. What we need is something that will attract the women voters. Something more traditional, more romantic.

SANCHO: Ah, a lover. (*He smiles meaningfully.*) Step right over here, señorita. Introducing our standard Revolucionario and/or Early California Bandit type. As you can see, he is well-built, sturdy, durable. This is the International Harvester of Mexicans.

SECRETARY: What does he do?

SANCHO: You name it, he does it. He rides horses, stays in the mountains, crosses deserts, plains, rivers, leads revolutions, follows revolutions, kills, can be killed, serves as a martyr, hero, movie star. Did I say movie star? Did you ever see *Viva Zapata? Viva Villa, Villa Rides, Pancho Villa Returns, Pancho Villa Goes Back, Pancho Villa Meets Abbott and Costello?*

SECRETARY: I've never seen any of those.

SANCHO: Well, he was in all of them. Listen to this. (*Snap.*)

REVOLUCIONARIO: (*Scream.*) ¡Viva Villaaaaa!

SECRETARY: That's awfully loud.

SANCHO: He has a volume control. (*He adjusts volume. Snap.*)

REVOLUCIONARIO: (*Mousey voice.*) Viva Villa.

SECRETARY: That's better.

SANCHO: And even if you didn't see him in the movies, perhaps you saw him on TV. He makes commercials. (*Snap.*)

REVOLUCIONARIO: Is there a Frito Bandito in your house?

SECRETARY: Oh yes, I've seen that one!

SANCHO: Another feature about this one is that he is economical. He runs on raw horsemeat and tequila!

SECRETARY: Isn't that rather savage?

SANCHO: Al contrario, it makes him a lover. (*Snap.*)

REVOLUCIONARIO: (*To* SECRETARY.) Ay, mamasota, cochota, ven pa 'ca! (*He grabs* SECRETARY *and folds her back, Latin-lover style.*)

SANCHO: (*Snap.* REVOLUCIONARIO *goes back upright.*) Now wasn't that nice?

SECRETARY: Well, it was rather nice.

SANCHO: And finally, there is one outstanding feature about this model I know the ladies are going to love: he's a genuine antique! He was made in Mexico in 1910!

SECRETARY: Made in Mexico?

SANCHO: That's right. Once in Tijuana, twice in Guadalajara, three times in Cuernavaca.

SECRETARY: Mr. Sancho, I thought he was an American product.

SANCHO: No, but . . .

SECRETARY: No, I'm sorry. We can't buy anything but American made products. He just won't do.

SANCHO: But he's an antique!

SECRETARY: I don't care. You still don't understand what we need. It's true we need Mexican models, such as these, but it's more important that he be American.

SANCHO: American?

SECRETARY: That's right, and judging from what you've shown me, I don't think you have what we want. Well, my lunch hour's almost over. I better . . .

SANCHO: Wait a minute! Mexican but American?

SECRETARY: That's correct.

SANCHO: Mexican but . . . (*A sudden flash.*) American! Yeah, I think we've got exactly what you want. He just came in today! Give me a minute. (*He exits. Talks from backstage.*) Here he is in the shop. Let me just get some papers off. There. Introducing our new 1970 Mexican-American! Ta-ra-ra-raaaa! (SANCHO *brings out the* MEXICAN-AMERICAN *model, a clean-shaven middle class type in a business suit, with glasses.*)

SECRETARY: (*Impressed.*) Where have you been hiding this one?

SANCHO: He just came in this morning. Ain't he a beauty? Feast your eyes on him! Sturdy U.S. Steel frame, streamlined, modern. As a matter of fact, he is built exactly like our Anglo model, except that he comes in a variety of darker shades: naugahide, leather or leatherette.

SECRETARY: Naugahide.

SANCHO: Well, we'll just write that down. Yes, señorita, this model represents the apex of American engineering! He is bilingual, college educated, ambitious! Say the word "acculturate" and he accelerates. He is intelligent, well-mannered, clean. Did I say clean? (*Snap.* MEXICAN-AMERICAN *raises his arm.*) Smell.

SECRETARY: (*Smells.*) Old Sobaco, my favorite.

SANCHO: (*Snap.* MEXICAN-AMERICAN *turns toward* SANCHO.) Eric? (*To* SECRETARY.) We call him Eric García. (*To* ERIC.) I want you to meet Miss JIM-enez, Eric.

MEXICAN-AMERICAN: Miss JIM-enez, I am delighted to make your acquaintance. (*He kisses her hand.*)

SECRETARY: Oh, my, how charming!

SANCHO: Did you feel the suction? He has seven especially engineered suction cups right behind his lips. He's a charmer all right!

SECRETARY: How about boards, does he function on boards?

SANCHO: You name them, he is on them. Parole boards, draft boards, school boards, taco quality control boards, surf boards, two by fours.

SECRETARY: Does he function in politics?

SANCHO: Señorita, you are looking at a political machine. Have you ever heard of the OEO, EOC, COD, WAR ON POVERTY? That's our model! Not only that, he makes political speeches.

SECRETARY: May I hear one?

SANCHO: With pleasure. (*Snap.*) Eric, give us a speech.

MEXICAN-AMERICAN: Mr. Congressman, Mr. Chairman, members of the board, honored guests, ladies and gentlemen. (SANCHO *and* SECRETARY *applaud.*) Please, please. I come before you as a Mexican-American to tell you about the problems of the Mexican. The problems of the Mexican stem from one thing and one thing only: he's stupid. He's uneducated. He needs to stay in school. He needs to be ambitious, forward-looking, harder-working. He needs to think American, American, American, American, American! God bless America! God bless America! God bless America! (*He goes out of control.* SANCHO *snaps frantically and the* MEXICAN-AMERICAN *finally slumps forward, bending at the waist.*)

SECRETARY: Oh my, he's patriotic too!

SANCHO: Sí, señorita, he loves his country. Let me just make a little adjustment here. (*Stands* MEXICAN-AMERICAN *up.*)

SECRETARY: What about upkeep? Is he economical?

SANCHO: Well, no, I won't lie to you. The Mexican-American costs a little bit more, but you get what you pay for. He's worth every extra cent. You can keep him running on dry Martinis, Langendorf bread . . .

SECRETARY: Apple pie?

SANCHO: Only Mom's. Of course, he's also programmed to eat Mexican food at ceremonial functions, but I must warn you, an overdose of beans will plug up his exhaust.

SECRETARY: Fine! There's just one more question. How much do you want for him?

SANCHO: Well, I tell you what I'm gonna do. Today and today only, because you've been so sweet, I'm gona let you steal this model from me! I'm gonna let you drive him off the lot for the simple price of, let's see, taxes and license included, $15,000.

SECRETARY: Fifteen thousand dollars? For a Mexican!!!!

SANCHO: Mexican? What are you talking about? This is a Mexican-American! We had to meld down two pachucos, a farmworker and three gabachos to make this model! You want quality, but you gotta pay for it! This is no cheap run-about. He's got class!

SECRETARY: Okay, I'll take him.

SANCHO: You will?

SECRETARY: Here's your money.

SANCHO: You mind if I count it?

SECRETARY: Go right ahead.

SANCHO: Well, you'll get your pink slip in the mail. Oh, do you want me to wrap him up for you? We have a box in the back.

SECRETARY: No, thank you. The Governor is having a luncheon this afternoon, and we need a brown face in the crowd. How do I drive him?

SANCHO: Just snap your fingers. He'll do anything you want. (SECRETARY *snaps.* MEXICAN-AMERICAN *steps forward.*)

MEXICAN-AMERICAN: ¡Raza querida, vamos levantando armas para liberarnos de estos desgraciados gabachos que nos explotan! Vamos . . .

SECRETARY: What did he say?

SANCHO: Something about taking up arms, killing white people, etc.

SECRETARY: But he's not supposed to say that!

SANCHO: Look, lady, don't blame me for bugs from the factory. He's your Mexican-American, you bought him, now drive him off the lot!

SECRETARY: But he's broken!

SANCHO: Try snapping another finger. (SECRETARY *snaps.* MEXICAN-AMERICAN *comes to life again.*)

MEXICAN-AMERICAN: ¡Esta gran humanidad ha dicho basta! ¡Y se ha puesto en marcha! ¡Basta! ¡Basta! ¡Viva la raza! ¡Viva la causa! ¡Viva la huelga! ¡Vivan los brown berets! ¡Vivan los estudiantes! ¡Chicano power! (*The* MEXICAN-AMERICAN *turns toward the* SECRETARY, *who gasps and backs up. He keeps turning toward the* PACHUCO, FARMWORKER *and* REVOLUCIONARIO, *snapping his fingers and turning each of them on, one by one.*)

PACHUCO: (*Snap. To* SECRETARY.) I'm going to get you, baby! ¡Viva la raza!

FARMWORKER: (*Snap. To* SECRETARY.) ¡Viva la huelga! ¡Viva la huelga! ¡Viva la huelga!

REVOLUCIONARIO: (*Snap. To* SECRETARY.) ¡Viva la revolución! (*The three models join together and advance toward the* SECRETARY, *who backs up and runs out of the shop screaming.* SANCHO *is at the other end of the shop holding his money in his hand. All freeze. After a few seconds of silence, the* PACHUCO *moves and stretches, shaking his arms and loosening up. The* FARMWORKER *and* REVOLUCIONARIO *do the same.* SANCHO *stays where he is, frozen to his spot.*)

JOHNNY: Man, that was a long one, ese. (Others agree with him.)

FARMWORKER: How did we do?

JOHNNY: Pretty good, look at all that lana, man! (*He goes over to* SANCHO *and removes the money from his hand.* SANCHO *stays where he is.*)

REVOLUCIONARIO: En la madre, look at all the money.

JOHNNY: We keep this up, we're going to be rich.

FARMWORKER: They think we're machines.

REVOLUCIONARIO: Burros.

JOHNNY: Puppets.

MEXICAN-AMERICAN: The only thing I don't like is how come I always get to play the damn Mexican-American?

JOHNNY: That's what you get for finishing high school.

FARMWORKER: How about our wages, ese?

JOHNNY: Here it comes right now. $3,000 for you, $3,000 for you, $3,000 for you and $3,000 for me. The rest we put back into the business.

MEXICAN-AMERICAN: Too much, man. Heh, where you vatos going tonight?

FARMWORKER: I'm going over to Concha's. There's a party.

JOHNNY: Wait a minute, vatos. What about our salesman? I think he needs an oil job.

REVOLUCIONARIO: Leave him to me. (*The* PACHUCO, FARMWORKER, *and* MEXICAN-AMERICAN ex*it, talking loudly about their plans for the night. The* REVOLUCIONARIO *goes over to* SANCHO, *removes his derby hat and cigar, lifts him up and throws him over his shoulder.* SANCHO *hangs loose, lifeless. To audience.*) He's the best model we got! ¡Ajúa! (*Exit.*)

DISCUSSION QUESTIONS

1. Describe Honest Sancho's business. What does he sell and to whom?
2. Discuss in small groups the character of Miss Jimenez. Whom does she represent? What does she represent?
3. Describe the three characters that are on sale. What does each have to do with the stereotyping of Mexican Americans?
4. Discuss the significance of the reversal at the end of this farce.

WRITING TOPICS

1. Imagine you are a theater critic for the newspaper and that you saw this play performed in a park. Write a review of the play.
2. Write a one-act play, a short farce, for radio. How do you change the visual aspects of humor for presentation for a sound-only medium?

MURRIETA ON THE HILL

Sergio Elizondo

Sergio Elizondo was born on April 29, 1930, in El Fuerte, Sinaloa, Mexico. He entered the United States illegally and lived by doing menial labor. In 1953 he turned himself in to the Immigration and Naturalization Service in order to regularize his status in the United States. Once done, he directed himself toward obtaining an education, earning degrees at Findlay College in Ohio (B.A., 1958) and at the University of North Carolina at Chapel Hill (M.A., 1961, Ph.D., 1964). He teaches at New Mexico State University and, through the literature he writes, seeks to open the minds of his Chicano students.

He has written four books that differ widely in style and technique. *Perros y antiperros; una épica chicana (Dogs and Antidogs; a Chicano Epic)* (1972) contrasts the dogs (Anglos) with the antidogs (Chicanos). To capture the flavor of popular speech, Elizondo avails himself of a very autobiographical book entitled *Libro para batos y chavalas chicanas (A Book for Chicano Guys and Gals)* (1977), writing at once as a wise teacher, lover, and introspective philosopher. *Rose, la flauta (Rose, the Flute)* (1980) explores the process of becoming Chicano for first-generation Mexicans like Elizondo: first you are Mexican, then you become a gringo, and then you get to be a Chicano. Finally, *Muerte en una estrella (Death in a Star)* (1984) is a story of two young second-generation Chicano protagonists. They share with their parents their nostalgic remembrance of their native land, though they themselves feel it only vicariously. The story relates the death of the two boys who, while enrolled in a Job Corps program, decide to steal a car and go to a march. They are caught and shot to death by a policeman. As they die, they communicate telepathically. While the narrative technique, consisting mostly of dialogue and stream of consciousness, may be full of artifice, the story is based on actual events.

"Murrieta on the Hill," translated by Gustava Segade, is a poem that is part of Sergio Elizondo's epic poem *Perros y antiperros (Dogs and Antidogs*). In this work Elizondo channels the anger of the Chicano youth of the early 1970s into the re-creation of legendary hero Joaquín Murrieta, who exacts payment for all injustice.

In eight and thirty six
through hills and curves of bald earth
crying ¡mulas![1]
Comes a muleteer along the hill
5   alone
a man
animals
the heart is sweating
lariats
10 sombrero
huaraches[2]
hide
he is the king of the trail.

If because I'm poor, and wear a sombrero,
15 Brother, you don't respect me . . .
Make way, ¡adios![3]
Drink of my water
smoke my tobacco
and, que te vaya bien, Güero.[4]
20 Between the sierra[5] and the sea
to Santa Barbara I bear my cargo.
I pass slowly.
I paint images with my solitude
between the heights and the sea.

25 I am quiet, a man of peace
but on my waist I strap
an onion-cutting knife;
on my shoulder, a horsehair lariat.
I have lived a hundred years,

---

[1] Mules!
[2] Sandal-like woven leather shoes.
[3] Good-bye!
[4] Godspeed, blonde one.
[5] Mountain range.

30 Califas is my home
and my Tata[6] lives in México.

In my Catholic faith
live I and my love;
the Holy Child looks over me
35 daily and at night;
through the Camino Real[7]
San Cristobal[8] of the muleteers
accompanies me
I'm going north.
I see.
40 They killed Cholos and Californios[9]
in the Sonora mines.
They were light-haired men with pistols
and insolence of heart.

The threads of Chicano murmur
45 wove stories about me.
They say I killed me many,
it is said I even wore
a Texas hat . . .
that I would cut ears off
50 to leave a sign
wherever I went.
They used to kill my brothers,
I left the gabas[10] a bit lopped off.

DISCUSSION QUESTIONS

1. How does the epic hero describe himself?
2. Discuss whether the image that he projects is one of peace, as he proclaims, or one of violence.
3. Compare his views of California and Texas as he describes them in this poem.

---

[6] Dad.
[7] Literally, the royal road—the historic highway of California.
[8] St. Christopher, patron saint of travelers.
[9] Hispanics/Latinos and Californians.
[10] *Gabas* is short for *gabachos*, meaning foreigners; here specifically whites—much like the word *gringoes*.

4. This nineteenth-century heroic figure appears in the form of a muleteer or mule driver. Discuss whether this appearance is appropriate for a hero.

WRITING TOPICS

1. Taking on the role of the epic hero, compose a toast (a poetic, bragging self-description) to yourself.
2. Write an essay discussing the function of heroes in our society. What special purpose might heroes serve in the Hispanic community?

ARISE, CHICANO

Angela de Hoyos

Born in Coahuila, Mexico, Angela de Hoyos displayed artistic inclinations from early childhood. During her youth, she was badly burned in an accident with a gas heater. To keep up her spirits as she recovered, she would speak to her inner voice in rhymes and verses. Later, her family moved to San Antonio, Texas. There, after an eclectic education at the University of Texas-San Antonio, San Antonio College, San Antonio Art Institute, and the Witte Museum, Angela de Hoyos began writing poetry for various publications and founded *Huehuetitlan*, a literary journal.

Her poetry, which has been translated into five languages, is included in a number of works such as the *Longman Anthology of World Literature by Women, 1875–1975, Mexican American Literature, The Third Woman: Minority Women Writers of the United States, Sotto Il Quinto Sole, After Aztlan: Latino Poets of the Nineties,* and other anthologies. She has also authored several collections of her poetry. *Arise, Chicano and Other Poems* (1975) calls for change in the social, economic, and political conditions of her people. Her second book, *Chicano Poems for the Barrio,* also published in 1975, explores identity. *Selecciones* (1976) frames social issues within a dialogue between life and death, ending with hope. Finally, *Woman, Woman* (1985) portrays the experiences of women in society.

Angel de Hoyos's "Arise, Chicano," translated by Mireya Robles, is the lead poem in the collection *Arise, Chicano and Other Poems,* though it appears in third position in the chapbook. The poem enjoins the listener, presumably a migrant worker, to reach inside and save himself.

In your migrant's world of hand-to-mouth days,
your children go unsmiling to a cold bed,
the bare walls rockaby the same wry song,
a ragged dirge, thin as the air . . .

5   I have seen you go down
under the shrewd heel of exploit—
your long suns of brutal sweat
with ignoble pittance crowned.
Trapped in the never-ending fields
10   where you stoop, dreaming of sweeter dawns,
while the mocking whip of slavehood
confiscates your moment of reverie.
Or beneath the stars, offended
by your rude songs of rebellion
15   . . . when, at last, you shroud your dreams
and with them, your hymn of hope.

Thus a bitterness in your life:
wherever you turn for solace
there is an embargo.
20   How to express your anguish
when not even your burning words
are yours, they are borrowed
from the festering barrios of poverty,
and the sadness in your eyes
25   only reflects the mute pain of your people.

Arise, Chicano—that divine spark within you
surely says—Wash your wounds
and swathe your agonies.
There is no one to succor you.
30   You must be your own messiah.

DISCUSSION QUESTIONS

1. Describe the plight of the farmworker as presented in this poem.
2. Discuss the problems faced by impoverished urban Hispanics as depicted by de Hoyos.
3. The poem begins by discussing the problems of the children. Examine the likelihood that the children can escape the poverty that their parents have known.
4. Discuss the solution to the farmworker's problems, as proposed by the poet.

WRITING TOPICS

1. Write an essay proposing specific social programs to reduce poverty and alleviate despair.
2. Write a journal entry from the perspective of an impoverished parent of young children.

I Am Joaquín

Rodolfo "Corky" Gonzales

Rodolfo "Corky" Gonzales was born on June 18, 1928, in Denver, Colorado. He grew up in a difficult neighborhood, raised with his five brothers and sisters by his father. Gonzales claims that these circumstances taught him early the importance of defending himself. He became interested in boxing in 1943, but did not compete until after World War II. He was quite successful in competition, with a record of sixty-five wins, nine losses, and one draw. In addition to competing as a boxer, he was a bail bondsman and the owner of "Corky's Corner"—a bar where he became an advisor to *barrio* people who needed his counsel. Around 1957, Gonzales became the first Mexican-American district captain for the Democratic Party in Denver. In 1959, he financed *Viva*, the first *barrio* newspaper in Denver. Soon after, he served as the Colorado coordinator of the Viva Kennedy presidential campaign and the chairman of the city's antipoverty program, as well as a general agent for Summit Fidelity and Surety Company of Colorado.

Los Voluntarios (The Volunteers), a politically activist unit formed to protect Chicano youth from the abuses of the system—particularly the police, was founded by Gonzales in 1963. It was funded by the government's Office of Economic Opportunity and provided low-income youth with employment. Gonzales continued his work for the inner-city youth of Denver, serving on the boards of a number of social service commissions, until 1966, when he was accused of discriminating against blacks and whites in favor of Chicanos. He responded by founding the Crusade for Justice and developing a program that would allow for the Mexicanization of Chicano culture and the political Americanization of his people. He went on to produce a manifesto called the "Plan of the Barrio," adopting the concept of Aztlán to identify Chicanos with their Mexican Indian heritage.

In 1972 Gonzales published *I Am Joaquín/Yo soy Joaquín*, an epic poem that some describe as a social document rather than art. The poem, however, is very much appreciated by Chicanos, because

it provided the revolutionary movement with a very succinct statement of Chicano nationalism and ideology. The following selection,
in effect, served as a battlecry to the Chicano movement and implied
an invitation to rebel.

◎

. . . Here I stand
                    before the Court of Justice
                            Guilty
for all the glory of my Raza[1]
5   to be sentenced to despair.
Here I stand
      Poor in money
      Arrogant with pride
                  Bold with Machismo
10   Rich in courage
                  and
            Wealthy in spirit and faith.
My knees are caked with mud.
My hands calloused from the hoe.
15 I have made the Anglo[2] rich
                  yet
      Equality is but a word,
            the Treaty of Hidalgo has been broken
            and is but another treacherous promise.
20 My land is lost
                  and stolen,
My culture has been raped,
            I lengthen
            the line at the welfare door
25 and fill the jails with crime.
            These then
are the rewards
            this society has

30 For sons of Chiefs
                  and Kings
                  and bloody Revolutionists.
Who
gave a foreign people
            all their skills and ingenuity

---

[1] Race.
[2] Whites.

35 to pave the way with Brains and Blood
for
those hordes of Gold starved
                                    Strangers
Who
40 changed our language
and plagiarized our deeds
                        as feats of valor
                        of their own.
They frowned upon our way of life
45   and took what they could use.
                    Our Art
                    Our Literature
                    Our music, they ignored
so they left the real things of value
50 and grabbed at their own destruction
                    by their Greed and Avarice
They overlooked that cleansing fountain of
                    nature and brotherhood
        Which is Joaquín
55   We start to MOVE.
        La Raza!
Mejicano!
    Español!
        Latino!
60   Hispano!
            Chicano!³
or whatever I call myself
                    I look the same
                    I feel the same
65   I cry
                        and
                    Sing the same

        I am the masses of my people and
        I refuse to be absorbed.
70   I am Joaquín
        The odds are great
        but my spirit is strong
                        My faith unbreakable
                        My blood is pure
75 I am Aztec Prince and Christian Christ
                    I SHALL ENDURE!
                    I WILL ENDURE!

---

³ Various groups/names within *La Raza* (the race): Mexicans, Spanish, Latino, Hispanic, Chicano.

DISCUSSION QUESTIONS

1. Describe where the poetic persona finds himself at the opening of the poem. Why is he there?
2. Discuss his description of his knees, his hands, his land, and his culture.
3. Consider the questions posed in lines 32 through 43 of the poem. Who is responsible for what?
4. What is the solution that the poet offers in closing? Discuss his affirmation.

WRITING TOPICS

1. Write an essay analyzing the poem in terms of "I" (yourself), and "the Other" (any other entity, such as your enemy, your "other" side, those people different from you, an institution, the government, and so on).
2. As a radio talk show host, write an interview with the poet.

CHAPTER TEN

DEFINING WOMANHOOD,
ASSUMING MANHOOD

In Hispanic societies the man's role traditionally has been defined as that of the macho. He was proud and in control. Any fears he had remained hidden beneath surface bluster. In his society, obedience from the women around him was expected. Women, on the other hand, balanced the *machismo* of men with *marianismo*. With the Virgin Mary as her model, a woman's role required that she be submissive, chaste, and respectful. The family's honor depended on her circumspect behavior and her strength of character.

Understandably, these traditional gender roles for Hispanic men and women were significantly changed by migration to an urban setting in an industrial economy. Some writers have addressed in their writings the nature of these role changes and their effect on the Hispanic family. For instance, the traditional societal role for the man was that of breadwinner and provider to his family. But today, a female left as head of a household does what she must in order to supply her children with the basics they need to survive. For example, in the selection by Nicholasa Mohr, the author pays tribute to the resourcefulness of a young widowed mother.

FILOMENA

Roberta Fernández

Roberta Fernández was born in Laredo, Texas, on November 17, 1940. She was raised and educated in the state, receiving her B.A. and her M.A. from the University of Texas at Austin. Subsequently, she earned her Ph.D. in romance languages from the University of Califor-nia at Berkeley (1990). Fernández has taught, researched, and lectured at many universities around the country, including Brown University, Carleton College, the University of California at Santa Barbara, the University of Massachusetts, Mills College, where she started a literary magazine entitled *Prisma: A Multicultural, Multilingual Women's Literary Review,* the University of Texas, and the University of Houston.

Her understanding and appreciation for the aesthetic possibilities of language are evidenced in her short stories, published both in English and in Spanish, in magazines such as *The Massachusetts Review, Fem,* and *Melquíades,* and in anthologies such as *Chicana Creativity* and *Criticism: Charting New Frontiers in American Literature and Hispanic Short Fiction.* In addition, Fernández edited *Contemporary Latina Writers of the United States: An Anthology* (1993).

Her greatest achievement in narrative, however, is her novel *Intaglio: A Novel in Six Stories* (1990), which was selected as best fic-tion for 1991 by Multicultural Publishers Exchange. Within the novel, "Filomena" is interwoven with five other stories. This particular story subtly explores death and rebirth in a divided family.

I

¹   Every year, in early November, the life of the dead assumed primary importance for Filomena and me, and in preparation for our commemora-

tion, we were making our purchases at the *mercado*.[1] All around us, pails of flowers—mostly *zempoalxochitles*,[2] the color of the sun—were displayed, as one vendor after another tried to entice us with the same statement: "*¡Flores para los muertos! ¡Flores para los muertos!*"[3] As we walked around, my arms formed a circle around the sweet-smelling clusters of flowers that Filomena had already picked out.

2   To get a little relief from the scent of the flowers, I turned my head upwards and saw that from the second floor of the *mercado*, sheets with large bold letters announced "*El 2 de noviembre—Día de los Muertos.*"[4] All over the signs, painted skeletons danced around a central figure who was draped over a chair with a scythe in his right hand. Years before, Filomena had told me his name—Mictlantecuhtli, the Lord of the Dead. "*Pobrecito*[5] *Mictlantecuhtli*," I thought to myself, "no one in school ever talks about you. Maybe they're all hiding from you." Looking at his bony figure, I whispered, "Ah, Mictlantecuhtli, you certainly are no stranger to Filomena and me."

3   I turned to Filomena to point out the skeletons on the sheets, then skipped the gesture. It was obvious she was through with her purchases and we were ready to go past the throng of celebrants choosing their offerings for the holiday. Awed with the beauty of the scene we would soon be leaving behind, I now took in one deep breath after another until I became intoxicated with the smell of the flowers. Like me, Filomena was holding the bouquets to her nose. Not wanting to break the spell of the moment, we walked in silence, content simply to be together.

4   Her house was only a few blocks from the marketplace, and as we approached it, I began to measure my steps by hers, giving her quick side glances. Today, as on most days, she had gathered her long dark hair at the nape of her neck with a black barrette. Her face was free of any make-up and she was wearing a gray rayon dress which came to her midcalf. No doubt it was this simplicity of manner that gave her a certain agelessness and enigmatic wisdom. My mother, who had just turned forty, had once told me that she and Filomena were about the same age. This I found hard to comprehend, for they seemed so different from each other. My mother had a certain quickness of manner, while Filomena moved in slow steady paces—one, a volatile, unpredictable spirit, the other, deeply rooted and steadfast.

5   As we walked along, I kept thinking of the three people we'd soon be honoring: Alejandro, Nalberto and Martín. In the four years I had been helping Filomena with the commemoration, I had picked up a lot of disjointed

---

[1] Market.
[2] Flowers—zinnias, marigolds.
[3] Flowers for the dead!
[4] November 2—Day of the Dead.
[5] Poor little . . . .

details about Nalberto, her father, who had been killed in a battle at Zacatecas, a few months before she had been born. Even though I knew an assortment of facts about his life, my sense of Nalberto was vague, no doubt because of Filomena's own sense of her father. Perhaps more confusing for me was the fact that Filomena was already fifteen years older than her father had been when a *federal*[6] had pierced his heart with a bullet. He looked so young in the only photograph she had of him that I kept imagining her as Nalberto's mother rather than his daughter.

6   In contrast to the indefiniteness that surrounded Nalberto, Martín had continued to maintain a presence in Filomena's life. They had been married in 1932, the year they settled in our area, and although she was always reticent about expressing her feelings verbally, she still had given me a sense of the undying love she felt for Martín. Often she described his fiery Pedro Armendáriz smile and his brawny body which heavy physical labor had made more sinewy. A deep sadness overtook her whenever she remembered the day he had been called to serve in the war, leaving her behind with the three children.

7   Every day she had gathered them in her little bedroom where she had set up an altar in honor of the *Virgen de San Juan de los Lagos*.[7] Her *altarcito*[8] had consisted only of a table with a small statue of the lovely dark-haired Virgin surrounded by her father's photograph and several snapshots of Martín. The altar had expanded, however, since she had added a small offering for every month Martín was gone. Then one day a young Marine had knocked on her door telling her that her husband had been wounded in Iwo Jima. A few days after that visit, she had quietly joined the legion of other women who mourned their loved ones with small black crosses on their windows.

8   Almost immediately she had enlarged her altar with a picture of the Sacred Heart of Mary. Her neighbors, knowing she found consolation through her sacred articles, had added two new pieces to her collection: a statue of the *Virgen de Guadalupe*[9] and a tin *retablo*[10] of the Holy Trinity, which she nailed to the wall, next to the images of the Virgin. In the evenings, after the children went to bed, she would spend hours kneeling in front of her altar, lighting and relighting candles, ridding herself of any accusations she might have made against God and the Virgin in the moments of initial grief. During the day as she cleaned houses she whispered away her sorrow: "and pray for us sinners, now and at the hour of our death. *Amén.*"

9   Slowly she began to realize that she could not take care of the children by herself, for the work she was able to do never yielded a sufficient income.

---

[6] Federal policemen.
[7] Virgin of San Juan de los Lagos.
[8] Little altar.
[9] Virgin of Guadalupe (patron saint of Mexico).
[10] Altarpiece.

Bureaucratic stipulations overwhelmed her and she was unable to handle the required paperwork for her widow's pension. So, on the day she finally came to terms with what she perceived as her only solution, she gently informed the children about her decision. Alejandro would be boarded in a Catholic school and Lucila and Mateo would be sent for a short while to live with relatives in Michoacán. As soon as she resolved her finances, she'd send for the younger two.

10   From then on she worked at various chores at once but her primary job consisted of helping my mother take care of me. Needing to activate her quiescent maternal feelings, Filomena showered me with affection and I, sensing her deep love, began to view her as my second mother. By the time I was five I knew all about the various saints she admired, and on many occasions I attended novenas with her. On the day she was initiated into the Marian Sodality, I too became one of the *Hijitas*[11] with the long white dresses and blue scapulars. Feeling that I was now connected to all the saints and martyrs who had ever lived and to the hundreds still to come, I began to listen with fascination to Filomena's endless references to an ever expanding pantheon of saints. I particularly enjoyed her descriptions of the religious festivals in which she participated every year when she and Alejandro went back to Michoacán to visit the other children.

11   Lucila and Mateo never came to visit Filomena, telling her they felt no need to leave the land of their ancestors where they were both quite happy. So Alejandro, Filomena and I spent more and more time together. During the summers and on holidays, Alejandro took a break from his tasks at boarding school and accompanied us to so many parish celebrations I soon began to feel like his littlest sister. I admired his gentle ways and considered him a good substitute for the brother I did not have.

12   When I was seven, Alejandro graduated from high school. Right away he got a job, hoping to reunite his brother and sister with his mother. By then, however, the seventeen-year-old Lucila had a *novio*[12] she did not want to leave behind; and Mateo, at fifteen, had clearly accepted his role as the youngest son in his aunt's family. Alejandro was truly disappointed at their decision, for it was unlikely he could join them in Uruapan, a place that had never been home for him. Filomena consoled Alejandro for the way things had turned out and affirmed that their lives were now to be spent in our city. Alejandro then wrote a long letter to his brother encouraging him to prepare himself scholastically so he could attend the university in Morelia. Then he dedicated himself to his role as breadwinner for his divided family. At that time he begged Filomena to take a rest while he provided for their needs. She agreed to remain at home but continued to take in ironing.

13   One afternoon while I was helping Filomena with her work, Alejandro

---

11 Little Daughters—members of the Sodality, a church organization.
12 Boyfriend, fiancé.

walked in with three white wrought iron birdcages. We both admired their unusual workmanship, following him to the tiny screened-in porch in the back of the house where he hung them next to the geraniums. They remained empty for several weeks and finally Filomena suggested using them as planters for more flowers. As soon as she said this, Alejandro told her that within a week he would make sure she would never again be alone during his absence. Much to my pleasant surprise, in exactly two days he filled the cages with a variety of finches, canaries and orange-breasted lovebirds which added a joyful twittering to the house. Filomena gave a name to each of the birds and began to note the unique characteristics she found in each one. I had never seen her so enthusiastic before and she admitted that Alejandro had given her the best present she had ever received.

14   "I'll have to give you an even better present," he had remarked.

15   Alejandro was true to his word, and on a bright September morning when Filomena and I had just returned from Mass, he asked us to step out to the porch. There in a huge domed cage was a radiant green macaw with a crimson breast and a yellow poll. When she saw us she squawked, "*¡Loro! ¡Loro! ¡Loro!*"[13] Then, as she walked along the dome of the cage gripping the roof with her large claws, she told us her name in a throaty voice: "¡Kika! ¡Kika!"

16   "Do you like her?"Alejandro asked with a glowing smile. "If you like her, she's yours."

17   "*Mira, nomás,*"[14] Filomena shook her head as if she could not take it all in.

18   "*Es tuya, Mamá.* She's yours," he repeated once again.

19   For a moment I was afraid Filomena was not going to accept Kika as she stood there with her arms crossed, shaking her head yet smiling as she inspected the parrot.

20   "Kika's an Amazona parrot from either the Yucatán or Central America," Alejandro explained. "I bought her from Mrs. Arzuela on the condition that I could take her back if you didn't like her."

21   Much to my relief, Filomena accepted Kika and since the *guacamaya*[15] had been well trained by Mrs. Arzuela, the bird was allowed free rein of the house. During the day, Kika flew from room to room but she always returned to her favorite perch, a swing Alejandro had hitched onto a corner of the ceiling in the livingroom. At night, on her own she walked into her cage. Then Filomena would cover it with dark towels, letting Kika know it was time to go to sleep. In the mornings when Filomena removed the towels from all four cages, she was immediately greeted by the happy trills of the finches and canaries and Kika would add to the rituals with her own rasping

---

[13] Parrot! Parrot! Parrot!
[14] Well, would you look at that!
[15] Macaw, a type of parrot.

sounds. Occasionally she also let out two or three whistles. The house which had been quiet for so many years had suddenly become alive again, thanks to Alejandro.

22   Unfortunately, Alejandro did not have enough time to enjoy the melodic pleasures he had brought to his home. Within six months after his graduation he was inducted into the service to fight the atheistic communists who, we were constantly reminded in school, wanted to take over the entire free world.

23   "Don't worry," Alejandro had said to his mother. "I'll be back. In the meantime you have Kika and the other birds to remind you of me. Every time you hear their singing, remember that my spirit will always speak to you through their songs."

24   And so Alejandro went away once again. Almost as soon as he left, Filomena taped a large map of Asia to the wall. In front of the map she placed a small statue of the *Santo Niño de Atocha*. The patron saint of travelers, she explained to me. And every night when she recited her prayers, she would look at the names of the strange-sounding places she heard pronounced on the radio and console herself with the thought that at least Alejandro might be fighting the heathens in some of those towns and villages whose names she herself did not try to articulate. In school we heard about the Yellow Peril that Alejandro had gone to fight, an enemy I tended to imagine as John Wayne riding over the eastern horizon with hordes of barbarians behind him, just as I had seen him do in "The Conqueror." As Filomena and I prayed for Alejandro, I would envision him as St. George slaying the dragon of the Mongolians. "Come home, Alejandro. Come home," I would repeat over and over after every prayer, hoping that when I opened my eyes, Alejandro would appear in the room with us.

25   Alejandro did not come back to us alive. Within a year of his departure he was sent home from Korea in a casket. I was so grief-stricken with his death and the denial of my supplications that for days I wept without stopping. All around me the neighbors shook their heads and said that fairness had betrayed herself when she had dealt with Filomena. Hearing this, I cried all the more, forcing my mother to keep me away from Filomena so that my lamentations would not add to her sorrow.

26   So, I only saw Filomena at the funeral where I was surprised that unlike the neighbors' strong reactions and my own uncontrollable sobbing, she seemed to respond to Alejandro's death with equanimity, for she only cried a little, both before and after the funeral, and then during the sounding of the taps. After that, she retired to her little room where once again she sat in front of her altar for long hours, praying for the souls of the three men in her family whose lives had been prematurely snuffed out in distant wars. This time Filomena's mourning period lasted through a month of solitary prayer and silent meditation.

27   At home, my mother recited stories to me about her own losses as a child and Tía Griselda told me about the way she had coped when her father had

died when she was ten. "Every time I'd shut my eyes," she'd say, "I would see my father behind a bright streak of light. So I would sit for hours with my eyes closed, trying to get a glimpse of his face behind the light." Even as she spoke, Alejandro's young face would appear before me, covered by a golden aura, which in my mind I would try to push up, away from his face. Little Adriana would touch my shoulder, then whisper in her little baby's voice, "He is up there. You can't see him but he sees everything you do. Don't cry anymore. He's going to be with you again." The matter-of-fact tone in which she made her prediction consoled me immensely and I resolved to keep the memory of Alejandro alive.

28   When my mother thought it was proper for me to resume my old habit of spending the late afternoons with Filomena, I found that she had completely reassembled and expanded her altar. The table had been replaced with a wooden pedestal on which she had crowded in her various statues. Green votive glasses with perpetually lit candles were interspersed between the photographs, and on the wall above the altar she had hung a large tin mirror on which the flickering of the candles was repeated in soothing rhythms. Zacarías, her neighbor, had attached thick hooks into the ceiling above the altar. There she had hung her bird cages, seemingly to include the birds' warbles and the parrot's noisy voice as part of her offering. Moved by the beatific spirit of Filomena's simple heart, I took off my gold chain with the tiny medallion of the *Virgen de Guadalupe*, then placed it on the altar in front of Alejandro's picture. After that I joined her in prayer every afternoon while the birds chirped softly above us. As I knelt there I began to realize that my prayers were no longer murmurs of petition; instead, they had become statements of resolution: "Thy will be done on earth as it is in heaven."

II

29   As the end of October approached, Filomena was planning a trip to Michoacán to participate in the traditional Tarascan rituals of the Day of the Dead. Part of her pilgrimage would include the observances on the island of Janitzio and she wanted me to benefit from them also. My parents, who had never allowed me to travel with any of my friends even to near-by places, surprised me by being open to Filomena's suggestion. The experience might be a good spiritual cleansing for me, they reasoned, as they discussed the trip with the rest of the family. As a result of the conversations, Griselda finally agreed to go with us. So, on the 28th of October, Griselda, Filomena and I set out to Morelia on the all-night express offered by Tres Estrellas de Oro.

30   In Morelia we made connections to Uruapan, where Mateo, Lucila and her *novio* Mauricio met us. At first I felt a bit uncomfortable with Filomena's real children, knowing that in the last several years I had spent more time with her than they had. Both were very amiable, however, trying their best to put me at ease. "Lucila and I speak Spanish and English," Mateo had let me know. "So you can speak to us in either language."

31   "Let's speak in both," I suggested. "Sometimes in English and some-times in Spanish. We can also use Tex-Mex." With that, we all laughed and settled down to the business of preparing the offerings we would be taking with us to Janitzio.

32   Rosa—Filomena's sister—and her husband had already taken care of the preliminary details. They proudly pointed to a five-foot cross made out of chickenwire which was ready to have the chrysanthemums mounted on it. Two days later, all the young people, including Rosa's and Arturo's three children, spent the morning in the adjoining field gathering the yellow flow-ers; later, we hooked them onto the cross with tiny wires. While we were busy with the cross, Filomena, Rosa and Griselda prepared the dishes we would be taking with us to the island. By mid-afternoon we were ready to set out in Arturo's truck to Pátzcuaro where we would be taking a small boat to the island.

33   Filomena and Griselda rode with Arturo while Lucila, Mateo and I sat in the bed of the truck holding on to the cross and other offerings. Along the way we took turns sprinkling water from a large bucket on the flowers. We also waved now and then to other families on the road who were as loaded down as we were.

34   "Alejandro would love all this," Lucila sighed. "He relished ceremonies. From the time we were very small, Mamá passed on to us a sense of ritual. Alejandro picked it up even more than I did. He loved getting dressed up in white during the month of May when he and all the other kids in the neigh-borhood would go to offer flowers to the virgin." She looked into the dis-tance, then repeated, "Alejandro loved ceremony."

35   Mateo must have noticed that I had gotten very quiet, for he suddenly asked me what single memory of his brother stood out the most for me. After a pause I described the day when Alejandro had brought Kika home to complete the household of birds. "The birds have now multiplied," I explained, "so that every time there's a new batch I realize that Alejandro's music will be with us forever. He gave your mother the perfect gift."

36   After a while Mateo said he was tired of only good memories. "Let's face it," he said, "Alejandro was mother's favorite and that's why she kept him with her."

37   "I used to get very jealous about that too," Lucila admitted, "but some-time in the last three years I realized that she really did want us all together. She just didn't have the slightest notion of how to go about supporting us. I think Mamá assumed we would all come together again at some point. But it just didn't work out that way. Or at least you and I wound up messing up her plan."

38   "*No. No. No.* We really should have all come back here together," Mateo insisted.

39   "Once Papi died, Mamá would not have left him back there all alone. Now, you know she'll stay there forever. She's got to take care of both Papi's and Alejandro's graves."

40   "At least we're all here now, Nenita," he patted my cheek just as Arturo knocked on the back window to let us know we had arrived in Pátzcuaro.

41   Before heading for the lake he whirled us through the town, stopping at the Zócalo where I was amazed at the size of the colonial plaza and the activity already underway for the big festivities. When we finally got to the lake, many small boats were setting out, just as a dozen or so Tarascan fishermen with their huge butterfly nets were riding in with the tide. Already I was beginning to feel more at peace than I had ever felt before.

42   "You're staying with our friends in Pátzcuaro tonight," Arturo told Griselda and me. "And tomorrow you're being taken across the lake to Janitzio." Then he turned to Filomena, "Tomorrow you'll have to leave by three o'clock. The lake will be full of boats by dusk."

43   The next day we were at the shores of Lake Pátzcuaro by two thirty, loaded down with all the offerings we were taking. The boatman, an experienced navigator of the lake, was not at all surprised with our cargo. Compared to other loads he had carried to Janitzio in other years, he thought ours was rather light. His small boat was built in such a way that the cross could easily go in an upright position in the middle section. Filomena, Griselda and I rode in the prow and the others in the stern. By three o'clock we were on our way, gliding on the tranquil waters of the lake. Already by then, other small craft like ours dotted the view clear to the horizon.

44   "I'm really on a pilgrimage," I thought to myself, and with the waters lapping the side of the boat, I gently closed my eyes promising myself I would accept whatever happened. Opening them a few seconds later, I saw slightly ahead of us a small crew of fishermen with giant butterfly nets gracefully dipping into the placid water for the white fish that had made the lake famous. Watching the fishermen line up their boats in a row while they dipped to the right, then to the left, I felt I was entering a state of blissful surrender. My parents had been right; I was definitely undergoing a spiritual cleansing. While in this peaceful state I glanced first at Filomena, then at Griselda and I realized that they too were in a sublime mood.

45   As we got closer to Janitzio we saw hundreds of pilgrims already milling around at the highest point of the island, where the cemetery was located. Griselda pointed to the terraced slopes we'd have to climb to reach the top, then sighed, looking at the steep stairway. "Don't worry," Filomena reassured her. It would be worth the effort. She promised that in the morning, after we finished with the ceremony, we could continue farther up the steps to the balcony where we would have a spectacular view. In the meantime we followed her as she made her way through the multitude of people heading towards the cemetery with their offerings.

46   Inching our way through the crowds, we finally located the spot where Arturo's father was buried, knowing it was the only grave we could rightfully claim. First Mateo dug a small hole at the head of the grave, where we immediately buried the stem of the cross. Upright on the grave we placed about a

dozen tall candles while Lucila arranged vases full of chrysanthemums here and there along the edges of the grave. The rest of us scattered yellow petals on the mound itself, where we then placed our photographs. When we were finished, Griselda rolled out a long cloth alongside the grave and Filomena gave each of us a small cushion.

47   As the evening wore on we took turns praying the rosary together, then relaxing, watching the people closest to us. All around us, crosses sheathed in golden blossoms let out a gentle fragrance and the glow of the candles added a sense of splendor against the darkness. Then, as the night emerged, the dewy wetness in the air became saturated with the pungent aroma of the flowers and the candles, and a sense of peace seemed to envelop the entire place.

48   After a while Filomena began to express the doubts we had each secretly started to feel. "None of them is buried here," she whispered. What if their spirits could not make their way back here as we believed they would? In the end, however, the joyous scene aroused our faith and we set aside our doubts, opening our baskets, and placing the food on top of the grave. Lucila poured water into glasses and hot chocolate into ceramic cups for our guests. Out of another basket we took out our own food and ate, keeping conversation to a minimum, and, although I was sure the others were as tired as I was, none of us lay down to sleep.

49   As the first light of day streaked the sky, the Indian flutes began to sound here and there throughout the cemetery. Their high monotones calling the spirits home dissipated any misgivings we ever had about our loved ones. I shut my eyes tightly, envisioning Alejandro smiling at me, with Kika perched on his shoulder. Then, just as quickly as he had appeared, his face was covered by a blaze of light. In the distance I could hear the chirping of the birds getting louder as he and Kika were suddenly absorbed by the sun. "I saw him," I whispered to Filomena as she gently nodded her head. Griselda, too, had an expression of bliss and even Mateo was very quiet, staring out into the distance.

50   Lucila got up to embrace her mother and Filomena extended her hand to Mateo. "*Hijitos*, now more than ever, I know I have to return to my little home up North. Why don't you come back with me?"

51   Lucila put her head against her mother's shoulder, whispering that just as her mother felt she belonged in *el norte*,[16] so she and Mateo now had their home in this beautiful land of perpetual springtime.

52   "Don't worry, Mamá. Everything is okay," Mateo murmured.

53   I kept looking at Filomena as we began to gather our things. This is the happiest I've ever seen her, I thought. Then she smiled at me, "Here we all find what we are looking for."

---

[16] The North.

III

54   For the next three years, in contrast to the public communal festivities in Janitzio, Filomena held a private observance of the Day of the Dead; as her assistant I was her only witness. We tried to keep our ceremonies as close as possible to those in Janitzio, even though we did not go into the elaborate preparations that had taken place there. Here we simply gathered the *zempoalxochitles* and other flowers at the market on the eve of the holiday. Lucila, who was now coming for yearly visits, was bringing us decorated bees-wax candles which Filomena stored in the refrigerator until we needed them. This was the one night she would leave the bird room lit up so that Kika's screeches and the other nocturnal sounds could also form part of the offerings. I loved our private ceremony but up to then, I had not been able to recapture the spirit of the Indian celebration on the island nor the strong connection I had felt to Alejandro as the sun broke out on that special morning of personal transcendence. Filomena reassured me that I would have that experience again whenever I opened up to the gift of faith as I had done in Janitzio.

55   Over the last three years, Filomena's birds had multiplied many times over and her small house had become a music box of magnificent proportions, especially in the early morning and at sunset. The daily concerts could be heard blocks away but no one ever complained about Filomena's happy birds. In fact, the other children from the neighborhood had started to flock to the house they were now calling "la Pajarera Blanca, the white home of the birds." At first, five or six children had gathered on the sidewalk at dusk as the birds warbled away. Then more youngsters began to huddle together. One day Filomena discovered close to twenty children mingling outside, delightedly listening to her birds. "If you promise to be quiet, I'll let you come in," she had cautioned the children who then tiptoed into her house in hushed whispers.

56   In her cage, Kika squeaked with excitement at the visitors. As if they could sense the pleasure the children were getting from their song, the birds twittered ceaselessly in splendid synchronism. From then on, Filomena routinely invited the little friends into her home. Once inside the house, the children became enthralled with the incandescent lights and incense beckoning them to Filomena's altar. First, one or two youngsters were invited to pray with us; then, five or six joined in. Pretty soon, as many children as could be accommodated in the little room could be heard reciting Filomena's litanies in soft, repetitive sounds.

57   For the celebration we would be observing in a few hours Filomena had invited everyone who had been in her house within the last month. Who would come would depend on the neighbors' willingness to give parental permission. As far as I knew, most of the children observed the occasion strictly as All Souls Day, as I had done in the past, and their main ritual would consist of visiting the cemetery with their parents, who would lay a wreath

on the grave of their own dear ones. Most of them had never participated in cerebrations as joyous and elaborate as the one Filomena and I had been sharing for so long.

58　　As we neared the house, we heard the sweet trills of the canaries and finches which now took up the entire back porch. Their harmonizing seemed to rise a tone or two as soon as we stepped into the house, and while we placed the flowers in the different containers already pre-arranged around the altar, Kika flew above us in anticipation of what was to follow.

59　　By sundown we finished with the basic assembling; next, we distributed the bread onto plates nestled here and there around the altar and then as darkness set in, we lit the candles which made the room take on a bright glow. In the back porch we lit the only lights in the house. Tonight we would not use any towels on the cages, for we hoped that as we pronounced our benediction our feathered friends would accompany us with their song.

60　　Before long the children started to arrive.

61　　First Rosita and Laura from next door appeared, bringing four white sugar skulls with our names written across the foreheads. Next, Pepe and his four brothers showed up, each bearing candleholders shaped like a tree of life, which immediately went upon the altar. Zacarías's son brought his flute made of bamboo and Micaela's daughters each carried a tambourine. My best friend Aura and her brothers gave Filomena miniatures of skeleton-musicians made of gesso and gayly painted in vivid colors. Patricia and Adriana brought a surprise especially for me: a small wooden cross which they had decorated with chrysanthemums to look like the crosses in Mexico I had described to them. Even Verónica joined us bringing exquisitely embroidered napkins to cover the bread. Before long, eighteen children were gathered in front of Filomena's shining altar.

62　　With Kika perched on her shoulder, Filomena invited everyone to kneel. As she recited the prayers for the dead, Marcos began to play on his flute and the Miranda girls gently sounded the tambourines which elicited the birds into song. Pretty soon we were enveloped into one voice, as the incense of the candles and the perfumes of the *zempoalxo-chitles* floated around the room. As the different timbres and vapors merged above my head, I became entranced with the joyous reverence around me, and slowly, slowly, a dream-like image of Alejandro began to take shape in front of me. At that instant I thought the birds' song had reached perfection. Accompanying them, the flute resounded higher and higher filling the room; then the sounds and scents seemed to swirl their way out the window, taking the birds' trills with them up, up, up into the night. Suddenly Kika left Filomena's shoulder and perched herself on the altar. I looked at her red lores and her blue cheeks while she positioned herself for a night's sleep, and I knew that just a few seconds before, Alejandro had finally come home once again. Rejoicing I prayed, *"Amen! Amen! Amen!"*

IV

⁶³   By coincidence, ten years later I was home on the day that Kika died of a sudden attack of pneumonia.

⁶⁴   "*Se murió la Kika anoche*,"¹⁷ Filomena told me when I came by unexpectedly in the late morning.

⁶⁵   "How can that be? What happened?" Aware of how long Amazona parrots are supposed to live, I had assumed that Kika would be around for years and years. In shock I let Filomena guide me into the kitchen where Kika was laid out in a bright lacquered wooden chest from Olinalá. Filomena had lined the box with Kika's grains, then laid her sideways on top of her food.

⁶⁶   My eyes filled with tears as I listened to the silence in the house and marvelled at how the other birds must be sensing the passing of their companion. The only sounds came from Filomena as she described her surprise at finding Kika on her back, her claws gripping the heavy air above her. Her first reaction had been to cradle Kika in her arms, and when she had finally accepted that her pet was dead, she had called a taxidermist in the hopes of giving her a new life. Now, quite resolutely she stated that her memories of her parrot would suffice. Kika's great bird nature had consisted precisely in her moving about from room to room, letting out her rasping screeches. "*Fue una buena compañera*. A wonderful present from my Alejandro."

⁶⁷   We took Kika's box to the back yard and buried her under a pecan tree. Then, as we were down on our knees patting down the mound, we began to hear the cooing of the finches. One by one the birds picked up the sounds. Suddenly they burst out into their usual song.

⁶⁸   "How lovely! They're saying good-bye to their friend," Filomena commented very matter-of-factly. Then, she traced the sign of the cross on the loose dirt. "*Requiescat in pacem*,"¹⁸ she murmured.

V

⁶⁹   For many hours Filomena and I conversed, reminiscing over the many memories we shared of Kika and of Alejandro. As we went over the old days, I felt somewhat reaffirmed in what I subconsciously had come to seek. Lately I had been feeling very uncomfortable in one of my first graduate classes at the university. A middle-aged professor-poet, already on his way to becoming one of the major voices in American letters, taught his literature class with a degree of cynicism that made me uncomfortable. His total rejection of spiritual epiphanies bothered other members of the class, as well, and so we had started to meet on our own to comment more freely on some of the

---

¹⁷ Kika died last night.
¹⁸ Rest in peace (Latin).

writers we were reading. Even with our more open discussions in the small group, I still felt I was losing my old sense of identity. At times I even felt that many new images were being imprinted on me and that I had not even had the chance to approve or reject what was happening.

70   A few days before coming home I had paid a visit to the campus chapel where I had sat by myself in the front pew for a long time, staring at the statues on the strangely austere altar, unable to draw out the familiar consolation I sought. "Maybe I'm becoming a non-believer," I had thought to myself as I gathered my things, then headed down the lonely, narrow aisle, never to come back. Outside, the bright afternoon light only emphasized my sadness which I tried to overcome by recalling the many happy hours I had spent with Filomena and Kika and the neighborhood children who had come to our novenas. The contrast between the past and the present was so immense that I began to question whether things had really been the way I was remembering them. I knew then that I needed to go home.

71   Now, even Kika was gone. As I faced Filomena I suddenly began to have an uneasy feeling which soon seemed to take control of me. Perhaps the visit was not doing me much good after all.

72   "She's too accepting of everything that happens to her," I complained to my mother. " '*Así lo quiere Dios*'[19] is always on her lips."

73   "That's true. But Filomena is truly one of the happiest people I know, in spite of all the blows life has given her," was my mother's response, adding to my emerging dissatisfaction with what I perceived as their lack of critical thinking.

74   When I left that weekend I was even more confused than when I had come. Kika's death saddened me tremendously, for she had been my direct link to the memory of Alejandro and to the saddest and the happiest moments of my childhood. I was also very disturbed with Filomena's resignation to the death of so many of her loved ones. How easily she seemed to have given up Kika. Perhaps she hadn't really cared deeply about her, after all. Nor about any of the people in her life. This might be the reason why she had been willing to part with her children so many years ago. Would she react the same way if I went away for good?

75   As a defense against my new confusion, I began to give myself full-heartedly to the ideas of writers I admired for asking the right questions about being and about giving meaning to one's life through action: Sartre, Camus, Sábato, Beckett. Still, I sensed that in the end their philosophical conclusion about the essence of life seemed so meaningless and absurd. How long could one really appreciate their principles? "At bottom, it's a decadent philosophy, isn't it? Their ideas strike me as the perspective of a world in agony," I commented to one of my favorite professors.

---

[19] That is what God wants.

76   "You do need to question the position of those writers," she advised. "Here. I think you'll enjoy reading this little story. From what you've told me about yourself, I think you'll relate to it." She smiled as she handed me a copy of *Trois contes*. "Read 'Un cöeur simple.' 'A simple heart.' It's Flaubert's masterpiece. As you read it you'll see why I'm suggesting it to you."

77   "This story is about Filomena," I said to myself as I mulled over every word about the simple-hearted Félicitè and the great love she bore for her parrot Loulou whom she eventually transformed into her own image of God. Always physically and psychologically isolated, Félicitè lived through a state of loneliness that became more acute as she got older. Loulou then assumed a position of paramount importance in her life, leading Félicitè to conclude that the bird that people usually identified with the Holy Ghost had mistakenly been seen as a dove when in reality she had actually been a parrot. Convinced that Loulou was really an extension of the deity, Félicitè managed to transform her parrot into the image of God at the moment of her own death. As her spirit entered heaven in a mist of incense, Flaubert describes the parting of the clouds and the emergence of a large parrot which opened its wings to welcome and embrace the soul of Félicitè. Touched, I closed the book, amazed that the cynical Flaubert had actually given such credence to the faith of a simplehearted maid.

78   What answer I had found I was not really sure, but for the moment I decided that I needed to put a halt to the years of abstract thinking and to involve myself more with tangible and communal action. For me these new interests became personified in community activities. I found a real sense of authenticity through new contacts in many different projects but it was in the community arts that I found my most meaningful outlet. For a long time I participated in colorful exhibits in the parks, poetry readings in community centers, sales of folk crafts, coordination of children's folkloric dances. I felt that these activities connected me back to the stimulating creativity of the people who had served as my mentors as I was growing up, at the same time that they satisfied my new needs to move away from an alienating individualism towards a public collectivism much more in keeping with the experiences of my youth.

79   For many years these activities fulfilled me. Then one day I came across a new folk art which caught me completely off-guard. There, on a table underneath a blossoming magnolia tree, I saw dozens of earrings made to resemble the folk altars that many contemporary artists were assembling and exhibiting in galleries and museums. As I approached the table, I noticed that the artist-vendor was wearing a pair. I stared at the leather-backed keychains on which she had pasted a laminated holy card of *la Virgen de Guadalupe*. Around the inch-square "altar," she had glued rhinestones, interspersed with red and green glass beads to resemble the lights around some village altars. Amazed at the creation, I listened to the artist describe how she had sold two dozen in just two hours. "But friends have been advis-

ing me never to wear these in Mexico," she laughed. "They tell me that people might get upset that I've taken their national symbol out of context."

80   "*Sabes*, I've never had any real objection to people wearing clothing that resembles the American flag," I quickly told her. "Somehow that seems pretty abstract to me. But I'll admit that the sight of your earrings really galls me. I find them to be very insensitive to the spiritual beliefs of the people in the *pueblos*. I have a dear friend who would probably feel pretty sad at seeing you make light of her deeply-felt respect for religious icons. It's terribly personal with her."

81   "Oh, no! *No entiendes*," she retorted. "This is my way of showing respect for your friend's faith. I grew up in this sprawling metropolis." She spread her arms to emphasize her point. "So I never had any direct contact with the traditional religious sentiment that you are talking about. This is my way of giving tribute to that experience."

82   "I'll believe you," I smiled as I opened my purse. "How much are you asking for a pair?"

83   With the earrings in my purse I made my way through aisles of tables filled with folkwares. As I walked around, I ran my fingers over the smoothness of the laminated cover on the icon. "Now, why did I spend my money?" I thought. "I wonder what Filomena would think if I gave them to her?" Immediately I felt ashamed for even allowing the thought to pass through my mind, then concluded, "Only someone from this centerless city could have come up with these gaudy creations!"

84   I paused to look around me, at one colorful table after another. Wafts of sweet-smelling grass drifted about everywhere. At the far end of the park, a combo was blaring out its electrical instruments. As I made my way through the people's artwork, I looked up to see dozens of colorful balloons which had just been released. For a long time I watched the balloons moving upwards until they disappeared into the distant air.

85   As I stood there, I kept wondering if I would forever go from one crisis to another. How unlike Filomena who had stood firm in the face of real calamities. Perhaps some day I would once again draw some strength from the little *altarcitos* that I had known in my childhood.

86   On the way home, I stopped at a dimestore to buy some crayons. For hours that evening I drew a huge image of Kika as I remembered her: thick green feathers, yellow poll, blue cheeks and crimson breast. Satisfied, I ran my fingers over the waxen image several times, then folded up my drawing into a thick square. Cramming it into a glass jar, I was ready to put the lid on it when I remembered the earrings. "They will serve a purpose after all," I thought, as I dropped them in the jar and headed towards my car, then drove to a nearby eucalyptus grove.

87   The scents from the eucalyptus trees became more pungent as I drove further into the grove, looking for just the right spot. In front of me, the road curved precariously but I drove slowly, knowing that no one was behind me. Suddenly the light of the moon filtering through the branches

lit the tallest tree up ahead and I knew I had found what I had been searching for. As I stepped out of the car, in the distance I heard an owl repeating the same sound over and over. What a contrast it made with the happy chirps of the birds that had been Filomena's and Kika's companions. The owl's song was supposed to announce an impending death, I remembered. I listened to the bird, recalling other sounds I had associated with Filomena. Suddenly, whispering voices came to me from among the trees.

88   "¡Flores para los muertos! ¡Flores para los muertos!"

89   The voices continued as I made a shallow hole beneath the tallest eucalyptus, where I buried the jar. Suddenly I thought I heard a loud screech like that of the white owl of my youth. Uncertain, I listened out there in the dark for a long time. But no. It had been only the brown barn owl after all. I stood up as the wind rustled through the branches and watched a lone lizard scurry up a tree.

90   As I headed to the car, a faint chant sounded behind me once again. "¡Flores para los muertos! ¡Flores para los muertos!" I did not look back.

DISCUSSION QUESTIONS

1. Describe the narrator's experience with Filomena and her family in the United States.
2. Describe the pilgrimage to Janitzio.
3. Discuss Filomena's sense of motherhood and her experience of it.
4. Analyze the narrator's encounter with the world of the cynical, critical thinkers at the university.
5. Discuss the similarities between "Filomena" and Flaubert's "Un cöeur simple."

WRITING TOPICS

1. Write an essay discussing the relationship the narrator had with Filomena.
2. Write an essay contrasting the customs of Halloween with the rituals associated with the Mexican celebration on November 2, the Day of the Dead.

SHOOTING STARS

Denise Chávez

Born August 15, 1948, in Las Cruces, New Mexico, Denise Chávez has established herself in the Chicano literary world. Influenced by her experience in a high school theater class, Chávez went on to obtain a B.A. degree in drama from New Mexico State University. In 1974 she was awarded a master's degree in drama from Trinity University and in 1984 a master's degree in creative writing from the University of New Mexico.

Chávez's interest in writing fiction led to *The Last of the Menu Girls* (1986), a series of seven interrelated stories that chronicle Rocío Esquivel's coming-of-age. Her latest book, *Face of an Angel* (1995), is a novel that centers on the ideology of the women's liberation movement as reflected in the life of Soveida Dosamantes. A waitress, Dosamantes also is an author who seems to be irresistibly drawn to unemployed, shiftless men. With great humor, Chávez moves along the bawdy story.

The following selection is excerpted from *The Last of the Menu Girls.* "Shooting Stars" deftly examines the creation of a sense of womanhood in Rocío's mind. Chávez reminisces about the physique, behavior, and personality of the girls and women whom she has known.

1   When I was a young girl, images were conjured up in the white walls in my father's old study room. Faces leaped out from the plaster's twists and turns. These imaginings consumed the lazy summer afternoons. I was supposed to have been napping, but inevitably I wandered back to the faces in the wall, to the vast ruminations of my adolescent self.

2   What did it mean to be a woman? To be beautiful, complete? Was beauty a physical or a spiritual thing, was it strength of emotion, resolve, a willingness to love? What was it then, that made women lovely?

3   The images in the wall receded and then like bright dancing beams of

light burst into my consciousness. I thought of Eloisa, Diana and Josie. One by one their faces broke out of the wall's textured surface and into my dreams to become living flesh and blood.

4   In my mind I was back in Texas, a place I always apologized for. It was a place removed from normal experience, the farthest spot away from my reality. As a part of that unvoiced obedience to parental rule, my sister and I spent a portion of each summer with my mother's Texas relatives.

5   One of our favorite pastimes was to sell wild flowers in a makeshift shop constructed by sticking clumps of stray flowers in my aunt's stone wall, with its cinderblock slots. We picked the flowers in a vacant lot sectioned off by a chain link fence that spiraled downward into an uncultivated field of wildflowers. Occasionally, the greyed and moving form of an old man materialized, alongside that of several angry dogs. Never was our flower industry totally shut down. The summer days passed this way, one upon another, in the ritual of the flower picking. No one knew of this flower industry, no one ever bought these flowers, but it mattered little to my sister and me. Each day we would set out our display, pricing and haggling between ourselves, then sitting down to wait for customers. It did not matter that our shop lay at the end of a dead-end street, or that the summer heat wilted customer and flower alike.

6   These days passed from the early morning obscurities of waking up, dressing, eating breakfast and wandering about the house to heightened afternoons of rummaging through my grandmother's shelves. They held warm, softened objects, handkerchiefs and embroidered limpiadores[1] with pale stitched roses on a fading background of days: Lunes, Martes, Míercoles.[2] In the corners, wrapped in filmy plastic bags, were peinetas[3] still holding tufts of strong, dark hair. Later I would go through my aunt's chest of drawers. Although it was never spoken of, I knew my aunt had cancer and was dying. In her drawers were pieces of paper with obscure names, felt bookmarkers and small handbound books with either God or Daisy in the title. I found one time a collection of *Fairy Tales*, all unread, that still haunt me today. In one story, several dogs, with eyes like huge, wild saucers, guarded a magic spell-bound castle. In another a mermaid whose fins were replaced by bleeding feet learned to walk on land, beside an unfeeling lover who did not know her pain of loving.

7   In those days of stories, there were mudpies and one summer, an infestation of worms to be killed ingeniously. Death by stomping. Death by stoning. Death by fire. Death by insecticide. Death by scalding.

8   The worms oozed their way into my aunt's stone house, crawling from the marble floors onto the walls, and hung there, seeking shade in the tor-

---

[1] Literally "cleaners," here, "doilies."
[2] Monday, Tuesday, Wednesday.
[3] Ornamental comb.

pid summer afternoons. Nearby, the bookshelf held *The Incredible Shrinking Man*, a book that I have regretted reading. As a child, I spent long hours imagining my disappearance in that ever fearful darkness children know so well.

9   In the evenings we slept outside, for it was always too hot in the house. Our adopted family consisted of my aunt, whose joys were watermelon and books, my silent and morose uncle, my two strange cousins, my grandmother, mother, Mercy and me. Each of us had our separate cot. Mine hugged the wall near the side of the house that faced the long hot highway that reached farther and deeper into Texas. It was a bit set off from the others. Lying down, I could see the low mountains in the horizon to my left and in front, the shadow of the straw roof that housed the makeshift barbecue pit that was used on fiestas, holy days. In the silent summer darkness, the imaginary aromatic memories of cabrito[4] floated to me, along with the sound of phantom voices, haunted guitars.

10   As the hot, steaming nights grew longer, everyone would gravitate outside to the back of the house. Each cot would be surrounded by watermelon seeds, the moist remnants of that evening ritual. My mother and aunt sat on cots facing each other, eating gleefully and laughing about some past episode in the life of their favorite uncle, the incomparable Acorcinio, who as a drunk was prone to tears and, who sober, was something to be reckoned with. My uncle would be napping inside, face down on his single bed. My two cousins were nowhere to be found. Mercy, busy with her watermelon, dangled her legs between the metal grating of the cot's side. Curled up in my sheet, I would stare up into the sky. Somewhere far away a lone and anxious coyote called to the moon.

11   One day we rode into a small, nearby town, to visit relatives: a small, old lady with a fifty-year-old retarded daughter and a talkative middle-aged man whose father had once been my grandmother's beau.

12   It was then that I came to know Eloisa, a local girl, the daughter of a family friend. Her aunt wore men's shirts and pants and bound her breasts with rags. One day I found that Eloisa's mother and aunt (half men to me), were relatives! This made Eloisa, too, part of my mother's family. Most of them were a queer, unbalanced lot.

13   Eloisa was sixteen, already a woman. It was she who instigated the beginning of our many walks around the town, a place of well-kept churches, with large, wide streets and tiny, wooden shacks, like the one my mother's aunt, Eutilia, lived in. The two sisters were clear proof of little change—one spoke English and was the Postmistress of the town, the other was poor, hunchbacked, private.

14   Up Main Street we would go, past the record shop, with its few forty-fives of Tiny Morrie and Dion, near the five and dime, past the Paisano

---

[4] Roasted young goat.

Hotel where the cast of *Giant* had stayed, the short but lovely Elizabeth Taylor and James Dean, who had allegedly wooed my teenage cousin, Zenaida. Up we'd go to the court house, and around the block, into familiar and dear streets. Our walks were without time or sense. They were talking walks, stopping walks. How I admired Eloisa! How grateful I was for her allowing me into her magical woman's world. Eloisa and I were bright girls, mature girls, and always trailing behind us was my little sister, Mercy.

15   Later, after the nightly watermelon, I would fall asleep under the stars thinking about Eloisa. She was Venus, I myself was a shooting star. The two of us were really one. We were beautiful girls, bright beautiful girls spitting out watermelon seeds. We were coyotes calling out to the moon.

16   That summer I carried Eloisa around with me—her image a holy card, revered, immutable, an unnamed virgin. That is, until the Jeff Chandler movie at the Pasatiempo Theatre.

17   Sitting in the darkness of the theatre, front row, little sister in tow, I saw, on my way to the candy counter, none other than Eloisa. She was sitting with friends. Smoke rose from their lips. My heart sank. I was sick with nicotine, faint with its smell. I wandered back to my seat. Jeff Chandler, tanned idol, a suddenly blanched earthworm. A nervous bull terrier yapped on the screen and I sank down in my seat, pretzel-like, sick to my heart. Eloisa smoked cigarettes!

18   When I had recovered from the shock, I stole my way back to the rear of the theatre, where Eloisa sat, chortling and braying like a rude goat. She was not alone, she was with a man, and he had his paws across her shoulder.

19   I crawled back to my seat again, faint with disappointment. I don't remember the rest of the movie, I barely remember Jeff Chandler was in it.

20   I do remember that we didn't take many other shortcuts through the sculptured lawns of the First Presbyterian Church. Fall was coming. I was to go home to New Mexico, my father, the sun.

21   To me, Texas signified queer days, querulous wanderings, bloody fairy tales, hot, moon-filled nights, earthworms and unbought flowers. Texas was women to me: my fading grandmother, my aunt dying of cancer, my mother's hunchbacked aunt and Eloisa. All laughing, laughing. Summer was a yapping dog and a dream of becoming ever smaller.

22   When I lay in the solemn shade of my father's study, I thought of myself, of Eloisa, of all women. The thoughts swirled around like the rusty blades of our swamp cooler. Each lugubrious revolution brought freshness, change. Shifting through the many thoughts, I heard voices in the afternoon silence. Perhaps someday when I grow older, I thought, maybe then I can recollect and recount the real significance of things in a past as elusive as clouds passing . . .

23   Diana was another of those young women who suddenly appeared in my life. Diana was lovely and apparently guileless. She did not smoke. She did have a boyfriend. One day I spoke of saving myself for marriage, and Diana said that yes, she too, was saved.

24   Ruben, her boyfriend, was a childhood sweetheart. They used to play together. He was steadfast, loyal, dark like Diana, and very smart. Anyone who loved Diana must surely be smart. Diana had manners, was so nice. Sí Señora this and Sí Señora that. Nice. Nice and with the ugliest sister this side of Texas. Her sister had flat feet, spider veins, droopy nalgas and empty, lagaña-ridden eyes.

25   New Mexico is as unlike Texas as the moon is unlike the sun.

26   Diana was the personification of all that her sister was not. She was, like her namesake, the huntress in her clear, animal grace. She was simply Diana, fresh, bright-eyed, hopeful and kind. Perhaps too kind. But this weakness of her spirit did not manifest itself at first. Diana was my older sister when my older sister married and was continually birthing nieces and nephews for me. She was my confidante, someone I looked up to, respected, loved. Unlike her Texas counterpart, Diana was first and foremost: a friend who could never betray, no never. Nor could she see the possibility of betrayal. In this assumption of hers and mine lies all the tragedy of young womankind.

27   What was it, then, that made Diana beautiful to me, I thought as I sat in the kitchen, facing her small, strong back. Her body darted across the room to pick up a stray cup, now a plate. The steaming hot water rose and frosted the windows, fogging the view of the fields, the world beyond.

28   Diana's beauty came out of a certain peacefulness, not her own, but mine, that lived and breathed when I was with her. To me, the crowded dirty kitchen, the smell of warmed food, the humid moistness of frosty windows, all this was peace to me. Peace and love. That crowded kitchen, always and forever was a reminder of Diana who filled that space with her high, bright laughter.

29   When Diana laughed, she laughed at all life, at all dirt. Her laughter echoed through the room, and then the house. It crossed the fields and fogged all consciousness. All memory became as the water beads on the glass panes: small, wet, persistent, clinging pools.

30   Who was this woman? My mother's brief assistant, our solitary sister for so short a while?

31   Beauty is silent, does not speak. For when Diana spoke, she was not beautiful, but naive, a little girl.

32   In observing Diana, I observed myself. I wanted physical beauty, and yet, I wanted to speak clearly, to be understood.

33   Eloisa, my earlier womanly model, had walked far into the stars, and then gotten lost in the sickening odor of cigarette smoke at the back of a crowded movie theatre. Diana now, too, was lost, but in words, words, the flow and sound of words. Her music was confused, jangled, unsure. Her thoughts were half syllables, monosyllabic utterings of someone dependent upon the repetitious motions of work, the body and its order.

34   The faraway fields outside the northern window opened up to other views, not of the sky, but of the fecund movements of the sweet earth's turning.

35   Now again that laugh.

36   It wasn't until later that I heard again of Diana. She and Ruben were run-
ning a home cleaning service, D and R Janitorial Service. They had two sons.
Ruben left her periodically to live with her former maid. One Sunday I saw
her in church, mustached, wrinkled, with frightened eyes. The dog-faced sis-
ter was nearby. She was now beautiful and happily married. La Comadre
Clara, Diana's mother, an old spotted monkey in ribbons, said to me, "Ay,
Rocío, aquí está la Diana! Diana! You remember her?" Mother of God,
Diana, the goddess, I thought, she's gone . . .

37   My speculations into womanhood seemed so far away from me at this point,
unreachable, hopeless. The face of Diana vanished into the concrete walls.

38   I closed my eyes. I imagined I was on La Calle del Encuentro going past
the Márquez house. In my waking life I never got inside.

39   Josie lived there with her mother and sister, Mary Alice. It was the same
street my uncle lived on, the uncle who had a swimming pool. As a result of
that, the street was revered in my mind. It was probably one of the widest in
town. It was a broad, empty street that lapped into the houses of my uncle,
the house of the transients (later to become the house of my cousin with the
gold toothpick) and the house of the Romanos. Every day paunchy and balding Mr. Romano would dash outside in his sleeveless t-shirt and khaki shorts
to get the evening paper and move the hose to the rosebushes. His was a
house where tragedy lived and bloomed, like the blood red roses in the front
yard. One of his children died by suicide, the other was run over by a truck.
His was a house, even in those early days, that echoed pain. Across the street,
the home of the druggist lay. Up from there, on the left, was the Márquez
house, a white temple of obscure shadows, a house of women.

40   It seems to me that as children we drove past the Márquez home either
on the way to school or back. I was always filled with unwhetted curiosity
about the house, its inhabitants. The front lawn was neat, sculptured. It was
apparent that no one spent much time in the yard. Too public. There was
also a barricaded backyard. I always tried to catch a glimpse behind curtains
or beyond the painted, white brick wall. I don't remember whether I saw
anything or not. Shadows of dark-haired women, perhaps, with gestures
half-completed, mouths open, in half-light. It was in this state of remembrance that I saw the form of Josie's mother. Mrs. Márquez was a tensely
correct and aristocratic woman who was too beautiful for her own good. She
usually spoke Spanish, a sound of clipped, sexual tension with no release. Her
hair was dark brown, not black, and it framed her buried, smouldering face.

41   And what of Mr. Márquez? Who was he? I never saw or even heard of
him, and yet, someone built that dream house. Who?

42   Josie's sister, Mary Alice, was a little replica of Mrs. Márquez. She was my
older sister's age and I was not close enough to that world of teenage concerns to be able to say that I knew her. The impression I have of her is of a
lovely dark-haired girl eating a hamburger in an ad in the Bulldog annual,

1956. The dark sister is munching happily, with three or four others, one a fellow with neat, greased-back hair, while two or three girls lean on a counter, in long, pleated skirts and tight, revealing sweaters and penny loafers. Perhaps this is not the real image of the older sister, perhaps it is she that sits at the Florist's Shop, ordering a boutonniere, or maybe it is she that thumbs through the racks in the Smart Shop ad. I don't know.

43 While the older sister remained an indecipherable mystery to me, as did the striking mother, it was Josie, the youngest Márquez, who unwittingly found herself the subject of my insatiable gleanings and continual speculations into the mysteries of womanhood. I began my questioning with Eloisa, continued it with Diana, and was left still unsure and trembling with unanswered questions about my own uncertain womanhood when I began to study the memorable, but very short Josie Márquez.

44 Josie had the finely chiseled Márquez nose and full, pouty lips. Her teeth were white and even, like a small rodent's. Her eyes were the eyes of a playful and willful child. Her hands were long and slender, the nails painted red. Josie's hair was black and she wore it in trained curls around her unusually long neck that would have been prized by Japanese men who admire such anatomy. Josie had a generously full and high bust. It seemed she always managed to push it out farther and fuller than even those women with pointy, elongated breasts. She took advantage of this asset as she grew older. The necklines plunged, the dresses accented her ripe cleavage, the whiteness of her skin. From the corner of blouses and wandering into that humid maze one could discern the turning of white skin, the white meat of Josie's pale, lovely breasts.

45 I used to see Josie at the dancing parties held in the neighborhood by groups of older teenagers and college students who would gather to dance in someone's parents' t.v. room or vacant rental. It was here that my cousins perfected the cha-cha steps, fanning out, then touching hands, and then cha-chaing back to their sophisticated partners. It was at one of these parties that my cousin, Lorraine, only a year older than I, surpassed me, my babyness, and found her way into the light of young adulthood. It was at these parties that the embodiment of all my womanly hopes, Josie Márquez, one-two-cha-chaed her way into eternity. I stood in the darkness near the punch bowl, humming a litany of displacement to myself.

46 Josie was always at these parties, and either seemed to be entering or exiting. Her voice rang out greetings, burbled and chortled hellos and good-byes. Her black spike heels clicked and turned and danced their way out the door with tall, handsome strangers, sophomores and juniors at the State University who belonged to the Newman Center and were majoring in Mechanical Engineering and who loved to dance.

47 Josie's closest friend was our neighbor, Barbara, who Ronelia says is doomed to her mother's face. I myself would never assign this dubious honor to her, and yet, it appears to be true. Her face, alas, was Texas stock, with a nose that would reach the horizontal boundaries of that beloved state.

48 Barbara was the person in those days who was always going from a tint

to a rinse, from blond to brunette, from streak to different colored streak. She was a tall and gangly woman who "did the best" with what she had, and somehow managed to effect an attractiveness from her almost horsey features. Later, when she married the man of everyone's dreams, perhaps her own, his name was Derrick and he was brought up around Amarillo, a tall, handsome and rugged ex-farmer, the epitome of masculine beauty to some, to most. Barbara was the same woman who slept in her makeup, her eyeshadow and her base. This was the same woman who wore tiny, tight, curlers, a fuzzy, pink bathrobe and cried on leaving her mother's house for her own, complete with swimming pool. "Goodbye, Mama, I'll miss you."

49   To see Barbara and Josie was to see two disparately different body types and souls. Yet, it seemed to me that the closest womanly ties were between these two women. Both were charming, vibrant, effusive bird creatures, caught and trapped in lovely, shiny cages. They did not have the spirit of Eloisa, the gentleness of Diana, but yet, they seemed so happy to sing! Theirs was the blinding, powerful song of women, sisters!

50   For most of us, choice is an external sorting of the world, filled with uncertain internal emptiness. Who was I, then, to choose as model? Eloisa, Diana, Josie or Barbara? None seemed quite womanly enough. Something seemed to be lacking in each of them. The same thing that was lacking in me, whatever it was.

51   As I grew older, matured, I became ever more the solitary observer of my changing womanhood. I was jealous of those women who had effected the change from girlhood to womanhood with ease. I was at the far end of a crystal punch bowl. I heard the faraway music, saw all the colors and the lights, and yet, I was unable to join the dance.

52   Eloisa's gross fulfillment of the flesh, coupled with Diana's shattered dreams, somehow intertwined with Josie's pattering, pounding rhythm. I was caught in Josie's dance, and when I spun loose of all the illusionary part- ners, students from State, majoring in life, I felt a vague, disconcerting lack of joy. Where was the joy?

53   In the quiet walks, in the long summer afternoons when Diana was at the sink, laughing, telling stories in a broken language that can never be repeated. Now Josie chortles hello. Hello.

54   In the hazy half-sleep of my daily nap, the plaster walls revealed a new face. Behind all the work of growing up, I caught a glimpse of someone strong, full of great beauty, powerful, clear words and acts. The woman's white face was reflected in the fierce, mid-day sun, the bright intensity of lov- ing eyes. Who was that woman?

55   Myself.

56   I thought about *loving* women. Their beauty and their doubts, their sure sweet clarity. Their unfathomable depths, their flesh and souls aligned in mystery.

57   I got up, looked in the mirror and thought of Ronelia, my older sister,

who was always the older woman to me. It was she whom I monitored last. It was she whose life I inspected, absorbed into my own.

58 It was my sister's pores, her postures that were my teachers, her flesh, with and without clothes, that was my awakening, and her face that was the mirror image of my growing older. To see her, was to see my mother and my grandmother, and now myself.

59 I recalled Ronelia standing with her back to me, in underwear. How I marvelled at her flesh, her scars. How helpless she was, how dear! It was she who grabbed me when I was fearful that I would never be able to choose, to make up my mind. One time she and another young married cornered me, picked over me, my skin. Her friend hissed at me to toe the womanly line. "For godsakes, Rocío, stand up straight, and do *something* about your hair!" I felt hopelessly doomed to vagueness. Everything seemed undefined, my hair, my skin, my teeth, my soul. I'm incapable of making decisions, Ronelia, I thought. Leave me alone. Why are you attacking me? Go on with your babies and your fetid errands! But instead of crying out, I sat forward, bit my lip, and allowed these two young matrons to attempt a transformation of me, an indecisive girl with bumpy skin.

60 The charting of my sister's body was of the greatest interest to me, I saw her large, brown eyes, her sensual lips (always too big for her) soften and swell into dark beauty. At the same time, I checked myself, measuring *my* attractiveness and weighing it against my other models: Eloisa, Diana and Josie. Looking in the mirror, I saw my root beer eyes (my sister's phrase) in front of me monitoring flesh and its continuance.

61 I never spoke of growing old, or seeing others grow older with any sense of peace. It was a subject that was taboo, a topic like Death.

62 I knew that we grew older, but how could I imagine that all the bright young girls, the Jennies and the Mary Lous, the Eloisas and Dianas and the Josies, with their solid B-cups, their tangle of lovers, their popularity and their sureness, would one day become as passing shadows on the white canvases of late afternoon dreams?

63 The turning, plaster waves revealed my sisters, my mother, my cousins, my friends, their nude forms, half dressed, hanging out, lumpish, lovely, unaware of self, in rest rooms, in the dressing rooms, in the many stalls and the theatres of this life. I was the monitor of women's going forth. Behind the mirror, eyes half closed, I saw myself, the cloud princess.

64 I addressed my body, the faint incandescent loveliness of its earliest but not dearest blooming. Could I imagine the me of myself at age twenty-one and thirty-one and so on . . .

65 I turned the mirror to the light. The loveliness of women sprang from depthless recesses; I thought, it was a chord, a reverberation, the echo of a sound, a feeling, a twinge, and then an ache . . . .

66 Always there is the echo of the young girl in the oldest of women, in small wrists encased in bulky flesh, in the brightest of eyes surrounded by wrinkles. There is beauty in hands tumultuous with veins, in my grandmother's flesh

that I touched as a child, flesh that did not fall, but persisted in its patterning. Her skin was oiled old cloth, with twists and folds and dark blue waves of veins on a cracked sea of tired flesh. On my dream canvas my grandmother pats her hands and says, "Someday, someday, Rocío, you'll get this way."

67   Women. Women with firm, sure flesh of that age in time. In dreams. Let them go. There were reflections of light, a child's imaginings at naptime, patterns on plaster walls, where shapes emerged, then receded into hazy swirls before the closing of an eye. They were clouds, soft bright hopes. Just as quickly as they were formed, they dissolved into vast pillows. Their vague outlines touched the earth and then moved on . . .

68   Sharp patterns on the walls and ceilings, faces in the plastered waves, all those women, all of them, they rise, then fall. Girls, girls, the bright beautiful girls, with white faces and white voices, they call out. They are shooting stars, shooting stars, spitting seeds. They are music, the echo of sound, the wind.

69   Somewhere very far away . . . a lone coyote calls out to the moon, her Mother.

DISCUSSION QUESTIONS

1. Describe Rocío's adolescent speculations about womanhood.
2. How does Rocío describe Eloísa, Diana, Josie, and Barbara?
3. Discuss Rocío's reaction to seeing Eloisa at the Pasatiempo Theatre. How did her regard for Eloisa change as a result?
4. Discuss Rocío's thoughts about women growing older. What does she mean by her statement "Always there is the echo of the young girl in the oldest of women . . ."?

WRITING TOPICS

1. Write a journal entry discussing physical likenesses that you and your parents and siblings share. Compare your image of your older self with the way a parent or grandparent looks.
2. Write an essay discussing your understanding of what it is to be a woman or a man and how that understanding changed as you grew.

A Thanksgiving Celebration (Amy)

Nicholasa Mohr

Wanting to offer a different view of El Barrio—one that is not centered on gangs and violence—Nicholasa Mohr writes of family-oriented, everyday characters with whom her readers can readily identify. Her characterization is deliberate, because she wants to break the minority stereotype that Nuyorican literature typically associates with Puerto Rican and Latino men and to focus, instead, on interpersonal relationships and emotions within the family and the community.

For more information, turn to the previous biography on page 200.

Excerpted from the powerful *Rituals of Survival: A Woman's Portfolio*, "A Thanksgiving Celebration (Amy)" poignantly tells the story of a mother who assumes her role even when she does not have the means to do so. Nicholasa Mohr's praise of the imagination of this Puerto Rican woman in New York, who desired to build a home environment for her children in the context of scarcity, makes for a touching tale of love and creativity.

AMY

1   Amy sat on her bed thinking. Gary napped soundly in his crib, which was placed right next to her bed. The sucking sound he made as he chewed on his thumb interrupted her thoughts from time to time. Amy glanced at Gary and smiled. He was her constant companion now; he shared her bedroom and was with her during those frightening moments when, late into the night and early morning, she wondered if she could face another day just like the one she had safely survived. Amy looked at the small alarm clock on the bedside table. In another hour or so it would be time to wake Gary and give him his milk, then she had just enough time to shop and pick up the others, after school.

2   She heard the plopping sound of water dropping into a full pail. Amy hurried into the bathroom, emptied the pail into the toilet, then replaced it so that the floor remained dry. Last week she had forgotten, and the water had overflowed out of the pail and onto the floor, leaking down into Mrs. Wynn's bathroom. Now, Mrs. Wynn was threatening to take her to small claims court, if the landlord refused to fix the damage done to her bathroom ceiling and wallpaper. All right, Amy shrugged, she would try calling the landlord once more. She was tired of the countless phone calls to plead with them to come and fix the leak in the roof.

3   "Yes, Mrs. Guzman, we got your message and we'll send somebody over. Yes, just as soon as we can . . . we got other tenants with bigger problems, you know. We are doing our best, we'll get somebody over; you gotta be patient . . .

4   Time and again they had promised, but no one had ever showed up. And it was now more than four months that she had been forced to live like this. Damn, Amy walked into her kitchen, they never refuse the rent for that, there's somebody ready any time! Right now, this was the best she could do. The building was still under rent control and she had enough room. Where else could she go? No one in a better neighborhood would rent to her, not the way things were.

5   She stood by the window, leaning her side against the molding, and looked out. It was a crisp sunny autumn day, mild for the end of November. She remembered it was the eve of Thanksgiving and felt a tightness in her chest. Amy took a deep breath, deciding not to worry about that right now.

6   Rows and rows of endless streets scattered with abandoned buildings and small houses stretched out for miles. Some of the blocks were almost entirely leveled, except for clumps of partial structures charred and blackened by fire. From a distance they looked like organic masses pushing their way out of the earth. Garbage, debris, shattered glass, bricks and broken, discarded furniture covered the ground. Rusting carcasses of cars that had been stripped down to the shell shone and glistened a bright orange under the afternoon sun.

7   There were no people to be seen nor traffic, save for a group of children jumping on an old filthy mattress that had been ripped open. They were busy pulling the stuffing out of the mattress and tossing it about playfully. Nearby, several stray dogs searched the garbage for food. One of the boys picked up a brick, then threw it at the dogs, barely missing them. Reluctantly, the dogs moved on.

8   Amy sighed and swallowed, it was all getting closer and closer. It seemed as if only last month, when she had looked out of this very window, all of that was much further away; in fact, she recalled feeling somewhat removed and safe. Now the decay was creeping up to this area. The fire engine sirens screeching and screaming in the night reminded her that the devastation was constant, never stopping even for a night's rest. Amy was fearful of living on the top floor. Going down four flights to safety with the kids in case of a fire

was another source of worry for her. She remembered how she had argued with Charlie when they had first moved in.

9   "All them steps to climb with Michele and Carlito, plus carrying the carriage for Carlito, is too much."

10   "Come on baby," Charlie had insisted "it's only temporary. The rent's cheaper and we can save something towards buying our own place. Come on . . ."

11   That was seven years ago. There were two more children now, Lisabeth and Gary; and she was still here, without Charlie.

12   "Soon it'll come right to this street and to my doorstep. God Almighty!" Amy whispered. It was like a plague: a disease for which there seemed to be no cure, no prevention. Gangs of youngsters occupied empty store fronts and basements; derelicts, drunk or wasted on drugs, positioned themselves on street corners and in empty doorways. Every day she saw more abandoned and burned-out sections.

13   As Amy continued to look out, a feeling that she had been in this same situation before, a long time ago, startled her. The feeling of deja vu so real to her, reminded Amy quite vividly of the dream she had had last night. In that dream, she had been standing in the center of a circle of little girls. She herself was very young and they were all singing a rhyme. In a soft whisper, Amy sang the rhyme: "London Bridge is falling down, falling down, falling down, London Bridge is falling down, my fair lady . . . ." She stopped and saw herself once again in her dream, picking up her arms and chanting, "wave your arms and fly away, fly away, fly away . . ."

14   She stood in the middle of the circle waving her arms, first gently, then more forcefully, until she was flapping them. The other girls stared silently at her. Slowly, Amy had felt herself elevated above the circle, higher and higher until she could barely make out the human figures below. Waving her arms like the wings of a bird, she began to fly. A pleasant breeze pushed her gently, and she glided along, passing through soft white clouds into an intense silence. Then she saw it. Beneath her, huge areas were filled with crumbling buildings and large caverns; miles of destruction spread out in every direction. Amy had felt herself suspended in this silence for a moment and then she began to fall. She flapped her arms and legs furiously, trying to clutch at the air, hoping for a breeze, something to get her going again, but there was nothing. Quickly she fell, faster and faster, as the ground below her swirled and turned, coming closer and closer, revealing destroyed, burned buildings, rubble and a huge dark cavern. In a state of hysteria, Amy had fought against the loss of control and helplessness, as her body descended into the large black hole and had woken up with a start just before she hit bottom.

15   Amy stepped away from the window for a moment, almost out of breath as she recollected the fear she had felt in her dream. She walked over to the sink and poured herself a glass of water.

16   "That's it, Europe and the war" she said aloud. "In the movies, just like my dream."

17   Amy clearly remembered how she had sat as a very little girl in a local movie theatre with her mother-and watched horrified at the scenes on the screen. Newsreels showed entire cities almost totally devastated. Exactly as it had been in her dream, she recalled seeing all the destruction caused by warfare. Names like "Munich, Nuremburg, Berlin" and "the German people" identified the areas. Most of the streets were empty, except for the occasional small groups of people who rummaged about, searching among the ruins and huge piles of debris, sharing the spoils with packs of rats who scavenged at a safe distance. Some people pulled wagons and baby carriages loaded with bundles and household goods. Others carried what they owned on their backs.

18   Amy remembered turning to her mother, asking, "What was going on? Mami, who did this? Why did they do it? Who are those people living there?"

19   "The enemy, that's who," her mother had whispered emphatically. "Bad people who started the war against our country and did terrible things to other people and to us. That's where your papa was for so long, fighting in the army. Don't you remember, Amy?"

20   "What kinds of things, Mami? Who were the other people they did bad things to?"

21   "Don't worry about them things. These people got what they deserved. Besides, they are getting help from us, now that we won the war. There's a plan to help them, even though they don't deserve no help from us."

22   Amy had persisted, "Are there any little kids there? Do they go to school? Do they live in them holes?"

23   "Shh . . . let me hear the rest of the news . . . her mother had responded, annoyed. Amy had sat during the remainder of the double feature, wondering where those people lived and all about the kids there. And she continued to wonder and worry for several days, until one day she forgot all about it.

24   Amy sipped from the glass she held, then emptied most of the water back into the sink. She sat and looked around at her small kitchen. The ceiling was peeling and flakes of paint had fallen on the kitchen table. The entire apartment was in urgent need of a thorough plastering and paint job. She blinked and shook her head, and now? Who are we now? What have I done? Who is the enemy? Is there a war? Are we at war? Amy suppressed a loud chuckle.

25   "Nobody answered my questions then, and nobody's gonna answer them now," she spoke out loud.

26   Amy still wondered and groped for answers about Charlie. No one could tell her what had really happened . . . how he had felt and what he was thinking before he died. Almost two years had gone by, but she was still filled with an overwhelming sense of loneliness. That day was just like so many other days; they were together, planning about the kids, living from one crisis to the next, fighting, barely finding the time to make love without being

exhausted; then late that night, it was all over. Charlie's late again, Amy had thought, and didn't even call me. She was angry when she heard the doorbell. He forgot the key again. Dammit, Charlie! You would forget your head if it weren't attached to you!

27   They had stood there before her; both had shown her their badges, but only one had spoken.

28   "Come in . . . sit down, won't you."

29   "You better sit down, miss." The stranger told her very calmly and soberly that Charlie was dead.

30   "On the Bruckner Boulevard Expressway . . . head on collision . . . dead on arrival . . . didn't suffer too long . . . nobody was with him, but we found his wallet.

31   Amy had protested and argued—No way! They were lying to her. But after a while she knew they brought the truth to her, and Charlie wasn't coming back.

32   Tomorrow would be the second Thanksgiving without him and one she could not celebrate. Celebrate with what? Amy stood and walked over and opened the refrigerator door. She had enough bread, a large pitcher of powdered milk which she had flavored with Hershey's cocoa and powdered sugar. There was plenty of peanut butter and some graham crackers she had kept fresh by sealing them in a plastic bag. For tonight she had enough chopped meat and macaroni. But tomorrow? What could she buy for tomorrow?

33   Amy shut the refrigerator door and reached over to the money tin set way back on one of the shelves. Carefully she took out the money and counted every cent. There was no way she could buy a turkey, even a small one. She still had to manage until the first; she needed every penny just to make it to the next check. Things were bad, worse than they had ever been. In the past, when things were rough, she had turned to Charlie and sharing had made it all easier. Now there was no one. She resealed the money tin and put it away.

34   Amy had thought of calling the lawyers once more. What good would that do? What can they do for me? Right now . . . today.

35   "These cases take time before we get to trial. We don't want to take the first settlement they offer. That wouldn't do you or the children any good. You have a good case, the other driver was at fault. He didn't have his license or the registration, and we have proof we was drinking. His father is a prominent judge who doesn't want that kind of publicity. I know . . . yes, things are rough, but just hold on a little longer. We don't want to accept a poor settlement and risk your future and the future of your children, do we?" Mr. Silverman of Silverman, Knapp and Ullman was handling the case personally. "By early Spring we should be making a date for trial . . . just hang in there a bit longer . . ." And so it went every time she called: the promise that in just a few more months she could hope for relief, some money, enough to live like people.

36   Survivor benefits had not been sufficient, and since they had not kept up premium payments on Charlie's G.I. insurance policy, she had no other income. Amy was given a little more assistance from the Aid to Dependent Children agency. Somehow she had managed so far.

37   The two food stores that extended her credit were still waiting for Amy to settle overdue accounts. In an emergency she could count on a few friends; they would lend her something, but not for this, not for Thanksgiving dinner.

38   She didn't want to go to Papo and Mary's again. She knew her brother meant well, and that she always had an open invitation. They're good people, but we are five more mouths to feed, plus they've been taking care of Papa all these years, ever since Mami died. Enough is enough. Amy shut her eyes. I want my own dinner this year, just for my family, for me and the kids.

39   If I had the money, I'd make a dinner tomorrow and invite Papa and Lou Ann from downstairs and her kids. She's been such a good friend to us. I'd get a gallon of cider and a bottle of wine . . . a large cake at the bakery by Alexander's, some dried fruits and nuts . . . even a holiday centerpiece for the table. Yes, it would be my dinner for us and my friends. I might even invite Jimmy. She hadn't seen Jimmy for a long time. Must be over six months . . . almost a year? He worked with Charlie at the plant. After Charlie's death, Jimmy had come by often, but Amy was not ready to see another man, not just then, so she discouraged him. From time to time, she thought of Jimmy and hoped he would visit her again.

40   Amy opened her eyes and a sinking feeling flowed through her, as she looked down at the chips of paint spread out on the kitchen table. Slowly, Amy brushed them with her hand, making a neat pile.

41   These past few months, she had seriously thought of going out to work. Before she had Michele, she had worked as a clerk-typist for a large insurance company, but that was almost ten years ago. She would have to brush up on her typing and math. Besides, she didn't know if she could earn enough to pay for a sitter. She couldn't leave the kids alone; Gary wasn't even three and Michele had just turned nine. Amy had applied for part-time work as a teacher's aide, but when she learned that her check from Aid to Dependent Children could be discontinued, she withdrew her application. Better to go on like this until the case comes to trial.

42   Amy choked back the tears. I can't let myself get like this. I just can't! Lately, she had begun to find comfort at the thought of never waking up again. What about my kids, then? I must do something. I have to. Tomorrow is going to be for us, just us, our day.

43   Her thoughts went back to her own childhood and the holiday dinners with her family. They had been poor, but there was always food. We used to have such good times. Amy remembered the many stories her grandmother used to tell them. She spoke about her own childhood on a farm in a rural area of Puerto Rico. Her grandmother's stories were about the animals, whom she claimed to know personally and very well. Amy laughed, recalling

that most of the stories her grandmother related were too impossible to be true, such as a talking goat who saved the town from a flood, and the handsome mouse and beautiful lady beetle who fell in love, got married and had the biggest and fanciest wedding her grandmother had ever attended. Her grandmother was very old and had died before Amy was ten. Amy had loved her best, more than her own parents, and she still remembered the old woman quite clearly.

44   "Abuelita, did them things really happen? How come them animals talked? Animals don't talk. Everybody knows that."

45   "Oh, but they do talk! And yes, everything I tell you is absolutely the truth. I believe it and you must believe it too." The old woman had been completely convincing. And for many years Amy had secretly believed that when her grandmother was a little girl, somewhere in a special place, animals talked, got married and were heroes.

46   "Abuelita," Amy whispered, "I wish you were here and could help me now." And then she thought of it. Something special for tomorrow. Quickly, Amy took out the money tin, counting out just the right amount of money she needed. She hesitated for a moment. What if it won't work and I can't convince them? Amy took a deep breath. Never mind, I have to try, I must. She counted out a few more dollars. I'll work it all out somehow. Then she warmed up Gary's milk and got ready to leave.

47   Amy heard the voices of her children with delight. Shouts and squeals of laughter bounced into the kitchen as they played in the living room. Today they were all happy, anticipating their mother's promise of a celebration. Recently, her frequent moods of depression and short temper had frightened them. Privately, the children had blamed themselves for their mother's unhappiness, fighting with each other in helpless confusion. The children welcomed their mother's energy and good mood with relief.

48   Lately Amy had begun to realize that Michele and Carlito were constantly fighting. Carlito was always angry and would pick on Lisabeth. Poor Lisabeth, she's always so sad. I never have time for her and she's not really much older than Gary. This way of life has been affecting us all . . . but not today. Amy worked quickly. The apartment was filled with an air of festivity. She had set the kitchen table with a paper tablecloth, napkins and paper cups to match. These were decorated with turkeys, pilgrims, Indian corn and all the symbols of the Thanksgiving holiday. Amy had also bought a roll of orange paper streamers and decorated the kitchen chairs. Each setting had a name-card printed with bright magic markers. She had even managed to purchase a small holiday cake for dessert.

49   As she worked, Amy fought moments of anxiety and fear that threatened to weaken her sense of self-confidence. What if they laugh at me? Dear God in heaven, will my children think I'm a fool? But she had already spent the money, cooked and arranged everything; she had to go ahead. If I make it through this day, Amy nodded, I'll be all right.

50   She set the food platter in the center of the table and stepped back. A

mound of bright yellow rice, flavored with a few spices and bits of fatback, was surrounded by a dozen hardboiled eggs that had been colored a bright orange. Smiling, Amy felt it was all truly beautiful; she was ready for the party.

51 "All right," Amy walked into the living room. "We're ready!" The children quickly followed her into the kitchen.

52 "Oooh, Mommy," Lisabeth shouted, "everything looks so pretty."

53 "Each place has got a card with your own name, so find the right seat." Amy took Gary and sat him down on his special chair next to her.

54 "Mommy," Michele spoke," is this the whole surprise?"

55 "Yes," Amy answered, "just a minute, we also have some cider." Amy brought a small bottle of cider to the table.

56 "Easter eggs for Thanksgiving?" Carlito asked.

57 "Is that what you think they are, Carlito?" Amy asked. "Because they are not Easter eggs."

58 The children silently turned to one another, exchanging bewildered looks.

59 "What are they?" Lisabeth asked.

60 "Well," Amy said, "these are . . . turkey eggs, that's what. What's better than a turkey on Thanksgiving day? Her eggs, right?" Amy continued as all of them watched her. "You see, it's not easy to get these eggs. They're what you call a delicacy. But I found a special store that sells them, and they agreed to sell me a whole dozen for today."

61 "What store is that, Mommy? " Michele asked. "Is it around here?"

62 "No. They don't have stores like that here. It's special, way downtown."

63 "Did the turkey lay them eggs like that? That color?" Carlito asked.

64 "I want an egg," Gary said pointing to the platter.

65 "No, no . . . I just colored them that way for today, so everything goes together nicely, you know . . ." Amy began to serve the food. "All right, you can start eating."

66 "Well then, what's so special about these eggs? What's the difference between a turkey egg and an egg from a chicken?" Carlito asked.

67 "Ah, the taste, Carlito, just wait until you have some." Amy quickly finished serving everyone. "You see, these eggs are hard to find because they taste so fantastic." She chewed a mouthful of egg. "Ummm . . . fantastic, isn't it?" She nodded at them.

68 "Wonderful, Mommy," said Lisabeth. "It tastes real different."

69 "Oh yeah," Carlito said, "you can taste it right away. Really good."

70 Everyone was busy eating and commenting on how special the eggs tasted. As Amy watched her children, a sense of joy filled her, and she knew it had been a very long time since they had been together like this, close and loving.

71 "Mommy did you ever eat these kinds of eggs before?" asked Michele.

72 "Yes, when I was little," she answered. "My grandmother got them for me. You know, I talked about my abuelita before. When I first ate them, I

couldn't get over how good they tasted, just like you." Amy spoke with assurance, as they listened to every word she said. "Abuelita lived on a farm when she was very little. That's how come she knew all about turkey eggs. She used to tell me the most wonderful stories about her life there."

73 "Tell us!"

74 "Yeah, please Mommy, please tell us."

75 "All right, I'll tell you one about a hero who saved her whole village from a big flood. He was . . . a billy goat."

76 "Mommy," Michele interrupted, "a billy goat?"

77 "That's right, and you have to believe what I'm going to tell you. All of you have to believe me. Because everything I'm going to say is absolutely the truth. Promise? All right, then, in the olden days, when my grandmother was very little, far away in a small town in Puerto Rico . . ."

78 Amy continued, remembering stories that she had long since forgotten. The children listened, intrigued by what their mother had to say. She felt a calmness within. Yes, Amy told herself, today's for us, for me and the kids.

DISCUSSION QUESTIONS

1. Describe the conditions in which Amy lived with her children.
2. Discuss the meaning of Amy's dream.
3. Does Amy have hope for a better future? What circumstances limit her?
4. What creative solution does she bring to her Thanksgiving table in the midst of her poverty? In small groups, discuss whether her idea works.

WRITING TOPICS

1. Write a proposal for an inexpensive alternate celebration of Thanksgiving for a family with young children.
2. Write an essay analyzing the plight of poor women. Discuss practical ways to offer them community assistance.

TO BE A MAN

Gary Soto

The writing style of Gary Soto is fresh and unadorned. Through sometimes terse description and matter-of-fact tone, he brings originality to familiar themes. He builds on ordinary, inconsequential events so that readers come to recognize their importance in developing a character's impression of something or someone. Soto is particularly skilled at examining doubt, uncertainty, and suffering.

For more information, turn to the previous biography on page 194.

"To Be a Man" presents a kind of double perspective—from the past, as a child anticipates being a man, and from the present, as a man wonders how he came to be who he is. Of interest is the very astute definition of manhood in a society that measures it not by one's valor or sexuality, but by how one provides for himself.

1   How strange it is to consider the dishevelled man sprawled out against a store front with the rustling noise of newspaper in his lap. Although we see him from our cars and say "poor guy," we keep speeding toward jobs, careers, and people who will open our wallets, however wide, to stuff them with money.

2   I wanted to be that man when I was a kid of ten or so, and told Mother how I wanted my life. She stood at the stove staring down at me, eyes narrowed, and said I didn't know what I was talking about. She buttered a tortilla, rolled it fat as a telescope, and told me to eat it outside. While I tore into my before-dinner-snack, I shook my head at my mother because I knew what it was all about. Earlier in the week (and the week before), I had pulled a lawn mower, block after block, in search of work. I earned a few quarters, but more often screen doors slapped shut with an "I'm sorry," or milky stares scared me to the next house.

3   I pulled my lawn mower into the housing projects that were a block from

where we lived. A heavy woman with veined legs and jowls like a fat purse, said, "Boy, you in the wrong place. We poor here."

4   It struck me like a ball. They were poor, but I didn't even recognize them. I left the projects and tried houses with little luck, and began to wonder if they too housed the poor. If they did, I thought, then where were the rich? I walked for blocks, asking at messy houses until I was so far from home I was lost.

5   That day I decided to become a hobo. If it was that difficult pulling quarters from a closed hand, it would be even more difficult plucking dollars from greedy pockets. I wanted to give up, to be a nobody in thrown-away clothes, because it was too much work to be a man. I looked at my stepfather who was beaten from work, from the seventeen years that he hunched over a conveyor belt, stuffing boxes with paperback books that ran down the belt quick as rats. Home from work, he sat in his oily chair with his eyes unmoved by television, by the kids, by his wife in the kitchen beating a round steak with a mallet. He sat dazed by hard labor and bitterness yellowed his face. If his hands could have spoken to him, they would have asked to die. They were tired, bleeding like hearts from the inside.

6   I couldn't do the same: work like a man. I knew I had the strength to wake from an alley, walk, and eat little. I knew I could give away the life that the television asked me to believe in, and live on fruit trees and the watery soup of the Mission.

7   But my ambition—that little screen in the mind with good movies—projected me as a priest, then a baseball coach, then a priest again, until here I am now raking a cracker across a cheesy dip at a faculty cocktail party. I'm looking the part and living well—the car, the house, and the suits in the closet. Some days this is where I want to be. On other days I want out, such as the day I was in a committee meeting among PhDs. In an odd moment I saw them as pieces of talking meat and, like meat we pick up to examine closely at supermarkets, they were soulless, dead, and fixed with marked prices. I watched their mouths move up and down with busy words that did not connect. As they finished mouthing one sentence to start on another, they just made up words removed from their feelings.

8   It's been twenty years since I went door to door. Now I am living this other life that seems a dream. How did I get here? What line on my palm arched into a small fortune? I sit before students, before grade books, before other professors talking about books they've yet to write, so surprised that I'm far from that man on the sidewalk, but not so far that he couldn't wake up one day, walk a few pissy steps saying, "It's time," and embrace me for life.

DISCUSSION QUESTIONS

1. Describe the narrator's experience when he went looking for landscaping work.
2. What attracted him to the life of a hobo?
3. Discuss his description of his stepfather.
4. What does it mean to be a man, according to Soto?

WRITING TOPICS

1. From the perspective of a parent, explain in a letter to your son what it means to be a man.
2. Think about the ways that movies and television convey what it is to be a man. Write an essay on the effect of those images on society.

WOMEN ARE NOT ROSES

Ana Castillo

Ana Castillo was born on June 15, 1953, in Chicago, Illinois, where she was raised. She received a B.A. from Northern Illinois University in 1975 and an M.A. from the University of Chicago in 1979. She went on to study at the University of California at Santa Barbara, where she was a dissertation fellow in Chicano studies from 1989 through 1990.

Her first book, *Zero Makes Me Hungry* (1976), was followed in 1977 by her first poetry chapbook, *Otro canto (Another Song)* , and in 1979 by a second chapbook, *The Invitation* (1979). *Women Are Not Roses* (1984) is her first poetry collection and includes some selections from her previous works. In addition, she has written two novels: *The Mixquiahuala Letters* (1986), an epistolary novel containing forty letters that explore gender relations, and *Sopogonía (An Anti-Romance in 3/8 Meter)* (1990), which returns to her gender relations theme from the male point of view. Her work has been honored with an Archive at the University of California at Santa Barbara and with numerous awards.

Ana Castillo's "Women Are Not Roses" bridles against the stereotypical male portrayal, ever present in poetry, that women are roses. Although her very brief poem does connect women to nature, the effect is something altogether different from the image of the rose.

Women have no
beginning
only continual
flows.

5 Though rivers flow
women are not
rivers.

Women are not
roses
10 they are not oceans
or stars.

i would like to tell
her this but
i think she
15 already knows.

DISCUSSION QUESTIONS

1. What aspects of a woman and her life can be described as "continual flows"? Explain your answer.
2. Who is the persona in this poem?
3. Discuss the metaphors of women as "the beginning," as "rivers," as "roses," and as "oceans." Why does the poet negate them all?
4. What does the poet mean by "I think she already knows"?

WRITING TOPICS

1. From the perspective of a parent, explain in a letter to your daughter what it means to be a woman.
2. Think about the ways that movies and television convey what it is to be a woman. Write an essay on the effect of those images on society.

THE GOAT INCIDENT

Virgil Suárez

Born in Cuba, Virgil Suárez emigrated to the United States in 1974 after spending four years in Spain. He completed his secondary education in Los Angeles, and received a B.A. in creative writing in 1984 from California State University–Long Beach. He also studied at the University of Arizona and earned his Master of Fine Arts degree from Louisiana State University in 1987. Suárez currently teaches writing at The Florida State University-Tallahassee.

Suárez has written three novels, *Latin Jazz* (1989), *The Cutter* (1991), and *Havana Thursdays* (1995), a novella and five stories collected in the volume *Welcome to the Oasis* (1992), a collection of Latino writing, *Iguana Dreams: New Latino Voices* (1992), and *Little Havana Blues: A Cuban American Literature Anthology.* Suárez has centered his literary creations on the stories of Cubans and Cuban families who had to abandon the island and come to live and work in the United States. Their struggle and their hopes are deftly portrayed in his books. For more information, turn to the previous biography on page 144.

"The Goat Incident" appears in *Spared Angola: Memories from a Cuban American Childhood* (1997), an autobiographical collection of stories and poems. In this story from his childhood in Cuba, Suárez considers some of the lessons he unconsciously learned about manhood, about violence, about power among males, about honor from the "macho" point of view, about women and their relation to men and to honor.

1   One of the biggest scars from my childhood comes at my most vulnerable moment. I'm still clueless about the reasons, though I have speculated: the government's torment of my father (he was going crazy, I remember, once having tried to set the house on fire, though that's another story), the friction between my mother and father due to my grandmother's illness, the

fact that my parents had been trying to leave the island for the last few years, since 1962 (the year I was born). They had left me in the care of my maternal grandparents in the little town of San Pablo, somewhere in the Province of Las Villas. I cannot remember how I got there, whether my parents brought me or somebody went to Havana and picked me up. Funny how memory fails one.

2   But the goat incident I remember well from all the years that I've had to carry it blazoned in my memory, though I once tried to purge myself of it in one of my books, my first novel, in fact, a pseudo autobiography, not mine but my father's. I claim this because I was too young to go through any of what the main character, Julián Campos in *The Cutter*, went through. But my father did. It was his life mostly that I tried to capture in that book. Anyway, I wrote a chapter about the goat incident, which I liked and my agent liked—she thought it added dimension—but when it came to my editor, he thought it didn't fit. So, I cut it out, for a few drafts, but then reworked it into another form. Having it printed in another form didn't resolve the scarring, so I've carried it with me since. I've carried it since 1968, when I was six and somehow I had ended up in the care of my maternal grandparents.

3   The incident begins very much like the chapter I wrote in the novel with an unknown voice. An unknown, unseen voice saying, "Let's go, let's go, there's a fight. Let's go see it." My grandfather, Domingo, white haired then (as he is now more than twenty years later), climbed onto his horse. My mother's brothers were there and they too got on their horses. I looked up at these giants sitting on these beasts. I wanted to go too. I voiced so to my grandfather. He turned the horse a few times, then he reached down and in one swoop he pulled me up and I found myself sitting behind him, holding on to him. They wasted no time going up to wherever it was the fight had broken out. I embraced my grandfather. I felt the horse hair sneaking in through my pants and irritating the skin on my legs. In the novel, the incident took place at night, but such violence was better seen by a child at night and then attributed to nightmares, but in broad daylight . . . what torment.

4   We arrived in the clearing which was surrounded by *bohíos*, which were thatched huts. A crowd of men made a circle. When we rode up, I was able to catch some of the action before my grandfather dismounted his horse and then pulled me off and asked me to stay away at a distance. There were two men, that much I saw. They stood in the circle, bare chested, shoeless. The circle of men expanded and contracted as the pushing and shoving continued. Again, the men in the circle. Another glimpse revealed the men, sweating, bestial, fighting each other with goats. With goats over their shoulders. Both goats had not made it. They were limp in death. One of the animals was white. The other spotted, or was that blood? I pulled my grandfather's

horse away. Both my uncles were pushing their way into the circle. I ran to a nearby guava tree, tied my grandfather's horse to it, and climbed up high on to one of the branches. A part of me didn't want to see, but the other did, and so I climbed higher, scraping the insides of my thighs against the knobby branches of the tree. I went up high enough to get a perfect view.

5   Inside the circle of spectators, the two men went about their fighting slowly. The fight had been going on for quite some time now, for the men moved sluggishly as if tired and worn out. One goat's belly had been gutted open by the horns of the other. The pink and reddish entrails dangled like rope out of the gaping wound. They oozed over the bare-backed man. The other goat had its fur stained. Their heads hung limp.

6   "I'll kill you," the man with the gutted goat said. "I'll teach you to respect a man." The other man did not respond. He charged and struck the other man with the goat. The other man lost his balance. He fell on his knees, but then got up quickly and charged. No one made an attempt to stop the two men from fighting. I hung tightly, wondering when my grandfather and uncles would come to the rescue. For the goats, they had arrived too late, but not for the men.

7   Someone threw in a knife. The one man with the spotted goat flung the carcass off his shoulders and picked up the knife. The men continued now with their death dance. The man with the knife kept stabbing at the goat. More blood, more entrails. Then a machete was thrown in to the other man. He let go of the mangled goat and grabbed the machete. Both men swung at each other. The one with the knife swung low at the other's stomach, each time missing, coming close the next. This went on and on until one of the men lost his balance, perhaps out of exhaustion, and fell on his back. The other man, the one with the machete, swung and cut the man on the arm. The sharp blade cut through the flesh down to the bone.

8   The crowd held its breath. For one long moment all sound escaped the scene. Then my grandfather fired a shot and the crowd parted. My uncles took their place by both men. Why my grandfather waited so long to fire, I still don't know. He and my uncles stood in the center of the circle and kept both men from starting again. My grandfather told everyone to go away, to go back to their homes. The men did reluctantly at first, but then, seeing my grandfather and uncles were serious, more quickly.

9   Then I can't remember much else, other than looking down and realizing how high in the tree I had climbed. How would I get down? I started to inch my way down slowly. My hands became tired and cramped. Slowly I came down, my inner thighs on fire, scraped and bruised. I made it down and grabbed the horse's bit and pulled him away from the tree. My grandfather and uncles returned. We all got on the horses and rode back to my

grandparents' house. I rode back holding on to my grandfather's waist, my head against his chest. I listened to him as he talked to my uncles about what had happened. Why the men had fought. The one man had caught the other with his wife. My uncles laughed and nodded their heads. "These *guajiros*,[1] my grandfather said, "they have too much time on their hands." My uncles nodded in agreement.

10   We arrived at the house, and the men told nothing to the women. The women, my aunts and grandmother, had heard the shots, so they wanted to know what happened. "Let's eat," my grandfather said. I wanted to hear it again, the whole story. Over dinner, my grandfather spoke up and told of what had happened, but I couldn't make it out, the conversation being too adult for my understanding. I kept waiting and waiting for him to mention the goats, but he didn't mention them. I kept hearing about violence, the violence of these men so secluded from society. This was the kind of violence, my grandfather must have said, that was brought about by the system. And much later that night I thought about the goats. As on so many other countless nights to follow, I thought about the dead goats. The way their heads dangled, eyes wide open, tongues sticking out from the corners of their mouths. Years later, when I saw Francis Ford Coppola's *Apocalypse Now*, in the scene where the natives kill the oxen during a ceremony, I thought of the goat incident again. I then realized what I believe about violence now: it is all irrational, it is not supposed to make sense after the fact. After so many years, even words, language fails to relate what really did happen, what memory and recollection choose to carve out into some deep recess of ourselves.

DISCUSSION QUESTIONS

1. In small groups, discuss the two incidents that scarred the author/narrator.
2. Discuss the author's failure to remember much about one of the incidents discussed above, while the other incident is vivid in his mind.
3. Discuss the intertexuality of this selection. To what other books or films does this story refer? Why?
4. Describe the central incident of the story. Why does it occur?
5. Discuss the link between violence and manhood. How does this relate to the appeal of violent sports?

---

[1] Hicks; peasants.

WRITING TOPICS

1. Write a description of an incident that you read about or observed in which violence played a central role. In your writing, discuss your response to the incident.
2. Write an explanation, from the traditional male point of view, of what happened in the story and why. Be sure to explain the men's motives for fighting and the grandfather's motives for intervening.

CHAPTER ELEVEN

CONSTRUCTING THE SELF

As human beings grow and mature, their images of self change. Experiences and emotional responses to them may lead an individual to reconsider his or her identity. For example, when responding to questions about one's race, ethnicity, language, culture, gender, religion, and so on, an individual inwardly examines himself or herself in developing a response. In doing so, that individual may reconstruct or revise his or her image of self.

The definition of individuals does not come only from self-examination, however, as illustrated by one of the following selections. Sometimes the self is defined by an individual's project for life. His or her commitment to a goal may well define self, as for "Corky" Gonzales. In addition, one's relationship to others may significantly affect one's image of self. A friendship such as that described in the selection by Piri Thomas leads to self-examination for two young boxing opponents.

Clearly, then, the self is not a given. It is not static and unchanging. It is who one is, and who one thinks one is. It develops over time and reflects one's responses to life and the people and circumstances one encounters.

SEEING SNOW

Gustavo Pérez Firmat

Gustavo Pérez Firmat was born in Havana, Cuba, on March 7, 1949, and moved as a youngster with his family to the United States. He studied in Miami, receiving his B.A. in English and his M.A. in Spanish from the University of Miami. Pérez Firmat went on to earn his Ph.D. in comparative literature from the University of Michigan in 1979. Since then, he has taught Spanish at Duke University.

As a professor, Pérez Firmat has contributed to scholarly dialogue with many interesting and thought-provoking books. These include *Idle Fictions: The Hispanic Vanguard Novel, 1926–1934* (1982), *Literature and Liminality: Festive Readings in the Hispanic Tradition* (1986), *The Cuban Condition: Translation and Identity in Modern Cuban Literature* (1989), and *The Cuban American Way* (1993). In addition, he has written two creative books of poetry: *Carolina Cuban*, which appeared in 1987 with two other collections of poetry in a volume entitled *Triple Crown: Chicano, Puerto Rican and Cuban American Poetry,* and *Equivocaciones (Equivocations/Mistakes),* published in 1989.

Pérez Firmat's works generally combine the Cuban exile theme with the experience of adjusting to life in America. "Seeing Snow" and "Dedication" link place and language to create the self the poet has become.

SEEING SNOW

Had my father, my grandfather, and his,
had they been asked whether I would ever see snow,
they certainly—in another language—
would have answered,
5   no. Seeing snow for me
will always mean a slight or not so slight
suspension of the laws of nature.
I was not born to see snow.
I was not meant to see snow.

¹⁰ Even now, snowbound as I've been
all these years,
my surprise does not subside.
What, exactly, am I doing here?
Whose house is this anyway?
¹⁵ For sure one of us has strayed.
For sure someone's lost his way.
This must not be the place.
Where I come from, you know,
it's never snowed:
²⁰ not once, not ever, not yet.

DEDICATION

The fact that I
am writing to you
in English
already falsifies what I
⁵ wanted to tell you.
My subject:
how to explain to you
that I
don't belong to English
¹⁰ though I belong nowhere else,
if not here
in English.

DISCUSSION QUESTIONS

1. Describe the feeling of the poetic persona upon seeing snow.
2. Discuss the connection that the poet feels to his father, grandfather, and great-grandfather. What does snow mean to the poet and to his family?
3. The poet's feelings about living with snow and writing in the English language suggest that he is an altered being. Discuss how this could be and how he feels about it.
4. What is the author's dilemma of being a Cuban and writing his poem "Dedication" in English? Discuss the implications.

WRITING TOPICS

1. Imagine that your family has moved to an exotic location to live. In a journal entry, describe your experience with the climate.
2. Write a poem about experiencing something that you never expected to encounter.

TO FREE CUBA

Evangelina Cossío y Cisneros

Evangelina Cossío y Cisneros was born in Puerto Príncipe, the capital city of the province of Camagüey, Cuba, in 1878. Her father, a widower since she was two years old, treated her like a boy, giving her opportunities to learn about his business and the politics of the time. She did not lack for feminine guidance, however, because her family included older sisters.

In 1895, her father was imprisoned for his role in a planned revolt to gain Cuban independence from Spain. He was to be executed by a firing squad. After much pleading, Evangelina and one of her sisters were able to have their father's death sentence commuted. His alternate punishment was imprisonment in the Spanish prison in Ceuta, North Africa. Later he was transferred to the Cuban Isle of Pines. The prison master there took a sexual interest in the girls, resulting in their incarceration in the Recogidas, a prison for women. Though her sister was freed three weeks later, Evangelina was detained for fifteen months.

Meanwhile, for the *New York Journal*, which was seeking to increase circulation and to promote a war in Cuba, Evangelina became a cause célèbre. Newspaper magnate William Randolph Hearst appealed to prominent women throughout the United States to write letters and sign petitions on her behalf. When this did not result in her release, Hearst had one of his reporters, Karl Decker, travel to Havana to help her escape. Dressed as a man, she managed to gain freedom, and her rescue and arrival in New York were widely celebrated. Subsequently, Cossío y Cisneros—the grandniece of a President of Cuba in Arms—set about writing her autobiography.

The Story of Evangelina Cisneros (1898) contains several accounts, including her autobiography. The following selection is an excerpt from her work. "To Free Cuba" focuses on her youth and the unique and close relationship she built with her father.

1   This is the story of my life. American women may find it interesting. It is at least true. I am not used to writing, but will tell my story as well as I can. I will try to make everything plain and easy to understand, although it will be hard for any one who has never lived in Cuba to believe that some of the things which I must tell could really happen so close to the free country of America.

2   To begin with, I am not a girl, as all the people who have been writing about me always say I am. I am a woman. I am nineteen years old.

3   I was born in Puerto Principe. Puerto Principe is the capital of a Province of Camiguey. It is a little city, where there were many happy people before the Revolution. Camiguey is said by Americans to be the Kentucky of Cuba. By that, I think, they mean that we have beautiful horses there, and that we are proud of the prettiest girls in Cuba. I am one of four sisters. My mother died before I can remember. They say she was a very little woman, and that she was exceedingly pretty. She had large eyes, and she was very slender, and she had the lightest foot in the dance of any girl in Camiguey. Her name was Caridad de Cisneros y Litorre. My father's name was Jose Augustine Cossío y Serrano. There were four of us children, all girls. Flor de Maria was the eldest. She it is who has told me so much about my mother. Then came Carmen and then Clemencia, and then I. We were all very happy when we lived in Camiguey. It was always warm and pleasant there, but sometimes the trade-wind blows, and then it is well to stay indoors.

4   We girls had a little garden, and it was our pleasure to make the flowers grow. Flor de Maria made it her especial business to raise the beans and the peppers and the many things that we of Cuba like to eat. My father had a little money, and we lived in a pretty house with thick walls to keep out the sun, and a court, with a fountain in it, where all of us children learned to walk. That is the first thing I can remember, the fountain. It leaped and sparkled in the sun, and I used to think it was alive and try to catch it, and make it stand still and talk with me. When I was in prison I often dreamt of the fountain which danced so gayly in the little court-yard.

5   My father was a good man, and he loved his children. It was always a holiday for us when he came home. But he was never happy in Camiguey after my mother died. He thought first of going one place and then to another. He could not bear to stay in the little home where he first took her as a bride. So he sold it, and we went with him from one place to another all over our beautiful Cuba. At last we came to Sagua La Grande, a seaport on the north coast of the island. There we found an old friend who had known my mother when she was a little girl; Rafael Canto y Nores was his name. He took us to his house, and his good wife was like a mother to us. My father went to a large sugar plantation close by and became weighmaster there, and for seven years I lived with Señora Nores. She was very good to me. By and by my father was sent for to come to Cienfuegos. Cienfuegos is on the south coast of Cuba, and there is an estate there which is the largest plantation on the island. It is called the Constancia estate. When he was settled at Constancia he sent for Carmen and me.

6   My other sisters stayed with Signora Nores.

7   My father had a pretty little house near the estate and Carmen and I kept it for him as well as we could. Señora Nores had taught me how to make *tortillas* and *arroz con pollo* and all of the good Cuban dishes. We had a happy time there in our little house; for Carmen and me, and it was almost like playing in a doll's house.

8   But my father was a strange man in some ways. He would have been better pleased if one of his children had been a son. He often looked at me, and took my head between his hands and said to me, "Evangelina, when I look at your brow it seems to me that you should have been my son and not my daughter," and then I would laugh and put my hands at my sides and pretend to whistle, and my father would cover my mouth with his hand, for in Cuba it is not good for a young girl to behave as the boys behave.

9   But for all that my father treated me more like a son than like a daughter. In the evening, when he had finished his supper, and we sat together he would talk to me about his business and his work at the plantation, and he would tell me of the things which vexed him, and of the things which had pleased him during the day. He talked much to me about Cuba, and many a time I have sat with my father until the moon arose, and listened to his stories of the ten-years' war against Spain, until every drop of blood in my veins was afire with the love of my brave country. My father told me how he had kissed my mother good-bye. She did not even weep, as she stood at the window, waving her hand to him and crying "Viva Cuba!" while he went down the path—out to fight for his country. Often he told me how she used to write to him, and tell him of his children at home, and what they did and said, and of how she missed him and prayed for him; but always he said the letters ended with the words, "Viva Cuba!"

10   When he had told me these things his voice would be a little rough sometimes, and he would speak quick, and I knew that he was trying hard to keep from crying; then I always went and sat by him, and held his hand against my face, and he told me that I had eyes like my mother's eyes—like hers!

11   In all these talks with my father he did not treat me as most Cuban fathers treat their daughters. He spoke to me freely and without reserve, and through him I knew something more of the world than most Cuban girls, who are brought up in the seclusion of their homes, ever dream of knowing.

12   One day (it was in May, a very hot day in 1895) Carmen and I had prepared supper and my father came home at his usual hour.

13   He did not kiss me when he came into the house, and when we were at the table he sat a long time without speaking.

14   I knew that there was to be war in Cuba. My father had told me so. I had heard his friends sitting in the shadow of the house and talking to him about it. When he did not speak to me as usual that night I knew that something had happened. I wished to ask him what it was, but I was afraid. All at once

he pushed away his plate, and jumped up from the table. He caught me by the shoulders and looked straight into my eyes.

15   "My little girl," he said, "I am going to fight for Cuba."

16   I put my arms round his neck and kissed him, and then, I think, I cried a little, and my father kissed me and did not speak.

17   "Father," I said, "I am going with you," and from that moment my father knew that my mind was made up.

18   He never tried to persuade me not to go. He told me again of my mother and of her courage and her devotion to the cause of Cuba, and of his young sister Soleded, who had fought by his side in the former war.

19   That night we sat late and talked of many things.

DISCUSSION QUESTIONS

1. The selection begins with a remonstration by the narrator that she is not a girl, but a woman. The excerpt concludes, however, with a conversation in which her father addresses her as "My little girl." Discuss the reasons for their differing perspectives.
2. Discuss why Cossío y Cisneros wants to share her story with readers.
3. What was the narrator's life like as she was growing up?
4. Discuss the reasons the narrator's father did not try to dissuade her from going to fight for Cuba. What response did he make after she declared her intention to go?

WRITING TOPICS

1. Make a list of significant events in your life that you would include in your autobiography.
2. Write an essay discussing your political convictions and how you came to develop them.

THE ANGEL JUAN MONCHO

Ed Vega

Edgardo Vega Yunqué (Ed Vega) was born in Ponce, Puerto Rico, on May 20, 1936. His family moved to the Bronx, New York, in 1949. The household in which he grew up was somewhat strict, as his father was a Baptist minister. As a child, Vega was surrounded by books and began writing in Spanish when he was young. After moving to New York, he completed his public education and entered New York University, where he obtained his B.A. (1969) with honors. He has been a full-time writer since 1982.

Vega writes prolifically, though not all of his work has been published. His short stories appeared in Hispanic magazines beginning in 1977. His first novel, *The Comeback* (1985), tells the story of a half-Puerto Rican, half-Eskimo ice hockey star who becomes enmeshed in an underground conspiracy to liberate Puerto Rico from the United States. The novel portrays the identity crisis of the protagonist within the bounds of an ethnic autobiography. At the same time, however, it satirizes the ethnic biography form itself, making a parody of its suppositions and assumptions about ethnic immigrants. *Mendoza's Dreams* (1987) is a collection of stories connected through a narrator, Alberto Mendoza, whose observations of the human condition are made from a kind concern for the human race. *Casualty Report* (1991), Vega's third published book, comprises another collection of short stories. Their focus, however, is on the despair felt by his community. The book chronicles the suicidal destruction brought on by drugs and violence and the escape they represent.

The following selection, "The Angel Juan Moncho," is from Vega's collection entitled *Mendoza's Dreams*. In the story, Juan Moncho intervenes in the life of Camacho. Vega's choice of the Christmas setting is particularly appropriate.

1   One day late last fall when the days were growing shorter and colder and I was preparing to lock myself up for winter to catch up on a backlog of dreams, some of the people came to me and said, "Mendoza, you're too serious when you tell our dreams. Although what you write about us is true, there are times when we would prefer hearing something humorous." I nodded and explained that the recounting of dreams was a serious matter and that there were inherent difficulties in turning dreams into comedy. They replied that words were words and since I was supposed to be the expert, it was my responsibility to produce some humor from dreams. Arguments are useless once the people have made up their minds, so I asked what they had in mind. They said Christmas was approaching and tradition dictated they listen to the story of the Three Kings and the Infant Jesus, which was a very spiritually uplifting story except that a few months later they had to make promises which they never kept anyway, which made them feel very badly. Patiently, I explained to them that the story of Jesus was part of the yearly cycle of death and rebirth. "It's a metaphor of the seasons, part of ancient myth and therefore extremely important to the collective psyche," I said. They said that I certainly talked beautifully but that they weren't interested in philosophy.

2   Instead, they wished me to recount a miracle. I said the birth of the Child Jesus was a miracle and that the resurrection was most certainly a prime example of the same. They agreed but said they wanted to hear about a modern Christmas miracle, but one which would not frighten them like most miracles tended to do. I attempted to explain that germane to the idea of a miracle was the awe which the miracle inspired. They said that awe or not most miracles frightened them. I was silent, hoping they would recognize the futility of their quest and allow me to return to the recording of their dreams.

3   But they remained and insisted that the least I could do was explain what had taken place last year with Paulino Camacho, the butcher. How was it, they said, that after spending all his money drinking, Camacho was able to place such beautiful gifts under the Christmas tree for his wife and children? Gifts like no one in the neighborhood had ever seen? Like beautiful electric trains, expensive bicycles, fire engines and trucks with real rubber wheels and hoses; and oh yeah, white dolls that seemed more alive than any white person they had ever seen, and doll houses with better furniture than the furniture in their own apartments, stuffed toys bigger than the children themselves, and clothes like they had never worn, and mind you, we're not jealous, they said, but to see his wife, Marta, in that mink coat Camacho gave her for Christmas just to go to the laundromat or the supermarket when it was 80 degrees was a little bit too much for any human being to have to endure. And how did that happen? they wanted to know.

4   I said I had no idea but that whatever had happened it certainly had the makings of miraculous intervention. "Well, there you have it," they said. I asked them if upon finding out that Camacho had been able to accomplish

this seemingly impossible feat, which had all the makings of a miracle, they hadn't been frightened. They said they had not, but that plenty of people had been angry with Camacho and some even began whispering that perhaps he wasn't really a butcher but spent his spare time dealing in drugs. I said I didn't know anything about that but that I seriously doubted it. "Well then, how do you explain Camacho's good fortune?" they said growing annoyed.

5   I again said I could not explain it, certainly not rationally, but that I thought perhaps an angel may have had a part in the matter. They then wanted to know if this angel I was talking about would frighten them. I said that angels were not generally intended to frighten people. They disagreed and were more annoyed than ever, insisting that angels, for the most part, came down to take people away and that the only reason they were dressed in white was so that people would be fooled and accompany the angel wherever it was he wanted to take them. "It's like doctors," they said. "As soon as you see them dressed in white, you think you're going to be all right and then before you know it they're sticking needles into you and cutting you open and who knows what else and that's the way angels are." I told them I disagreed, that angels were inoffensive, ethereal beings and that I couldn't guarantee that Camacho's story would be as humorous as they wanted. They said that just as long as the angel wasn't frightening and they could at least smile a few times I could do whatever I wanted, as long as I only explained how Camacho had gotten away with what he did. I said I'd do my very best.

6   So, I began by saying that it was the night before Christmas and all through El Barrio everybody was stirring, including Camacho. Especially Camacho and most certainly Camacho. Because, I mean, Christmas only comes once a year and what the hell: *Felicidades y Japi Nu Yial.* Right? You see, you have to understand something about Camacho. Camacho enjoyed drinking. Not to excess but in the tradition of comradery, which dictates that whenever and wherever men gather bottle and glasses be on hand. So on this most festive of nights, Camacho was sitting at the long brown bar of *La Estrella de Borinquen,* on Lexington Avenue up the street from the subway station, and things were heating up. He was what we call *picao.* Somewhere between feeling mellow and passing out.

7   If you had seen Camacho you would've loved him immediately. He'd remind you of your father, all chubby and brown, sporting his big moustache and looking out into the world through those serious, sad eyes which used to make you shake when you were a child and made you say, penitently, "*Sí, papi,*" and "*No, papi.*" So, there was Camacho hitting on a bottle of Bud saying things like: "Dis Bod for jew," and laughing, and every once in a while one of his *panitas*[1] would buy him a shot of Bacardí and down the

---
[1] Buddies.

hatch it went. And Camacho would feel so grateful for his friend's generosity that he'd slap a ten or twenty dollar bill on the bar and buy everyone a drink. No doubt about it. It was absolutely the best of nights, this *Nochebuena*.² The jukebox was playing *salsa* and *aguinaldos*³ and one time when the disco version of "I'm Dreaming of a White Christmas" came on, Camacho got silly and danced, his belly hanging out and sweat rolling off his face.

8   About nine o'clock, as if everyone were hooked into the same circuit, men started making excuses about having to get home and be with their families. Snow was falling quite heavily and the streets gleamed brightly. Words went back and forth and in each one there was the aroma of *pernil, arroz con gandules, pasteles, salmoreja de jueyes, empanadas, alcapurrias, morcillas, mofongo, arroz con dulce, majarete, tembleque, almendras, nueces, turrón de alicanti, turrón de jijona de mazapán*⁴ and to top it all off *coquito*.⁵ *Ay, madre santísima*.⁶ You couldn't believe how tongues were watering as men wished each other *Felicidades*.⁷

9   Camacho snapped to. Oh, man, he thought. I've done it this time. He looked into his pockets and extracted three crumpled up dollar bills and some change. His stomach turned over a few times and he felt as if his legs would buckle and he'd fall over in a faint. All at once the Christmas decorations on the bar window became blurred and Camacho's eyes rolled up into his head. Holding on to the bar with both hands, he tried to steady himself. A feeling of complete desolation and regret hit him, tears came into his eyes, and then a long sobbing sound, which to the remaining patrons of the bar sounded like the flushing of the toilet, escaped from his chest.

10   One of Camacho's buddies, Epifanio Marrero, whom everyone knew as Ponce, came over and put his arm around Camacho's shoulder. Ponce was a worthless drunk, a piece of human driftwood, but the best guitar player in all of El Barrio. He lived for his art and if anyone had ever suggested that he take money for his music he would have been insulted.

11   "What's the matter, Camacho?" he said, tipping back a bottle of beer. "Don't cry. If it's a woman, forget her. If it's money, we'll rob a bank. Cheer up! It's *Nochebuena*,⁸ man!"

12   All Camacho could do was shake his head and another agonizing sob escaped from his chest. Why had he been so careless? The children were expecting so much this year. He had meant to get them all something earlier

² Literally, beautiful night; here, meaning Christmas Eve.
³ A type of Caribbean dance music and Christmas carols.
⁴ Roast pork leg; Puerto Rican dish of rice and peas; Puerto Rican tamales; crab sauce made with oil, vinegar, salt and pepper; pastry rolls filled with meat and vegetables; another type of tamale; blood sausages; mashed boiled plantain baked with pork rinds; rice pudding; pudding made of milk, sugar and corn; coconut pudding; almonds; walnuts; hard nougat (candy) served at Christmas; soft nougat—marzipan, served at Christmas.
⁵ A coconut and pineapple juice mixed with rum.
⁶ Oh, holiest of mothers.
⁷ Greetings of the season.
⁸ Christmas Eve.

in the week but he'd never had a free moment at the butcher shop to get away and buy the presents. He should've let Marta buy the gifts but she always complained that whatever she bought for them they were never satisfied with. The kids would just say Santa Claus was cheap. But that wasn't it. It was all his fault and, rather than being a man and doing his best, he had squandered all his money on drink.

13   "What am I going to do?" he said holding his head in both hands.

14   "You're drunk," said Ponce peering into Camacho's face.

15   "Yes, I know," said Camacho. "Leave me alone, Ponce. I'm no good. No good at all. I feel like dying."

16   "Well, in that case, let me have the rest of your beer and I'll sing at your funeral. What would you like me to sing? A *bolero*?[9] Maybe a *guaracha*?[10] I know, I know. You're from the mountains, right? Good, good. *Un seis chorreao*."[11] And having said this, Ponce kicked off his shoes, removed his socks, rolled up his pants to the calves and began singing *a seis*, introducing the song with that high pitched nasal *lelo-lai-lelo-lai*[12] of the *jíbaros*.[13] For Camacho all it did was to give him a headache and make him feel as if his friend were mocking him.

17   "This is no laughing matter, Ponce," said Camacho regaining some of his composure.

18   "No, of course not, *compadre*,"[14] Ponce replied. "When it comes to my music I'm very serious. It's a pity that just this morning I had to hock my guitar."

19   "I'm in trouble," said Camacho.

20   "We all are, my friend. Plenty of trouble. Each day I'm faced with the same question. Should I go on living or should I step out in front of the Lexington Avenue Express and get it over with."

21   "Do you think that's what I ought to do?"

22   "Are you crazy? What kind of a man are you? What will people say. 'Camacho? He was a coward.' That's what they will say."

23   "Well, maybe they won't. You can be my witness. You will tell them I was very drunk and fell on the tracks."

24   Ponce held up his hand and shook his head violently.

25   "No, I will not be a part to deceiving people. I will not join you in this scheme to make them believe that you died accidentally. How would I face Chu Chu Barbosa down at Florindo's bar. He takes his job seriously. Suppose it is he that is driving the train and you jump out in front of it. Am I supposed to make him believe it was an accident? No way. *De ninguna manera*."[15]

---

[9] A slow song and dance tune.
[10] An old Spanish and, now, popular dance.
[11] A Puerto Rican folk dance and its music.
[12] Puerto Rican humming sound in a song, much like "dooby-dooby-do" in English.
[13] Puerto Rican peasant.
[14] Godfather or father, in relation to one another; or buddy.
[15] No way.

26   "But he drives on the D Line, not the Lexington."

27   "It doesn't matter. He will ask questions. No, I won't do it. It is nothing but cowardice to kill yourself. Have another drink. Whatever it is, it will pass. It always does."

28   "You're no help," said Camacho, and stumbled forward out of the bar and into the snow, his jacket open. "No help at all," he yelled as he skidded on the sidewalk.

29   The snow was coming down harder, the wind blowing in wild gusts that made the snow drift up against cars and buildings. Camacho staggered forward, oblivious to the cold and snow. Which way was home? Yes, First Avenue. He must walk towards Third. No matter what happened he had to get home. What time was it? Ten o'clock. Should he pray? Maybe if he prayed hard enough a miracle would take place. What was he talking about? He didn't believe in any of that stuff. That was for old women. What did he care if Paco Miranda had seen a vision of the Virgin holding up a piece of cardboard with a number and then played it and hit for almost $600. Or stupid Gloria Franco, ugly as sin, praying every single day at Saint Cecilia's for 20 years to get married, and having that rich Cuban with the two restaurants up in Washington Heights courting her like she was a princess and then marrying her and buying her a damn condominium downtown. Everybody said that was a miracle. Maybe he should pray.

30   Rather than going down the subway stairs and perhaps as a deterrent against his original plan to do away with himself, he began walking towards what he thought was First Avenue, where he had grown up, but not where he now lived. He also walked west rather than east. He crossed Park Avenue and then Madison. Halfway down the block between Madison and Fifth Avenues, near an empty lot next to an abandoned building, Paulino Camacho slipped and fell banging his head against an iron railing and passing out in a deep snow drift. The street was deserted and no one saw him.

31   No one that is, except Juan Ramón Burgos, scanning the city of New York, at the Puerto Rican Department of the OFFICE FOR THE PROTECTION AND SALVAGE OF WAYWARD MORTALS. Dressed in his blue velvet V-neck robe, his beautiful blue wings tucked safely in a nonflying position, he was sitting at his monitor when he caught a brief glance of Camacho slipping and falling. Damn, he thought, another drunk. He'd come back to him later. He went on further south where in the Lower East Side a woman was threatening a man with a broken beer bottle and further on in Brooklyn someone was about to pass out on his bed with a lighted cigarette. What the hell were they doing down there! . . . they were worse than ever this year.

32   He pushed a couple of buttons and made the woman throw down the bottle in disgust and walk away. He then pushed another button and the man with the cigarette suddenly sat up and started screaming for his wife to hurry up and come to bed. Finally, he came back to Camacho but couldn't find him in the snow. He tried a closeup but still couldn't locate him. The

scanner showed that he was there but he couldn't see him and therefore couldn't help him. He pushed a button and Camacho's data showed up on the screen.

33 . . . He'd have to go down there.

34 He picked up the phone and dialed his supervisor's number. The phone rang a few times before he got an answer. He then explained that it was imperative that he go down.

35 "It's an emergency, Tillary," he said.

36 "Emergency? What kind of emergency?" his supervisor said.

37 "I got a drunk that fell into a snow drift in Manhattan. It's really coming down hard. There's a blizzard down there. What the hell are those people in weather doing! Tell them I don't appreciate their humor."

38 "I have nothing to do with the weather department," Tillary said.

39 "Well, I gotta go down and help this guy out."

40 "Maybe he got up?"

41 "Tillary, the scanner goes right to the spot. The board's lit up. It's an emergency. Take my word. He's there all right. I just can't see him."

42 "Can't you just scrape the snow away?"

43 "Scanners can't do that, Tillary. The Old Man's inventing all this electronic stuff but somehow he hasn't figured this one out yet."

44 "Have you tried everything?"

45 "Everything, Tillary. Bad dreams, sirens. Nothing. If every red light on my board's lit up, he's in trouble. It's all in the regulations. I have to go down."

46 "I can't let you go. There's nobody to run the scanner in your department."

47 His supervisor's response made Burgos angrier than he'd ever been in all the time he had been in heaven. It made him reflect again on why he had ever volunteered for this kind of duty. It was all guilt about the way he had lived down on earth and how just before he had died he had promised to reform. He died anyway and rather than going down he went up. Big deal! Boring and thankless work. Day and night rescuing idiots from their stupid mistakes.

48 "Give me a break, Tillary," he said. "This guy's gonna die. He'll freeze to death."

49 "Maybe I can put in a call to the old man and He can talk to him. He'll repent, die and you got somebody you can train."

50 "Tillary, this guy's got five kids to support. We're not talking about some worthless drunk. He's a hard worker, loves his wife and worships those five kids. He just screwed up, period."

51 "Worships?" Tillary said.

52 "Cut out the doctrinal stuff, okay? You know what I mean."

53 "Is he worth saving?"

54 ". . . Damit, Tillary! What in the hell . . ."

55 "Careful, Burgos."

56   "Sorry, Tillary. I know, I know. Language. Regulations and all that. Okay, okay. Yeah, he's worth saving. He just screwed up and spent all his money drinking and now he can't buy anything to put under the Christmas tree. He's really a good guy. Just got carried away. Can't you get Blaisdell from the Wasp Department to help out. God, they're. . . . Sorry. I mean, they're overstaffed over there."

57   "I'm sure you can understand that," Tillary said. "There are a lot more wasps than there are Puerto Ricans."

58   "Sure, I'm not gonna deny that. You don't even have anybody covering Puerto Ricans in Boston or Philly."

59   "They're covered. We got them split up. The Polish department's got some and the Irish, the rest. We're doing our best."

60   But a 1 to 3 ratio, Tillary? One damned angel . . . oops . . . one angel to watch every three wasps and I gotta bust my hump watching all the Puerto Ricans in New York City to make sure they survive all this holy day crap . . ."

61   "Burgos!"

62   "Okay, okay. So it's the Kid's birthday and the Old Man's not gonna like it if I talk that way. But have a heart. I did the computations, and even if I'm at my best, I'm gonna lose at least a hundred people before the New Year comes in. People leaving kids alone and the building going up in flames, arguments that turn into murder, overdoses, people falling into subway tracks. A hundred souls and the way they're carrying on not one of them's got a chance to make it up here. It isn't easy, Tillary. Get me one of the guys from the Wasp Department. Some sociology professor that would enjoy slumming."

63   "They don't understand Spanish. It's in the regulations. The guy that runs the scanner has to speak Spanish. Your people got the thing passed last year as part of that affirmative action package."

64   Burgos thought for a moment.

65   "What about Sinclair?" he said. "He was a Peace Corps volunteer in South America. Some guerrillas blew him up."

66   "Speaks Quechua."

67   "Yes . . . sorry. What about Garrison? I've spoken Spanish with him. He was with the Lincoln Brigade. Got killed outside of Madrid back in the thirties."

68   "Burgos, you're jeopardizing the welfare of an entire community. The man is not well. Still carries on conversations with Hemingway, even though we have no communication channels with those people below."

69   "He'll have to do. Just send him down and I'll explain the whole scanning procedure to him. I'll have to take my chances."

70   "Okay, he'll be at your shop in five minutes."

71   "Five minutes? He's gotta be here now. I'm leaving."

72   "I'll do my best."

73   "Thanks, Tillary. Just keep me posted on who else is down in New York in case I need help. Log me off in five minutes."

74   A few moments later a pale young man entered the glass enclosed quarters where the giant Puerto Rican scanner was located and greeted Burgos in Spanish. Burgos explained everything very quickly, patted him on the back and thanked him.

75   "Just make sure that on each ten minute round you scan The Bronx, Manhattan and Brooklyn first. Don't worry too much about Staten Island. We don't have too many there. In Queens most of the people are pretty middle class. Once in a while there's the makings of a traffic accident or a faulty wire on a Christmas decoration, but nothing major. Just keep your eye on the upper and lower ends of Manhattan, the South Bronx and the four different locations in Brooklyn marked in blue. All right?"

76   The young man saluted and Burgos went off running into the decompressing chamber. He pushed several buttons for dress and stepped into the converter. Within seconds his blue robe and wings were off and he was dressed in the same clothes he'd worn that fateful night ten years before when, after celebrating his third round knockout of Bobby Russo in his fifth pro fight as a lightweight, he'd gone drinking and stepped out in front of a car going 80 miles an hour on the Grand Concourse and that was the end of Juan Moncho, as his mother had called him. He looked in the mirror and felt ashamed of the raggedy clothes, torn by the scraping metal, but he felt the blood pumping in his body and a fraction of a second later he was standing on the corner of Madison Avenue and 111th Street.

77   The snowfall was now a blizzard, obscuring objects no more than a foot away. Looking down through the snow at his locator he finally found the spot where Camacho had fallen and began shovelling away the snow with his bare hands. After a few minutes he found Camacho's chest. His heart was still beating but he was already stiff. He got him out of the snow and slung him over his shoulder. As he walked he called his own number at the Department and Garrison answered.

78   "*Teniente Garrison a sus órdenes,*"[16] Garrison said.

79   "Garrison, this is Burgos. Screen up the file on Paulino Camacho, butcher."

80   "I'm afraid I would need a direct communication from control in order to do that."

81   "Garrison, knock off the . . . . This is life and death."

82   "Regulations are regulations and I really don't feel I should jeopardize this operation by bending the rules."

83   "Garrison, screen up the . . . file or I'm gonna spread it around that you got shot in the back outside Madrid because you were scared . . . and were running from the fascists, damnit. Screen up that information."

84   "Yes, sir," Garrison said.

85   "Thank you."

---

[16] Lieutenant Garrison, at your service.

86   "Here it is. Camacho, Paulino. Occupation, butcher. Age 38. Born, Cacimar, Puerto Rico. Married. Wife, Marta. Five children. Address, 405 East 6th Street, Apt. 4. Last Mass attended 4/17/77."

87   ". . . He's all the way down there? I thought he lived in El Barrio. Thanks. I'll see you later."

88   As he walked he applied heat to Camacho's body with the hand resuscitator. By the time they were back on Lexington Avenue, Camacho was moaning. The angel Juan Moncho looked for a cab but there was no traffic at all on the street. They would have to take the subway. As they reached the subway stairs Camacho came to and began struggling.

89   "Let me down, Ponce," he said. "I can make it down the stairs by myself. What the hell are you doing, anyway? You're right, I would be a coward to kill myself. Are you gonna throw me in front of a train, you idiot? Let me down."

90   The angel Juan Moncho propped Camacho up against the wall and Camacho all of a sudden opened his eyes and peered into Burgos' face.

91   "Hey, you're not Ponce," he said. "Who the hell are you and where were you taking me? You were trying to mug me and then throw me in front of a train, right? You're a junkie."

92   "Just take it easy."

93   . . . Camacho . . . took a wild swing at the angel Juan Moncho.

94   Juan Moncho slipped the punch easily and pushed Camacho up against the wall.

95   "Hey, I told you to take it easy, Ace. You're in a lot of trouble and all I was doing was trying to help you. You fell in the snow and I'm trying to get you home."

96   The liquor having worn off somewhat, it once again dawned on Camacho what he was facing when he arrived home. He burst out crying and began pounding the wall near the token booth.

97   "I can't go home," he bawled. "My kids. I got nothing to put under the tree. I don't care what Ponce said, I'm gonna jump in front of the train."

98   And off he went crawling under the turnstile with the angel Juan Moncho behind him after slipping two dollars into the booth's window. He grabbed Camacho and pushed him down on a bench with the specific instructions that if he got up he'd feel a lot worse than if the train had run over him.

99   "Hey, I don't wanna hurt you, but if I have to I'm gonna knock you into next year if you keep it up. Now get a hold of yourself . . . Okay?"

100   "Okay, okay. Boy, you're pretty strong for a little guy. What's your name?"

101   "Juan Moncho," said the angel.

102   Camacho peered into the angel's face and then at his clothes.

103   "You look familiar as hell. Like you was in the newspaper or something. Ain't you cold in those summer clothes?"

104   "I'm fine. Don't worry about it."

105   "Hey, I'm in trouble, man."

106   "I know all about it. Here comes the train."

107   They got on the Lexington Avenue local, changed at 86th Street and got on the Express train, and all along Juan Moncho reassured Camacho that everything was going to be all right.

108   "How? Man, I spent all my money and those kids are gonna be disappointed as hell in the morning"

109   "Don't worry about it," Juan Moncho said. "We'll pick something up on the way there. There's gotta be a toy store or two down in the Village."

110   "Everything's closed right now, man. I really blew it."

111   "We'll find a way. Just leave it to me."

112   "What you gonna do, break into a toy store?"

113   "Just don't worry."

114   At that point, as the train was leaving 59th Street, Juan Moncho got a call from Tillary. He closed his eyes and concentrated on silent receiving and sending.

115   "Yeah, Tillary?"

116   "How's it going with the job?"

117   "Pretty good. We're going down to the Village and see if we can transmit some stuff to his Christmas tree. Another hour or so of work and I'll be back up there. How's Garrison doing?"

118   "No complaints yet. He hasn't called in any emergencies, but I had to send O'Brien from the Irish Department to show him how to operate the console. There was some party up in the Bronx and a bunch of people crashed it and all hell broke loose. Guns, knives, the whole works. O'Brien patched the cops and they just happened to show up in time to put a stop to the whole thing."

119   "Good, good. Well, I'll see you later. Thanks for calling."

120   Juan Moncho was about to click off when all at once Tillary was talking very fast and giving him orders.

121   "Slow down, Tillary. Slow down. Who?"

122   "Mandlestein. Mandlestein," Tillary said. "He's gotten himself involved with those idiotic Guardian Angels. Go see what's going on."

123   "I can't do that! Where the hell is he?"

124   "Two cars down from yours."

125   "On the same train? You sure?"

126   "Of course I'm sure. Go! I'll monitor and send help if it's needed."

127   Juan Moncho clicked off, shook Camacho awake and told them they had to go.

128   "Where? We getting off?" Camacho said.

129   "Let's go. Follow me."

130   They went through a couple of nearly empty cars and then into a third one and there was six foot one Bryan Mandlestein, dressed in gold lamé from head to toe, cape and all, bleached blond hair to his shoulders and made up like he was being photographed for the cover of Vogue. Around

him six red berets in feathers and buttons, all of them with logoed t-shirts over their winter clothing, were shoving and pushing as they tried to get at Mandlestein. As soon as Mandlestein saw Juan Moncho coming he began clapping his hands. He then jumped up on one of the seats of the train.

131   "Oh, thank goodness you've come, Robin," he said, sighing. "Please explain to these cretins that they're tastelessly and abominably dressed. Tacky, tacky, tacky," he added, turning to them and pointing his finger at the startled Guardian Angels. "Tell them, okay? I mean you speak their language. Oh, and add that if they're Guardian Angels, then I'm Marlene Dietrich." And then oblivious to their growing anger he went into the singing of some current popular song while gyrating sensuously atop the subway seat 'Marlene watches from the wall, her mocking smile says it all . . .'"

132   "Let me at him, José," said one of the Guardian Angels. "I'll kick his . . ."

133   "Word," said a couple more.

134   "Yo, what's going on, brother," said Juan Moncho. "Chill out."

135   "Hey, mind your own business, shorty" said one of the Guardian Angels. "Or ama bust you upside the head."

136   "Just take it easy," Juan Moncho said.

137   Two of the Guardian Angels moved towards Juan Moncho, adopting karate stands, their fingers curled as they crouched.

138   "My, my," said Mandlestein from his perch. "How grossly butch. Let me turn them into Michael Jackson teeny boppers, Burgos."

139   Juan Moncho waved Mandlestein off and as soon as the first one made his move, consisting of a high kick, he stepped under and inside, jabbed three times with his left, crossed over with his right and knocked the Guardian Angel out before he hit the floor of the subway car with a thud. The other five Angels rushed Juan Moncho, but as he was getting ready to deliver his next blow, the five turned into young screaming teenage girls made up in punk outfits, their hair chopped in mohawks or dyed the most awful shades of green, orange and red, and their clothes looking like they had shopped at the Salvation Army. The subway car doors opened and Mandlestein jumped off the seat.

140   "Let's go, you beast. You could've hurt that boy. You Latins are so impulsive."

141   Out the three of them went at Grand Central Station. Camacho was totally sober but nearly in shock. He kept looking from Mandlestein to Juan Moncho, unable to say anything. He was sure the little guy was Johnny Burgos, the lightweight that had gotten killed about ten or eleven years ago.

142   Mandlestein explained how he'd been sitting up in his cubicle, monitoring the gays in the Village when all of a sudden a friend he knew from fifteen years before when he died was about to commit what amounted to suicide by getting involved with somebody who had been diagnosed as having AIDS.

143   "Like I couldn't blame him because this boy was divine. I mean, can we talk? Tab Hunter move over, okay? But I couldn't let my friend, Donald, do it and he wouldn't respond to anything I sent down and Tillary told me

under no circumstances was I to come down and I told him to buzz off, know what I mean? And now I'm in all sorts of trouble and he's going to report me and I'll probably have to go in front of the All Powerful and all that other garbage. Oh, I'm getting so depressed. Look at me. Still dressed in this tacky outfit which is strictly passé. So, what brings you down here?"

144   Juan Moncho explained about Camacho.

145   "I'm just gonna stop off at a toy store and get some stuff for his kids. We'll just beam it under their Christmas tree and then get a dress or something for his wife and get him home."

146   Mandlestein was shocked.

147   "You have to be kidding. I know what you're thinking. Just cheap stuff and get it over with, right? I know you got it hard with so much responsibility but, puleeze. Okay? Can I speak frankly without you going into your Rocky or Rambo thing, or whatever fantasy it is you think you're playing out?"

148   "Sure, go ahead," Juan Moncho said.

149   Camacho couldn't take it any longer.

150   "Say, who are you guys?"

151   "Quiet, Pancho," Mandlestein said. "Everything's under control."

152   "My name's not Pancho" Camacho said.

153   "Okay, then Cisco," Mandlestein said. "Just don't get your panties in a wad, all right?"

154   "What?" Camacho said, feeling insulted.

155   "That's okay, Camacho," Juan Moncho said. "Let me handle this," and turning to Mandlestein, told him to go ahead.

156   Mandlestein explained that part of the reason Puerto Ricans were in such bad shape was because they felt all this guilt about one thing or another and therefore didn't believe they deserved the very best the society had to offer. And that here Juan Moncho had a chance to do it up big and really bring about a miracle and he was settling for some cheap toys and a $19.95 dress for Camacho's wife.

157   "What did you have in mind?" said Juan Moncho.

158   "Don't get me wrong, Sheena of the Jungle," Mandlestein said. "I know I'm being a bit selfish because I haven't been shopping in so long but, like how does FAO Schwarz, Bergdorf Goodman, Bloomies and Fred the Furrier sound to you?"

159   "Are you crazy?" Juan Moncho said.

160   "Of course I am, but it's your holy day not mine. I'm already in trouble, so let them put it on my tab. Come on. Get out your scanner and get sizes on Lola or Conchita or whatever her name is. What's your wife's name, darling?" he said, turning to Camacho.

161   "Don't call me that, okay?" said Camacho, going into an extremely awkward boxing stance. "I don't let *patos*[17] talk to me like that."

---

[17] Literally ducks; here, slang for homosexuals.

162   "Oh, my!" said Mandlestein, backing off as if he were frightened. "Mucho macho! Get out your scanner, Burgos. Although Pancho Villa here doesn't seem to appreciate our effort."

163   Juan Moncho went into his pocket and retrieved his miniature scanner and punched in Camacho's address. Immediately the screen showed Camacho's living room with the kids sitting around the Christmas tree in their pajamas and Marta Camacho sitting on the sofa crying. Mandlestein snatched the pocket scanner away from Juan Moncho and shoved it at Camacho.

164   "Take a look, big man," he said.

165   "Oh, my God," said Camacho. "I'm gonna jump in front of a train."

166   "No, you're not, sweetie," said Mandlestein. "You're going shopping, whether you like it or not."

167   "What's he talking about?" Camacho said, turning to Juan Moncho.

168   "Just do as he says. Don't worry. We'll have you home in less than an hour."

169   "Oh, goody," said Mandlestein. "Let's get out of here and get a cab. Burgos, make sure they all go to sleep before we start."

170   Juan Moncho pushed a couple of buttons on his pocket scanner and watched as the kids kissed their mother and went off to bed. Unable to resist the angel induced sleep, Marta Camacho turned off the lights and also went to bed.

171   Within minutes they were inside FAO Schwarz and Camacho was going crazy picking out toys for Alicia, Betty, Rodolfo, Kevin and the baby, Nilsa. He couldn't believe it. He picked out a stuffed elephant the size of a great dane for the baby. Juan Moncho aimed the transporter at the gray form and it disappeared.

172   "See," Mandlestein said, pointing to the scanner.

173   "Wow," said Camacho, watching as the elephant ended up against the couch where Marta had sat. "You guys are too much! Listen, I'm sorry about what I said about *patos*," he said to Mandlestein.

174   "That's okay, ducky," Mandlestein said. "Just keep shopping."

175   From the FAO Schwarz they went to Bloomingdale's and then to Bergdorf Goodman, then to Cartier's where they picked out a watch for Marta and then off to Fred the Furrier where Mandlestein chose a full length sable for her. He wrote down a name and address on a piece of paper and gave it to Camacho.

176   "Your wife's not half bad," he said, "but she's got to do something about her hair and makeup. Have her go see my friend, Alonzo in the Village. We do miracles, but what he does with women is truly heavenly, okay, sweetie?"

177   "Sure," said Camacho.

178   And so it went. When they were finished they stood out in the street with the snow still falling. Juan Moncho told Mandlestein that he had to get Camacho home. Mandlestein said he was absolutely exhausted. Since they should both be getting back up, Juan Moncho said, why didn't they use the transporter to get Camacho home. Mandlestein agreed.

179   "Okay, Camacho," Juan Moncho said. "We gotta go. Merry Christmas and Happy New Year."

180   "But who are you?" Camacho said.

181   "If anybody wants to know, just tell them, you met your guardian angel," Juan Moncho said laughing.

182   Before Camacho could say another word, the angel Juan Moncho pushed three buttons and Camacho found himself in bed next to Marta. He slipped quietly out of bed, tiptoed out of the bedroom, looked in on the children and then peeked into the living room. By the light of the lamppost outside the window he saw dozens of boxes next to the Christmas tree and against the sofa, the outline of the huge elephant.

DISCUSSION QUESTIONS

1. Analyze Mendoza's function in this story. Why was he reluctant to recount a modern miracle?
2. Discuss Camacho's dilemma on Christmas Eve.
3. Describe Juan Moncho's role in this story. Why does he act as he does?
4. Describe the miracle told by Mendoza. Why is it a miracle? Do you detect some criticism in this story? To whom is it directed? Why?

WRITING TOPICS

1. Write a continuation of this selection in which you describe Camacho's family's response to their Christmas presents and Camacho's explanation of them.
2. Write a story about a guardian angel's intervention in your life.

FROM *BECKY AND HER FRIENDS*

Rolando Hinojosa

Hinojosa, raised in the border culture of southern Texas, has written a number of works on the struggles of Texas Mexicans (tejanos). In a familiar and confiding tone, his characters relate their experiences with relatives and neighbors, discuss the politics of their community, and speak matter-of-factly about their own and other people's shortcomings.

For more information, turn to the previous biography on page 172.

In this selection, Rolando Hinojosa's character Becky, from *Becky and Her Friends*, has her say. Prior to this chapter in this carefully crafted novel, the other characters have expressed their opinions of Becky and her behavior. Now readers hear her side, related in an autobiographical tone that is intimately deceptive, yet revealing of a woman who confesses her flaws as she rationalizes her actions.

Becky. The listener has nothing to add here. Nor does the listener intend to add a colophon, a coda. Becky, and it's high time, too, should speak for herself.

1   Years ago, Daddy decided to Mexicanize himself, and so much so that he's not an Anglo anymore, a *bolillo*[1] as Jehu says.

2   As a kid, when I was with the Scholastics and later on at St. Ann's, we used English and nothing but . . . I spoke English to Mama, and she'd answer me in Spanish. That's pretty normal for Valley *mexicanos*. Besides, Mama prefers Spanish, and that's it.

3   Daddy is the sweetest, dearest thing there is. He's a good man in the good sense of the word. Oh, I know what people say, and I've heard it all my life: "All he does is hunt and fish." That's just talk. And Mama? She adores him, and I do too. He is something that people wish they were: kind, giving, and—a word not much in currency—virtuous.

---

[1] An Anglo, a white person.

4   People. People say Mama pushed me into marrying Ira. That's partly true, but I'm the one who made that mistake. I thought I loved Ira, convinced myself I did, and for a long time, too.

5   And what's the big to-do? Is there a mother who doesn't want her daughter well off? Comfortable? But it happens that I let myself, had placed myself there. I wanted to marry Ira. That I don't love him as a husband now, or that I don't want him to live with me and the kids, that is something I decided as well. I made a mistake a long time ago, and it was up to me to correct it.

6   Can't I be allowed to make a decision? Must I always accommodate myself, every time?

7   And I certainly didn't talk the divorce over with Mama and Dad beforehand. The difficulty, but difficult only in broaching the subject, was in talking to the kids. Sarah was eight at the time, and Charlie going on eleven. They love their Father, as they should. I insist on it. But they can also see that this is another life, that their Mom has remarried. That Mom works, and that there's nothing wrong in it. As far as I know, the kids have not had the divorce thrown in their faces. If someone were to, old or young, the kids know what to say to that. Now then, that Jehu and I married a year and a half after the divorce is as much our business as it is Charlie's and Sarah's, but no one else's.

8   Jehu prefers straight talk. I do too, although I had to learn that for myself. It was hard going, but that wasn't Jehu's fault.

9   And this is what people must understand: Jehu is not the kids' Father; he's their Dad. There shouldn't be any mistake on that score, I don't think. They both love and respect Jehu, and he loves them. When they're not with me or when I can't take them to work with me, Jehu leaves the bank, takes them to the park, to Mom's house, or to see Rafe or Rafe's nephews out at the farm.

10   The first visits to Mom's house were strained. And why shouldn't they have been? But Time's a great leveler; it's like money, says Jehu. And he laughs when he says it; I do too. And in time, Mom's learned to come around. Mama is a snob, but is that a high crime? Aren't there worse things?

11   It seems almost a hundred years ago that Ira and I moved to Klail. And then, straight away, Noddy decided that Ira was to run for the Commissioner's post . . . even before we left Jonesville for Klail. Many things happened back then. Personal things.

12   Among them, I lied for Jehu. I lied to Mr. Galindo. To Noddy. To myself. But I didn't know Jehu then, and I had no way of knowing that Jehu was, is, capable of defending himself, from any quarter. But I lied because I already loved him, and so I sought to protect him from Ira, from Noddy. *That's* funny.

13   Ollie San Esteban. I do not, nor will I ever, speak ill of Ollie San Esteban or her memory. Never. I was a spoiled, silly, nattering little fool, but with all of that, I sensed somehow that changes had to be made. I knew I wanted Jehu. That's a difference. And we made love; he wanted to, and I wanted to. I wanted to see him, be with him, hold him. I was indiscreet, of course, but I wasn't a fool. All he saw in me was a pretty face. I knew that. But he had to know who I was, what I was.

14   As for those changes, I didn't have the nerve, the courage, or even the imagination to figure them out. But I learned. Now, alone or with Jehu, here, in our home, I think about what held me back from seeing the changes. It was fear. Finally, one day, I asked myself what it was I feared. The answers came tumbling out, hundreds of them, But then, at that time, I hadn't learned about ultimate questions . . . oh, yes. When I asked myself the ultimate question, and I answered yes to myself, and I knew I was dead serious, fear, or whatever it was, flew out that front door, through the porch, and away from this house . . .

15   That day, the kids came in from school, and I prepared some limeade for the three of us. Sarah brought the cookies, I remember, and Charlie set the table . . . He was about to go upstairs for his shorts and sneakers, ready to go out and play, but I asked them to sit. For a talk. I had no idea what they'd say, how long I would talk, but talk I did and all of us cried, too. And then we waited for Ira . . .

16   I sat there, I thought I'd done a selfish thing, that I was the same old Becky. And I cried. Just then, Sarah moved over and told me not to cry. And she was just eight-years-old, you understand. Charlie then ran upstairs and put on some long pants and a shirt. We waited. The car, the door, the front porch . . .

17   We were a long way from the first day we'd moved to Klail . . . I cut a ridiculous figure. And for a while there, I even pretended to myself that I wasn't Elvira Navarrete's daughter, as if Ira's mother had raised me. Denial, of course; nothing else but.

18   I had made myself into another person, and, too, I was such a fool I couldn't see Sammie Jo's friendship when it was offered.

19   And Sammie Jo and I are friends. She's something. *Es persona*. And that is how she saw me. As a person, but I couldn't see myself.

20   But getting back to Jehu. I was just one more conquest, but hardly that, since there'd been no resistance on my part. I went to him, even when I knew he loved Ollie San Esteban. And why shouldn't he love her, and yes, I also knew about him and Sammie Jo . . . And well, was I any better?

21   But I didn't love Ira. And there were the kids. And people. And Mom . . . And then the ultimate question . . . what would I do for Jehu to know me so that he would then love me. And so I told Ira that I'd decided he was not to live with us anymore.

22   That man Jehu . . . He called on the San Esteban family for over a year after Ollie's death. A man of responsibilities, you see. And then, twelve months to the very day of the decision, on a day like today, a bit gray and overcast, somewhat windy, hurricane weather, he showed up. There, on the porch.

23   We sat, and I couldn't stop talking. Poor Jehu. But I didn't care what he thought of me then and there. What I wanted to know, all I wanted to know, was did he love me, did he love me as I loved him? But thank God Jehu is the way he is. He nodded and looked at me for the longest time. I couldn't know, of course, but I felt it.

24   I don't know about you, but have you ever had someone look at you, up close, eye to eye? A clear, unclouded, an almost unblinking look at you? Jehu looked at me that way that afternoon.

25   I didn't ask him to say he loved me, I wasn't a kid. But he said it anyhow. One surprise after another, that man.

26   And then? He said to call the kids, to go out, for a walk, on the sidewalk, around the block. And Sarah, who'd never seen him, took his hand, hugged him. Sarah! Yes. And kissed him. Even the weather helped; the wind calmed down, as calm as the kids.

27   Charlie? Charlie ran up to his room and brought back a sketch he'd drawn at the Scholastics. When Jehu smiled, Charlie gave it to him: a present. I don't think they said a word between them.

28   Since much Spanish common property law prevails in Texas, the management and apportionment of property took time. It was Jehu who suggested that Romeo Hinojosa represent me. Jehu then said it would be better if he didn't call on me until after the divorce. He then explained this to the kids: clearly, simply, no embellishment. Well, Mr. Hinojosa made an excellent case for me and the kids, although I must say that Ira behaved like a pig in this. Kept bringing up the fact, his lawyer did, that Jehu had called on me. Poor Ira! He still doesn't understand a thing.

29   That's been two years now, and the trouble with Ira is that he can't see beyond tomorrow. The kids are growing up, and they may wind up not loving Ira because of Ira's behavior. Jehu, now, he will not allow the baby, Sarah, or Charlie either, for that matter, he won't allow them to speak disrespectfully about Ira. Jehu says that isn't done. He, too, never says a word against Ira, and so, the kids follow his example: no criticism.

30   Don't mistake what I say, though. Jehu knows Ira for the fool he is. And he knows that Noddy controls Ira, who doesn't know the first word about banking or little else. Jehu says Noddy knows this, and since Ira likes the easy way out of things, Noddy keeps him under wraps.

31   As for Noddy, he can throw both Jehu and Ira out of the banking business and into the streets any time he wants to. It's his bank. But Jehu doesn't care, and poor Ira does care. That's the difference.

32   And this is my new life, and it's the best one I could have chosen. There's no set routine to our lives . . . As I said earlier, Jehu comes home at noon, on a Wednesday, say, he'll call the bank and say he won't be back that afternoon. He'll drive to Klail Mid-School, sign out for the kids, and if I've got nothing pressing at the moment, we'll drive out to El Carmen Ranch and visit a while.

33   That's Jehu, impromptu. It's the same with the few parties we give at home. A few people we know, mostly family.

34   For Jehu it's always the family. Me. The children, that's the first family. And then the other family, Rafe, who's more than just a cousin. They're like kids, they call each other on the phone.

35   And speaking of Rafe, Jehu wanted to postpone the wedding, and I was for it. Rafe was recuperating from his eye trouble again, but Rafe wouldn't hear of it. Got me on the phone, "*No lo dejes,*"[2] is what he said.

---

[2]Do not postpone it.

36   People who don't know Rafe think he's reserved; that's the word I always hear. He's quiet, sure, and he's certainly that way in public. He's funny, though. Like Jehu, he laughs, he can tell a joke . . .

37   To me, Jehu is the reserved one. And patient? I think that's why the kids also love him. He's incredibly patient . . . and you know, it takes a good business head and sense to be patient. I learned that on my own.

38   I won't talk about my work or what I do at Barragán Enterprises. It's boring to talk about it, but it's something else to live it. It's my professional life; that's all there is to that.

39   Viola? I was wrong about her as I was wrong about many things. She loves me as if I were her own daughter, had she had one . . . I learned the business by watching her, by being there . . . and I remember my first important lesson in business: *Yes* means *yes*, and *no* means *no*. Negotiations are always preliminaries, but the yeas and nays are the finalities . . .

40   I talked to few people about what I wanted to do . . . I talked to Mrs. Campoy, a hundred if she's a year, and bright and lucid . . . I also talked to Viola. Before I talked to Mama. See? And Viola? She cried. But do you see? We're talking about a fearless woman here. And she was the first to see what was in me, before I could even see for myself. Saw it before Jehu, too.

41   And that's it. I'm not a woman who was saved, redeemed. I saved myself. With help, of course. With love and good will, too, and all the rest. But if I couldn't save myself, if I couldn't save me from myself . . . But why go on?

42   Let's say I saved myself, and let it go at that.

43   Yes, the listener will also let it go at that.

DISCUSSION QUESTIONS

1. Discuss Becky's marriage to Ira Escobar.
2. Becky decides to divorce Ira. Discuss her motives in doing so.
3. What is Jehu's role in the story that she tells? How does he behave toward Becky, her children, Ira, and others in the community?
4. Becky's most interesting comments concern herself. Analyze her own self-consideration and examination.

WRITING TOPICS

1. Write a first-person account about a mistake you made in a relationship with a friend and what you did to rectify it.
2. Write an article about Becky for the social pages of your local newspaper.

AMIGO BROTHERS

Piri Thomas

Born in New York City in 1928, this child of El Barrio (Spanish Harlem) grew up during the Depression in the oppressive poverty of New York's meanest streets. Although John Peter (Piri) Thomas identified himself with the native homeland of his mother (Puerto Rico) and the adoptive country of his Cuban-born father, American society regarded him as African-American. His alienation from his family led him to run away from their new Long Island home and to return to the Barrio, where he led the life of an addicted dope dealer and armed robber. Later, after serving a seven-year sentence in a maximum-security prison in the late fifties, Thomas began working with young people both in New York and in Puerto Rico to try to prevent drug involvement and gang membership.

He began writing his autobiography in the early sixties with a grant from the Louis Rabinowitz Foundation. Five years later Thomas's novel *Down These Mean Streets* (1967) was published and was received with great favor. Thomas began to make public appearances and to do television interviews speaking out about community issues. *Saviour, Saviour Hold My Hand* (1972) continues his autobiographical account and is followed by *Seven Long Times* (1974).

Stories from El Barrio (1978), a collection of eight short stories, affirms the positive in New York's Hispanic youth. In "Amigo Brothers," Piri Thomas recounts the tale of two seventeen-year-old friends—*amigos*. Their determination to be their best while preserving their friendship will inspire readers.

1   Antonio Cruz and Felix Vargas were both seventeen years old. They were so together in friendship that they felt themselves to be brothers. They had known each other since childhood, growing up on the lower east side of Manhattan in the same tenement building on Fifth Street between Avenue A and Avenue B.

2   Antonio was fair, lean, and lanky, while Felix was dark, short, and husky.

Antonio's hair was always falling over his eyes, while Felix wore his black hair in a natural Afro style.

3   Each youngster had a dream of someday becoming lightweight champion of the world. Every chance they had the boys worked out, sometimes at the Boys' Club on 10th Street and Avenue A and sometimes at the pro's gym on 14th Street. Early morning sunrises would find them running along the East River Drive, wrapped in sweat shirts, short towels around their necks, and handkerchiefs Apache style around their foreheads.

4   While some youngsters were into street negatives,[1] Antonio and Felix slept, ate, rapped, and dreamt positive. Between them, they had a collection of *Fight* magazines second to none, plus a scrapbook filled with torn tickets to every boxing match they had ever attended, and some clippings of their own. If asked a question about any given fighter, they would immediately zip out from their memory banks divisions, weights, records of fights, knock-outs, technical knockouts, and draws or losses.

5   Each had fought many bouts representing their community and had won two gold-plated medals plus a silver and bronze medallion. The difference was in their style. Antonio's lean form and long reach made him the better boxer, while Felix's short and muscular frame made him the better slugger. Whenever they had met in the ring for sparring sessions, it had always been hot and heavy.

6   Now, after a series of elimination bouts, they had been informed that they were to meet each other in the division finals that were scheduled for the seventh of August, two weeks away—the winner to represent the Boys' Club in the Golden Gloves Championship Tournament.

7   The two boys continued to run together along the East River Drive. But even when joking with each other, they both sensed a wall rising between them.

8   One morning less than a week before their bout, they met as usual for their daily work-out. They fooled around with a few jabs at the air, slapped skin, and then took off, running lightly along the dirty East River's edge.

9   Antonio glanced at Felix who kept his eyes purposely straight ahead, pausing from time to time to do some fancy leg work while throwing one-twos followed by upper cuts to an imaginary jaw. Antonio then beat the air with a barrage of body blows and short devastating lefts with an overhand jaw-breaking right.

10   After a mile or so, Felix puffed and said, "Let's stop a while, bro. I think we both got something to say to each other."

11   Antonio nodded. It was not natural to be acting as though nothing unusual was happening. . .

12   They rested their elbows on the railing separating them from the river. Antonio wiped his face with his short towel. The sunrise was now creating day.

---

[1] *Street negatives,* undesirable or delinquent behavior.

13   Felix leaned heavily on the river's railing and stared across to the shores of Brooklyn. Finally, he broke the silence.

14   " . . . I don't know how to come out with it."

15   Antonio helped. "It's about our fight, right?"

16   "Yeah, right." Felix's eyes squinted at the rising orange sun.

17   "I've been thinking about it too, *panín*.[2] In fact, since we found out it was going to be me and you, I've been awake at night, pulling punches on you, trying not to hurt you."

18   "Same here. It ain't natural not to think about the fight. I mean, we both are *cheverote*[3] fighters and we both want to win. But only one of us can win. There ain't no draws in the eliminations."

19   Felix tapped Antonio gently on the shoulder. "I don't mean to sound like I'm bragging, bro. But I wanna win, fair and square."

20   Antonio nodded quietly. "Yeah. We both know that in the ring the better man wins. Friend or no friend, brother or no . . ."

21   Felix finished it for him. "Brother. Tony, let's promise something right here. Okay?"

22   "If it's fair, *hermano*,[4] I'm for it." Antonio admired the courage of a tug boat pulling a barge five times its welterweight[5] size.

23   "It's fair, Tony. When we get into the ring, it's gotta be like we never met. We gotta be like two heavy strangers that want the same thing and only one can have it. You understand, don'tcha?"

24   "*Sí*, I know." Tony smiled. "No pulling punches. We go all the way."

25   "Yeah, that's right. Listen, Tony. Don't you think it's a good idea if we don't see each other until the day of the fight? I'm going to stay with my Aunt Lucy in the Bronx. I can use Gleason's Gym for working out. My manager says he got some sparring partners with more or less your style."

26   Tony scratched his nose pensively. "Yeah, it would be better for our heads." He held out his hand, palm upward. "Deal?"

27   "Deal." Felix lightly slapped open skin.

28   "Ready for some more running?" Tony asked lamely.

29   "Naw, bro. Let's cut it here. You go on. I kinda like to get things together in my head."

30   "You ain't worried, are you?" Tony asked.

31   "No way, man." Felix laughed out loud. "I got too much smarts for that. I just think it's cooler if we split right here. After the fight, we can get it together again like nothing ever happened."

32   The amigo brothers were not ashamed to hug each other tightly.

33   "Guess you're right. Watch yourself, Felix. I hear there's some pretty heavy dudes up in the Bronx. *Suavecito*,[6] okay?"

---

[2] *Panín* (pä nēn'), Puerto Rican slang for *buddy*.

[3] *Cheverote* (chā vā rō'tā), Puerto Rican slang for *super; great*.

[4] *Hermano* (er mä'nō), brother or pal. [*Spanish*]

[5] *Welterweight*, in boxing, a division between the lightweight and heavyweight divisions. Antonio is thinking of the tug boat as medium-sized.

[6] *Suavecito* (swä vā sē'tō), Take it easy. [*Spanish*]

34   "Okay. You watch yourself too, *sabe*?"[7]

35   Tony jogged away. Felix watched his friend disappear from view, throwing rights and lefts. Both fighters had a lot of psyching up to do before the big fight.

36   The days in training passed much too slowly. Although they kept out of each other's way, they were aware of each other's progress via the ghetto grapevine.

37   The evening before the big fight, Tony made his way to the roof of his tenement. In the quiet early dark, he peered over the ledge. Six stories below the lights of the city blinked and the sounds of cars mingled with the curses and the laughter of children in the street. He tried not to think of Felix, feeling he had succeeded in psyching his mind. But only in the ring would he really know. To spare Felix hurt, he would have to knock him out, early and quick.

38   Up in the South Bronx, Felix decided to take in a movie in an effort to keep Antonio's face away from his fists. The flick was *The Champion* with Kirk Douglas, the third time Felix was seeing it. . . .

39   Felix became the champ and Tony the challenger.

40   The movie audience was going out of its head, roaring in blood lust at the butchery going on. The champ hunched his shoulders grunting and sniffing red blood back into his broken nose. The challenger, confident that he had the championship in the bag, threw a left. The champ countered with a dynamite right that exploded into the challenger's brains.

41   Felix's right arm felt the shock. Antonio's face, superimposed on the screen, was shattered and split apart by the awesome force of the killer blow. Felix saw himself in the ring, blasting Antonio against the ropes. The champ had to be forcibly restrained. The challenger was allowed to crumble slowly to the canvas, a broken bloody mess.

42   When Felix finally left the theater, he had figured out how to psyche himself for tomorrow's fight. It was Felix the Champion vs. Antonio the Challenger.

43   He walked up some dark streets, deserted except for small pockets of wary-looking kids wearing gang colors. Despite the fact that he was Puerto Rican like them, they eyed him as a stranger to their turf. Felix did a fast shuffle, bobbing and weaving, while letting loose a torrent of blows that would demolish whatever got in its way. It seemed to impress the brothers, who went about their own business.

44   Finding no takers, Felix decided to split to his aunt's. Walking the streets had not relaxed him, neither had the fight flick. All it had done was to stir him up. He let himself quietly into his Aunt Lucy's apartment and went straight to bed, falling into a fitful sleep with sounds of the gong for Round One.

---

[7] *Sabe?* (sä'bā), Understand? [*Spanish*]

45   Antonio was passing some heavy time on his rooftop. How would the fight tomorrow affect his relationship with Felix? After all, fighting was like any other profession. Friendship had nothing to do with it. A gnawing doubt crept in. He cut negative thinking real quick by doing some speedy fancy dance steps, bobbing and weaving like mercury. The night air was blurred with perpetual motions of left hooks and right crosses. Felix, his *amigo* brother, was not going to be Felix at all in the ring. Just an opponent with another face. Antonio went to sleep, hearing the opening bell for the first round. Like his friend in the South Bronx, he prayed for victory, via a quick clean knockout in the first round.

46   Large posters plastered all over the walls of local shops announced the fight between Antonio Cruz and Felix Vargas as the main bout.

47   The fight had created great interest in the neighborhood. Antonio and Felix were well liked and respected. Each had his own loyal following. Betting fever was high and ranged from a bottle of coke to cold hard cash on the line.

48   Antonio's fans bet with unbridled faith in his boxing skills. On the other side, Felix's admirers bet on his dynamite-packed fists.

49   Felix had returned to his apartment early in the morning of August 7th and stayed there, hoping to avoid seeing Antonio. He turned the radio on to *salsa* music[8] sounds and then tried to read while waiting for word from his manager.

50   The fight was scheduled to take place in Tompkins Square Park. It had been decided that the gymnasium of the Boys' Club was not large enough to hold all the people who were sure to attend. In Tompkins Square Park, everyone who wanted could view the fight, whether from ringside or window fire escapes or tenement rooftops.

51   The morning of the fight Tompkins Square was a beehive of activity, with numerous workers setting up the ring, the seats, and the guest speakers' stand. The scheduled bouts began shortly after noon and the park had begun filling up even earlier.

52   The local junior high school across from Tompkins Square Park served as the dressing room for all the fighters. Each was given a separate classroom with desk tops, covered with mats, serving as resting tables. Antonio thought he caught a glimpse of Felix waving to him from a room at the far end of the corridor. He waved back just in case it had been him.

53   The fighters changed from their street clothes into fighting gear. Antonio wore white trunks, black socks, and black shoes. Felix wore sky blue trunks, red socks, and white boxing shoes. Each had dressing gowns to match their fighting trunks with their names neatly stitched on the back.

54   The loudspeakers blared into the open windows of the school. There were speeches by dignitaries, community leaders, and great boxers of yesteryear. Some were well prepared, some improvised on the spot. They all

---

[8] *Salsa* (säl'sä) *music*, lively dance music.

carried the same message of great pleasure and honor at being part of such a historic event. This great day was in the tradition of champions emerging from the streets of the lower east side.

55   Interwoven with the speeches were the sounds of the other boxing events. After the sixth bout, Felix was much relieved when his trainer Charlie said, "Time change. Quick knockout. This is it. We're on."

56   Waiting time was over. Felix was escorted from the classroom by a dozen fans in white T-shirts with the word FELIX across their fronts.

57   Antonio was escorted down a different stairwell and guided through a roped-off path.

58   As the two climbed into the ring, the crowd exploded with a roar. Antonio and Felix both bowed gracefully and then raised their arms in acknowledgment.

59   Antonio tried to be cool, but even as the roar was in its first birth, he turned slowly to meet Felix's eyes looking directly into his. Felix nodded his head and Antonio responded. And both as one, just as quickly, turned away to face his own corner.

60   Bong—bong—bong. The roar turned to stillness.

61   "Ladies and Gentlemen, *Señores y Señoras.*"

62   The announcer spoke slowly, pleased at his bilingual efforts.

63   "Now the moment we have all been waiting for—the main event between two fine young Puerto Rican fighters, products of our lower east side."

64   "Loisaida,"[9] called out a member of the audience.

65   "In this corner, weighing 134 pounds, Felix Vargas. And in this corner, weighing 133 pounds, Antonio Cruz. The winner will represent the Boys' Club in the tournament of champions, the Golden Gloves. There will be no draw. May the best man win."

66   The cheering of the crowd shook the window panes of the old buildings surrounding Tompkins Square Park. At the center of the ring, the referee was giving instructions to the youngsters.

67   "Keep your punches up. No low blows. No punching on the back of the head. Keep your heads up. Understand. Let's have a clean fight. Now shake hands and come out fighting."

68   Both youngsters touched gloves and nodded. They turned and danced quickly to their corners. Their head towels and dressing gowns were lifted neatly from their shoulders by their trainers' nimble fingers. Antonio crossed himself. Felix did the same.

69   BONG! BONG! ROUND ONE. Felix and Antonio turned and faced each other squarely in a fighting pose. Felix wasted no time. He came in fast, head low, half hunched toward his right shoulder, and lashed out with a straight left. He missed a right cross as Antonio slipped the punch and countered with one-two-three lefts, that snapped Felix's head back, sending a mild

---

[9]*Loisaida* (lō ē sīdə), a dialectal pronunciation of *Lower East Side.*

shock coursing through him. If Felix had any small doubt about their friendship affecting their fight, it was being neatly dispelled.

70   Antonio danced, a joy to behold. His left hand was like a piston pumping jabs one right after another with seeming ease. Felix bobbed and weaved and never stopped boring in. He knew that at long range he was at a disadvantage. Antonio had too much reach on him. Only by coming in close could Felix hope to achieve the dreamed-of knockout.

71   Antonio knew the dynamite that was stored in his *amigo* brother's fist. He ducked a short right and missed a left hook. Felix trapped him against the ropes just long enough to pour some punishing rights and lefts to Antonio's hard midsection. Antonio slipped away from Felix, crashing two lefts to his head, which set Felix's right ear to ringing.

72   Bong! Both *amigos* froze a punch well on its way, sending up a roar of approval for good sportsmanship.

73   Felix walked briskly back to his corner. His right ear had not stopped ringing. Antonio gracefully danced his way toward his stool none the worse, except for glowing glove burns, showing angry red welts against the whiteness of his midribs.

74   "Watch that right, Tony." His trainer talked into his ear. "Remember Felix always goes to the body. He'll want you to drop your hands for his overhand left or right. Got it?"

75   Antonio nodded, spraying water out between his teeth. He felt better as his sore midsection was being firmly rubbed.

76   Felix's corner was also busy.

77   "You gotta get in there, fella." Felix's trainer poured water over his curly Afro locks. "Get in there or he's gonna chop you up from way back."

78   *Bong! Bong!* Round two. Felix was off his stool and rushed Antonio like a bull, sending a hard right to his head. Beads of water exploded from Antonio's long hair.

79   Antonio, hurt, sent back a blurring barrage of lefts and rights that only meant pain to Felix, who returned with a short left to the head followed by a looping right to the body. Antonio countered with his own flurry, forcing Felix to give ground. But not for long.

80   Felix bobbed and weaved, bobbed and weaved, occasionally punching his two gloves together.

81   Antonio waited for the rush that was sure to come. Felix closed in and feinted with his left shoulder and threw his right instead. Lights suddenly exploded inside Felix's head as Antonio slipped the blow and hit him with a pistonlike left, catching him flush on the point of his chin.

82   Bedlam broke loose as Felix's legs momentarily buckled. He fought off a series of rights and lefts and came back with a strong right that taught Antonio respect.

83   Antonio danced in carefully. He knew Felix had the habit of playing possum when hurt, to sucker an opponent within reach of the powerful bombs he carried in each fist.

84 A right to the head slowed Antonio's pretty dancing. He answered with his own left at Felix's right eye that began puffing up within three seconds.

85 Antonio, a bit too eager, moved in too close and Felix had him entangled into a rip-roaring, punching toe-to-toe slugfest that brought the whole Tompkins Square Park screaming to its feet.

86 Rights to the body. Lefts to the head. Neither fighter was giving an inch. Suddenly a short right caught Antonio squarely on the chin. His long legs turned to jelly and his arms flailed out desperately. Felix, grunting like a bull, threw wild punches from every direction. Antonio, groggy, bobbed and weaved, evading most of the blows. Suddenly his head cleared. His left flashed out hard and straight catching Felix on the bridge of his nose.

87 Felix lashed back with a haymaker, right off the ghetto streets. At the same instant, his eyes caught another left hook from Antonio. Felix swung out trying to clear the pain. Only the frenzied screaming of those along ringisde let him know that he had dropped Antonio. Fighting off the growing haze, Antonio struggled to his feet, got up, ducked, and threw a smashing right that dropped Felix flat on his back.

88 Felix got up as fast as he could in his own corner, groggy but still game. He didn't even hear the count. In a fog, he heard the roaring of the crowd, who seemed to have gone insane. His head cleared to hear the bell sound at the end of the round. He was . . . glad. His trainer sat him down on the stool.

89 In his corner, Antonio was doing what all fighters do when they are hurt. They sit and smile at everyone.

90 The referee signaled the ring doctor to check the fighters out. He did so and then gave his okay. The cold water sponges brought clarity to both *amigo* brothers. They were rubbed until their circulation ran free.

91 *Bong!* Round three—the final round. Up to now it had been tic-tac-toe, pretty much even. But everyone knew there could be no draw and that this round would decide the winner.

92 This time, to Felix's surprise, it was Antonio who came out fast, charging across the ring. Felix braced himself but couldn't ward off the barrage of punches. Antonio drove Felix hard against the ropes.

93 The crowd ate it up. Thus far the two had fought with *mucho corazón*.[10] Felix tapped his gloves and commenced his attack anew. Antonio, throwing boxer's caution to the winds, jumped in to meet him.

94 Both pounded away. Neither gave an inch and neither fell to the canvas. Felix's left eye was tightly closed. Claret red blood poured from Antonio's nose. They fought toe-to-toe.

95 The sounds of their blows were loud in contrast to the silence of a crowd gone completely mute. The referee was stunned by their savagery.

---

[10] *Mucho corazón* (mü chō kō rä sōn'), much courage.

96   *Bong! Bong! Bong!* The bell sounded over and over again. Felix and Antonio were past hearing. Their blows continued to pound on each other like hailstones.

97   Finally the referee and the two trainers pried Felix and Antonio apart. Cold water was poured over them to bring them back to their senses.

98   They looked around and then rushed toward each other. A cry of alarm surged through Tompkins Square Park. Was this a fight to the death instead of a boxing match?

99   The fear soon gave way to wave upon wave of cheering as the two *amigos* embraced.

100   No matter what the decision, they knew they would always be champions to each other.

101   *Bong! Bong! Bong!* "Ladies and Gentlemen. *Señores* and *Señoras.* The winner and representative to the Golden Gloves Tournament of Champions is . . ."

102   The announcer turned to point to the winner and found himself alone. Arm in arm the champions had already left the ring.

DISCUSSION QUESTIONS

1. Describe the friendship between Antonio Cruz and Felix Vargas.
2. Discuss Antonio's and Felix's dreams regarding the elimination match.
3. Discuss their dedication to boxing and their sportsmanship.
4. Describe Tompkins Square Park, the fight, and the outcome.

WRITING TOPICS

1. Write your plan for accomplishing an important task. Address the preparations you will make and the consecutive steps you will take to complete the job.
2. Write a column for the sports section of your local newspaper on the fight between Cruz and Vargas for the Golden Gloves championship. Use descriptive language and include details about the personal lives of the fighters.

CHAPTER TWELVE

THE COSMIC RACE

Some years ago a magazine called *Nuestro* featured on its cover a drawing of a Hispanic boxer. In designing the cover art, the illustrator had to make some decisions about the physical characteristics of a Hispanic man. Of course, they would depend upon whether the boxer was from the Caribbean, perhaps of the black race, or from the Southwest, and of Mexican/Indian ancestry. The illustrator, uncertain about the appropriate combination of characteristics to convey a Hispanic, compromised by drawing the boxer in silhouette, thus skirting the issue. The difficulty for the artist was how to portray a Hispanic because, in fact, Hispanics come from many races and frequently have mixed racial backgrounds.

Hispanics define their race in terms of language and culture. During the 1960s and 1970s the influx of Hispanics to the United States resulted in an explosion of urban growth. The print media that developed in response depicted the Hispanic communities as having unique identities somewhat like the *barrios* of most American cities in the nineteenth century. The writings addressed race, color, language, and culture in establishing self-images for these displaced Hispanics whose common experience was migration, yet whose backgrounds and appearances were widely varied.

Mexican American writer José Vasconcelos coined the phrase "the cosmic race" to refer to an ideal—a mixture of races and cultures in Latin America that could coexist peacefully without regard to differences among them. Hispanics in the United States also recognize the possibility of a cosmic race in which their varied traditions, definitions, and races will come together. Some Hispanic writers today have embraced this idea, finding hope in the desire to unite and work together to solve problems that are not limited to race, but, in fact, besiege society as a whole.

LA DOCTORA BARR

Mary Helen Ponce

Mary Helen (née Merrihelen) Ponce was born on January 24, 1938, in the San Fernando Valley in southern California, the youngest of seven sisters and three brothers. One sister belonged to the Book of the Month Club and introduced her to literature. Years later, Ponce went on to attend California State University at Northridge, where she obtained her B.A. and her M.A. in Mexican American Studies. Subsequently, she enrolled at UCLA to obtain a second M.A. in history. She left UCLA in 1984 to pursue a doctorate in American studies from the University of New Mexico.

Her writing reflects her experience of living in a Mexican-American area of California, and Ponce has undertaken its documentation through fiction. Her first book, *Recuerdo: Short Stories of the Barrio* (1983), is full of autobiographical first-person accounts. *Taking Control* (1987) includes not only her view of women, but writing in which poor victims of oppression end up taking control of their lives. *The Wedding* (1989), a novel set in the 1940s and 1950s in the San Fernando Valley, is the story of a young woman, Blanca, and her experiences as she grows up and anticipates her wedding.

Mary Helen Ponce's "La Doctora Barr" brings tradition to modernity and vice versa. The birthing rites of the middle-class community are contrasted with those of the traditional poor Indian woman and the modern physician.

1   My earliest memory is of when I was about three, when my brother Joey was born. Joey was delivered at home by 'la Doctora Barr' who had also delivered me. She practiced medicine in the nearby city of *Burbanke,* as we called Burbank, and also came to the homes of *la gente mexicana*[1] of Pacoima to dispense medicine and deliver babies.

---

[1] The Mexican people.

2   She was of medium height, a bit plump, with soft brown hair worn in a bun from which wispy tendrils escaped to form a halo around her cheerful face. She wore little makeup; she needed none for her ruddy, healthy cheeks were a bright red so that when she smiled it appeared she had two apples for cheeks. She wore glasses with wire frames which often slipped to her nose so that she appeared to peer at us in a friendly way.

3   "Well, playing ball again I see."

4   "Sí Señora Barr." "Yes Mrs. Doctor." "Oh yes ma'am."

5   "Yes ma'am, I wash dishes, sweep the kitchen and make the beds."

6   "Liar, I make the beds."

7   "No she doesn't, I do. She makes them too messy—I have to make them over," I would protest to *la doctora*[2] as she disappeared into the doorway of a nearby house.

8   Most of the time Dr. Barr would not be consulted by the expectant mother until the pregnancy was well into its final month. Most of the women had an idea of what to do during *un embarazo*.[3] The women continued with their work, caring for home and children until the first labor pains would signal an imminent birth. A neighbor was first alerted, she in turn would notify *un señor*[4] who would rush off to the one public phone booth located on Van Nuys Boulevard to call the doctor. In the meantime the neighbor women would bring out *sábanas limpias*,[5] put water to boil and farm the kids out to neighbors or relatives so as to spare them the confusion that accompanied *un parto*,[6] as at times the younger children slept in the same room as the parents, even shared the same bed; thus it was neither advisable nor practical to have them around.

9   When Dr. Barr arrived all was in readiness; the expectant mother lay on clean, white sheets, her face washed, hair combed back in a *chongo*[7] or *una trenza*,[8] in her hand, a clean rag to bite on when the pain became unbearable as it was thought to be *muy ranchera*[9] to scream out. The *señoras*[10] made sure *una botella de alcohol*,[11] *toallas limpias*[12] and a pan for the afterbirth were nearby along with a supply of clean white rags to be used as sanitary napkins as few women of the *barrio*[13] could afford to buy this

---

[2] The woman doctor. Barr is the doctor's last name.
[3] A pregnancy.
[4] A gentleman.
[5] Clean sheets.
[6] A birth.
[7] Bun.
[8] A braid.
[9] Very low class.
[10] Ladies.
[11] A bottle of alcohol.
[12] Clean towels.
[13] Neighborhood.

item at *la Tienda Blanca*, an item not to be found *en la tienda de Don Jesús*.[14]

10   Not all of the women believed in a scientific approach to childbirth; among these was a neighbor *la Juana*,[15] said to be *una india*[16] because of her dark skin, high cheekbones, black slanted eyes, and the facility for delivering babies every nine months without a fuss. *La Juana* never 'showed' until she was in her eighth month; somehow she carried her babies in such a manner that her stomach did not protrude.

11   One time I was playing ball with my best friend Chelo, when her mother was summoned to help *la Juana*[17] who was about to give birth.

12   "Doña Placencia, Doña Placencia, dice la Juana que ya es tiempo."[17]

13   "Avísale que ya voy."[18]

14   Upon hearing this exchange Chelo and I quickly volunteered to help carry the towels and alcohol as we were curious to be around someone who was about to give birth, a subject that was discussed by our mothers with sighs of *Jesús, María y José*[19]—and ended abruptly when we were within earshot. Once at the house we were not allowed inside but chose to remain outside in hopes of being asked inside or to run *un mandado*.[20] Chelo and I soon got bored waiting for something to happen. We left but later returned on the pretext of wanting permission to go to *la Tienda de Don Jesús*. Chelo's mother pretended to be pleased at our request since we never asked but *told* her where we were going, only her smiling eyes gave her away. She quickly let us in—as she went to find the handkerchief where she kept her money rolled in a tight knot. While Chelo stood and waited for her mother to return *con un cinco*,[21] I tiptoed into the next room and peeked inside the bedroom. The room was dark; I could barely make out the figures of two women, *la Juana*, bent over, a woman standing immediately behind her, towels at her feet, hands outstretched.

15   "Puje, puje, un poquito más."[22]

16   "Ay, cómo duele."[23]

17   "Pues eso ya sabía—si no es el primero."[24]

18   "Ya sé . . . ojalá sea el último."[25]

19   "Sí, pero primero pújele."[26]

---

[14] At Don Jesús's store, as opposed to *la Tienda blanca*, the "white" store.
[15] Juana or Joanna, the English version of the name.
[16] An (American) Indian woman.
[17] "Doña Placencia, Doña Placencia, Juana says that it is time."
[18] "Let her know I am on the way."
[19] "Jesus, Mary, and Joseph."
[20] An errand.
[21] "With a five" (could be a nickel or a five-dollar bill).
[22] "Push, push a little more."
[23] "Oh, this hurts a lot."
[24] "Well, you knew that—this is not your first."
[25] "I know . . . I hope it will be my last."
[26] "Yes, but first, push."

20   I stood mesmerized, staring into the room, trying to see more but was forced to move quickly into the next room when I heard Chelo's mother approaching from another direction. She gave me a look that spoke volumes; I believe she saw me coming out of the room. However she said nothing, handed Chelo two dimes, then quickly shooed us out the door. Later that evening we heard that a son had been born to Juana. Early the next day she was seen outside, new baby strapped to her back, hanging clothes on the line, looking not as if she had just given birth. The *señoras* of the neighborhood shook their heads in wonder (and disgust) at *los modos rancheros de la Juana*[27] who neither asked for *la doctora* nor followed *la dieta* afterwards.

21   One of the areas of conflict experienced by Dr. Barr and the women of our barrio dealt with the special diet that new mothers were supposed to follow. *La Dieta* pertained not only to diet but to after-care following a birth. For all her goodness, Dr. Barr would become exasperated when her patients insisted on following the traditions and customs inherent in Mexican culture rather than her own instructions, which she felt were more scientific and "wholesome." Dr. Barr encouraged *las señoras* to bathe and wash their hair soon after *un parto*; however Mexican custom dictated otherwise. In order not to catch *frío*,[28] a woman was supposed to refrain from bathing for at least six weeks. Along with this, the new mother should avoid eating certain foods such as *limones*,[29] *avocados* y *carne de puerco*;[30] foods that would sour her milk. In addition the new mother was made to wear a heavy *banda* around her stomach, a band made of old sheets cut into strips which was wound around her stomach immediately after she had expelled the afterbirth and which was expected to remain for the same six weeks to ensure that *la matriz*[31] would quickly contract and return to its normal size. Heavy lifting was prohibited as was heavy housework such as the washing of clothes *en el lavadero*,[32] the mopping of floors and hanging washclothes on the line. This then was a time when a woman like my mother who worked hard most of her life was allowed to rest and be waited on by family and neighbors. However in time the custom of *la dieta* was either modified or abolished as not everyone could afford the luxury of lying in bed for six weeks. In time the younger women wanted to be *como las americanas*[33] and soon did as *la doctora* suggested: got up on the third day, took a bath and continued with their daily chores. It seems that *la Juana*, an illiterate woman, knew what she was doing all along.

---

[27] Juana's low-class ways.
[28] Cold.
[29] Lemons.
[30] Avocados and meat of the pig; pork.
[31] The womb.
[32] In the laundry room.
[33] Like the American (Anglo) women.

DISCUSSION QUESTIONS

1. Describe the traditional way Mexican-American women prepared for a childbirth in their community.
2. In what ways did Doctora Barr's methods differ from the customs of the Mexican-American community?
3. Describe the strategies of the narrator and Chelo for witnessing "la Juana" in childbirth.
4. Discuss the issue of tradition versus modernization regarding childbirth and other events in the Mexican-American community.

WRITING TOPICS

1. After interviewing your mother or another female relative, write an account of childbirth from the mother's perspective.
2. Write an essay about adherence to tradition in your family or community.

SAN ANTONIO PHANTASMAGORIA

Ricardo Sánchez

The youngest of thirteen children, Ricardo Sánchez was born on March 29, 1941, in a rough district of El Paso, Texas, known as the Barrio del Diablo (The Devil's Neighborhood). As a young man Sánchez dropped out of high school, feeling lost in what he would later call a "racist" educational system, and enlisted in the U.S. Army. Later he served time in prison. After his parole in 1969, Sánchez earned his high school equivalency and subsequently received grants from the Ford Foundation. He obtained a Ph.D. in American studies from the Union Graduate School with his dissertation entitled "CUNA: The Barrio and the Poetics of Revolution."

Before his death in 1995, Sánchez, a prolific poet, was recognized as a creator of Chicano literature. In particular, he was known for his bilingual poetry. Among his books are *Canto y grito mi liberacion (y lloro mis desmadrazgos)* [I Sing and Shout My Liberation (and Cry About My Mistakes)] (1971), *Hechizospells: Poetry/Stories/Vignettes/Articles/Notes on the Human Condition of Chicanos & Picaros, Words & Hopes within Soulmind* (1976), *Milhuas Blues and Gritos Norteños* (1980), *Brown Bear and Honey Madnesses: Alaskan Cruising Poems* (1981), *Amsterdam Cantos y Poemas Pistos* (1983), *Selected Poems* (1985), and *Eagle Visioned/Feathered Adobes: Manito sojourns and pachuco ramblings* (1989). He also prepared an anthology with Abelardo Delgado entitled *Los cuatro* (The Four) (1971) and wrote a screenplay for *Entelequia* (1979).

Sánchez worked as a free-lance writer and journalist, as well as founder and editor of Míctla Publications (El Paso), *La Luz* (Denver), and *Ins and Outs* (Amsterdam, Holland). He prepared special issues of *Wood/Ibis* (Austin), *". . . ?" Magazine* (Venice, Italy), and *De Colores: Journal of Emerging Raza Philosophies* (Albuquerque). In addition, he taught at Washington State University—until the time of his death. At the University of Wisconsin-Milwaukee, he helped to organize the first Canto al Pueblo Festival (Song to the People) in the mid-seventies.

Sánchez will always be remembered for his "unbridled linguistic inventiveness," as one critic puts it. The following three selections are representative of the unique style that became a trademark of the poetry he wrote for oral performance. In the following selections the poet speaks to racial pride, human dignity, and a future of hope.

The first poem, "San Antonio phantasmagoria," focuses on an exhibit of constantly shifting scenes (a phantasmagoria) as a group of midwestern tourists visits San Antonio, and the Alamo, the fortress symbolizing Texan independence, comes into view.

SAN ANTONIO PHANTASMAGORIA

sitting beside dr. gardéa
with abner haynes'[1] voice reverberating,
this is a grimey city
as we go to hear música
5   and partake of mexican refín.[2]

ciudad de san antonio[3]
with pantheon of the alamáo/mamáo ÁLAMO,

false glory
midst ethnic ululation,[4]
10   cry of adulation,

death still haunts
brown/black people,
slavery is real,
       but now it's called pobreza . . .[5]

15   sit and talk,
pillars of grand society,
band-aid ills and miseries,

we shall eat/hear mariachis[6]
and rap about funds

---

[1] Abner Haynes, along with Dr. Gardéa, are names of the characters in the scene.
[2] Mexican-American expression for food.
[3] City of San Antonio (Texas).
[4] Wailing; howling.
[5] Poverty.
[6] Mexican street bands.

20 that abner says will come
from his friends
at zale foundation[7]
                    (which i doubt!)
and we shall nonetheless
25 continue seeking out
an answer to the ills
deracinating raza. . . .[8]

BARRIOS OF THE WORLD

barrios[1] of the world
where we live and strive,
where rich and poor separate
                    their worlds
5 into different realities;
barrios of the world,
paradoxes
seething with rage/unsanity

a new world cometh,
10 world of awareness,
plagueless world,
spectral world,
love-struck world,
composite of man's humanity
15 cauldron of sister/brother-hood.

el chuco, los,[2] alburque, denver,
san anto, el valle, laredo,
the midwest, borícua harlem,
change is coming to you
20 birdlike, vibrant, vehemently virile

la voz del Chicano[3] proclaims
hermandad—carnalismo—humanidad,[4]
like bumper stickers cauterizing
gods of all dimensions,

---

[7] A philanthropic foundation.
[8] A reference to the taking away of racial identity ("deracinating") of the *raza*—the race, here the Mexican-American people.

[1] Neighborhoods; Spanish-speaking quarters of a community.
[2] The Latino, from . . .
[3] The voice of the Chicano.
[4] Different Spanish words for humanity.

25   god is chicano, mexican, hispano,
          cholo, pocho,[5] mexican-american,
          american of spanish surname (ASS!),
          borícua, puertorro,[6] and a host
          multihued
30   proclamando[7] divinity, dignity,
          humankind moving forth . . .

For us, there is our reality,
it is real and virile/fertile,
simplicity unadorned,
35 scorched by sun and drenched in love,
Chicano destiny being created,
carnales[8] one and all, we do not fear
the providence others claim,
we just seek our own horizons;
40 peaceful people that we are,
we'll defend our right to live,
somos la raza, hogan/jacal[9] creators,
pyramid builders, cathedral makers,
living en el diablo, siete infiernos,[10]
45 coronado, la loma, y kern place,[11]
creators of our destinies
desde barelas a maravilla. . . .[12]

LATINOS

latinos meeting,
     borícuas/chicanos,[1]
striving to create
way out
5   from social quagmire
where we
stand viewing
others making it
while we hungrily

---

[5] Various terms for Latinos or Mexican Americans.
[6] Other Hispanic ethnic groups—here from Puerto Rico or of Puerto Rican descent.
[7] Proclaimed.
[8] Sensual.
[9] "We are the race." A hogan or jacal is a Mexican-style hut.
[10] In the devil; seven hells.
[11] A reference to the Spanish explorer of the U.S. Southwest, Francisco Vásquez de Coronado; the hill; and the place of "kern"—origination.
[12] From one place to another place of wonder.

[1] Puerto Ricans/Chicanos (Mexican-Americans).

10   scratch souls,
     and our guts shrivel
     for hope luxuriates
     only in the minds
     of those
15   who've made it

                    (we all carry contradictions
                    within the chaos of our poverty!) . . .

     can we dare hope
     to somehow band
20   into a force/a wedge
     to open doors
     where we might thrive?

     we dare do more,
     we must do more
25   than hope and wait
     and trust in fate
     or hibernate!

     we must define
     just who we are
30   and struggle on
     as comrades must
     to thus express
     that we shall live
     as human beings
35   with dignity,
     but dignity only comes
     when we have taken on
     the course of liberation
     and conquered fears
40   and slave mentality. . . .

DISCUSSION QUESTIONS

1. Analyze the motif of poverty in Sánchez's construction of Hispanic identity.
2. These poems are about representative people and symbolic places. Discuss the meaning of the poems in relation to these aspects of the poetry.

3. Discuss the future of Hispanics/Latinos in general in the United States, according to Sánchez.
4. Does Sánchez believe that the white community will assist the Hispanic community? Give examples from the selections to support your answer.

WRITING TOPICS

1. Write an essay about the future of Hispanics in the United States. You may relate to the history of Latinos in the U.S. in your essay.
2. Construct a fictional interview with the late Ricardo Sánchez about his poetry.

A CHILD TO BE BORN

Alberto Urista (Alurista)

Born in Mexico City on August 8, 1947, Alberto Urista would become an important voice in Chicano poetry in the seventies. His delight in linguistic playfulness has always been in direct contrast with the formal education he pursued in the United States when his family arrived in 1960. He obtained his B.A. (1970) and his M.A. (1972) from San Diego State University and his Ph.D. from the University of California, San Diego (1983).

It was in the mid-sixties, when he saw César Chávez leading the striking farmworkers, that Alurista decided to write and to reflect his identity in terms of the Chicano experience. His first book, *Floricanto in Aztlán* (1971) conveys his identification with the workers and their struggle, creating a connection to the Mexican pre-Columbian past. That work was immediately followed by *Nationchild Plumaroja, 1969–1972* (1972), a book of one hundred poems—each divided into five Mayan *katunes* (units of twenty) marked by a flower or animal symbol. *Timespace Huracán: Poems, 1972–1975* (1976) abandons the bilingual poetry so characteristic of Alurista for a book of poems composed wholly in Spanish. The work experiments with poetic form (concrete poetry, serial poems, prose poems, and haiku). In contrast, *Return: Poems Collected and New* (1982) contains a more accessible poetry that leaves experimentation behind.

Alurista's "A Child to Be Born" is a bilingual poem that links the image of the plumed serpent god of the ancient Mayas (Kukulcán) and of the ancient Aztecs (Quetzalcoatl) to the future. (From Aztlán, their mythical home, now within the southwestern United States, the Aztecs moved to found Mexico City, where the eagle ate the serpent—an image of the loftiness of the eagle conquering the base instinct of the serpent.) Here Alurista senses the germination of that future.

A child to be born
　　　　pregnant is the continente[1]
el barro y la raza[2]
　　　　to bear Aztlán[3] on our forehead
5　el niño que como pájaro[4]
　　　　en su vuela de colores cantos[5]
　　　　　　guió a Tenoch hacia el águila[6]
el niño dentro del vientre semilla[7]
　　　　un madretierraroja le acaricia[8]
10　Aztlán, Aztlán of the continent that bears child
　　　　tu madres es – el continentetierraroja[9]
where the crickets call the birth
　　　　and the ranas arrullan al nacido[10]
y las víboras del mar siguen a la campanita[11]
15　　　　por donde pueden pasar los de adelante[12]
and the ones in the back se quedarán[13]
　　　　　　Aztlán, Aztlán
the semilla que plantó nuestro padre Quetzalcoatl[14]
　　　　ya germina[15]
20　　　en el vientre de nuestra[16]
　　　　　　madrecontinentetierra, Amerindia[17]
nationchild de su padrecarnalismo Kukulcán[18]

---

[1] Continent.
[2] The mud and the Mexican people.
[3] The mythical home of the Aztecs, now Southwestern United States.
[4] The male child that like a bird.
[5] In his flight of colors sings.
[6] Guided Tenoch toward the eagle.
[7] The male child within the womb seed.
[8] A red-earth-mother caresses him.
[9] Your mother is the red-earth-continent.
[10] And the frogs lull the child borne.
[11] And the seasnakes follow the little bell.
[12] Where the forward ones can pass.
[13] Will remain behind.
[14] The seed that our father Quetzalcoatl [plumed serpent god of the Aztecs].
[15] Planted.
[16] Already bears fruit.
[17] In the womb of our mother-continent-earth, Indoamerica.
[18] Nationcihld of his father-brotherhood Kukulcán [the Mayan version of the plumed serpent-god].

Discussion Questions

1. Describe the events in preparation for the birth of the child in this poem.
2. What images does Alurista call to mind in the construction of this birth?
3. Discuss the connections between this Hispanic child's birth and the land from where he comes, Aztlán.
4. Analyze the references to the animals and their role in this birth and those of the gods mentioned in the poem.

Writing Topics

1. Write a letter announcing the birth of a brother or sister to a friend.
2. Write an essay analyzing the poem's imagery.

PUERTO RICAN

Tato Laviera

Tato Laviera's poetry celebrates the culture and strength and spirit of Puerto Ricans in the United States. He focuses on the multiethnic aspects of American society, intertwining lyrics from popular music with voices from the *barrio* in some of his works to reflect the many facets of Puerto Ricans in New York.

For more information, turn to the previous biography on page 82.

Tato Laviera's "puerto rican" summarizes the identity of Puerto Ricans within the context of the cosmic race, enumerating the races and colors of their nature.


```
       silk
       smooth
       ivory
       polished
    5  into
       brown
       tan
       black
       soul
   10  leaning
       back
       looking
       proud
       sharp
   15  answers
       casual
       community
       conversations
       based
```

20 in
mental
admiration
how
highly
25 we
claim
our
worth
conceiving
30 new
society
inside
cemented
hard
35 core
beauty
chanting
snapping
beats

DISCUSSION QUESTIONS

1. Laviera includes some conceptions of race in his construction of a Puerto Rican. Analyze his references to race.
2. Describe the demeanor of Laviera's Puerto Rican.
3. Discuss the mental nature of the Puerto Rican in the poem.
4. What are Laviera's conceptions concerning society and beauty?

WRITING TOPICS

1. Write a poem constructing a person who is representative of your own ethnic group.
2. Compose a fictional interview with Laviera in which you discuss with him race and community, art and beauty, and intelligence and pride.

MY RACE

José Martí

José Martí is best known as a poet and a patriot. A political exile from Cuba, Martí was an intellectual whose writings frequently appeared in U.S. newspapers published in Spanish. He wrote in support of independence for Cuba and Puerto Rico.

For more information, turn to the previous biographies on pages 45 and 112.

The following selection is an essay in which race is examined with regard to racism. The piece, written in 1893, anticipates a future of freedom in which the races will be united.

1   The word *racist* has fallen prey to confusion, and its meaning must be clarified. Men have no special rights because they belong to one race or another: the word *man* defines all rights. The Negro, by being a Negro, is neither superior nor inferior to any other man. The white man who says "my race" is redundant; so is the Negro who says "my race." Everything that divides men, everything that sorts, separates, and categorizes them, is a sin against humanity. What sensible white man prides himself on being white, and what can the Negro think of one who harbors such a conceit, and thinks that being white gives him special privileges? What must the white man think of the Negro who prides himself on his color? Constant harping on racial divisions and the differences between the races in the case of an already divided people impedes the attainment of national and individual well-being, which are to be secured by the greatest possible coming together of the racial elements that form the nation. If it is said that the Negro has no inherent weakness, and no virus that incapacitates him for the fullest realization of his human soul, one speaks the truth, and it must be said and proved, for the injustice of this world is great, as is the ignorance of many who pass for sages, and there are many who still honestly believe that the Negro is incapable of the intelligence and spirit of the white man. If that defense of nature is called racism, well and good, for it responds to the natural fitness of things, and is

the voice that wells from the breast of a man moved by the spirit of peace who seeks the welfare of his country. If a Negro asserts that slavery does not in itself demonstrate an inferiority in the enslaved race, since the white Gauls, of blue eyes and golden locks, were sold in chains in the Roman markets, that is good racism, because it is eminently just and helps to jar the ignorant white man out of some of his prejudices. But just racism ends with the Negro's right to maintain and prove that his color does not deprive him of any of the capabilities and rights of the human race.

2   With what justice can the white racist, who believes his race to be superior, complain of the Negro racist who considers his race specially privileged? How can the Negro racist, who insists on the special character of his race, complain of the white racist? The white man who rates himself superior to the Negro because of his race admits of the idea of race, incites the Negro racist, and gives him grounds for a like position. The Negro who proclaims his race, although it may be his mistaken way of proclaiming the spiritual identity of all races, provokes and justifies the white racist. Peace asks that the universal rights of Nature be recognized; discriminatory rights, which are contrary to Nature, are enemies of peace. The white man who isolates himself, isolates the Negro. The Negro who isolates himself moves the white man to isolation.

3   There is no danger of war between the races in Cuba. Man means more than white man, mulatto, or black man. Cuban means more than white man, mulatto, or black man. The souls of white men and Negroes have risen together from the battlefields where they fought and died for Cuba. Alongside every white man there was always a Negro, equal in loyalty, brotherhood, and cunning for the daily tasks of war. Negroes, just like white men, align themselves with the different parties in which men are grouped along lines of character, timid and valiant, selfless or grasping. Political parties are aggregates of preoccupations, hopes, interests, and personal qualities. The essential element in a party is to be sought and discovered beneath surface differences: the common motive is the fusion of the fundamental in analogous characters, who may differ in view on incidentals or details. To sum up, similarity of character is decisive and dominant in the formation of parties and outweighs the internal bonds that stem from man's variable color, or antagonisms that differences of pigmentation sometimes arouse. Affinity of character is stronger in men than affinity of color. The Negro, relegated to the thankless and unequal employments of the human spirit, could not, and would have no desire to, join forces against the white man similarly employed. The Negroes are too tired of an imposed slavery to enter voluntarily into a slavery of color. Pompous or self-seeking men will gravitate toward one party, regardless of their color, and generous, disinterested men will enter the other. Men worthy of the name will show each other loyalty and tenderness, for merit's own sake, and from pride in everything that honors the land in which they were born, black or white. The word *racist* will drop from the lips of the Negroes who use it today in good faith when they

realize that it is the only semblance of a valid argument that sincere, but timorous, men can adduce to deny the Negro his full rights as a man. Both racists are equally at fault: the white racist and the Negro racist. Many white men have already forgotten their color, as have many Negroes. They work together, blacks and whites, for the improvement of their minds, the propagation of virtues, and the triumph of the creative act and charitable spirit.

4   There will never be a war between the races in Cuba. The Republic cannot take a step backward; and the Republic, from the drafting of the first constitution of independence on October 10, 1868, in Guaimaro, which is the only day of redemption the Negro has known in Cuba, has never spoken of either blacks or whites. The civil rights conceded by the Spanish government now for astutely political reasons, which have long been in practice among the people, will never be taken from the Negro, either by the Spaniard who will maintain them while he breathes Cuban air to continue dividing the Cuban Negro from the Cuban white man, or by the independence, which could not deny in the hour of liberation what the Spaniard conceded in the hour of slavery.

5   When the independence comes, every individual will be free in the sanctity of the native home. Merit, the tangible, cumulative of culture, and the inexorable play of economic forces will ultimately unite all men. There is much greatness in Cuba, in both Negroes and whites.

DISCUSSION QUESTIONS

1. Discuss Martí's analysis of racism.
2. Analyze his conception of justice implied throughout this essay.
3. In 1912 there was a race war in Cuba, and in the United States the "Negroes" did enter into a community based on color. Discuss Martí's predictions with regard to these two events.
4. Given the dated nature of his ideas about the historical future and remembering that this essay was written in 1893, why is his analysis of racism important?

WRITING TOPICS

1. Write an essay about racism in America today.
2. Imagine a future in which race is no longer as important as it is today. Write a story in which some other issue has become more important.

ACKNOWLEDGMENTS

Anaya, Rudolfo. Chapter 1 from *Bless Me, Ultima*. Copyright © Rudolfo Anaya 1974. Published in hardcover and mass market paperback by Warner Books, Inc. 1994; originally published by TQS Publications. Reprinted by permission of Susan Bergholz Literary Services, New York. All rights reserved.

Anonymous. "La Llorona," retold by Bernal Díaz del Castillo, from *Chicano Literature: Text and Context*, eds. Antonia Castañeda Shular, Tomás Ybarra-Frausto, Joseph Sommers, Prentice-Hall, Inc, 1972.

Báez, Joan. "Thoughts on a Sunday Afternoon" by Joan Báez in *The Chicanos: Mexican American Voices*, ed. Ludwig and Santibañez, Penguin Books, 1971. Reprinted by permission of Joan Báez.

Cabeza de Vaca, Álvar Núñez. Chapters 10–14 from *The Account: Álvar Núñez Cabeza de Vaca's Relación* by Álvar Núñez Cabeza de Vaca are reprinted with permission from the publisher (Houston: Arte Público Press-University of Houston, 1993).

Cabrera, Lydia. "The Prize of Freedom" by Lydia Cabrera from *Beyond the Border: A New Age in Latin American Women's Fiction*, ed. Erro-Peralta and Silva-Núñez, Cleis Press, 1991. Copyright © 1991 by Nora Erro-Peralta and Caridad Silva-Núñez. Reprinted by permission.

Castillo, Ana. "Women are Not Roses" by Ana Castillo from *My Father was a Toltec*. Copyright © 1995 by Ana Castillo. Published by W.W. Norton. Reprinted by permission of Susan Bergholz Literary Services, New York.

Chavez, Denise. "Shooting Stars" by Denise Chavez is reprinted with permission from the publisher of *The Last of the Menu Girls* (Houston: Arte Público Press-University of Houston, 1986).

Chávez, Fray Angelico. "A Romeo and Juliet Story in Early New Mexico" in *The Short Stories of Fray Angelico Chávez*, ed. Genaro M. Padilla, University of New Mexico Press, 1987. Reprinted by permission of Thomas E. Chávez on behalf of the Chávez family.

Cisneros, Sandra. "My Name" from *The House on Mango Street*. Copyright © 1984 by Sandra Cisneros. Published by Vintage Books, a division of Random House Inc., and in hardcover by Alfred A. Knopf, 1994. Reprinted by permission of Susan Bergholz Literary Services, New York. All rights reserved.

Cofer, Judith Ortiz. "Progress Report for a Dead Father" by Judith Ortiz Cofer, edited by Evangelina Vigil-Píñon, is reprinted with permission from the publisher of *Woman of Her Word: Hispanic Women Write* (Houston: Arte Público Press-University of Houston, 1987). "To My Father" by Judith Ortiz Cofer is reprinted with permission from the publisher of *Terms of*

Survival (Houston: Arte Público Press-University of Houston, 1987). "Tales Told Under the Mango Tree" by Judith Ortiz Cofer is reprinted with permission from the publisher of *Silent Dancing: A Partial Remembrance Of A Puerto Rican Childhood* (Houston: Arte Público Press-University of Houston, 1990).

Colón, Jesús. "Bitter Sugar: Why Puerto Ricans Leave Home" by Jesús Colón, edited by Edna Acosta-Belén and Virginia Sánchez Korrol, is reprinted with permission from the publisher of *The Way It Was and Other Writings* (Houston: Arte Público Press-University of Houston, 1993).

Cossío y Cisneros, Evangelina. "To Free Cuba" from *The Story of Evangelina Cisneros* by Evangelina Betancourt Cossío y Cisneros, B.F. Johnson Publishing Company, 1897.

Cruz, Victor Hernández. "Borinkins in Hawaii" in *By Lingual Wholes,* Momo's Press, 1982. Copyright © 1982 by Victor Hernández Cruz. Reprinted by permission of Victor Hernández Cruz.

de Hoyes, Angela. "Arise, Chicano" originally published in *Arise, Chicano and Other Poems* by Angela de Hoyos, Backstage Books, 1975, reprinted with permission from the publisher of *Selected Poems of Angela de Hoyes* (Houston: Arte Público Press-University of Houston, yet to be published).

Elizondo, Sergio. "Murrieta on the Hill" by Sergio Elizondo in *Perros Y Antiperros,* Quinto Sol Publications, 1972. Reprinted by permission of Sergio Elizondo.

Esteves, Sandra María. "Transference" by Sandra María Esteves, edited by Evangelina Vigil-Piñón, is reprinted with permission from the publisher of *Woman of Her Work: Hispanic Women Write* (Houston: Arte Público Press-University of Houston, 1987).

Fernández, Roberta. "Filomena" by Roberta Fernández is reprinted with permission from the publisher of *Intaglio: A Novel in Six Stories* (Houston: Arte Público Press-University of Houston, 1990).

Firmat, Gustavo Pérez. "Seeing Snow" and "Dedication" by Gustavo Pérez Firmat from *Triple Crown: Chicano, Puerto Rican, and Cuban-American Poetry,* eds. Roberto Durán, Judith Ortiz Cofer, Gustavo Pérez Firmat. Copyright 1987 by Bilingual Press/Editorial Bilingue. Reprinted by permission.

Gonzales, Rodolfo. "I Am Joaquín" from *I Am Joaquín/Yo Say Joaquín: An Epic Poem* by Rodolfo "Corky" Gonzales, as published in *Chicano Literature:* Prentice-Hall, Inc., 1972. Copyright © 1967 by Rodolfo Gonzales.

Herrera-Sobek, María. From *Northward Bound: The Mexican Immigrant Experience in Ballad and Song* by María Herrera-Sobek, Indiana University Press, 1993. Reprinted by permission.

Hijuelos, Oscar. Excerpt from *Our House in the Last World* by Oscar Hijuelos, copyright © 1983 by Oscar Hijuelos. Reprinted by permission of Persea Books, Inc.

Hinojosa, Rolando. Excerpts (Letters 1 and 2) from *Dear Rafe* by Rolando Hinojosa are reprinted with permission from the publisher (Houston: Arte Público Press-University of Houston, 1985). Excerpt ("Becky") from *Becky and her Friends* by Rolando Hinojosa is reprinted with permission from the publisher (Houston: Arte Público Press-University of Houston, 1990).

Hospital, María Carolina. "Dear Tía" by María Carolina Hospital from *Cuban American Writers: Los Atrevidos, Ediciones Ellas,* Linden Lane Press, 1988. Reprinted by permission of Maria Carolina Hospital.

Laviera, Tato. "familia" and "puerto rican" by Tato Laviera are reprinted with permission from the publisher of *Enclave* (Houston: Arte Público Press-University of Houston, 1985).

Martí, José. "Our America" and "My Race" from *The America of José Martí* by José Martí, translated by Juan de Onís. Translation copyright © 1954 by The Noonday Press. Translation copyright renewed © 1982 by Farrar, Straus & Giroux, Inc. Reprinted by permission of Farrar, Straus & Giroux. "The Indian Ruins" by José Martí from *The Golden Age* by José Martí, 1984 edition, Milos Inc. Reprinted by permission.

Mohr, Nicholasa. "An Awakening . . . Summer 1956" by Nicholasa Mohr, edited by Evangelina Vigil-Piñón, is reprinted with permission from the publisher of *Woman of Her Word: Hispanic Women Write* (Houston: Arte Público Press-University of Houston, 1987). "Early November, 1941" by Nicholasa Mohr is reprinted with permission from the publisher of *Nilda* (Houston: Arte Público Press-University of Houston, 1986). "A Thanksgiving Celebration (Amy)" by Nicholasa Mohr is reprinted with permission from the publisher of *Rituals Of Survival: A Woman's Portfolio* (Houston: Arte Público Press-University of Houston, 1985).

Moraga, Cherríe. "For the Color of My Mother" in *This Bridge Called my Back: Writings of Radical Women of Color,* Kitchen Table: Women of Color Press, 1983. Copyright © 1983 by Cherríe Moraga and Gloria Anzaldúa, eds. Reprinted by permission of the author and Kitchen Table: Women of Color Press, P.O. Box 40-4920, Brooklyn, NY 11240-4920.

Muñoz, Elías Miguel. Excerpt from "Five" by Elías Miguel Muñoz is reprinted with permission from the publisher of *The Greatest Performance* (Houston:Arte Público Press-University of Houston, 1991).

Parades, Américo. "The Ballad of Gregorio Cortez" from *With his Pistol in his Hand: A Border Ballad and its Hero* by Américo Paredes, Copyright © 1958, renewed 1986. Reprinted by permission of the author and the University of Texas Press.

Pérez de Villagra, Gaspar. "Canto III", by Gaspar Pérez de Villagrá from *Historia de la Nueva México,* ed./tr. Encinias, Rodríguez, Sánchez, University of New Mexico Press, 1992. Reprinted by permission.

Pietri, Pedro. "Black & White Photo" in *Traffic Violations* by Pedro Pietri, Waterfront Press, 1983. Reprinted by permission of Pedro Pietri: "Dedicated to my sister Carmen Pietri. Written at Mt. Olivet Cemetery at the grave of my father, Francisco Pietri."

Ponce, Mary Helen. "La Doctora Barr" by Mary Helen Ponce in *Woman Of Her Word: Hispanic Women Write,* edited by Evangelina Vigil-Piñón, Arte Público Press-University of Houston, 1983. Reprinted by permission of Mary Helen Ponce. (Mary Helen Ponce is the pen name of Merrihelen Ponce, Ph.D. Ponce is currently working on biographies of women writers of Mexico.)

Portillo-Trambley, Estela. "Sun Images" by Estela Portillo-Trambley in *Nuevos Pasos: Chicano and Puerto Rican Drama,* eds. Kanellos and Huerta, Arte Público Press-University of Houston, 1989. Reprinted by permission of Estela Portillo-Trambley.

Rivera, Tomás. "Eva and Daniel" and "The Night Before Christmas" by Tomás Rivera, both edited by Julián Olivares, are reprinted with permission from the publisher of *Tomás Rivera: The Complete Works* (Houston: Arte Público Press-University of Houston, 1992).

Salazar, Rubén. Excerpts from "A Stranger in One's Land" by Rubén Salazar, *U.S. Commission on Civil Rights Clearing House Publication, No. 19* (May 1970). Published by the U.S. Government Printing Office.

Sánchez, Ricardo. "San Antonio phantasmagoria," Barrios of the world," "Latinos" from *Hechizospells* by Ricardo Sánchez, Chicano Studies Center, University of California Los Angeles. Copyright © 1976 by Ricardo Sánchez. Reprinted by permission of Maria Teresa Sánchez.

Soto, Gary. "First Love" and "To Be A Man" from *Small Faces* by Gary Soto. Copyright © 1986 Gary Soto. Used with permission of the author and Bookstop Literary Agency. All rights reserved.

Suárez, Virgil. "A Perfect Hotspot" by Virgil Suárez is reprinted with permission from the publisher of *Welcome to the Oasis and Other Stories* (Houston: Arte Público Press-University of Houston, 1992). "The Goat Incident" by Virgil Suárez is reprinted with permission from the publisher of *Spared Angola* (Houston: Arte Público Press-University of Houston, 1997.)

Thomas, Piri. "Amigo Brothers" from *Stories from el Barrio* by Piri Thomas. Copyright © 1978 by Piri Thomas. Reprinted by permission of the author and Charlotte Sheedy Literary Agency.

Urista, Alberto (Alurista). "A Child to be Born" by Alurista from *Nationchild Plumaroja,* Toltecas en Aztlan, 1972. Reprinted by permission from Alurista.

Valdez, Luis. "Los Vendidos" by Luis Valdez is reprinted with permission from the publisher of *Luis Valdez Early Works: Actos, Bernabé and Pensamiento Serpentino* (Houston: Arte Público Press-University of Houston, 1971).

Vando, Gloria. "Nuyorican Lament" by Gloria Vando is reprinted with permission from the publisher of *Promesas: Geography of the Impossible* (Houston: Arte Público Press-University of Houston, 1993).

Vega, Bernardo. "The customs and traditions of the tabaqueros and what it was like to work in a cigar factory in New York City" in *Memoirs of Bernardo Vega,* ed. César Andreu Iglesias, Monthly Review Press. Copyright © 1984 by Monthly Review Press. Reprinted by permission.

Vega, Ed (Edgardo Vega Yunque). "The Angel Juan Moncho" from *Mendoza's Dreams* by Edgardo Vega Yunque, Arte Público Press-University of Houston, 1990. Reprinted by permission of Edgardo Vega Yunque.

Vigil-Piñón, Evangelina. "night vigil" by Evangelina Vigil-Piñón is reprinted with permission from the publisher of *Thirty An' Seen a Lot* (Houston: Arte Público Press-University of Houston, 1982).

Viramontes, Helena Maria. "The Moths" by Helena Maria Viramontes is reprinted with permission from the publisher of *The Moths and Other Stories* (Houston: Arte Público Press-University of Houston, 1985).

AUTHOR-TITLE INDEX

Account, The, 2
Amigo Brothers, 379
Anaya, Rudolfo A., 100
Angel Juan Moncho, The, 360
Arise, Chicano, 296
Awakening. . . Summer 1956, An, 152

Báez, Joan, 265
Ballad of Gregorio Cortez, The, 58
Barrios of the world, 397
Becky and Her Friends, 374
Benítez, José Gautier, 142
Bitter Sugar: Why Puerto Ricans Leave Home, 237
Black & White Photo, 89
Bless Me, Ultima, 101
Borinkins in Hawaii, 269

Cabeza de Vaca, Álvar Núñez, 2
Cabrera, Lydia, 70
Cadilla de Martínez, María, 62
Canto III, 14
Castillo, Ana, 343
Chávez, Denise, 321
Chávez, Fray Angélico, 178
Child to Be Born, A, 402
Cisneros, Sandra, 131
Cofer, Judith Ortiz, 85, 120
Colón, Jesús, 237
Corridos, 75
Cossío y Cisneros, Evangelina, 355
Cruz, Victor Hernández, 269

de Hoyos, Angela, 296
Dear Rafe, 173
Dear Tía, 91
Dedication, 353
Doctora Barr, La, 390
Doubt, 142

Elizondo, Sergio, 292
Esteves, Sandra María, 186
Eva and Daniel, 189

***f**amilia,* 83
Fernández, Roberta, 304
Filomena, 304
Firmat, Gustavo Peréz, 352
First Love, 195
For the Color of My Mother, 246

Goat Incident, The, 345
Gonzales, Rodolfo "Corky," 229
Greatest Performance, The, 158

Herrera-Sobek, María, 74
Hijuelos, Oscar, 248
Hinojosa, Rolando, 172, 374
Hospital, Carolina, 91

***I** Am Joaquín,* 300
Indian Ruins, The, 112
Indigenous Profile, 62

***L**lorona, La,* 79
Latinos, 398
Laviera, Tato, 82
Los Vendidos, 281

Martí, José, 45, 112, 406
Memoirs of Bernardo Vega, The, 39
Memorial, 27
Mohr, Nicholasa, 151, 200, 331
Moraga, Cherríe, 245
Moths, The,
Muñoz, Elías Miguel, 158
Murrieta on the Hill, 293

My Name, 131
My Race, 406

Night Before Christmas, The, 135
night vigil, 165
Nilda, 200
Nuyorican Lament, 278

Our America, 45
Our House in the Last World, 249

Paredes, Américo, 57
Pérez de Villagrá, Gaspar, 13
Perfect Hotspot, A, 144
Pietri, Pedro, 89
Ponce, Mary Helen, 390
Portillo-Trambley, Estela, 207
Prize of Freedom, The, 71
Progress Report for a Dead Father, 85
puerto rican, 404

Rivera, Tomás, 134, 189
Romeo and Juliet Story in Early New Mexico, A, 179

Salazar, Rubén, 229
San Antonio phantasmagoria, 396
Sánchez, Ricardo, 395

Seeing Snow, 352
Shooting Stars, 321
Solís de Merás, Gonzalo, 27
Soto, Gary, 194, 340
Stranger in One's Land, A, 229
Suárez, Virgil, 144, 345
Sun Images, 207

Tales Told Under the Mango Tree, 120
Tato Laviera, 404
Thanksgiving Celebration (Amy), A, 331
Thomas, Piri, 379
Thoughts on a Sunday Afternoon, 265
To Be a Man, 340
To Free Cuba, 356
To My Father, 87
Transference, 186

Urista, Alberto (Alurista), 401

Valdez, Luis, 281
Vando, Gloria, 277
Vega, Bernardo, 38
Vega, Ed (Edgardo Vega Yunque), 399
Vigil-Piñón, Evangelina, 165
Viramontes, Helena María, 93

Women Are Not Roses, 343